BIBLICAL PROPHETS AND
ENVIRONMENTAI

Biblical Prophets and Contemporary Environmental Ethics

Re-Reading Amos, Hosea, and First Isaiah

HILARY MARLOW

UNIVERSITY PRESS

OXFORD
UNIVERSITY PRESS

Great Clarendon Street, Oxford, OX2 6DP,
United Kingdom

Oxford University Press is a department of the University of Oxford.
It furthers the University's objective of excellence in research, scholarship,
and education by publishing worldwide. Oxford is a registered trade mark of
Oxford University Press in the UK and in certain other countries

First published 2009
First published in paperback 2015

Published in the United States of America by Oxford University Press
198 Madison Avenue, New York, NY 10016, United States of America

British Library Cataloguing in Publication Data
Data available

Library of Congress Cataloging in Publication Data
Data available

ISBN 978–0–19–956905–2 (Hbk.)
ISBN 978–0–19–874510–5 (Pbk.)

Foreword

Jews and Christians who want to ground a concern for ecology in the Old Testament face a formidable task, because so many influential voices claim that this is the very document that lies at the root of human exploitation of the natural world. Sir David Attenborough (quoted by Hilary Marlow in her Introduction) takes it as simply obvious that the command in Genesis for humans to have 'dominion' over the world of nature is a licence to exploit it, quaintly arguing that this is an idea of 'desert-dwellers' (not too many desert-dwellers wrote the Old Testament!). He expresses a cultured though poorly informed contempt for the Bible very common among modern intellectuals, and blames it for many of our environmental ills. This belief has become so entrenched in the modern ecological debate that one despairs of ever eradicating it. But if the attempt fails, it will not be for want of trying on the part of biblical scholars, and among them Hilary Marlow represents a powerful and independent voice.

In this important monograph she examines the consensus represented by Attenborough very thoroughly, and shows it to be mistaken. At the same time she argues, through a thorough survey of the teachings of patristic, Reformation, and modern theologians that theological discussion has indeed often tolerated the exploitation of the natural world—in this falling short of the ideal actually expressed in Genesis, which is one of responsible stewardship. This is the most complete survey of such theological opinion to date, and it will prove very useful as a resource for future discussions.

But Marlow also breaks new ground in finding fruitful material in the books of the eighth-century prophets Amos, Hosea, and Isaiah. Here there emerges an idea that she calls 'interconnectivity', whereby the relations of people to God, to each other, and to the creation come together to form an organic whole. This is a theologically sophisticated model, and one that provides a basis for a much more nuanced understanding of the Old Testament's contribution to thinking about ecology. In a field where there is a lot of careless writing about what the Bible says, Marlow's work is a model of clarity and good sense, and I hope it will be widely read—not only within the 'guild' of biblical scholars, but even (though this may be a forlorn hope) by distinguished TV presenters.

John Barton

Preface and Acknowledgements

This project was conceived from the desire to bring together two significant interests of mine. The first was a growing concern about the environmental degradation occurring throughout the world, and the negative impact of human lifestyles and activities upon the earth. The second was my interest in the prophets of the Old Testament, and in particular their use of metaphors, themes, and language connected with the natural world. Was there a way in which these two interests could be fruitfully combined in a way which neither did disservice to the ancient texts, nor trivialized the scale of the current problem? The attempt to answer that question has led, ultimately, to this book, which began life as my doctoral thesis for the University of Cambridge.

Some of those who encountered the project in its early months were sceptical about the task, regarding environmental issues as only of marginal interest and of little relevance to a biblical studies research project, or indeed to the Christian church. As time wore on and the challenges of global warming were often headline news, some of those same sceptics became enthusiastic supporters, pointing me in the direction of useful articles and news reports. Hopefully, as the book now goes to press, there are few who doubt that the world faces a serious problem—one that raises important ethical issues that demand a response from those with religious convictions and those with none.

My heartfelt thanks are due to a number of people. In the early stages, the project was gently guided by my supervisor, Katharine Dell. My examiners, John Barton and Graham Davies, provided wise comments on the thesis and encouraged me towards publication. Since then, many of the suggestions of those who read the manuscript in its draft form have been taken on board. In particular, Graham Davies continued to offer perceptive and invaluable comments as he re-read the manuscript chapter by chapter. John Barton graciously agreed to write a foreword to the book and I am grateful for his generous endorsement. The book would be all the poorer without Walter Houston's insight and eye for detail. John Brooke, Judith Lieu, and Jason Rampelt have each provided helpful comments on individual chapters. Numerous inconsistencies in style, syntax, and spelling were pointed out by my father, Eric Jay, whose editing skills have not diminished with time. Lizzie Robottom, Tom Chandler, and others at OUP have been supportive and patient with the questions of a first-time author. Without all these wise and willing partners, the book would be much the poorer. As it is, responsibility for its remaining shortcomings and mistakes lies fully with the author. Other people have provided invaluable ongoing support and confirmation that this is a project worth pursuing. In particular thanks go to Peter Harris, founder of the conservation charity A Rocha, for his encouragement that the book will have interest and relevance for those outside the world of academic biblical studies. I have greatly appreciated the interest and involvement of my colleagues at the Faraday Institute for Science and Religion, where I now continue my research on the Old Testament and environmental ethics. However, the biggest expression of gratitude goes to my family, especially my mother Muriel, husband Ian, and our children Andy, Jo (and husband Simeon), Rosie, and Carrie, for their encouragement, love, and support throughout the project. I dedicate this book to them and to our first grandchild who will have made his entry into the world by the time of publication.

H.F.M.

Cambridge, 2009

Table of Contents

List of Figures

List of Abbreviations

AB	Anchor Bible
ABR	*Australian Biblical Review*
AHR	*American Historical Review*
ANET	*Ancient Near Eastern Texts Relating to the Old Testament*, ed. J. B. Pritchard, 3rd edn. Princeton, 1969
ArBib	The Aramaic Bible
AsTJ	*Asbury Theological Journal*
ATANT	*Abhandlung zur Theologie des Alten und Neuen Testaments*
AUSS	*Andrews University Seminary Studies*
BASOR	*Bulletin of the American Schools of Oriental Research*
BDB	F. Brown, S. R. Driver, and C. A. Briggs, *A Hebrew and English Lexicon of the Old Testament*. Oxford, 1907
Ber	*Berytus*
BHS	*Biblica Hebraica Stuttgartensia*, ed. K. Elliger and W. Rudolph. Stuttgart, 1983
BHT	Beiträge zur historischen Theologie
Bib	*Biblica*
BJRL	*Bulletin of the John Rylands University Library of Manchester*
BKAT	*Biblischer Kommentar, Altes Testament*, ed. M. Noth and H. W. Wolff
BN	*Biblische Notizen*
BRev	*Bible Review*
BS	Biblical Seminar
BZ	*Biblische Zeitschrift*
BZAW	Beihefte zur Zeitschrift für die alttestamentliche Wissenschaft
CAT	Commentaire de l'Ancien Testament
CBQ	*Catholic Biblical Quarterly*
CCC	Concordia Classic Commentary
Cels.	*Against Celsus*

Civ.	*City of God*
Conf.	*Confessions*
CSR	*Christian Scholar's Review*
de Princ.	*First Principles*
DSD	*Dead Sea Discoveries*
ERT	*Evangelical Review of Theology*
EvT	*Evangelische Theologie*
ExAud	*Ex auditu*
ExpTim	*Expository Times*
FAT	Forschungen zum Alten Testament
FC	Fathers of the Church. Washington, D.C., 1947–
FoiVie	*Foi et Vie*
FOTL	Forms of the Old Testament Literature
GAT	Grundrisse zum Alten Testament
Gen. Imp.	*Literal Interpretation of Genesis (unfinished)*
Gen. Litt.	*Literal Meaning of Genesis*
Gen. Man.	*Genesis Against the Manicheans*
GK	*Gesenius' Hebrew Grammar*, 2nd edn., ed. E. Kautzsch. Oxford University Press, 1910
Haer.	*Against Heresies*
HBT	*Horizons in Biblical Theology*
HCOT	Historical Commentary on the Old Testament
Hex.	*Hexaemeron*
HeyM	Heythrop Monograph
HTR	*Harvard Theological Review*
HUCA	*Hebrew Union College Annual*
ICC	The International Critical Commentary
Int	*Interpretation*
JBL	*Journal of Biblical Literature*
JETS	*Journal of the Evangelical Theological Society*
JNES	*Journal of Near Eastern Studies*
JNSL	*Journal of Northwest Semitic Languages*
JOTT	*Journal of Translation and Textlinguistics*
JQR	*Jewish Quarterly Review*

JSOT	*Journal for the Study of the Old Testament*
JSOTSup	Journal for the Study of the Old Testament: Supplement Series
JSPSup	Journal for the Study of the Pseudepigrapha: Supplement Series
JSS	*Journal of Semitic Studies*
JSSMS	Journal of Semitic Studies Monograph Series
JTS	*Journal of Theological Studies*
LCBI	Literary Currents in Biblical Interpretation
LCC	Library of Christian Classics. Philadelphia, 1953–
LCL	Loeb Classical Library
LHBOTS	Library of Hebrew Bible/Old Testament Studies
LXX	The Septuagint
MT	Masoretic Text
NAC	New American Commentary
NCB	New Century Bible
NICOT	New International Commentary on the Old Testament
NPNF[1]	*Nicene and Post-Nicene Fathers*, Series 1
NPNF[2]	*Nicene and Post-Nicene Fathers*, Series 2
NRSV	New Revised Standard Version
OBT	Overtures to Biblical Theology
Opif.	*On the Creation of the World* (Philo)
Opif.	*On the Making of Man* (Gregory)
OTL	Old Testament Library
OTM	Oxford Theological Monographs
OtSt	Oudtestamentische Studiën
PEQ	*Palestine Exploration Quarterly*
PER	*Perspectives*
PIBA	*Proceedings of the Irish Biblical Association*
Pol.	*Politics*
PSB	*Princeton Seminary Bulletin*
RA	*Revue d'assyriologie et d'archéologie orientale*
RB	*Revue Biblique*
RevExp	*Review and Expositor*
RNBC	Readings: A New Biblical Commentary
SBL	Society of Biblical Literature

SBLABib	Society of Biblical Literature Academia Biblica
SBLDS	Society of Biblical Literature Dissertation Series
SBLMS	Society of Biblical Literature Monograph Series
SJOT	*Scandinavian Journal of the Old Testament*
SJT	*Scottish Journal of Theology*
SOTSMS	Society for Old Testament Studies Monograph Series
SSN	Studia semitica neerlandica
ST	*Studia theologica*
Sum. Theol.	*Summa Theologica*
Syr.	Peshitta (Syriac)
TDOT	*Theological Dictionary of the Old Testament*, ed. G. Johannes Botterweck, Helmer Ringgren, and Heinz-Josef Fabry, trans. David E Green, vols. 6–15. Grand Rapids, Mich.: Eerdmans, 1990–2006
Tg.Isa.	*Targum Isaiah*
Them	*Themelios*
ThTo	*Theology Today*
TOTC	Tyndale Old Testament Commentaries
TRE	*Theologische Realenzyklopädie*, ed. G. Krause and G. Müller. Berlin, 1977–
TynBul	*Tyndale Bulletin*
TZ	*Theologische Zeitschrift*
VT	*Vetus Testamentum*
VTSup	Supplements to Vetus Testamentum
WBC	Word Biblical Commentary
WMANT	Wissenschaftliche Monographien zum Alten und Neuen Testament
ZAW	*Zeitschrift für die alttestamentliche Wissenschaft*
ZTK	*Zeitschrift für Theologie und Kirche*

English translation of the principal texts under consideration is the author's own unless otherwise specified. All other translations are NRSV.

The MT versification is prioritized throughout with the English versification, where different, in square brackets, e.g. Hos 2:23 [21].

Introduction

> [T]he impacts of global warming are such that I have no hesitation in describing it as a weapon of mass destruction.
>
> Sir John Houghton, *The Guardian*, 2003

THE FUTURE OF THE PLANET

Human impact on the natural world is unsustainable and has costly implications for our survival and that of numerous other species. Ever-increasing industrialization, population expansion, and patterns of consumption are placing enormous stresses on the earth's resources and its capacity to provide for its inhabitants. Concerns for the well-being of the planet in the face of these human-generated pressures began to receive world-wide attention in the last decades of the twentieth and the first decade of the twenty-first century. At the Earth Summit (the United Nations Conference on Environment and Development, UNCED) in Rio de Janeiro in 1992, the UK Government's submission stated that 'the ways we multiply, produce energy, use natural resources and produce waste threaten to change fundamentally the balance of our global environment'.[1] Since then attention has focused on anthropogenic climate change, and we have seen the publication of increasingly grave scientific predictions about the future consequences of global warming, together with research

[1] Department of Environment, *This Common Inheritance*, 9.

demonstrating the economic consequences of failure to tackle the problems.[2]

During this period, environmental issues have been brought under the public spotlight by the attention given them in the world's press. Rather than being the concern of a few keen scientists, generally regarded as rather obsessive or suspect, the well-being of the planet now features in dinner-party conversation and being 'green' is regarded by some celebrities as an essential fashion accessory. Such media hype has certainly brought to public attention the seriousness of global warming. But there is a danger that it also trivializes an issue that has been growing in seriousness over a long period, to the extent that the general public either assumes it is just another problem with a technological solution or, as a result of media 'fatigue', ceases to take sufficient notice of the gravity of the situation.

Since 2008, a series of global economic 'crises' have culminated in the collapse of major financial institutions and businesses in a number of countries and precipitated a worldwide recession. The consumer dream of the West seems to have evaporated, and amid rising unemployment and economic uncertainty, people are increasingly feeling the need to reduce outgoings on food, fuel and other consumables. Our reliance on fossil fuels to service our apparently insatiable demand for energy—for industry, transport, and domestic heat and light—is coming under question. The high carbon emissions generated by coal-fired power stations, together with rapidly dwindling resources of gas and oil mean that finding alternatives to fossil fuels has become rather more urgent for governments worldwide, and for an increasing proportion of the general public.[3] Just as serious but less well reported is the growing global food shortage, as

[2] See the Intergovernmental Panel on Climate Change (IPCC), '4th Assessment Report' and HM Treasury, *Stern Review.* In March 2009 an international gathering of climate scientists, meeting in advance of the December 2009 United Nations Copenhagen Convention on Climate Change, presented evidence that climate change is accelerating faster than anticipated and stressed the urgent necessity of political action (http://unfccc.int).

[3] In 2008 the International Energy Agency drastically reduced its estimate of the capacity of global oil resources to meet demand, suggesting that peak oil production will happen in 2020 rather than 2030–50 as previously predicted (George Monbiot, *The Guardian*, 18 Dec. 2008).

the world population soars, and deteriorating soil quality and extreme weather events adversely affect productivity in many parts of the world.[4] These issues draw attention both to the speed of change, and the cumulative and wide-scale effects of unprecedented human population growth and human induced climate change.[5]

RELIGION, ETHICS, AND ENVIRONMENTAL CONCERN

As awareness of the seriousness of environmental problems has grown, the challenge facing the earth and its inhabitants has been taken up by numerous voices calling for moral accountability. Moral theologian Daniel Maguire puts it succinctly, 'If current trends continue, we will not. And that is qualitatively and epochally true. If religion does not speak to [this] it is an obsolete distraction'.[6] In his most recent book, theologian and ethicist Michael Northcott suggests climate change is a 'novel moral problem'. Although in previous centuries human beings have altered and even damaged local climates, 'never before have they been responsible for planetary climate change'.[7] He argues that '[t]he strongest moral case for mitigating global warming is that it is already life-threatening to those who are least able to defend themselves, and have no responsibility for its causation'.[8]

The call to find common ground between contemporary environmental issues and religious traditions is not something that is purely the concern of religious adherents or members of faith communities. The recognition that spiritual concerns might have a part to play in environmental ethics is increasingly found among some ecologists, whether or not they have religious allegiance themselves, as the

[4] E.g. in May 2008 a serious typhoon in Burma, followed by a major earthquake in central China, seriously affected the food production capacities of those two nations.

[5] World population currently stands at just over 6 billion, and is projected to rise to 9 billion by 2050 (Population Reference Bureau, www.prb.org; Optimum Population Trust, www.optimumpopulation.org).

[6] Maguire, *Moral Core*, 13.

[7] Northcott, *Moral Climate*, 55.

[8] Ibid. 55–6.

following statement by Maurice Strong, former UN Under-Secretary General demonstrates:

In the final analysis, our economic and social behavior is rooted in our deepest moral and spiritual motivations. We cannot expect to make the fundamental changes needed in our economic life unless they are based on the highest and best of our moral, spiritual and ethical traditions, a reverence for life, a respect for each other, and a commitment to responsible stewardship of the earth.[9]

More specifically, the World Bank programme on Faiths and Environment is convinced that

[r]eligious organisations and leaders can play a role in influencing peoples' perspectives on [the environment]...based upon and rooted in their own understanding of the relationship between humanity and the rest of nature.[10]

As a result of this conviction the programme has facilitated a wide range of discussions on how religions can work in partnership with secular agencies engaged in environmental and development work, and has enabled the formation of new partnerships between governments, NGOs, and faith communities.[11]

In the US context, where the Republican government of George W. Bush was notable in its reluctance to acknowledge the seriousness of global climate change, the debate has traditionally polarized along religious, specifically Christian, lines.[12] This perceived antipathy between conservative Christianity and the concerns of environmentalists is increasingly being challenged. In early 2007 a consultation

[9] Strong, 'Beyond Rio'.

[10] Whitten and Morgan, *Faiths and Environment*, 1.

[11] Ibid. 2.

[12] E.g. Orr, 'Armageddon'. His particular focus is the American right-wing evangelical belief (held by a number of members of the administration of George W. Bush) that environmental concern is unnecessary in the light of the imminent 'end times'. A response to his paper by a number of Christians with professional involvement in conservation-related disciplines urges dialogue, and a recognition of the resources that Christian theology can bring to environmental problems (Stuart et al., 'Conservation Theology'). There was a slight change of mood in the White House at the end of Bush's term, with President Bush acknowledging the reality of climate change. It remains to be seen what effect the election of President Barack Obama will have.

between a group of leading scientists led by the atheist evolutionary biologist E. O. Wilson and US evangelical leaders pledged a joint commitment to 'save' the living world:

> We agree not only that reckless human activity has imperiled the Earth—especially the unsustainable and short-sighted lifestyles and public policies of our own nation—but also that we share a profound moral obligation to work together to call our nation, and other nations, to the kind of dramatic change urgently required in our day.[13]

In the UK, there is neither such a strong tradition of hostility between environmental and Christian concerns, nor the same political resistance to change. All the major political parties and church denominations have produced policy statements on climate change and environmental responsibility. More insidious is the combination of apathy among the general population and lack of unified political policy to foster radical lifestyle and economic changes. Among ecologists there has been prejudice and cynicism over the contribution organized religion might make to raising environmental awareness. For a number of environmentalists the Judaeo-Christian tradition, in particular the Old Testament, is part of the problem.[14] This perspective is epitomized by naturalist and broadcaster Sir David Attenborough's response to an interview question about the reasons for the separation between people and nature:

> Judeo-Christians believe . . . people who lived in the desert believed that nature was hostile. You can see in the old testament [*sic*] that the natural world was there to exploit—it was there for their benefit. That has cast a long shadow.[15]

[13] Ball and Bauma-Prediger, 'Scientists and Evangelicals Unite', 1. See also the 2006 statement by the Evangelical Climate Initiative (www.christiansandclimate.org/statement).

[14] The Christian Old Testament is of course also the Hebrew Scriptures or Hebrew Bible of the Jewish tradition. The decision to use the term Old Testament throughout this volume reflects that fact that much of the discussion is concerned with biblical interpretation and ethical reflection within the Christian tradition.

[15] Attenborough, 'Natural World', 18. His perspective undoubtedly draws on the criticism of the Judaeo-Christian tradition made by Lynn White Jr. in his now infamous article, 'The Historical Roots of our Ecologic Crisis,' which will be discussed in more detail in the following chapter.

WHY THIS BOOK?

Sir David's comments highlight an important and potentially damning indictment of the biblical text—from someone who has probably not read it very thoroughly. Yet similar perspectives are evident in those who *do* read it, and who teach it to others.[16]

It is the contention of this volume that such perspectives represent a serious misunderstanding of the Old Testament writers' approaches to the natural world, one that is potentially damaging to any attempt to ground an environmental ethic in the sacred scriptures of the Jewish and Christian traditions. Although recent years have seen a proliferation of books in the realm of eco-theology, there is comparatively little that engages in a sustained way with the biblical text itself.[17] Yet biblical exegesis still features in many undergraduate theology degrees; it forms an important part of the curricula of many Christian seminaries and is regarded as a foundational component of theological reflection. The Hebrew Scriptures also form the cornerstone for almost all aspects of Jewish Studies—religious and ethical as well as literary and historical. The field of theology and religious studies is increasingly broadening to include study of the impact of religion on contemporary culture. Evaluating the biblical traditions for their potential contribution to contemporary issues such as environmental debates is an important part of this process, and one that will form the major part of this volume.

In the light of increasing concerns about the future of our planet, what insights might a close study of the biblical texts yield, and is there a viable ecological hermeneutic to be derived from such readings? What principles derived from the texts might inform discussions in environmental ethics, and conversely, how might the issues faced today influence reading of the texts? The aim of this book is to use the tools of biblical studies to provide an in-depth exegesis of part of the Old Testament, namely some of the prophetic books, to answer

[16] E.g. Clayton, *God and Contemporary Science*, 33–4; Godfrey, *God's Pattern for Creation*.

[17] One exception is the work of the Earth Bible Project, which will be discussed in a later chapter.

such questions. More simply put, it will explore two fundamental questions through the lenses of the biblical prophets: how have we got into this mess—and how do we get out of it?

At its heart this book is concerned with the relationship between people and the earth. Ecology is defined as the study of relationships between living organisms—including humans—and their environments. In the Old Testament a third participant is involved and takes centre stage, namely YHWH, the God of Israel. So the textual analysis that follows will be concerned with relationships between God, human beings and the earth, whether expressed in literary terms, by means of a particular theme, motif or metaphor, or in conceptual ones, as Israel's prophets define their identity with respect to YHWH and to the land that sustains them.

TERMINOLOGY

Before embarking on this course one potential difficulty must be addressed, namely that of terminology. It will become apparent that scholars and commentators of the Old Testament adopt a wide variety of terms to denote the world in which we live, ranging from the broad (and ambiguous) 'earth' to the cumbersome 'non-human creation' and the shorter, but arguably more functional, 'nature'. There are a number of issues here. To start with, there is no Hebrew equivalent for the concept of nature, which has its origin in Greek philosophy.[18] To refer to nature in the Old Testament may imply a Platonic divide between mind and matter, which is foreign to Hebrew thought. While a functional view of the world that desacralizes creation and reduces it to an object of human study is appropriate in a biology book, it is perhaps less applicable in the theological context of the text. Then there is the question of distinguishing between human and non-human life, which is important for the exegetical

[18] Rogerson, 'Nature'. For discussion of the various Greek concepts of nature, *physis*, in different philosophical schools, see Annas, 'Naturalism in Greek Ethics'; Laks, 'Commentary on Annas'; and for wider discussion see McGrath, *Nature*, 88–102.

method adopted in this study. The nouns 'creation' and 'the created world' could reasonably be assumed to denote all that God has made—i.e. his human and non-human creation. However, in practice, many people use these phrases to refer to everything *apart from* humans—a synonym for the natural world. Thirdly, on a more practical level and for the sake of smoothly flowing English, there is need to employ a variety of synonyms and to avoid the tedium of qualifying every expression, or always using clumsy speech forms such as 'non-human creation'. Hence in this book, terms such as 'the natural world' and 'the earth' as well as 'non-human creation' have been used to signify the concept of creation apart from humanity; and the broader term 'creation' is used primarily to denote the whole of the created order, including humanity. Use of the word 'nature' has been kept to a minimum, apart from the section in Chapter 2 that discusses the dichotomy between nature and history in biblical theology.

Perhaps a more fundamental issue about terminology concerns the relationship between contemporary notions of the environment and the biblical understanding of the natural world. In one sense, the difference is huge—the biblical authors, and indeed all pre-technological human societies, could not have envisaged the enormous capacity of twenty-first-century human beings to control and alter their physical environment in the way we have done. The dangers of anachronism—of reading back into the text our contemporary perspectives—are real ones and to be taken seriously. As Cyril Rodd points out, we do the text a disservice if we read into it an understanding of the ancient Israelites as environmentalists.[19]

There is another sense in which the difference is not perhaps so great as one might envision, as helpfully articulated by Simon Hailwood, who uses the term 'landscape' rather than environment to denote the point at which culture and nature intersect.[20] In the Bible, just as much as in today's world, human society and the natural

[19] Rodd, *Glimpses of a Strange Land*, 249.

[20] Hailwood, *Green Liberal*, 24–5. He draws on Rolston's distinction between four different categories, environment (the current field of significance for a living being), ecology (the interactive relationships between an organism and its environment), nature (the entire system of things that follow natural law and happen spontaneously) and landscape (the local scope of nature, modified by culture). He

world encounter one another in a variety of ways. This encounter may be one that is mutually beneficial, or may result in tension or even in collision between different and potentially hostile spheres.[21] The exegetical chapters of this book are particularly concerned to explore what happens at the boundaries between human and non-human creation: in other words, what the text tells us of the landscape inhabited by the ancient Israelites, and how this may resonate with or differ from contemporary understandings of environment.

One further potential area of confusion concerns use of the word 'anthropocentric'. This term has been frequently used in environmental ethics to denote an instrumental or exploitative attitude towards the natural world, a usage that is increasingly being questioned.[22] Since, as Hailwood notes, 'in some of its senses, anthropocentrism—human centredness—is ineliminable and benign', we need to distinguish carefully between the inevitable human-centredness that arises from human capacity for self-consciousness and rationality and the anthropocentrism that assumes that the value of the world is derived from, or reducible to, the needs of human beings.[23] The preferable and more accurate way of describing the latter, which will be followed wherever possible in this volume, is an 'instrumental' approach to the world or one that is 'exploitatively anthropocentric'.

However, 'instrumental' and 'benign' anthropocentrism are not two clear-cut and easily separable concepts but represent opposite ends of a spectrum, with a range of positions in between. This is especially the case in some Christian theological traditions where a focus on human relationship to God is often combined with a

notes that 'humans have both natural and cultural environments; landscapes are typically hybrids' (Rolston III, 'Aesthetic Appreciation', 379).

[21] See Simkins's threefold sociological model of human relationship to the natural world, mastery over it, peaceful coexistence with it, or subjugation under it (Simkins, *Creator and Creation*).

[22] See e.g. de-Shalit, *Theory and Practice*; Eckersley, 'Beyond Human Racism'; Hayward, *Political Theory*. Lodge and Hamlin note that a non-anthropocentric perceptive is practically as well as conceptually unavailable to us 'because humans have disturbed the environment so pervasively that even those parts of it which we allow to be "natural" bear the human stamp and constantly require managerial decisions'. Lodge and Hamlin, *New Ecology*, 288.

[23] Hailwood, *Green Liberal*, 2.

profound appreciation of the natural world. For some of these positions, anthropocentrism is neither benign nor hostile to the non-human creation. Yet such ambivalence easily creates a blind spot as far as the effect of human action on the non-human world is concerned, and this quickly turns into the worst kind of anthropocentrism, that which is exploitative and instrumental. With this in mind, in the next chapter we shall look in more detail at some of the charges levelled against organized religion and whether these can be substantiated.

1

Creation in Church History

I'm truly sorry man's dominion
Has broken nature's social union,
An' justifies the ill opinion
Which makes thee startle
At me, thy poor, earth-born companion,
An' fellow-mortal!
(Robert Burns, *To a Mouse*)

CHRISTIANITY: THE ROOT OF THE PROBLEM?

In the Introduction it was noted that a number of environmental scientists and theologians view the Judaeo-Christian tradition with suspicion, even hostility, and that some lay the blame for the current environmental situation at the door of Christianity. In this section we shall discuss what the origins of these perceptions are, apart from a general antipathy towards religious belief itself. One of the earliest and most notorious public expressions of such views is that of the American historian of science Lynn White Jr. who, in 1966, gave a paper to the American Association for the Advancement of Science entitled 'The Historical Roots of our Ecologic Crisis'.[1] In it White severely criticizes Judaeo-Christian religious beliefs for their contri-

[1] White Jr., 'Historical Roots'. White was by no means the first modern writer to draw attention to the ecological problems caused by modern technology. Probably the best known of these is the biologist Rachel Carson whose 1962 book on pollution did more than any other to awaken the world to this crisis (Carson, *Silent Spring*).

bution to the emerging environmental crisis.[2] He does this in a number of ways. First he traces western leadership in the realms of science and technology back to the Middle Ages, and suggests that the adoption of early forms of technology in agricultural practice during this period led, for the first time, to an exploitative relationship between humans and the land they farmed. White makes an intrinsic connection between this exploitative attitude and the domination of Christianity over paganism in the western world.

Secondly, White evaluates the Christian view of the relationship between humanity and the environment. His brief retelling of the Genesis creation accounts prompts the assertion that creation is planned by God 'explicitly for man's benefit and rule: no item in the physical creation had any purpose save to serve man's purposes'.[3] His unequivocal conclusion is that 'Christianity is the most anthropocentric religion the world has seen'.[4] Thirdly, since from the thirteenth century onwards scientists have tended to explain their motivation in religious terms—'thinking God's thoughts after him'—White argues that it was 'the dynamism of religious devotion, shaped by the Judeo-Christian dogma of creation' that gave modern western science its impetus.[5] The inevitable conclusion for White is that Christianity carries a huge burden of guilt for the current ecological effects of the scientific and technological revolutions.

In mitigation, White offers a few qualifications of this sustained attack. He cautions against making sweeping generalizations (having done just that himself!), and draws a distinction between the scientific view of the natural world espoused by the western (Latin) Church and the more artistic, symbolic conception of nature in the

Her book was not well received by fellow scientists (at the time a predominantly male constituency), who castigated her work for being emotive and unscientific. Sadly, Carson died from cancer in 1964 without realizing the prophetic nature of her writing.

[2] Although White directs his critique to Judaeo-Christian beliefs, it is evident that he is primarily concerned with developments in the western Christian tradition.

[3] White Jr., 'Historical Roots', 1205.

[4] Ibid.

[5] Ibid. 1206.

early church and throughout the Eastern (Greek) Church. White also praises the thirteenth-century saint, Francis of Assisi, as a model of radical humility with respect to humanity's place in the natural order. His final proposition is that 'since the roots of our problem are so largely religious, the remedy must also be essentially religious'.[6] However, he does not define this, except negatively: 'We shall continue to have a worsening ecologic crisis until we reject the Christian axiom that nature has no reason for existence save to serve man.'[7]

White's short paper has prompted reactions both from those who endorse his opinions and from those who disagree. His conclusions have undoubtedly contributed to the growing, but largely unexamined, assumption among those in a wide range of disciplines (ecology, history, and philosophy as well as theology) that 'the Western theological tradition is ecologically bankrupt'.[8] In particular, the cultural historian Thomas Berry has an essentially pessimistic view of the biblical traditions, suggesting that they are so radically orientated away from nature that they must be discarded.[9]

White's paper has also has been widely criticized on a number of counts by historians, scientists, and theologians.[10] This is not without positive effects on western theological thinking since it has prompted a re-examination of both the biblical texts, and the history and theology of the Christian tradition, from the perspective of modern environmental problems.[11] As theologian Robert Leal puts it,

> The challenge posed by White has in the past three decades . . . played its part in the constitution of ecotheology as a viable branch of study [that has]

[6] Ibid. 1207. Francis of Assisi is discussed later in this chapter.

[7] Ibid.

[8] Santmire, *Travail of Nature*, 1.

[9] T. Berry, *Dream of the Earth*, 148–50. See discussion in Hiebert, *Yahwist's Landscape*, 14; Hendry, *Theology of Nature*.

[10] R. J. Berry, *God's Book of Works*, 38, 44–5. This has not been the result of collaboration between biblical scholars and environmentalists, nor does it arise out of shared contexts, aims or methods in interpretation. Rather, as Hiebert points out, 'their presuppositions and attitudes about biblical life and thought intersect at important points' (Hiebert, *Yahwist's Landscape*, 4).

[11] E.g. Hiebert, *Yahwist's Landscape*; Simkins, *History and Nature in Joel* and the work of the Earth Bible Project (Habel, *Readings*).

become a spur to a fundamental questioning of much of traditional theology itself.[12]

Issues arising from White's paper

White's controversial paper raises a number of interesting questions that will be explored in this volume. The first is concerned with the reasons behind the functional and exploitative use of the earth's resources that has characterized human society for the past two hundred years or more. Can the blame be laid at the feet of the Judaeo-Christian tradition in such a simplistic manner as White suggests? Secondly, and closely linked with this, is the question to what extent religious thought and particularly Christian theology over the centuries has contributed to such an instrumental perception of the world. In what ways have theological understandings of human relationship to the natural world promulgated the idea, particularly in western theological thinking, that it is ours to do what we like with? Thirdly, although White's paper lacks credibility from a biblical studies perspective, it raises questions about the biblical text and whether it is intrinsically hostile to or exploitative of the natural world.[13] What alternative insights might an in-depth analysis of specific biblical texts yield, and is there a viable ecological hermeneutic to be derived from such readings? Finally, since he suggests, albeit grudgingly, that religious belief might help to remedy the problems, the possibility that the biblical texts, or at least a contemporary interpretation of them, might have something to offer in environmental debates is important. What principles derived from the texts might inform discussions in environmental ethics? And conversely, how might the issues faced today influence reading of the texts?

[12] Leal, *Wilderness*, 9. For examples of such questioning see Hessel, *Christianity and Ecology*; Primavesi, *Sacred Gaia*; Ruether, *Gaia & God*.

[13] White's only reference to the Bible is to the Genesis creation texts to which he devotes a brief (less than half a page) and cursory summary, conflating the two accounts, which cannot properly be described as exegesis (White Jr., 'Historical Roots', 1205). Callicott suggests that whilst White set the agenda for environmental philosophy, he also set 'a low standard of biblical scholarship for critically glossing the environmental message of Genesis' (Callicott, *Beyond the Land Ethic*, 198).

Each of these issues is developed further in the chapters that follow. This chapter begins with an evaluation of White's thesis and the dangers of attributing ecological problems to a single causative agent. It then looks back into the history of the church to examine different ways in which theologians have construed human relationship with the rest of creation and evaluates to what extent these may have contributed to a negative perception of the created world.

Chapter 2 explores the changes in human perception of the natural world that came about with the rise of modern science from the sixteenth century onwards, before narrowing its focus to the academic study of the Hebrew scriptures from the late nineteenth century onwards. The marginalization of creation that emerged from early biblical scholars in this period will be contrasted with the alternative, more positive perspectives that began to emerge at the end of the twentieth century, including contemporary theological responses to environmental issues such as the development of eco-theology and eco-feminism.

In Chapter 3, the ecological hermeneutics of the Earth Bible Project, which represents the most serious and sustained attempt to engage with the biblical texts from an ecological perspective, will be discussed. The chapter will explore ancient Israelite views of the world before articulating its own ecological paradigm, that of the ecological triangle, which will be the lens through which the texts of the prophets are read in the ensuing chapters.

The three exegesis chapters, Chapters 4–6, consist of a detailed study of Amos, Hosea, and Isaiah 1–39 respectively, exploring the interrelationships in each of the texts between God, humanity, and the non-human creation. The texts are read with a number of questions in mind: what understanding of the non-human creation (whether cosmic or local) does the text present, what assumptions are made about YHWH's relationship to the created world and how he acts within it, and what effect do the actions and choices of human beings have on the non-human creation and vice versa?

The final chapter, Chapter 7, engages with the knotty problem of how, if at all, it is possible to derive contemporary ethics from biblical texts. It discusses the rise of interest in the ethics of the Old Testament over recent years and then provides a brief summary of contemporary ethical principles, including the development of environmental ethics. Finally the chapter explores connections that can be drawn between the ancient texts and contemporary environmental ethics, and proposes a new model for a biblical environmental ethic, one that integrates the intrinsic worth of all creation with human need for community and response to God.

Critique of White

Probably the greatest weakness of White's attack on Christian religion is its generalization and oversimplification. Indeed his is one of a number of attempts to attribute environmental degradation to a single variable, when in reality the causes of such a complex issue as this are themselves inevitably complex and multifaceted.[14] Theologian Michael Northcott maintains that 'the roots of the [environmental] crisis lie in a range of changes and social processes which together presage the beginnings of modern history, and that form of human society known as modernity, in which the human relation to nature is radically transformed'.[15] He cites various contributory factors: the agricultural revolution, the 'commodification' of nature, the rise of industry and technology, and the moral climate of modernity. Northcott suggests that the disruption to harmonious human relations with the natural world brought about by the developments of post-Reformation Europe was a departure from the conserving function of religion found in many of the medieval monastic orders, and indeed until recently in many non-western cultures.[16]

However, Northcott concedes that White is not entirely wrong in his analysis, since, alongside the growth of industrialization and the market economy, a contributory factor in the demise of nature was the new form of European Christianity that arose during the Enlightenment and increasingly viewed the natural world from an

[14] Other examples include Ehrlich who cites unsustainable population expansion (Ehrlich, *Population Explosion*) and Attfield who blames the unremitting pursuit of progress (Attfield, *Environmental Concern*). See Northcott, *Environment*, 40–1.

[15] Northcott, *Environment*, 41.

[16] Ibid. 83–4; see also Barr, 'Man and Nature', 27–8.

instrumental perspective. In Britain it was the Protestant tradition, with its focus on individual salvation as the primary purpose of God and its stress on the fallenness of the natural world, together with the subsequent Protestant work ethic, that paved the way for the economic changes that were the precursors of the Industrial Revolution.[17]

Like Northcott, Paul Santmire suggests a number of interrelated cultural forces that impacted western civilization in the period immediately following the Reformation, and that influenced Protestant thinking about the world. These include the rise of the natural sciences, the philosophy of Immanuel Kant and the socio-political effects of modern industrialization. He suggests that,

> [w]ith their vision of reality influenced by these trends, many nineteenth- and twentieth-century Protestant thinkers came to view nature no longer as a theatre of God's glory and power in which humanity is essentially embodied.... Nature now was approached as a self-enclosed, machinelike structure without any value or life of its own before God, set apart from both God and humanity.[18]

Although the development of modern science had its origins in Christian thought, the influence of the Kantian mechanistic view of nature and the dualism of Descartes precipitated the separation of science from religion that has characterized the succeeding centuries.[19] Whilst this 'de-deification' of the natural world was considered admirable in the mid-twentieth century, by the end of the century, as the extent of the environmental crisis unfolded, it was increasingly viewed as problematic.[20]

A slightly modified version of this process of change is adopted by Harvey Cox. Rather than science taming nature, he suggests that it was the desacralization of nature that took place as theologians in the twentieth century reframed biblical religion to fit the modern western culture, which provided an essential precondition for the

[17] Northcott, *Environment*, 53–4.
[18] Santmire, *Travail of Nature*, 133.
[19] Ibid. 134–5.
[20] Hiebert, *Yahwist's Landscape*, 13, see also the discussion in Barr, 'Man and Nature'.

development of modern science and urbanization.[21] Interestingly Cox also notes that this 'disenchantment of nature', a phrase originally coined by Max Weber, occurred as a result of the rise of Communist ideology, as well as changes in Christian thinking. Similarly Jean Dorst suggests that the tendency towards human domination of the natural world is found in materialistic philosophies as well as in religions and is derived from 'the European philosophy whence our technical civilisation was derived'.[22] The current contribution of emerging economies, such as India and China, to environmental degradation suggests that exploitative attitudes to the earth are also found in non-western ideologies as well as western ones.[23] This is acknowledged by environmental scientist Daniel Hillel in his response to Lynn White:

> Although a partial and hence misleading reading of the biblical message has been used as an excuse to exploit rather than to protect the environment, the primary impulse to do so does not come from religion. In the rich industrialized societies, it often comes from sheer greed, while in poverty-ridden societies, it comes from sheer necessity in the seeming absence of an alternative.[24]

It seems therefore that the degradation and destruction of the world that is now posing such a challenge is neither exclusively the result of a particular belief system nor wholly attributable to technological developments or market forces. Since the beginning of the nineteenth century a variety of different contexts and ideologies have combined with economic, political, and social factors to create conditions in which the earth serves human need and human greed.

THEOLOGICAL PERSPECTIVES ON CREATION

This is not, however, a reason to let theology off the hook. Despite the fact that destructive attitudes to the natural world characterize secular

[21] Cox, *Secular City*, 19–21.
[22] Dorst, *Before Nature Dies* cited in Barr, 'Man and Nature', 17.
[23] Environmental Audit Committee, 'Keeping the Lights On', 58.
[24] Hillel, *Natural History*, 245–6.

ideologies as well as religious ones, religious belief has undoubtedly played a role in framing human relationship with the non-human world. Moreover, in the light of the profound influence that Christianity has exerted on the history and culture of the western world, the contribution made by Christian theology to perceptions of the cosmos warrants further exploration.

As we have seen, Lynn White and Michael Northcott have focused on different historical periods in the search for moral and religious roots to the current environmental situation. White regards the Middle Ages as a catalyst for the development of the anthropocentric Christianity which, in his view, is entirely to blame for the exploitative attitudes to the natural world over the past two centuries. Northcott's more nuanced analysis considers that the legitimation of economic activity and individualism that Protestant Reformation theology encouraged played a significant part. Yet these periods in the history of the church do not stand alone, but are part of a long process of developing ideas and theological traditions, both before and after them, that have contributed to contemporary understandings of the created world and human place within it. The rest of this chapter will examine more closely the development of some of these perspectives in the Christian tradition and in particular in the Western Church.[25] Of course theological interpretations concerning the created order differ from age to age, as do the type of questions that are asked about the physical universe. Exploring some of these differences will provide a framework for understanding the unparalleled changes in religious thinking and in science that have come about since the Enlightenment.

Not surprisingly, this takes us back to the earliest centuries of the church and the cultural and philosophical milieu out of which it developed. Early Christian theologians responded in diverse ways to the challenges of their time—we shall explore the writings of just a few of the most influential of these to see how this happened. The aim is not to provide a comprehensive survey or an exhaustive

[25] This is not to deny the validity of the rich and varied interpretations of creation in Jewish traditions, merely that space precludes detailed examination of these. For a detailed study of the interpretation of creation texts (particularly Gen. 1:28) in Jewish literature, see Cohen, *Be Fertile & Increase*, and Neusner, *Story of Creation*.

discussion of each figure's writings; rather it is to highlight certain aspects of their theology that may subsequently have influenced later perceptions of the world and human place within it. For this reason we shall focus primarily on their understanding of the teleology of the non-human creation, both its material purposes and its eschatological future. This is because neither a teleology that has a functional, utilitarian view of the non-human, nor an eschatology predicated on the complete destruction of the present world in favour of a spiritual rest for the human soul is likely to provide a firm foundation for an ethic that values the natural world. In addition, since a major criticism of Lynn White's work is his sweeping generalizations from Genesis, where applicable we will consider the exegesis of the biblical creation texts undertaken by these theologians.[26]

Our exploration of the creation theology of key figures in the history of the church will continue through the medieval period as far as the Reformation. Although some of the major doctrinal questions that faced the early centuries of the church are no longer at issue, these periods in the history of the western Christianity are critical for understanding subsequent developments in theological thought that have contributed to contemporary perceptions of the world.

Theology rarely, if ever, develops in isolation. Rather it emerges in dialogue with individuals and groups, and as a response to a wide range of religious, political, and social factors. In addition, theologies of nature or creation derive their impetus from observations and questions concerning the natural world and human place within it. In the discussion that follows, all these factors will be seen to have played a part in the unfolding story of the church—the cultural, philosophical, and social contexts within which various theologies developed, the search for explanations of the physical attributes of the cosmos, and the unique factors that prompted individual theologians' responses to the challenges of their day.

There are three further points to note about this analysis of church history. First, by the very nature of their task, these theologians

[26] Primarily studies on the texts of Genesis 1–3, favoured by early exegetes, but also those on Psalm 104 which is a rich description of creation and the purposefulness of the natural world.

operate from a *theocentric* perspective. God (however conceptualized) is centre of their thought, and their understanding of the world is explored within this theocentric framework. Any charge that they are anthropocentric must be tempered by this realization. Secondly, just as the exegesis chapters of this volume offer a re-reading the Old Testament through the lenses of contemporary environmental concern, so too this exploration of church history self-consciously does the same. Both the questions and the agendas that we bring to texts now are very different from those of previous centuries, but it remains valid and important to note where commonalities exist and to ask what we can learn from them. Thirdly, the relationship between historical theological understandings of the world and the present situation does not represent a linear development, nor does it always follow a clear sequence. The discussion that follows is concerned rather to chart the ideas of a number of theologians across the centuries around the common motif of the teleology of creation, and to see to what extent they endorse the view that the primary function of the non-human creation is to provide for human need.

The influence of Greek philosophy

The vast and complex body of ideas that comprises Greek philosophy of the classical and Hellenistic periods exercised significant influence on early Christian theology, not least in relation to the natural world.[27] The quest for knowledge about the origin and function of the material universe as well as discussion on more abstract concepts played a significant part in the work of several Greek philosophers, including Plato and Aristotle. To Plato is generally attributed the classic dualism of soul and body, mind and matter, a concept that would be exceedingly influential in Christian thought over the centuries, and that has undoubtedly contributed to a disregard for the material world in certain Christian theologies.[28] Aristotle's interest in

[27] See Procopé, *Greek Philosophy*; McGrath, *Nature*.

[28] E.g. Plato, *Phaedo*, 80c–81c, 83a–b. There are subtle but important differences between the dualism of Greek philosophy and that of the 17th-century philosopher Descartes, who identified the mind with consciousness.

the natural world led him to produce some of the first systematic studies of the physical nature of animals, and perhaps the finest before the rise of modern natural sciences.[29] Yet his functional and utilitarian view of the non-human world is a perspective that surfaces in theological thinking across the centuries.[30] Stoic philosophy also contributed its own ideas on the philosophy of nature. Whilst it has not had the same lasting effect on Christian theology as either Plato or Aristotle it was extremely influential in the Graeco-Roman world of the early common era.[31]

THE EARLY CHURCH

The early centuries of the Christian church saw extensive and at times heated debate on a wide range of issues, both theological and practical, not least of which was the creation of the world.[32] In this creative and exciting period in the history of Christianity the emerging church sought to establish its identity with respect to the Judaism from which it emerged, and to define orthodoxy in the face of challenges from within and without.[33] In addition to the various Hellenistic philosophical ideas in circulation, the Graeco-Roman world of the day was rife with a plethora of mystery religions and temple cults celebrating various Greek and Roman gods. Pelikan suggests that '[t]he apologetic war of the early church was fought

[29] Raven, *Natural Religion*, 41.

[30] He writes 'we must suppose plants to be for the sake of animals and animals for the sake of humans...[Nature] has necessarily made all these things for the sake of human beings' (Aristotle, *Pol.* 1.6.1256b). As Glacken notes, '[i]n this anthropocentric conception of interrelationships in nature, the distribution of plants and animals is directly related to the needs and uses of man' (Glacken, *Rhodian Shore*, 48).

[31] As Long notes, '[m]any of the Christian fathers were more deeply affected by Stoicism than they themselves recognized' (Long, *Hellenistic Philosophy*, 107). See also Martin, 'Graeco-Roman Philosophy'.

[32] In particular Plato's contention that the universe is formed out of eternal pre-existent matter (e.g. Plato, *Timaeus*, 28c), which is addressed at length by Christian theologians as the doctrine of 'creation from nothing' is established (see May, *Creatio Ex Nihilo*).

[33] McGrath, *Historical Theology*, 17.

simultaneously on two fronts', namely the dispute with Judaism and the attack of Graeco-Roman paganism.[34]

The influence of Philo

The perceived superiority of Platonic and Stoic ideas over these mystical myths resulted in the espousal of Greek philosophy by many of the early apologists.[35] In this they were followers of, and often indebted to, Philo of Alexandria, the first-century CE Jewish scholar who interpreted the Greek Bible in terms of Hellenistic philosophy.[36] His influence on Clement and Origen is such that Berchman suggests: 'Alexandrian Judaism and the philosophical activity of Philo prepared the way for Clement and Origen to express Alexandrian Christianity in the cultural system of Hellenism and the conceptual systems of Judaic and Hellenic Platonism.'[37] Philo's work on the Genesis creation story, *On the Creation of the Cosmos according to Moses* (*De opificio mundi*), represents the earliest in a long tradition of exegesis of the Genesis creation accounts.[38] The philosophical

[34] Pelikan, *Christian Tradition*, 1. 27. Neither the Judaism nor the Hellenistic philosophy of the period was monolithic. As Lieu notes, they should be construed 'not in terms of opposition and negation so much as in terms of trying to plot continuities and discontinuities' (Lieu, *Neither Jew nor Greek*, 1).

[35] Olson, *Christian Theology*, 54–6; Pelikan, *Christianity and Classical Culture*, 95–7. Some, such as Clement of Alexandria, considered that the ideas in Plato's Timaeus were derived from the Hebrew Scriptures (Clement, *Protr.* 6, see discussion in Droge, *Homer or Moses?*). Although like many theologians of the early church, Clement is eager to refute aspects of Platonic cosmogonies which describe the world as crafted by a demiurge from eternal matter, the influence of Platonism unquestionably permeates his writing (Pelikan, *Christian Tradition*, 1 35–6, see also Northcott, *Environment*, 211–21).

[36] Aitken, 'Jewish Tradition', 89. See also Siegert, 'Early Jewish Interpretation', 162–89.

[37] *From Philo to Origen*, 295. For an extensive discussion of the relationship between Philo and Plato's *Timaeus* see Runia, *Philo and Timaeus.*

[38] A tradition which includes some of the patristic writers, as will be seen, and, according to some scholars, extends as far as Milton's *Paradise Lost* (Robbins, *Hexaemeral Literature*). The classification 'Hexaemeral' was coined by Robbins and other nineteenth and early twentieth century scholars to denote exegetical treatments of the six days of creation in Genesis 1. Although the term is no longer used in Patristic scholarship, it continues to surface in other literature (e.g. Glacken, *Rhodian Shore*; Harrison, 'Subduing the Earth').

background for his interpretation is drawn from Plato's *Timaeus* and it is clear from early in the exegesis that 'Philo perceives a far-reaching parallelism between the Mosaic creation account and Plato's famous mythic cosmogony'.[39]

Philo employs both accounts of creation to postulate a doctrine of double creation whereby God first creates the intelligible world, 'as a [*sic*] incorporeal and most god-like paradigm',[40] which is 'nothing else than the Logos of God'.[41] The Logos of God is the architect of the cosmos, a secondary, corporeal world that is a younger image of the intelligible world.[42] From his exegesis of the creation of animals it is clear that Philo, like Plato before him and Origen and others after him, considers human beings to be the crown of creation, by virtue of possessing the highest level of soul (that is, intellect).[43] Moreover, everything else is created in advance for them: 'for the living being which was dearest and closest to him in nature he made everything [so that] . . . he would lack nothing that was required both for life and for the good life, the former furnished by the abundant supply of things that give enjoyment, the latter by contemplation of the heavenly realm'.[44] As Runia comments, 'The anthropocentrism which marks the design and structure of the *Timaeus* is taken over by Philo, and is exploited to the full in his exegesis of the Mosaic cosmogony'.[45]

As well as colouring the exegesis of leading Alexandrian theologians such as Origen, the influence of Philo's reading of Genesis reaches well beyond the limits of Alexandria. The perception that human beings represent the pinnacle of the creation, which itself exists to supply human requirements, is echoed in a number of later theologians, including Gregory of Nyssa, Aquinas, and Luther. When coupled with the rapid expansion of scientific and technological endeavours from the eighteenth century onwards it is not hard to

[39] Runia in Philo, *Creation of Cosmos* (Runia), 32.

[40] Ibid. §50.

[41] Ibid. §51.

[42] Ibid. § 51. Williams notes Philo's ambiguity regarding the concept of the Logos (R. Williams, *Arius*, 118–19).

[43] 'To crown all he made man' (Philo, *Opif.*, 65, 66; see Runia's comment on the Greek *ἐπὶ δὲ πᾶσιν* in Philo, *Creation of Cosmos* (Runia), 216).

[44] Philo, *Creation of Cosmos* (Runia), §77.

[45] Runia, *Philo and Timaeus*, 465.

see how such a perception offers a theological basis for a view of the world that is not only anthropocentric, but also legitimizes the indiscriminate use of earth's resources in the pursuit of enjoyment and economic gain.

Irenaeus's rebuttal of Gnosticism

By no means all the Church Fathers incorporate Platonic cosmogony into their writings. An early exception to this tendency is Irenaeus, Bishop of Lyons, one of the most influential theologians of the second century. Irenaeus wrote his five-volume treatise *Against Heresies* in order to refute the various forms of Gnosticism that were gathering popularity in both the Greek and Roman churches, which has been described as 'the first and most dangerous heresy among the early Christians'.[46] In the light of the complex and dualistic account of the creation of the world endorsed by Gnosticism, Irenaeus is concerned to stress the goodness and supremacy of the one God as Creator, Sustainer, and Redeemer of the heavens and earth, and the goodness of God's creation.[47]

Against Heresies begins with an articulation of God as Creator: 'Him who founded and adorned the universe . . . God, who created the heavens and the earth and all things that are therein.'[48] Book II specifically refutes the Gnostic view that the world is intrinsically evil, created by other powers or angels (demiurges) with no knowledge of the supreme Being, by stressing the apostolic belief in God the Father who created the world and is revealed in it.[49] This belief is foundational for Irenaeus, and is frequently reiterated in his treatment of other key doctrines.[50] The creation itself is evidence of God's wisdom, benevolence, and glory:

[46] Filoramo, *History of Gnosticism*, 2. Although Irenaeus addressed his remarks primarily at the Valentinians, he also cited earlier Gnostic myths as the 'source and root' of the Valentinian heresies (Irenaeus, *Haer.*; see Grant, *Irenaeus*, 41).

[47] See Scheffczyk, *Creation and Providence*, 68–9.

[48] Irenaeus, *Haer.* I.Pref.1.

[49] Ibid. II.1–10.

[50] E.g. Ibid. III.4.2.

His wisdom [is shown] in His having made created things parts of one harmonious and consistent whole; and those things which, through His super-eminent kindness, receive growth and a long period of existence, do reflect the glory of the uncreated One, of that God who bestows what is good ungrudgingly.[51]

Although Irenaeus makes comprehensive use of scriptural texts he never attempts a systematic exegesis of the Genesis creation accounts, preferring to view Adam typologically, as the forerunner to Christ, the second Adam of Pauline theology.[52] This highlights one of his primary concerns—the nature of the Fall and Jesus Christ as the divinely ordained means of salvation. In this respect then, though he emphasises the creative goodness of God in bringing *all* things into being, his focus is essentially the human story, and human progression towards the divine.[53] Although for Irenaeus the purpose of the created world is not solely to benefit humanity, it is arranged by God to offer blessings to humans and to communicate salvation, a 'functional anthropocentrism' rather than an ontological one.[54]

Irenaeus's understanding of eschatological fulfilment is, like that of human redemption, firmly rooted in his conviction of the earth as the good creation of a good God, and of Christ as not only Redeemer of humanity, but 'the Perfecter of creation'.[55] He envisages not the destruction of the created world, but its ultimate restoration to its primeval condition, resulting in the fecundity and harmony prophesied in Isaiah.[56] In this he differs from both Origen and Augustine, for whom the present world is transient and will be superseded by the eternal resting place of human souls.

Both Irenaeus's soteriology and his eschatology are predicated upon his theology of creation, although the latter is never fully developed by him in its own right. His understanding of God as 'maker of heaven and earth' is the driving thought behind *Against Heresies*, and the *sine qua non* of his rebuttal of Gnosticism. His

[51] Ibid. IV.38.3.
[52] E.g. Ibid. III.23.
[53] Osborn, *Irenaeus*, 84–6.
[54] Santmire, *Travail of Nature*, 42.
[55] Ibid.
[56] Irenaeus, *Haer.* V.32.1, V.33.3.

insistence on 'the intrinsic goodness and redeemability of the generate order' is in stark contrast not only to the Gnostic view of the world but also to Platonic ideas of the inferiority of the corruptible order.[57] Nevertheless, the non-human creation features as just one part of his account of human relationship with the divine, namely as a means of divine revelation.[58]

The philosophical dualism of Origen

Origen, writing a few decades later than Irenaeus, attempted to blend classical Greek philosophy (in particular Neoplatonism) with biblical Christian beliefs.[59] His high regard for Scripture combined with his training as a grammarian meant that he brought to Christian interpretation of the Old Testament 'a precision and clear-sightedness which had previously been lacking'.[60] Although he suggested that the biblical text should be understood both literally and 'spiritually', he gave primacy to the spiritual interpretation, such that much of his exegesis of texts is allegorical.[61]

[57] Norris, *God and World*, 75.

[58] E.g. 'the manifestation of God which is made by means of all creation' (Irenaeus, *Haer.* IV.20.7).

[59] To what extent this was a commendable enterprise, and whether or not he succeeded in it, is much debated. Certainly Origen was condemned as a heretic from the fourth century onwards, and his work hotly criticised on a number of counts. But some modern commentators have adopted a more nuanced position, pointing out that some of Origen's most fundamental ideas can be found in earlier Christian writings such as Clement (see Chadwick, *Early Christian Thought*, 72, 74). In the introduction to his translation of *de Principiis*, Butterworth suggests that Origen was 'an orthodox defender of the faith . . . [attempting] to work out its implications for the educated world of his time' (Origen, *De Princ.*, xxxi). Trigg notes that whereas modern theologians sometimes accentuate the incompatibility of biblical thought and Platonic philosophy, for Origen it was the compatibility of the two in the face of Gnosticism that was compelling (Trigg, *Origen*, 71).

[60] Carleton Paget, 'Alexandrian Tradition', 501. Origen's interest in textual matters led to the first known Christian attempt to establish an accurate text of the LXX and resulted in the production of the Hexapla.

[61] Carleton Paget notes of Origen's exegesis that 'it is by no means always clear how the spiritual interpretation is linked to the literal, and at times Origen is too swift in dismissing or passing over the literal interpretation' (ibid. 526; see also 508–25).

In *First Principles*, Origen begins his restatement of traditional apostolic doctrines by expressing belief in a single benevolent creator God to whose nature the beauty of creation testifies, and who has revealed himself in the Christian Scriptures. However, this forms but a brief part of his schema, and he makes scant reference to God as Creator as the argument unfolds.[62] Origen has problems reconciling divine goodness and providence with the diversity of spiritual beings (angelic, human, and demonic) operating in the world. He resolves this by adding the Christian concept of free will onto the Platonic idea of the pre-existence of rational beings. The fall of some of these rational beings before the creation of the world, according to Origen, accounts for the 'diversity of natures', rational and divine, in the world.[63] Although the material world is not evil *per se*, it exists (albeit as a result of divine benevolence) to provide these fallen 'rational spirits' with a home while they wait to be returned to their original state in eternity.[64]

For Origen this hierarchical view of the world accounts for differences in social status (slavery or authority), race (barbarian or Greek), and health (invalid or healthy). The non-human creation, which is comprised of 'irrational beings', barely figures in his schema:

> As for dumb animals and birds and creatures that live in water, it seems superfluous to enquire about them, since it is certain that they should be regarded as of contingent and not primary importance.[65]

Origen's relegation of the non-human creation to a subsidiary position is reinforced in his apologetic work, *Against Celsus*, in which he draws on the Stoic view that 'providence has made everything primarily for the sake of the rational nature' to insist on the superiority of rational beings over irrational and inanimate ones.[66]

[62] Origen, *De Princ.* I.1.6. Scheffczyk notes that by the 3rd century, Christian theology's preoccupation with Trinitarian and Christological questions meant that creation ceased to be such an important issue (Scheffczyk, *Creation and Providence*, 82).

[63] Origen, *De Princ.* II.1.1.

[64] Ibid. I.8.1 (Greek text). Only about one sixth of Origen's writings are still extant in the original Greek text. See introduction by Butterworth in Origen, *De Princ.* xix–xxx.

[65] Origen, *De Princ.* II.9.3.

[66] Origen, *Cels.* IV.74.

To suggest, as Celsus does, that grass and plants might exist for the benefit of animals as well as humans, is according to Origen, tantamount to saying that they exist by chance rather than through God's providence.[67] Instead he applies his own thoroughly instrumental focus to all aspects of the non-human creation: 'the Creator, then, has made everything to serve the rational being and his natural intelligence.'[68]

Given the views outlined above, it is unsurprising that Origen's eschatology gives little importance to the material world. Since bodily existence represents a form of bondage, Origen suggests that at the 'consummation' rational beings will revert to the incorporeal state they enjoyed as eternal beings before the creation.[69] He attributes the groaning of creation in Romans 8 to the possession of materiality, even by the sun, moon, and stars, and explains the 'freedom of creation' as a time '[w]hen at the end and consummation of the world souls and rational creatures have been released as it were from their bars and prisons by the Lord'.[70]

The influence of Origen and his Platonic world view surfaces in fourth century scholars such as Basil of Caeserea and Augustine as well as in later centuries.[71] R. J. Berry suggests that 'Origen introduced a distinction between creation and God's saving work, which became ever stronger through Renaissance, Reformation and Enlightenment, and is only now beginning to break down'.[72] Glacken maintains that Origen's view is more nuanced, citing evidence from *Contra Celsum* that Origen accepted the notion of divine

[67] Ibid. IV.75.

[68] Ibid. IV.78.

[69] Origen, *De Princ.* III.6.1. This bondage extends to the sun, moon and stars which Origen counts as rational beings (Origen, *De Princ.* I.7.3). There is evidence of some ambiguity in this, since earlier in the same work he suggests that only God can be truly incorporeal, hence bodily matter would continue to exist. Origen, *De Princ.* I.7.3.

[70] Origen, *De Princ.* I.7.5.

[71] It can be seen in Augustine (e.g. Augustine, *Civ.* XI.23) and Aquinas (e.g. Aquinas, *Sum. Theol.* Q. 65, Art. 2). For discussion of the relationship between Origen and Augustine's views of creation see Vannier, 'Origène et Augustin'. However, from the end of the 4th century some of the theological thinking associated with Origen (Origenism), began to be considered heretical and Origen himself was discredited and anathematized in the 6th century for these views.

[72] R. J. Berry, *God's Book of Works*, 42.

intentionality behind the creation, albeit as a home for humankind. For Origen, suggests Glacken, '[t]he earth and nature do not exist for men for a narrow utilitarian reason, but because God favours the rational over the irrational'.[73] However, it is unclear how Glacken distinguishes between narrow utilitarianism and favouring the rational, since both presuppose that the non-human creation is of lesser value than human beings. In the end, Glacken's discussion does little to soften the functional anthropocentrism of Origen's thought.

Already two strands of thought are emerging concerning the relationship between human beings and the rest of creation. The first is the sense of the earth as a temporary abode for humanity—one planned by God, but which fades into insignificance beside the greater glory of human ascent towards the divine. The second is that human beings represent the crown of creation, and that all else in the created world serves to reveal God to humans and to provide for their daily needs. Although there is little to suggest an explicit concern to dominate nature in a negative or exploitative fashion, implicit in such writings are ideas of human superiority and likeness to the divine that will influence future centuries—both within the church and outside it.

Basil of Caesarea: Homilies on Genesis

In the *Hexaemeron*—a series of nine homilies on the six days of creation addressed to his congregation in clear and simple language—Basil of Caesarea (*c.*331–79) rejects the allegorical approach favoured by Origen in favour of a strongly literalistic exegesis.[74] He explains from Gen. 1: 1 that the order visible in the world is evidence of its divine origin, refuting pagan and 'atheistic' beliefs that the world came about by chance.[75]

[73] Glacken, *Rhodian Shore*, 185. His discussion is based on *Contra Celsum* and makes little reference to *de Principiis.*

[74] Carleton Paget, 'Alexandrian Tradition', 539. However allegorical tendencies may be seen in his homilies on the Psalms, which probably date from a similar time period, suggesting that the literalism of the *Hexaemeron* may derive in part from his interest in scientific matters, coupled with the simple audience it is addressed to (Carleton Paget, 'Alexandrian Tradition', 540).

[75] Basil, *Hex.* 1.5.

Basil emphasizes the revelatory potential of the creation by a series of analogies (such as that of a work of art demonstrating something of the artist), and describes its beauty in eulogistic manner:

I want creation to penetrate you with so much admiration that everywhere, wherever you may be, the least plant may bring to you the clear remembrance of the Creator.[76]

However, a more limited perspective is evident in his discussion of the phrase 'it was good' (ὅτι καλόν), where Basil maintains that the goodness of creation is functional rather than aesthetic and that the created world is conceived by God as a training ground for the soul.

[T]he world was not conceived by chance . . . but for a useful end . . . since it is really the school where reasonable souls exercise themselves, the training ground where they learn to know God; since by the sight of the visible and sensible things the mind is led . . . to the contemplation of invisible things.[77]

Hence his discussion of the purposefulness of all creation is primarily in the context of providing for human requirements and, while not relegating the created world to the extent found in Origen, has a utilitarian focus in which the non-human creation functions as a tool for human use, whether for practical or revelatory purposes.[78] This is offset, at least in part, by his evident appreciation of the natural world and his reflections on the biological questions of the day, including migration and the cycle of predation, which leads Glacken to comment that 'Basil's physico-theology is the best of its kind until the works of Ray and Derham in the late seventeenth and early eighteenth centuries'.[79]

Gregory of Nyssa

Basil profoundly influenced the work of his contemporaries, including his brother, Gregory of Nyssa, who himself wrote a treatise

[76] Ibid. 5.2.
[77] Ibid. 1.6, 4.6.
[78] E.g. his eulogy on the variety of trees (ibid. 5.7; see also Basil, *Hex.* 5.3, 5.7).
[79] Glacken, *Rhodian Shore*, 194.

entitled *On the Making of Man* to supplement the Genesis Homilies of Basil.[80] In it he defends Basil against his critics as well as engaging in detailed discussion of relatively small points of disagreement between them.[81] Gregory's fundamental view of the ontological divide between the uncreated Trinity and the created order means that, for him, God is utterly unknowable. But human beings, by virtue of the *imago dei*, are on the border between uncreated and created beings and they alone have the capacity to approach God such that they become aware of his unknowability.

This elevated view of humanity leads Gregory to emphasize the superiority of human nature over the rest of creation.[82] Man was created last, he maintains, in order that God could prepare the earth as 'a royal lodging for the future king'.[83] His destiny is to rule over the rest of creation and to enjoy its wonder and beauty and thus to better understand the power of God. As Moore and Wilson note in their introduction to *On the Making of Man*, 'The narrative of the creation of the world is not discussed in detail: it is referred to, but chiefly in order to insist on the idea that the world was prepared to be the sphere of man's sovereignty.'[84] Gregory goes so far as to turn a human being's lack of the natural protective covering of fur and his inability to defend himself against predators into a rationale for human dominion over 'subject animals'.[85] Human upright stance and unique ability to walk on two legs rather than four like other creatures are evidence for Gregory of 'marks of sovereignty which show his royal dignity'.[86]

Gregory, along with a number of early theologians, is well aware of human capacity to change the earth and regards human activity such as agriculture and domestication of animals as not only necessary but part of the creator's intention.[87] In this they undoubtedly draw on

[80] According to Robbins, Gregory of Nyssa 'ranks only second to Basil' as a source for later Greek 'hexaemeral' works (Robbins, *Hexaemeral Literature*, 54).

[81] Quasten, *Patrology*, 3: 263.

[82] See Glacken, *Rhodian Shore*, 298.

[83] Gregory of Nyssa, *Opif.* II.1.

[84] Ibid. 386.

[85] Ibid. VII.2.

[86] Ibid. VIII.1.

[87] Glacken, *Rhodian Shore*, 295–7.

Philo's explanation of human relationship with creation which likens the human to a pilot or driver, charged with the care of plants and animals and accountable to God.[88] This understanding of dominion as responsibility and care is one which gradually alters in the subsequent centuries of the church to include notions of 'man as modifier of nature, as an agent of God in furnishing and finishing creation'.[89]

Ambiguities in Augustine regarding the created order

Augustine's influential role in western theology is exemplified both by his own prodigious writings, and by the sheer volume of secondary literature portraying him in both a positive and a negative light. Augustine's interest in Genesis leads him to produce no fewer than four commentaries on Genesis, one of which, *On the Literal Interpretation of Genesis*, would prove to be exceptionally influential for medieval Latin writers on creation.[90] In addition to his commentaries, the most relevant of his writings for this discussion are *Confessions* and *City of God*, although it should be noted that in these, as in his other works, creation theology forms an extremely small part of the whole.

Augustine was converted to Christianity from Manichaeism, a third-century Persian religion based on a dualistic cosmology. As a reaction against this and in a desire for intellectual understanding of how God made the world, he attempts to marry the philosophical reasoning and scientific knowledge of his day with Christian doctrines that are, for him, articles of faith.[91] Central to his doctrine are the two essential themes of knowing God, and knowing humanity as the image of God.[92] Although this focus does not exclude awareness of the created world, in the words of Trapè, '[it] places it within a

[88] Philo, *Creation of Cosmos* (Runia), §88.

[89] Glacken, *Rhodian Shore*, 301.

[90] Robbins, *Hexaemeral Literature*, 64; see also D. F. Wright, 'Augustine', 727–30.

[91] Trapè, 'Augustine', 403. Manichaean teaching posits two eternal and equal forces of good and evil in perpetual combat. Like Gnosticism, matter as the creation of the evil force is itself evil; good is spirit—the creation of the good God of heaven.

[92] Ibid. 409–10. Raven suggests that in his later life, especially in *City of God*, Augustine returns to a Manichaean understanding of the physical world (Raven, *Natural Religion*, 51–2).

hierarchy and orders it toward man who is its crown and end'.[93] Nevertheless, Augustine opposes Origen's view of creation as a prison for fallen rational beings, and acknowledges the goodness and immanence of God as demonstrated in the beauty and completeness of creation: 'there was no other cause of the world's creation than that good creatures should be made by a good God.'[94]

In those of his commentaries on Genesis that are predominantly literal rather than allegorical Augustine adopts a meticulous exegetical method using grammatical and rhetorical tools as well as the scientific knowledge of his day to explain the literal meaning of the text.[95] Augustine's systematic hermeneutical method, which was to prove extremely influential in the Middle Ages, attempts to balance literal and spiritual readings of the texts.[96] His extensive treatment of the creation story in these works demonstrates a profound awareness of the mystery and detail of the created world.[97] However, it would be misleading to suggest that Augustine's interest here lies in any real way with the rest of the created world *per se*. The primary focus in his Genesis commentaries is, as elsewhere, on the relationship between the human self and God the Creator, in particular the human need to find self-fulfilment by turning to God.[98]

His focus on humanity as the image of God predisposes Augustine towards a hierarchical view of the created order. In this structural

[93] Trapè, 'Augustine', 409. See Augustine, *Conf.* X.vii.12–15, XIII.xxxii.47–xxxiii.48.

[94] Augustine, *Civ.* XI.23.

[95] Augustine, *Gen. Litt.*; Augustine, *Gen. Man.* It is evident that even in his literal commentaries, Augustine reverts to allegorical interpretation at various points. His interpretation of Gen. 1:28 explains human dominion over animals by virtue of human rationality, but he also reads this verse as an encouragement to 'hold in subjection all the affections and emotions of our soul, which are like those animals' (Augustine, *Gen. Man.* 2, 1.20.31). For discussion of literal versus allegorical interpretations see Trapè, 'Augustine', 377–8 and the Introduction by Teske in Augustine, *Gen. Imp.* That Augustine himself is aware of this issue is clear from the opening chapter of *The Literal Meaning of Genesis* (Augustine, *Gen. Litt.* I.1.1).

[96] In the end the spiritual reading is prioritized by most medieval commentators, thus reducing the natural world to a series of 'signs' whose explanation is to be found by reference to the scriptures (Harrison, *Protestantism and the Rise of Natural Science*, 30).

[97] Augustine, *Gen. Litt.* III.14.22; Augustine, *Gen. Man.* I. 25–6.

[98] See 'General Introduction' by Hill in Augustine, *On Genesis*, 14–15.

approach, which owes much to Neoplatonic ideas as well as dualistic influences from Augustine's past, the animate is superior to the inanimate, and intelligent and immortal beings are above all others, with the human race occupying the prime position in creation as 'its greatest ornament'.[99] The relationship of human beings to the non-human is explained further in Augustine's exegesis of Gen. 1:26–7. The image of God is not based on corporeal likeness, but 'on account of that power by which he surpasses the cattle'.[100] Both the rationality that distinguishes humans from animals and their upward stance, that brings them closer to heaven, represent for Augustine the 'likeness and image and wisdom of the Father'.[101] In the light of this understanding, it is unsurprising that Augustine should devote most of his theological attention to the higher, intelligent beings, and especially to human endeavour with respect to God. The fundamental aim of these literal interpretations of the Genesis creation account is, in the words of one scholar, 'a metaphysical meditation on the being and order of creation' rather than an account of the significance of creation in the divine purpose.[102]

Augustine's eschatology, like that of Irenaeus, is focused on the future culmination of history, in particular the destiny of rational beings, both human and angelic. His rejection of Platonic ideas that deny bodily resurrection in favour of the immortality of the soul leads him to identify the resurrection body fully with the earthly body.[103] However, Augustine's understanding of the resurrection of the body is less than corporeal.[104] Though he considers the wonders of creation to be a blessing in the present life, he does not conceptualise the blessings of the perfected soul in terms of renewal and perfection of the earth.[105] In the end, for Augustine the ultimate goal

[99] Augustine, *Civ.* XIX.13, IX.16.

[100] Augustine, *Gen. Man. 2*, 1.17.28.

[101] Augustine, *Gen. Imp.*, 60.

[102] Hill in Augustine, *On Genesis*, 20.

[103] Augustine, *Civ.* XXII.11. However, even in his mature thought, Augustine did retain some elements of his earlier, Platonic alienation from the human body, particularly from human sexuality (Santmire, *Travail of Nature*, 68–9). Robbins goes further, suggesting that 'Platonism in its derivative forms . . . became an integral part of Augustine's interpretation, and through the latter to a certain extent colored all later thought'. Robbins, *Hexaemeral Literature*, 11–12.

[104] See e.g. Augustine, *Civ.* XXII.21.

[105] Ibid. XXII.24.

of the human soul is the eschatological City of God; human life lived in the world in the present time, and by implication the whole of the created world, is merely a bridge over the gap between the past and the future.[106]

Augustine regards the world as beautiful and ordered, designed and created by a benevolent God, and at times lapses into lyrical prose to show how the order and beauty of the universe can lead human beings to a knowledge of God.[107] However this is not his main focus. As Glacken notes, for Augustine 'the most important idea concerning man's relation to the Creator and to the rest of the creation is that men become gods' by participation in the one true God.[108] This elevation of humanity to quasi-divine status is exacerbated by Augustine's move later in life back towards a more dualistic frame of reference that leads him to deny the importance of bodily existence in favour of spiritual reality.[109] His separation of creation from christological and pneumatological considerations is an example of 'the divorce of the willing of creation from the historical economy of salvation' which, according to Gunton, lies at the root of the modern separation between God and nature.[110] Augustine's legacy as one of the most influential theologians of the early church is, on the whole, one in which the created world is regarded as temporary and subsidiary to human relationship to God, and one that can only contribute to the alienation between human and non-human creation in later Christian thinking.

[106] See Gunton, *One, Three and Many*, 82–4.

[107] Glacken, *Rhodian Shore*, 200.

[108] Ibid. (from Augustine's *Expositions on the Psalms*).

[109] Scholars are divided over Augustine's legacy. Gunton suggests that Augustine's doctrine of creation is, in the end, Neoplatonic rather than Trinitarian, resulting in a separation of the creation of the world from its redemption. (Gunton, *One, Three and Many*, 54–5, see also the discussion in Northcott, *Environment*, 215–17). Raven, citing Augustine's last great work, *The City of God*, as well as his later Anti-Pelagian treatises, suggests that in his later life he returned to his Manichaean roots and espoused a wholesale condemnation of the secular realm, including by implication the natural world (Raven, *Natural Religion*, 51–2), whilst both O'Meara and Santmire reach more positive conclusions concerning his view of creation (O'Meara, *Augustine*, 122–30; Santmire, *Travail of Nature*, 70–3).

[110] Gunton, *One, Three and Many*, 55.

CONTRASTING PERSPECTIVES IN THE MIDDLE AGES

As well as drawing a strong distinction between human beings and the rest of the created world, the exegetical literature of the patristic period contributed two further and potentially conflicting ideas about the natural world that would become important to the understanding of human relationship with both Creator and creation in the Middle Ages and beyond.[111] The first is that of the natural world as God's book, supplementing revelation through Scripture as a means of knowing God, which provided the rationale for natural philosophers in the early decades of scientific investigation to 'think God's thoughts after him'.[112] This quest would eventually be a motivation behind the endeavours of numerous scientists of the seventeenth and eighteenth centuries to engage in empirical study of nature. The second idea concerns attempts to account for the struggles and lack of harmony in nature, including the presence of poisonous and harmful plants and animals, by means of theological reflection on the effect of human sin and the Fall on the natural world.[113] The apparent moral disjuncture that affected the whole created order, coupled with the medieval experience of the natural world as a harsh and hostile place, combined to produce a culture in which 'taming nature' was regarded as a wholesome, even morally superior act.[114]

The so-called Dark Ages are perhaps not as dark as some have suggested, although the inhospitable landscapes and weather conditions of western and northern Europe may have contributed tendency to regard nature as the enemy of civilization and in need of 'taming'.[115] The natural world was the subject of fascination for writers and artists alike resulting in the rich literature of legends and allegories and the skilled animal depictions of the bestiaries, with

[111] Glacken, *Rhodian Shore*, 202–3.

[112] The notion of the natural world as one of two books (the other being the Bible) was popularized in the Middle Ages by a number of writers (Harrison, *Protestantism and the Rise of Natural Science*, 44).

[113] Glacken, *Rhodian Shore*, 205–6.

[114] Northcott, *Environment*, 47.

[115] Glacken, *Rhodian Shore*, 172–3.

their moralistic overtones.[116] This literature, notes Glacken, 'kept alive the notion of the earth as the home of man, even if it were little more than an anteroom to the next world'.[117]

The growth of the monastic movement, in particular Benedictine monasticism, exemplifies the ambiguity in relationships between humanity and the natural world. Northcott notes that many of the monastic communities were 'models of sustainable farming, of self-sufficiency and self-government which ... reflected a spirituality of nature and land which was marked by gratitude for creation as the gift of God, and a careful quest to nurture its natural fruitfulness'.[118] Although this perspective demonstrates a more positive view of the natural world, the monastic transformation of the wilderness resulted in the development of labour-saving new agricultural implements, which were the precursor to the industrialization of agriculture, and which, according to Lynn White, contributed to the commodification of nature.[119]

The breadth of understanding regarding the created world in the Middle Ages is exemplified in the different approaches of two of its leading figures, Francis of Assisi and Thomas Aquinas. Francis is known as the founder of the Franciscan monastic order and for the wealth of legend concerning his extraordinary relationship with animals and his ability to perform miracles. The work of Aquinas reflects the tendency of the period to engage in theological debates from a philosophical perspective, which included a primarily metaphysical approach to creation.[120]

Francis of Assisi: the brotherhood of creation

Francis of Assisi's love of the natural world reflects that of the Celtic Christians of the preceding centuries. Indeed, there is some evidence that Francis and the Franciscans may have been influenced by the practices and ideas of the Irish monks who travelled to Europe on

[116] Raven, *Natural Religion*, 58–9.
[117] Glacken, *Rhodian Shore*, 207.
[118] Northcott, *Environment*, 47; see also McDonagh, *Care for the Earth*, 130–1.
[119] White Jr., 'Historical Roots'.
[120] Scheffczyk, *Creation and Providence*, 121.

pilgrimage.[121] Following several profound religious mystical experiences, Francis took a vow of poverty and chastity, and devoted his life to itinerant preaching and teaching, and to caring for society's outcasts, particularly lepers.[122] His biographers note that his dedication to Christ motivates not just his compassion for the poor but also a profound love and respect for all creation.[123] Bonaventure suggests that Francis's tendency to address animals as brother or sister is due to his conviction that all creation is created by God, and should therefore return due praise to the Creator.[124] But the natural world is also a means by which Francis encounters God.

> He exulted in all the works of the Lord's hands, and penetrated through those pleasant sights to their Life-giving Cause and Principle. In beautiful things he recognised Him who is supremely beautiful. . . . Everywhere he followed the Beloved by the traces he has impressed on all things; he made for himself a ladder whereby he might reach the Throne.[125]

For Francis then, God is the source of all life and goodness and there is no dichotomy between material and spiritual: '[B]y the power of his extraordinary faith . . . he seemed to perceive a divine harmony in the interplay of powers and faculties given by God to his creatures.'[126]

The writings attributed to him include a series of Admonitions, Rules, and Letters, addressed to members of the order and other devout followers, which are essentially didactic or devotional in nature, rather than presentations of systematic theology.[127] Whilst

[121] E. A. Armstrong, *Saint Francis*, 34–41.

[122] Knowledge of Francis's life and work is only available from the colourful and glowing accounts of early hagiographies. See Celano, *S. Francis*; Bonaventure, *Soul's Journey*; and St Francis, *Little Flowers*.

[123] Armstrong suggests that Francis' relationship to animals should be understood in the light of his 'essentially pastoral outlook' reflected in his compassionate dealings with people (E. A. Armstrong, *Saint Francis*, 109). However, it is notable that Celano's biography gives more space to animal stories than teachings on poverty, suggesting that to his contemporaries this aspect of Francis' life took precedence (Celano, *S. Francis*).

[124] Bonaventure, *Soul's Journey*, 8.6.

[125] Ibid. 9.1.

[126] Robson, *St Francis*, 238.

[127] For a full set of the writings of Francis see R. J. Armstrong and Brady, *Francis and Clare*.

his writings and those of his close followers are full of biblical quotations and allusions, he differs from many of the others in this study by the absence of any exegesis of texts or systematic theological discussion. In *Admonitions* his only reference to the creation is to suggest that his human audience have no grounds to boast in their creation in the image and likeness of God, since 'all creatures that are under heaven, according to their constitutions serve, acknowledge and obey their creator better than you'.[128] By far the most significant of his works, not least from the perspective of creation theology, is his *Canticle of Brother Sun*.[129] This hymn of praise to God as Creator, in the somewhat effusive description by Armstrong,

> expresses the mystical vision of the Saint of Assisi and, since it springs from the depths of his soul, provides us with many insights into the profundity of his life and faith in the Triune God, Who so deeply enters into creation. In this vision, . . . the Little Poor Man . . . [b]ecomes so intimate and familiar with the wonders of creation that he embraces them as 'Brother' and 'Sister,' that is, members of one family.[130]

Francis exhibits compassion to all creatures, but this is especially marked towards those which bear sacramental symbolism such as lambs and doves.[131] He also respects inanimate objects, in particular those associated with biblical imagery, for example rocks or fire.[132] His early biographers cite numerous occasions on which he preaches to animals and birds, urging them to praise and love God.[133] Other stories present him encouraging animals to live at peace with human beings and vice versa, including his legendary pact with a wolf not to terrorize the human population, which suggests,

[128] Karris, *Admonitions*, 78. However, Karris goes on to observe that in his citation of Gen. 1:26 in this admonition, Francis is not interested in its context or meaning in Genesis. Rather he is employing a medieval, monastic interpretation.

[129] Also called *Canticle of Creatures*.

[130] R. J. Armstrong and Brady, *Francis and Clare*, 38. Almost without exception the secondary literature on Francis, most of which originates within the Franciscan order of the Catholic Church, is couched in pietistic and eulogizing terms.

[131] E. A. Armstrong, *Saint Francis*, 106; see also R. J. Armstrong, *Francis of Assisi*.

[132] Bonaventure, 'Mirror of Perfection', 293; Robson, *St Francis*, 241.

[133] Robson suggests that in so doing Francis places a literal interpretation on the closing injunction of Mark's gospel that the disciples should preach to *every* creature (Robson, *St Francis*, 242).

according to some modern commentators, the attribution of a capacity for moral responsibility to animals.[134] For Lynn White, Francis represents 'the greatest revolutionary in history: he forced man to abdicate his monarchy over the creation, and instituted a democracy of all of God's creatures'.[135]

Francis of Assisi is unique in his appreciation of the natural world yet firm in his refusal to deify it, and it is with some justification that White dubs him the 'patron saint of environmentalists'.[136] His perspective on the world is thoroughly relational, as Armstrong notes: 'Enthralled by the beauty and mystery of Creation, he believed and showed that the love of God, love of man, and love of nature were not only compatible with one another but the natural, divinely purposed state of humanity.'[137] Although he set an example of poverty, love, and humility that inspired many and founded one of the best known monastic orders of the Catholic Church, his impact on the theological development of the western church is perhaps less obvious. It is for the extraordinary example of his life rather than for the theological profundity of his writings that he is remembered, and as such he is an inspirational rather than influential figure.

Anthropocentricity in Aquinas

Far more influential than Francis of Assisi, both in the Middle Ages and beyond, is the scholastic theologian Thomas Aquinas. He is one of the finest examples of medieval scholasticism's desire to use human reason to discover the answers to theological and philosophical questions and to trace the relation between Aristotelian philosophy and divine revelation.[138] Aquinas engages with both the Scriptures and earlier theologians, particularly Augustine, to explore

134 Hughes, 'Diversity of Creation', 315.

135 White Jr., 'Natural Science', 433.

136 White Jr., 'Historical Roots', 1207.

137 E. A. Armstrong, *Saint Francis*, 242.

138 Olson, *Christian Theology*, 311–13. Scheffczyk notes that although Aquinas's thought is steeped in Aristotelian ontology and logic, evidence of Platonic influence can also be detected in his understanding of creation (Scheffczyk, *Creation and Providence*, 149).

and refute some of the philosophical speculations of his day, most of which are not particularly concerned with the relationship between human and non-human creation.

When it comes to discussion of creation, Aquinas starts from the idea of God as efficient cause of the universe, with all creatures originating 'on account of God's goodness' and reflecting this divine attribute.[139] Scheffczyk notes that this metaphysical approach has the effect of detaching creation somewhat from the wider perspective of redemption and eschatology, and tends to 'represent Creation as somewhat self-contained, an isolated event in the past, to treat it as a mere object of rational analysis'.[140] Nevertheless Aquinas affirms the purpose of God in bringing diversity of creatures into existence, 'in order that his goodness might be communicated to creatures and be represented by them; and because his goodness could not be adequately represented by one creature alone'.[141]

The official church of Aquinas's day was especially concerned with the doctrines of angels and ecclesiology, each based on a hierarchical understanding of reality derived from the mystical theology of Pseudo-Dionysius.[142] This preoccupation surfaces in Aquinas and is influential in his hierarchical understanding of the working of the universe. That he views the world as a strictly tiered structure can be clearly seen in his discussion of Genesis 1, where he states that fish are superior to plants, land animals to fish and birds, and where he distinguishes humanity as 'the most perfect grade', created as a direct result of God's action.[143] Because of this hierarchy the lower orders are subordinate to and governed by the higher ones, with angels

[139] Aquinas, *Sum Theol.* Q. 65, Art. 2; see also Q. 47, Art. 1.

[140] Scheffczyk, *Creation and Providence*, 151.

[141] Aquinas, *Sum Theol.* Q. 47, Art. 1. For discussion of Aquinas's distinction between natural and revealed knowledge of God see Nichols, *Discovering Aquinas*, 37–47.

[142] Pelikan, *Christian Tradition* 3, 293–94. In his *Celestial Hierarchy* and *Ecclesiastical Hierarchy* Pseudo-Dionysius is preoccupied with angelic beings and humans as rational souls. Although he avers that all creation, including soulless and lifeless matter, owes its state of existence to the Good (*Divine Names*, 3.696D), the assumption in his hierarchies (e.g. *Celestial Hierarchy*, 2.3.140b; 2.4.144b) is that so-called irrational animals and other matter are ranked below rational and supernatural beings (Pseudo-Dionysius, *Complete Works*).

[143] Aquinas, *Sum Theol.* Q. 72, Art. 1.; Q. 96, Art. 1.

ultimately mediating God's rule in the world.[144] The latter idea gives Aquinas difficulty in explaining divine providence and the immanence of God in creation and is, according to Scheffczyk, illustrative of the tendency to transcendentalism that characterizes the period.[145]

Furthermore, Aquinas maintains that the ultimate purpose of the lower beings is to serve the higher ones: 'lifeless beings exist for living beings, plants for animals, and the latter for man', concluding that 'the whole of material nature exists for man, inasmuch as he is a rational animal'.[146] For him 'it is in keeping with the order of nature that man should be master over animals' since this is part of the 'order of Divine Providence which always governs inferior things by the superior'.[147] This sits uneasily with his understanding of creation reflecting God's goodness and marks a shift from the Augustinian appreciation of nature as a subject in its own right. As Santmire suggests, '[d]ominion over nature is, in Thomas's thought, in the process of becoming domination of nature. Nature is seen more as an object for human use, which satisfies biological needs and serves spiritual knowledge, than as a subject in its own right.'[148]

Aquinas's instrumental view of the world is further demonstrated in his eschatology. He maintains that, although the creation of the universe is good, it is only the 'first perfection' of nature. At the end of the world, only the spiritual beings, humans and angels, will be perfected by grace.[149] Since the heavenly movements that maintain 'corruptible' things such as plants and animals will cease, 'plants and animals will altogether cease after the renewal of the world'.[150] Such a

[144] Ibid. Q. 72, Art. 1.

[145] Scheffczyk, *Creation and Providence*, 136.

[146] Aquinas, *Sum Theol.* Q. 96, Art. 1; Aquinas, *Compendium of Theology* 1, 148 (see Santmire, *Travail of Nature*, 91).

[147] Aquinas, *Sum Theol.* Q. 95, Art. 1 & 2.

[148] Santmire, *Travail of Nature*, 92. Santmire notes the inherent ambiguity between this aspect of Aquinas' thought and his theocentric view of the diversity and gradation of creatures, all of which are created to mirror God's goodness (ibid.).

[149] Aquinas, *Sum Theol.* Q. 73, Art. 1.

[150] Aquinas, *Sum Theol. III (Supp.)* Q. 91, Art. 5.

denial of any purpose for the rest of creation in the final consummation would seem to contradict his view of the goodness and purposefulness of the material world.[151]

The work of Aquinas reflects the fact that in the Middle Ages, as in previous centuries, reflection on the created world primarily inspired theological comment about the nature of God, and moralistic and allegorical teachings. Interest in nature in its own right was remote from the popular themes of personal piety and the inner life, and hence regarded with suspicion by many.[152] From the end of the thirteenth century onwards however, this began to change as observations and depictions of the natural world became increasingly naturalistic.

Aided by the translation of major studies of natural history such as Aristotle's *De Partibus Animalium*, a number of medieval scholars compiled their own encyclopaedias, albeit based on exegesis of these ancient documents rather than their own observations.[153] Now the natural world ceased to be merely symbolic of deeper, religious realities; it became important and interesting in its own right.[154] This trend paved the way for the separation of secular learning in the natural sciences from theology, the queen of sciences, a separation that 'liberated natural science and . . . permitted it to develop as an autonomous human endeavour'.[155] Nevertheless, it was not until the Enlightenment that empirical study of the natural world, in the form of observation in the field and collection of specimens, became an accepted and valued part of scientific endeavour.[156]

[151] Santmire, *Travail of Nature*, 92–3.

[152] Hendry, *Theology of Nature*, 16. Aquinas devotes a vast amount of *Summa Theologica* to discussion of virtues, passions, and habits.

[153] Harrison, *Protestantism and the Rise of Natural Science*, 67–8.

[154] White Jr., 'Natural Science', 428–9. Francis of Assisi is, according to White, a pioneer in this move. However, for him, as we have seen, interaction with the creation is a profound theological experience rather than a distancing of the natural from the supernatural.

[155] Ibid. 432.

[156] Harrison, *Protestantism and the Rise of Natural Science*, 78.

THE MARGINALIZATION OF CREATION THEOLOGY IN REFORMATION THOUGHT

The Protestant reformation of the sixteenth century was such an important milestone in the journey of the church that its effect must be considered here, even though the doctrine of creation was not an area of major disagreement and hence received relatively little attention. The central preoccupation of the reformers was with challenging the authority and theology of the Catholic Church, including its insistence that the Scriptures could only be interpreted by the magisterium.[157] One of the characteristics of the work of the reformers was their insistence on the right of individuals to read and interpret the Bible for themselves, free from the dictates of priest or pope. Whilst this freedom is commendable and paved the way for the rise of critical scholarship and of contemporary methods of biblical studies, it nevertheless produced a focus on human beings and their individual relationship to God, a trend within Protestantism which would by default relegate the natural world to a peripheral and incidental place.

Martin Luther

Occasional references to Luther's understanding of the created world can be found in his works, but do not form a significant part of his doctrine.[158] His concern is rather with the Augustinian theme of God and the self, a focus on human salvation that effectively means that '[c]reation is merged with providence, and virtually disappears behind it'.[159] This is exemplified in his verse by verse exegesis of Genesis, in which he maintains that the essential purpose of creation

[157] McGrath, *Nature*, 173.

[158] His observations of nature are often used as an illustration for human conduct (e.g. Luther, *Sermon on the Mount*, 196–200), and function to express his distaste for the practice of astrology (e.g. Luther, *Table Talk*, 172); see Bornkamm, *Luther's World*, 185–96; and Elert, *Lutheranism*, 343.

[159] Hendry, *Theology of Nature*, 17.

is to meet human need and ultimately to point humanity to God.[160] Writing on Genesis 1:14 he states:

> God created all these things in order to prepare a house and an inn, as it were, for the future man, and . . . He governs and preserves these creatures by the power of his Word . . . that we may learn that the divine providence for us is greater than all our own anxiety and care.[161]

Luther draws a great distinction between human beings and other animals, on the basis of the human capacity to count and to measure time, which for him is evidence of the immortality of the human soul.[162] In keeping with many of his contemporaries, he views the world as a threatening and hostile place suffering under the curse of the Fall.[163] This negative view of creation is reflected theologically in his suggestion that the hostility of nature, which like human beings 'bears the traces of God's wrath', has the effect of drawing sinners to seek God's mercy.[164] As Santmire puts it, in Luther's doctrine of soteriology, nature functions as 'an essential springboard for grace'.[165] Yet Luther also suggests that even the prelapsarian intention for humanity is orientated towards the immaterial future: 'we were created for a better life in the future than this physical life would have been, even if our nature had remained unimpaired.'[166]

[160] Much of Luther's work is in the form of lectures, sermons, and homilies, often based on detailed exegesis of biblical books, which were subsequently edited and published. There is some debate over the authenticity and integrity of some of the published material, since in some cases comparison of Luther's own notes with the printed version suggests that extensive editorial reworking of the source material was carried out by second generation Lutherans. In the case of the Genesis lectures, for which Luther's own notes are not extant, Jaroslav Pelikan urges some caution, but concludes that 'the *Lectures on Genesis* are an indispensable source for our knowledge of Luther's thought' (Pelikan, 'Introduction', in Luther, *Genesis* XII). However, it is in his polemic works, against Catholic theologians such as Eck and Emser and against his fellow reformers such as Zwingli, that his influential reformatory doctrines were articulated most clearly and fully.

[161] Ibid. 47.

[162] Ibid. 46.

[163] His own decision to become a monk was triggered by being caught in a storm in an isolated location (Santmire, *Travail of Nature*, 148).

[164] Luther, *Genesis*, 208.

[165] Santmire, *Travail of Nature*, 125.

[166] Luther, *Genesis*, 56. He cites approvingly the more explicit affirmation by an earlier scholar (probably Lombard), 'Even if Adam had not fallen through his sin,

Although Luther eschews the strongly allegorical interpretation of the Bible favoured by earlier centuries of church tradition, his desire to read the Old Testament as the history of the Christian church, and not just of the people of Israel, leads to 'an exegesis of the Scriptures which seems to modern eyes allegorical or at least typological'.[167] As Pelikan notes, this is found par excellence in his exposition of Genesis[168] and a further example may be seen in his interpretation of Psalm 104, in which the entire exegesis is based on typologies and imagery, with no reference to the creation order.[169]

Luther's view of the world as God's good creation can without doubt be substantiated from many of his works. But the wider theological framework in which this is incorporated is the problem of human sinfulness in the face of the wrath of God, and the unmerited grace of God in dealing with the human condition. The dominance of Luther's 'theanthropocentric' perspective,[170] which will have an influential role in the development of Protestantism, means that any theology of creation fades completely into the background. As Hendry puts it, in Luther's teaching about creation, 'he reduced the whole world of nature to a repository of goods for the service of man'.[171]

still, after the appointed number of saints had been attained, God would have translated them from this animal life to the spiritual life'. (Cf. Lombard, *Sententiarum libri quatuor*, II, Distinctio XX, Patrologia Latina).

[167] Pelikan, *Luther the Expositor*, 90. Despite the sheer volume of the exegetical material, Pelikan suggests that 'much of Luther's exegesis was undistinguished, and even more of it was a product of the exegetical tradition that preceded him' (Pelikan, *Luther the Expositor*, 38).

[168] Pelikan, *Luther the Expositor*, 90–3.

[169] E.g. in his exegesis of Ps. 104 Luther suggests that 'the heavens' of v. 2 refer to the scriptures of the Old Testament, and the 'springs and waters' in v. 10 represent apostles and teachers sent by God to 'tame' the nations (Luther, *Psalms* II, 318–19, 326–27). A similar exegetical method may be found in his commentary on other creation psalms, e.g. Psalms 8 and 19 (Luther, *Psalms I*).

[170] A word given currency in the twentieth century by Karl Barth (Santmire, *Travail of Nature*, 124, 220 n. 20.

[171] Hendry, *Theology of Nature*, 17.

John Calvin

The other great Reformer of the sixteenth century, John Calvin, provides a more systematic account of Protestant theology in *The Institutes of the Christian Religion.* Although *Institutes* begins with a discussion of God as Creator, Calvin, like Luther, is primarily concerned with human relationship to God and major sections of his book cover the means of knowing God, the corruption of sin, justification by faith and divine election of the righteous, and the relationship between church and state.

Calvin does not deny the revelation of God in the wonders of creation, viewing God as the great Artificer and maintaining that 'upon his individual works he has engraved unmistakable marks of his glory, so clear and so prominent that even unlettered and stupid folk cannot plead the excuse of ignorance'.[172] He endorses study of natural phenomena by means of the natural sciences but warns against the neglect of divine providence in so doing.[173] He is vehemently opposed to those who equate creation with Creator or introduce the notion of nature as intermediary, and strongly refutes the pantheistic ideas of Greek philosophy.[174] For Calvin human beings are the supreme example of the divine creative wisdom, since '[man] is a rare example of God's power, goodness, and wisdom, and contains within himself enough miracles to occupy our minds'.[175]

In the brief discussion of the six days of creation in *Institutes* Calvin maintains that the order and functioning of the universe have human well-being as their goal.[176] God's goodness towards humanity is demonstrated by the provision of a world fully equipped to meet human needs: 'before having created man, he

[172] Calvin, *Institutes I*, I.v.1. See also I.xiv.20–21 on the goodness of creation and God as Artificer.

[173] Ibid. I.v.2.

[174] Ibid. I.v.5. In this section of the *Institutes* Calvin vehemently condemns Plato, Aristotle, and the Stoics in equal measure! Natural revelation is, however, not sufficient to bring knowledge of God, since due to 'human superstition and the error of the philosophies' (I.v.12) 'God bestows the actual knowledge of himself upon us only in the Scriptures' (I.vi.1).

[175] Ibid. I.v.3.

[176] Wendel, *Calvin*, 170. See Calvin, *Institutes I*, I.v.7.

made ready for him everything which, as he foresaw, would be useful or beneficial.'[177] Human superiority over animals is demonstrated by the human capacity to worship God and to aspire to immortality.[178] This narrowly anthropocentric perspective continues in Calvin's discussion of God's providence, which is particularly extended to human beings since 'the universe was established especially for the sake of mankind'.[179]

Calvin's doctrine of the fall and original sin is significant for his view of creation. His assertion of 'the hereditary depravity and corruption of our nature' has implications for the non-human creation.[180] For Calvin 'ever since man declined from his high original, it became necessary that the world should gradually degenerate from its nature', a process that accounts for 'the existence of fleas, caterpillars, and other noxious insects'.[181] His view of the world's 'fallenness', as McGrath suggests, introduces the idea that disorder in the world is ontologically present and pre-exists human awareness of such disorder.[182] In the context of his prioritization of the doctrine of human redemption, this understanding lays the groundwork for a perception of the non-human creation as 'fallen' and in need of mastery that surfaces later in the sixteenth and seventeenth centuries.

Calvin's commentary on Genesis adds nothing further to the views outlined above, affirming as it does the indisputable goodness of creation, yet also emphasizing the superiority and dignity of humanity compared with other creatures.[183] Moreover, his teleology of creation is also utilitarian: 'And hence we infer what was the end for which all things were created; namely, that none of the conveniences and necessaries of life might be wanting to men.'[184] In Calvin's exegesis and his theology he presents a view of the world that centres round human identity and God's activity in history. In

[177] Calvin, *Institutes I*, I.xiv.22; see also fn. 32 and I.xiv.2.
[178] Ibid. I.iii.3, see also fn. 14.
[179] Ibid. I.xvi.6.
[180] Ibid. II.i.8.
[181] Calvin, *Genesis*, 104.
[182] McGrath, *Nature*, 174–6.
[183] Calvin, *Genesis*, 97.
[184] Ibid. 96.

such a focus, perhaps inevitably, the natural world plays an incidental and utilitarian role.

DOMINATION NOT DOMINION

Despite their different perspectives and approaches, many of the influential theologians that have been surveyed here display certain common features in their approach to the created world and God's relation to it. Their primary concern is with human relationship to the divine, and within this matrix, the non-human creation, even though for some it is the gift of a good Creator, has a functional role with regard to human beings. With the exception of Francis of Assisi, the overall trend is away from the integrated view of the world presented by Irenaeus, towards one that marginalizes and will ultimately commodify the non-human world.[185] This culminates in the thinking of both Luther and Calvin which focuses extensively on God and humanity, a 'theanthropocentric' theology reflecting the post-Augustinian trend towards preoccupation with soteriology. As Northcott summarizes:

> The early Christian schema of creation/redemption is gradually eclipsed under the influence of Hellenistic philosophy and in particular of Platonism, and the good and salvific purposes of God for any part of the created order other than human souls are further eclipsed in Protestant theologies of election.[186]

As noted in the Introduction, the narrowly anthropocentric focus of Protestant thought, coupled with an increase in individualism and the rise in scientific questioning (of the existence of God as well as of the nature of the physical world), will ultimately play their part in the modern technological domination of nature. The focus on the

[185] Whether Harrison is correct in asserting that prior to the early modern era there is no *explicit* connection made between the Genesis creation accounts and the exploitation of nature, an instrumental view of the natural world is *implicit* in commentators' perception of the superiority of human beings and the functional teleology of the rest of creation (Harrison, 'Subduing the Earth').

[186] Northcott, *Environment*, 221.

human story in theological discourse and biblical exegesis will continue to feed the view that the non-human creation is of secondary or marginal importance. In the following chapter we will explore changes that took place from the sixteenth century onwards in both the natural sciences and theology, and, following the emergence of biblical criticism, in biblical studies.

2

Nature versus History
An Artificial Divide?

Because it is now deeply entrenched in our thought, it is easy to forget that the tendency to view all matters in terms of their histories may itself have a history.

(Mandelbaum, *History, Man and Reason*)

For the Old Testament the world is the field of man's experience, the stage on which his work and destiny are played out. Man is not interpreted in the light of the world, but the world in light of man.

(Bultmann, *Primitive Christianity*)

THE GROWTH OF MODERN SCIENCE

Few of the theologians discussed in the preceding chapter denied the role of natural theology in providing knowledge of the divine, and many positively endorsed it. However, this is by no means the same as an appreciation of the created order as a whole in its own right. The natural world was perceived as having 'purposes which, in one way or another, related to the human race and its welfare'.[1] Although from the thirteenth to fifteenth centuries there was growing interest in understanding how the world functioned, scientific

[1] Harrison, *Protestantism and the Rise of Natural Science*, 177.

study during this period was by and large subordinated to theological interests.[2]

The years between the Reformation and the start of the nineteenth century were a time of revolutionary scientific discoveries coupled with great intellectual and philosophical questioning, in which the authority of the political and religious *status quo* was radically challenged.[3] Although it is by no mean possible here to do justice to the complexities of this period in European history, a number of factors can be indentified that were influential in challenging the theological presuppositions of previous centuries, in particular with regard to the created world. The Copernican revolution radically altered the prevailing perception of the universe from a geocentric to a heliocentric one in which planets revolved around the sun.[4] In the light of this displacement of the earth from the centre of the universe, writes Harrison, 'no longer could its inhabitants claim to be the sole end of the created order'.[5] The seventeenth century saw a tremendous upsurge in interest in natural history and the flourishing of empirical study of the natural world.[6] For many of its proponents, nature was one of two 'books'—the other being Scripture—in which God revealed himself to humankind. Discovering new insights from God's 'book of works' was therefore, for some at least, a religious responsibility. Yet such a focus on nature did not necessarily result in a

[2] Brooke, *Science and Religion*, 53.

[3] Rhodri Lewis suggests that although the term Enlightenment may be a helpful shorthand to describe the work of thinkers during the latter part of this period, it is better to think in terms of a number of overlapping yet discreet 'Enlightenments' (Lewis, 'The Enlightenment', 99; see also Kent, 'Eighteenth Century'). The complexities of Enlightenment thought and its influence on the place of the Bible in the modern world are discussed in Sheehan, *The Enlightenment Bible.*

[4] Copernicus finally published his ground-breaking work *De revolutionibus orbium coelestium* in 1543, near the end of his life, but his theory was only accepted slowly by his contemporaries (Dampier-Whetham, *History of Science*, 119–24). For an engaging and readable account of responses to *De revolutionibus*, see Gingerich, *The Book Nobody Read.* On the relation between Copernican cosmology and biblical interpretation, see Howell, *God's Two Books.*

[5] Harrison, *Protestantism and the Rise of Natural Science*, 181.

[6] The development of the modern sciences of botany and zoology from the work of these early naturalists is a fascinating one but beyond the scope of this volume. For detailed discussion, see e.g. R. J. Berry, *God's Book of Works*; Harrison, *Protestantism and the Rise of Natural Science*; McGrath, *Nature.*

respect for other creatures. Cruelty towards animals, both for scientific research and for entertainment, was culturally acceptable, and by the Victorian era, zeal for hunting and collecting wild animals resulted in the extinction of many species.[7]

One rationale for scientific investigation and innovation as well as for human use of natural resources was provided by the notion of human beings as perfecters of a fallen creation.[8] This regarded the human quest for knowledge of the material world as a means of addressing one of the fundamental problems posed by the beginning of Genesis, namely repairing the loss of dominion engendered by Adam's 'Fall'.[9] The centuries following the Reformation saw a great interest in these early chapters of Genesis, resulting in numerous commentaries that built on the work of better known biblical commentators of preceding generations, such as Luther and Calvin.[10] Many of these were by scholars and clergymen who are relatively unknown today, but their influence is felt in some of the great literary works of the period, not least Milton's masterpiece *Paradise Lost* and the poetry of Spencer, Donne, and Dryden.[11]

The Genesis creation accounts were appealed to by these commentators as evidence of the superiority of human beings over other creatures, as Williams explains: 'Man is the colophon, the epitome, the masterpiece of all creation.'[12] Moreover, for several seventeenth-century authors, the stories of the Fall, the Flood, and the tower of Babel were evidence of human loss of knowledge concerning the material world: 'in the state of innocency in the first creation, man had perfect naturall knowledge of all naturall things, arising and springing immediately from his naturall soule.'[13] Scientific endeavour was regarded as a means of recovering this lost

[7] Thomas, *Man and the Natural World*, 17–30.

[8] See Harrison, *Fall of Man*.

[9] Although generally ascribed to Francis Bacon, the roots of this concept are in the earlier (9th century) writings of John Scotus Eriugena (Harrison, *Protestantism and the Rise of Natural Science*, 61).

[10] Arnold Williams calculates that approximately forty commentaries on Genesis appeared in Europe and England between 1527 and 1633 (Williams, *Common Expositor*, 6).

[11] Ibid. 29.

[12] Ibid. 68.

[13] George Walker, *History of the Creation* (1641), cited in Harrison, *Protestantism and the Rise of Natural Science*, 211.

understanding. Harrison notes that it is as these literalistic readings of the Genesis texts replaced the more allegorical ones of pre-Reformation Britain that ideas of human dominion over the natural world started to gain greater ascendancy: 'the literal approach to texts precipitated this change of attitude towards the world, while the literal content of key passages of the Bible further motivated natural philosophers in their quest to master nature.'[14]

This period also saw the beginning of a shift in perceptions of the relationship between science and theology. Philosophers such as Descartes who rejected the search for a 'final cause' which had characterized Aristotelian science, regarded science as increasingly separate from religion.[15] By contrast, early natural historians such as John Ray, writing in the late seventeenth century, integrated their scientific endeavour with a devout Christian belief in God's providence as well as his creative power.[16] Likewise, Isaac Newton, whilst he scrupulously tried to avoid allowing religious prejudices to colour his scientific theorems, considered that 'in the last analysis, the realm of science was dependent on the God of religion, and led the reverent mind to a fuller assurance of his reality and a readier obedience to his commands'.[17] However, the trend towards a mechanistic view of the world raised questions about God's role within it and eventually resulted in a deism which viewed God solely as initial creator of a system governed by unchanging laws.[18] Such a perception is epitomized by William Paley writing in the late eighteenth and early nineteenth century, who used the analogy of a watch to articulate in a lucid and compelling fashion the classic statement of the 'argument from design'—that the natural world was the careful and deliberate work of a cosmic designer.[19] In the Industrial Revolution

[14] Harrison, 269, see also 206–07.

[15] Brooke suggests that this process represents a new differentiation between science and religion rather than complete separation of the two. Brooke, *Science and Religion*, 16–42.

[16] Ray, *Wisdom of God*.

[17] Burtt, 'The Metaphysics of Newton', 132.

[18] Even so, many of those who used mechanical analogies, including Descartes and Boyle, saw ideas of design and God's sovereignty in their view of a mechanized universe (Brooke, *Science and Religion*, 118).

[19] Paley, *Natural Theology*, 3–31.

of the following century, the mechanical analogy had great appeal for the Victorian middle classes, ultimately contributing to the functional approach to the earth's natural resources that has characterized the industrial and technological era.[20]

RISE OF ROMANTICISM

Alongside the loss of respect for, and consequent exploitation of, the natural world in the scientific and industrial revolution of the west, a counter-trend can be identified, namely the search for moral purpose and aesthetic value in nature that characterized the Romantic Movement of the eighteenth and nineteenth centuries, and is epitomized in the works of the great Romantic poets such as Blake, Shelley, and Wordsworth. At the same time as the natural world was increasingly subject to exploitation to meet the needs of industrial and consumerist societies, 'philosophers, poets and ordinary people increasingly came to regard the natural world as a source of beauty, pleasure and moral guidance'.[21] Rather than the practice of reason which characterized Enlightenment thought, the Romantics used imagination and the expression of feeling to make 'the otherwise incongruous alliance between the infinite, their simulacrum of God and the natural'.[22] For most Romantics this resulted in a kind of 'natural supernaturalism' whereby God becomes naturalized and the natural world divinized.[23]

Although Romanticism did not have a profound effect on the prevailing Protestant theology of the church in Britain, its influence is visible in some of the hymn-writers of the eighteenth and nineteenth centuries, including Isaac Watts and John Keble, and most notably Fanny Alexander, the author of 'All things bright and beautiful'.[24] The Romantic enjoyment of the natural world

[20] McGrath, *Nature*, 250–1. However, Paley did not himself directly equate human mechanical and industrial endeavour with the world of nature.

[21] Northcott, *Environment*, 89.

[22] Masson, 'Romanticism', 118.

[23] Ibid. 119.

[24] Brooks, *Hymns as Homilies*.

resulted ultimately in the establishment of numerous voluntary organizations that are concerned for the protection of areas of natural beauty, like the Lake District in England and Yellowstone Park in the USA, and societies such as the Royal Society for the Protection of Birds (RSPB) devoted to the conservation of species and habitats. Yet despite the large numbers of people who today belong to such organizations or enjoy the open spaces they aim to protect, sensitivity to the magnitude of the environmental problems facing the world remains elusive.[25]

BIBLICAL EXEGESIS IN THE TWENTIETH CENTURY

Passmore contends that it is the influence of Greek thought rather than the Bible itself that promoted the view that human beings can do what they like with the world.[26] The writings of some of the patristic and medieval theologians discussed in the preceding chapter have hinted at this tendency. The ensuing biblical exegesis of the western Protestant tradition further helped to relegate the natural world to an incidental and functional position, and both drew from and fed the rise of science and the economic progress of the Industrial Revolution. The next question concerns the extent to which those exegetical traditions have continued and have coloured approaches to the natural world in contemporary understanding.

The interest in biblical theology of the mid-twentieth century produced a number of influential scholars who stressed the importance of human history within the biblical tradition and in so doing, it could be argued, relegated creation to a secondary position. However, since the 1990s, the priority and even exclusivity of the human story in the biblical traditions has come under question as a new wave of scholars has challenged this traditional viewpoint. The

[25] An estimated 3.5 million people belong to the National Trust, and 1 million to the RSPB. Although discussion of this disinterest is beyond the remit of this volume, it suggests there is a wide gulf between many westerners' enjoyment of the natural world as a leisure activity and their willingness to make lifestyle choices or advocate costly concrete political change in order to preserve it.

[26] Passmore, *Man's Responsibility*, 27.

following section will assess the work of von Rad and others for their contribution to the marginalization of creation theology within biblical studies and then consider a number of contemporary approaches, some arising as a direct response to the current rise in environmental awareness, that offer an alternative perspective.

The Influence of Hegelian Philosophy

One of the significant influences on the development of modern Old Testament theology is the German idealism that flourished in the nineteenth century, in particular the writings of the philosopher G. W. F. Hegel. In his *Philosophy of Religion*, Hegel draws on the dualistic distinction prevalent in western philosophical thought between mind and matter, spiritual and material, to propose a dichotomy between Spirit and nature. He regards religious development as a process of evolution from primitive religion of nature to religion of humanity and, ultimately to the 'perfect religion', namely Christianity.[27] Ancient Israelite religion marks the second stage of this development and is distinct from the nature religions of the ancient Near East by virtue of its sharp division between natural and spiritual. The result, maintains Hegel, is that '[n]ature is now degraded to the condition of something powerless, something dependent relative to the underived Power'[28] and '[n]ature is represented as thus entirely negated, in subjection, transitory'.[29] In contradistinction, humankind as the image of God is elevated: 'Man is exalted above all else in the whole creation. He is something which knows, perceives, thinks.'[30]

A similar dichotomy is articulated in Hegel's work on the philosophy of history in which he suggests that history develops by means of a dialectic progression of thesis, antithesis and synthesis.[31] The

[27] Hegel, *Philosophy of Religion*, 330.
[28] Ibid. 128.
[29] Ibid. 189.
[30] Ibid. 198.
[31] Hegel exalted Germany as the pinnacle of this progression, using utopian nationalist language, 'The German Spirit is the Spirit of the new World. Its aim is the realisation of absolute Truth as the unlimited self-determination of Freedom'. (Hegel, *Philosophy of History*, 341). Hegel's conception of the state and citizens'

cultures of the ancient 'Oriental' world are identified with the first, primitive, phase of history in which 'the Spiritual is limited by Nature'.[32] In ancient Judaea, the progression of history means that nature is displaced from its primary place in Eastern thought to 'the condition of a mere creature',[33] and '[t]he Spiritual develops itself in sharp contrast to Nature'.[34]

This dualistic understanding of both religion and of history, and the assumption of human superiority over nature have, in the words of Theodore Hiebert, 'provided the categories and language for much of the traditional biblical scholarship that has emphasized Israel's new historical consciousness and its subordination of nature'.[35] Hegel's dialectical scheme of development in history was applied to the Old Testament by Vatke, who was the first to suggest that the writings of the classical prophets predated the Pentateuch and who produced 'the first truly historical Old Testament theology'.[36] Vatke's work in turn anticipated much of Wellhausen's account of the development of the history and religion of Israel from primitive naturalism to the ethical monotheism of the priests and law codes via the religion of the prophets.[37] A number of contemporary studies have noted that, contrary to some accounts, Wellhausen did not himself espouse the philosophical underpinnings of Hegelianism.[38] This is notwithstanding von Rad's contention that Wellhausen '[was] strongly influenced by Hegel: he looked on Israel's history as a history of ideas, and presented it above all from the standpoint of spiritual evolution'.[39]

relationship with it is regarded by many as prefiguring 20th-century totalitarianism, including the nationalism that gave birth to the Third Reich. Conversely, as will be seen, his prioritization of history over nature was influential in attempts by von Rad and others to counter the tendencies of German National Socialism by their stress on salvation history (see Brueggemann, 'Loss and Rediscovery'; Peet, 'Protestant Churches'; Pois, *National Socialism*).

32 Hegel, *Philosophy of History*, 195.

33 Ibid.

34 Ibid.

35 Hiebert, *Yahwist's Landscape*, 17.

36 Morgan and Barton, *Biblical Interpretation*, 63.

37 Wellhausen, *Prolegomena*.

38 Morgan and Barton, *Biblical Interpretation*, 69; see also Perlitt, *Vatke und Wellhausen*; Oden, *Bible without Theology*.

39 Von Rad, *Old Testament Theology* 1, 113.

FOCUS ON SALVATION HISTORY (HEILSGESCHICHTE)

The growing interest in biblical theology in the mid-twentieth century produced a significant number of scholars on both sides of the Atlantic who viewed the Old Testament as the first part of the Christian canon and were concerned to read it not just as an account of ancient Israelite religion, but in terms of what is normative for Christian belief.[40] Of these perhaps the best known is the German scholar Gerhard von Rad, whose two-volume *Old Testament Theology* has greatly influenced subsequent decades of biblical studies. As already noted, von Rad speaks inaccurately and rather disparagingly of Wellhausen's Hegelianism yet displays the influence of Hegelian thought in his own perpetuation of a dualistic distinction between nature and history.[41] In one of his earlier articles, 'The Theological Problem of the Old Testament Doctrine of Creation', he maintains that 'in genuinely Yahwistic belief, the doctrine of creation never attained to the stature of a relevant, independent doctrine'.[42] Rather it 'performs only an ancillary function' as a stimulation to faith in the redemptive acts of God in Israel's history.[43] This conclusion is elaborated in his *Old Testament Theology* in which he asserts that,

> The Old Testament writings confine themselves to representing YHWH's relationship to Israel and the world in one aspect only, namely as a continuing divine activity in history.... In principle Israel's faith is grounded in a theology of history.... [and] regards itself as based upon historical acts.[44]

Von Rad considers that the earliest confessional statements about YHWH are those rooted in historical declaration (e.g. Deut. 26:5–9) and that this early 'Credo' is subsequently added to, to include, among other things, the accounts of creation and the primeval

[40] For a discussion of the development of biblical theology and its relationship to the history of religion school, see Perdue, *Collapse of History*, 19–68; Perdue, *Reconstructing Old Testament Theology*, 25–43.

[41] Simkins, *History and Nature in Joel*, 19–22.

[42] Von Rad, 'Doctrine of Creation', 142.

[43] Ibid. 134.

[44] Von Rad, *Old Testament Theology* 1, 106.

history.[45] Although von Rad considers it probable that belief in YHWH as creator predated the seventh century BCE, he maintains that this was not theologically integrated into the 'salvation history' religion of Israel until later, and that most Old Testament creation texts are of a late date.[46] In his concern to identify the primary theological tenets behind Israelite religion, von Rad appears to be drawing a distinction between belief and theology that cannot be substantiated from the texts.[47]

Von Rad's focus on salvation history leads him to the conclusion that neither Genesis nor Second Isaiah testify to the importance of creation for its own sake. Although he draws attention to the very many differences between the J and P creation narratives, he suggests that they are both based upon a soteriological understanding of creation, such that 'creation is part of the aetiology of Israel'.[48] The aim of Genesis 1 and 2 is not faith in creation; '[r]ather, the position of both the Yahwist and the Priestly document is basically faith in salvation and election.'[49] Interestingly for this analysis, but almost as a throwaway remark, von Rad asserts an anthropocentric focus for both accounts, 'Both . . . are at one in understanding creation as effected strictly for man's sake, with him as its centre and objective.'[50] Likewise the creation texts in Second Isaiah portray YHWH's creative activity as subordinate to his soteriological acts, and thus reinforce confidence in YHWH's power to save by presenting the creation as a saving event in itself.[51] In a number of these passages, according to von Rad, creation and redemption converge and virtually coincide.[52]

[45] Ibid. 121–4.

[46] Ibid. 136. He enumerates a few 'decidedly old' texts indicating an early belief in creation, although he does not define the phrase. The implication is that these fragments pre-date even the J creation account, since von Rad subsequently deals with this text in more depth (von Rad, *Old Testament Theology* 1, 140–1).

[47] Von Rad, 'Doctrine of Creation', 131.

[48] Von Rad, *Old Testament Theology* 1, 148. Somewhat at odds with his treatment of the J creation account is his earlier decision to '[leave] the Jahwist out of account, since he does not in fact treat of the creation of the world at all' (von Rad, *Old Testament Theology* 1, 136).

[49] Von Rad, *Genesis*, 46.

[50] Von Rad, *Old Testament Theology* 1, 150.

[51] E.g. Isa. 44: 24; 51: 9f; 54: 5.

[52] Von Rad, *Old Testament Theology* 1, 137.

In some of his later writings von Rad adopts a more nuanced view and cautions against reading the Old Testament exclusively from the perspective of historically conditioned theology.[53] In a discussion on the prohibition of images in his essay on the ancient Israelite world view he suggests that the distinction between history and nature is a modern and anachronistic one—in the Old Testament they are regarded as 'one single area of reality under the control of God'.[54] With reference to the wisdom literature von Rad argues that Job 28, Proverbs 8, and Ben Sira 24 each seek to portray the deity revealed in creation as the same God who is instrumental in Israel's historical development.[55] Nevertheless he still maintains that the creation accounts serve the purpose of furthering Israel's self-understanding, rather than presenting an understanding of the world.

This more positive evaluation of creation theology is developed by von Rad in his monograph on the wisdom literature, in which he identifies a soteriology brought about by means of the creation itself that is in tension with the earlier historical-salvation ideas of traditional Yahwism.[56] Texts such as Proverbs 8 and Ben Sira 24, which describe wisdom in terms of the created order, and Job 12 and certain Psalms which speak of the self-revelation of creation (e.g. Psalms 97, 145, 148) articulate a relationship between humankind, the world and God that differs from both that of the surrounding nations and from earlier Israelite religion. In von Rad's opinion, the sages who authored such texts were not intending them as a polemic against the earlier traditions. Rather 'the voice of this revelation filled a gap and satisfied a theological need that had begun to be felt'.[57]

Von Rad concludes his monograph on wisdom with a series of positive statements concerning creation, suggesting that, ontologically, 'creation ... vindicated every form of trust', and 'creation was an

[53] Von Rad, 'Old Testament World View', 144.

[54] Ibid. 155.

[55] Ibid. 163.

[56] Von Rad, *Wisdom in Israel*, 314.

[57] Ibid. 164. It is evident in this monograph that von Rad regards the wisdom literature as a fully integrated part of Israelite life and thought (von Rad, *Wisdom in Israel*, 174–5). This represents a departure from his earlier view that the wisdom literature '[is] an Egyptian outlook passed on to Israel by travelling teachers of wisdom' (von Rad, 'Doctrine of Creation', 142).

unlimited sphere of activity for the divine will'.[58] He hints at the endeavour of the sage to understand humanity, not in isolation from the world, but 'tied to an environment in which he found himself both as subject and object, active and passive'.[59] Unfortunately despite this moderation of his earlier, more negative, views of Israelite creation theology, it is generally those views for which he is remembered, and which have exerted a profound influence on scholarship.

The 'uniqueness' of Israelite religion

The desire among scholars of this period to distinguish Israel from her ancient Near Eastern neighbours and stress the uniqueness of her religion has contributed to the focus on YHWH as the God of history to the exclusion of creation.[60] In comparing biblical creation myths with those from other ancient Near Eastern civilizations, a number of scholars highlight the dissimilarity between Hebrew thought and that of the surrounding nations in order to demonstrate the 'universal and divinely sanctioned dogmas' behind the biblical text.[61] One such is von Rad's contemporary and compatriot, Walter Eichrodt, whose *Theology of the Old Testament* came to be regarded as 'one of the true classics of biblical studies'.[62] In volume two of this work, Eichrodt compares the biblical creation accounts specifically with the Babylonian creation myth, Enuma Elish.[63] Although he sees some external areas of agreement, he highlights a number of significant distinctive features of the Israelite concept of God, in particular the rejection of a 'naturalistic' understanding of the relationship between creator and creation.[64] His discussion of Genesis 1 concludes with the assertion that the divine command of Gen. 1:28 sums up the goal of creation and the purpose of human existence and activity, and finds its expression in history: '[God] ... subordinates Man to the mighty

58 Von Rad, *Wisdom in Israel*, 298.

59 Ibid. 314–15.

60 The influence of Mowinckel's work comparing Israelite religion with other ancient Near Eastern religions may be seen here.

61 Perdue, *Reconstructing Old Testament Theology*, 31.

62 Ibid. 41.

63 Eichrodt, *Old Testament Theology* 2, 93–117.

64 Ibid. 100, see also 16.

teleological world movement, which by its own inner logic moves inexorably towards the concept of history'.[65]

Eichrodt's discussion of the relative superiority of humanity over other creatures stresses both the alien remoteness of the natural and the gulf separating human beings from the world in which they live.[66] The result of such de-divinization of the physical world and elevation of humanity is outworked in the unique and universal mandate given to humanity: 'subjugation of the earth and dominion over its creatures bestows on the human race a common universal task.'[67] This task is to be accomplished without bounds: 'Man has authority over a wide sphere of activity. Here he rules in the fullness of his own power, installed as Lord over the created world, called by the divine blessing at creation to people the earth by virtue of his natural fertility, and equipped to overthrow all obstacles to the spread of his sovereignty.'[68]

This apparent mandate for human mastery of the natural world is only slightly nuanced by Eichrodt's assertion that the biblical text portrays 'Nature' as a living thing, with its own relationship with YHWH, and, particularly in the prophetic texts, to God's operation in the realm of nature as well as in history.[69] For Eichrodt the purpose of even the most impressive natural phenomena is not to have independent significance, but to be revelatory, as 'witnesses to the infinite power and wisdom of the one Lord'.[70]

Eichrodt has some difficulty holding together these two concepts relating to the natural world, on the one hand asserting human superiority over other creatures, on the other stressing the 'alien and incomprehensible quality of the cosmos' and its capacity to reveal something of God.[71] Although they cannot be seamlessly

[65] Eichrodt, *Old Testament Theology* 2, 110.

[66] Ibid. 118–31.

[67] Ibid. 127.

[68] Ibid. 151.

[69] Ibid. 152–62. Eichrodt suggests that in Second Isaiah the descriptions of nature function not only as proof of God's greatness and superiority over heathen gods, but are in themselves 'an actual source of revelation, on which faith in God's power and will to redeem can feed' (Eichrodt, *Old Testament Theology* 2, 159).

[70] Ibid.

[71] Ibid. 161.

harmonized, he suggests that they unite to form 'the inseparable and mutually indispensable aspects of a religious interpretation of Nature based on the revelation of the covenant God'.[72] It could be argued that Eichrodt wants to have his cake and eat it.

The rise of German National Socialism

The emphasis on human history that characterizes the biblical interpretation of both Eichrodt and von Rad takes on a particular significance when considered in the light of the political context of the time. Both were living and writing in Germany in the 1930s at a time of unique and intense pressure as German National Socialism came into the ascendency. Following the end of the First World War, the unfavourable terms of the Versailles Peace Treaty had meant loss of power and prestige for the German nation and empire, and heralded an economic collapse in which poverty and mass unemployment were rife. The post-war Weimar government comprised a coalition of socialists and Catholics, leaving Protestants feeling unempowered and disillusioned. The Protestant Church responded by idealizing the time of *Kulturprotestantismus* that they had enjoyed under Bismarck and in due course welcoming with open arms their new 'saviour', Adolf Hitler, who promised a return to conservative, paternalistic, and imperial Germany, and ostensibly at least, a Christian state.[73] Although a few Protestant church leaders spoke up against the increasingly nationalist and racist pronouncements of the Nazi regime, most were apparently unaware or indifferent to such trends—or were too afraid to challenge them.[74]

[72] Ibid. 162.

[73] Part of the Protestant Church's unquestioning allegiance to the state as an expression of God's will was a desire to return to the 19th-century *Volk* religion espoused by Hegel and others. This emphasis suggested that the Germans were the super race (*Herrenvolk*), that Christ came to enable the German nation to triumph in its struggles and in so doing bring the highest religion (Christianity) to other peoples, and that '[war] would bring the greatest folk of all, the Germans, to full fruition as rulers of lesser peoples and churches and religions' (Peet, 'Protestant Churches'; see also Pois, *National Socialism*).

[74] Peet notes that 'There was no excuse for this mass approval of Nazism by the German Protestants or, for that matter, by any other German group. They could have

Historian Robert Pois notes the irony that it was in part a reaction against the 'despiritualization' of the world of nature and the other-worldliness of the Judaeo-Christian tradition that led German National Socialism to call for a return to nature and to espouse belief in a 'natural mysticism', in which the pure Aryan German race would emerge as superior.[75] He concludes: 'National Socialism was the result of a process of disenchantment or demystification which, ironically enough, came out of that Judaeo-Christian tradition which it was seeking to extirpate.'[76]

In turn, von Rad, like his contemporaries Eichrodt and the theologian Karl Barth, interpreted the Old Testament in reaction against the nature religion espoused by National Socialism with its emblem, the swastika, derived from an ancient eastern symbol of fertility. Brueggemann notes of Barth and von Rad that both scholars 'have as their formative context the capacity of Hitler to use "religion" for purposes of state ideology'.[77] The resultant separation of nature from history, he suggests, is one of the prime reasons for the marginalization of creation in Old Testament studies.[78]

The American biblical theology movement

The biblical theology movement in America, which gained strength in the years immediately following World War Two, was dependent on the European interest in biblical theology whilst developing its own unique characteristics.[79] Within this movement, two biblical theologians stand out for their overall contribution to Old Testament studies and also for their different perspectives on the importance of creation in the Old Testament. The first of these, G. E. Wright, echoes

been aware of Hitler's ideology and aims, he had revealed much of them in his autobiography *Mein Kampf*, published in the twenties' (Peet, 'Protestant Churches').

75 Pois, *National Socialism.*

76 Ibid. 149.

77 Brueggemann, 'The Uninflected Therefore of Hosea 4:1–3', 232.

78 Ibid. 231.

79 Childs, *Biblical Theology*, 18–27. He considers that 'there never was a Biblical Theology Movement in Britain or Europe which was similar to that in America' (ibid. 22).

and develops the negative approach to creation that characterizes German biblical theology, whilst Bernhard Anderson is among those who have contributed to the rediscovery of creation theology in the latter half of the twentieth century—although, as we shall see later in this chapter, not without inconsistencies.

Like Eichrodt, G. E. Wright is concerned to draw a sharp distinction between 'biblical faith' and that of 'pagan' religions. Israel's understanding of God, he argues, is predicated 'not on the cycle of nature, but on what God had done, was doing and was yet to do according to his declared intention'.[80] He draws on a Hegelian dichotomy between nature and history to relegate the former to the role of 'a handmaiden, a servant of history',[81] maintaining that 'the realism of the Bible consists in its close attention to the facts of history and of tradition because these facts are the facts of God'.[82] The Israelite understanding of God, suggests Wright, is especially predicated on the deliverance of the Exodus; to such descriptions are added nature imagery borrowed from Canaanite religion. Furthermore, the anthropomorphic language used of God—as Judge, King, Shepherd, etc.—testifies that his primary relation is to history and human society.[83] Wright fails to acknowledge that the biblical texts also use images of nature to describe God, or to distinguish biblical ideas of divine self-revelation through natural phenomena from the identification of gods with elements of nature that characterizes other ancient Near Eastern religions.[84]

In his later work, *The Old Testament and Theology*, Wright articulates more specific differences between Israelite understanding of creation and that of her polytheistic neighbours. The creation myths of the ancient Near East lie outside of time, while Israelite creation stories function in the context of Israel's history and of God as her Redeemer, and are therefore located within the concept of time. Not only is the Creator and the Redeemer one and the same God, the creation itself is the first of God's mighty acts in history,

[80] G. E. Wright, *God Who Acts*, 25.
[81] Ibid. 43.
[82] Ibid. 38.
[83] Ibid. 49.
[84] As noted by Fretheim, 'Psalms', 24–7.

which 'identifies history's Lord and releases into time [his] judging and redeeming power'.[85] Humanity as God's servant has responsibility for ruling over the earth, an understanding, maintains Wright, that is 'the beginning of the demythologising of nature, on which our modern western world of history and science rests'.[86]

It is clear that on both sides of the Atlantic, the prevailing tendency in biblical theology of the mid-twentieth century was towards a marginalization of creation texts and creation ideas in the biblical traditions and an elevation of the human story. This is not from any specific desire to legitimize exploitative environmental practices, nor because of a total disregard for the natural world. In Europe the German political regime was undoubtedly a contributory factor in this emphasis on human history as the means of God's revelation; in America, there is perhaps less excuse.[87] Brueggemann sums it up thus:

> I do not suggest that Barth, von Rad, or Wright intended such an anthropocentric mode of interpretation, but only that the end result of that mode of theological interpretation was the abandonment of serious theological thinking about creation in the face of the powerful claims of 'objective' science.[88]

History of religions

The tendency to marginalize the significance of creation in the biblical narrative is not limited to biblical theology, but is found in the work of those scholars who were more interested in the study of

[85] G. E. Wright, *Old Testament Theology*, 95.

[86] Ibid. 72. Such a positive affirmation of a strong causal connection between the Bible and modern science and technology was first propounded by M. B. Foster in the 1930s, and more fully articulated by Harvey Cox (Foster, 'Doctrine of Creation', 'Science of Nature I', 'Science of Nature II'; Cox, *Secular City*). As Barr notes, this theory is not only questionable from the biblical evidence itself, but attributing the achievements of science to Judaeo-Christian religion is, in the light of the environmental crisis, a dubious endorsement (Barr, 'Man and Nature', 14–19).

[87] To what extent the desire of the American Biblical Theology Movement to distinguish itself from more liberal agendas may have contributed to its emphasis on revelation through history is open to question (see Perdue, *Collapse of History*, 223). It may be that, as with Karl Barth, it was the notion of *revelation* which was attractive.

[88] Brueggemann, 'The Uninflected Therefore of Hosea 4:1–3', 233.

the history of religions. These include H. and H. A. Frankfort whose comparative study concludes that Hebrew thought is characterized by its dissimilarity from Egyptian and Mesopotamian beliefs, since YHWH is not *in* nature, but is *sui generis*. They also suggest that humankind and nature are both equally valueless in Israelite religion, 'in view of the unique significance of the divine'.[89] However, this view is moderated by their suggestion that humankind has both new freedom and new responsibilities as the interpreter of God's acts in Israelite history, which has replaced cosmic phenomena as the arena of God's activity.[90] In the end, it seems that for them only nature is, in fact, valueless.[91]

Sigmund Mowinckel, despite his sympathetic exploration of ancient Near Eastern cosmological myths, likewise draws a sharp distinction between the historical basis of Israelite religion and those of surrounding nations: 'On the whole this historical character is a really fundamental feature in the religion of Israel....this is what has made Israelite religion something essentially different from the "natural" religions and "nature-religions" of the Near East.'[92]

A more moderate position is found in the writings of Robert Cohn, who draws on the work of Mircea Eliade in the study of religions to examine the concepts of sacred space and sacred time with respect to Israel's Yahwistic faith.[93] Cohn concludes that the idea of space has been neglected in favour of YHWH's actions in time, since even 'the historical deeds of Yahweh' are intimately concerned with the geography of Israel.[94] However, despite Cohn's concern for sacred space, and his endorsement of Albrektson's suggestion that other ancient Near Eastern deities apart from YHWH are also concerned with history, he still maintains that for Israel, history was 'the

[89] Frankfort et al., *Before Philosophy*, 243.

[90] Ibid. 245.

[91] Other comparative studies include that of the Israeli scholar, Yehezkel Kaufmann, who argues that the Israelite understanding of God as a non-mythological, transcendent and supreme being was in contrast to the deities of the surrounding nations, and who presents Israelite religion entirely as a historical development (Kaufmann, *Religion of Israel*; see also Eliade, *Eternal Return*; Gottwald, *Tribes of Yahweh*).

[92] Mowinckel, *Psalms*, 139.

[93] Cohn, *Shape of Biblical Space*; Eliade, *Eternal Return*.

[94] Cohn, *Shape of Biblical Space*, 2.

organising principle for communicating the Israelite experience of Yahweh in the Hebrew Bible'.[95] His subsequent exploration of the religious meanings of certain key elements of biblical geography is predicated upon and therefore coloured by this assumption.

In all these various attempts to understand Israelite religion, whether from a theological perspective or in the history of religions context, one fundamental problem remains. The categories adopted by Hegel that have subsequently been absorbed into the thinking of twentieth-century biblical scholarship are modern ones. Neither 'nature' nor 'history' can be represented by comparable terms in biblical Hebrew. This does not mean that the ancient Israelites had no understanding of these spheres, rather that their perspective on the world may not have been categorized in this way. As Hiebert notes,

> [o]ne finds in Israelite literature words for the earth and its features and for political entities and social institutions, but no words that divide these matters conceptually and absolutely into two different spheres and orders of reality as do the modern words 'nature' and 'history'.[96]

REDISCOVERING CREATION THEOLOGY

Whilst a focus on Israel's history has not entirely vanished from studies of the Old Testament, the tide has turned in favour of a new appreciation of the biblical creation traditions. Two scholars can be particularly credited for their contribution to the rediscovery of creation theology in the latter half of the twentieth century—Claus Westermann and, as already noted, Bernhard Anderson. Westermann is well known for his three-part commentary on Genesis, the first volume of which provides a detailed and masterful examination of the primeval narratives.[97] He has also written perceptively concerning the interactions between the Church and post-Enlightenment science, noting that 'once theology has imperceptibly become detached from

[95] Cohn, *Shape of Biblical Space*, 1; see Albrektson, *History and the Gods*, esp. 11–15.
[96] Hiebert, *Yahwist's Landscape*, 17.
[97] Westermann, *Genesis 1–11*.

Creator-Creation, the necessary consequence is that it must gradually become an anthropology and begin to disintegrate from within'.[98] Westermann observes that the Bible never proposes belief in a Creator-God as an article of faith, since in the Old Testament world, this is presupposed.[99] This is in direct contrast to the biblical concept of salvation: 'In the Old Testament an alternative to belief in Creation or Creator is quite unthinkable.... God's saving action can be an object of belief; Creation cannot.'[100] By refusing to compare creation and salvation as like with like, Westermann effectively counters von Rad's contention that Israelite religion is concerned primarily with salvation and not creation. Although his remarks are not specifically articulated in the context of environmental issues, his argument that belief in creation is a fundamental premise of biblical religion provides a sound basis for such discussions.

Bernhard Anderson, writing against the backdrop of the American biblical theology movement, relates his work more specifically to environmental issues. He examines the nature of Israelite creation faith in the light of these concerns and of the increase in dialogue between science and theology, in two major works published in 1987 and 1994 respectively.[101] In *Creation versus Chaos* Anderson draws heavily on Gunkel's history of religions approach, which suggests that the primeval traditions of early Genesis are early Israelite adaptations of Mesopotamian creation myths.[102] However, Anderson is keen to stress the distinctiveness of Israel by virtue of its historical consciousness, suggesting that 'the Bible sets forth a historical drama—a *Heilsgeschichte*—in which man becomes "truly himself" as a historical being who decides and acts in response to the action of God in history'.[103]

[98] Westermann, *Creation*, 3. It is evident from the context that Westermann uses 'Church' to denote post-Reformation Protestantism.

[99] Ibid. 5.

[100] Ibid. 114.

[101] Anderson, *Creation Versus Chaos*, and *From Creation to New Creation*. Anderson also edited a collection of essays on various aspects of Israelite creation theology, *Creation in the Old Testament*.

[102] Anderson, *Creation Versus Chaos*, 23–6; Gunkel, *Schöpfung Und Chaos*.

[103] Anderson, *Creation Versus Chaos*, 30.

Likewise, in *From Creation to New Creation* Anderson begins by noting that faith in God as creator is the source of meaning for both human history and the natural world.[104] But he asserts that it is Israel's election faith, 'that is, the conviction that God has chosen the history of Israel as the special medium of divine revelation', that is presupposed by both creation accounts.[105] Like von Rad before him, Anderson suggests that creation and redemption belong together: 'in the Bible creation is not an independent doctrine but is inescapably related to the basic story of the people in which Yahweh is presented as the actor and redeemer.'[106]

Anderson stresses the uniqueness of human beings, made in God's image, who are not bound by the natural order but are 'decisional beings, summoned into dialogue with their Creator', and contrasts them with the animals that experience 'no greater demand upon them than to adjust harmoniously to the rhythms of nature'.[107] However, he also argues that the anthropocentric thrust of much twentieth-century theology, such as Bultmann's existentialist approach and Barth's rejection of natural theology, has perpetuated the sharp dichotomy between science and religion and led to an abdication of responsibility for the environment.[108]

Much of Anderson's work comprises detailed and perceptive exegesis of creation texts, in particular the primeval narratives. Where relevant he discusses the hermeneutical implications in the light of environmental issues. Yet there remains a fundamental ambivalence in his work, based upon his espousal of the biblical text as primarily an account of God's revelation in history. Despite appearing to advocate a responsible approach towards the environment, Anderson's focus, even when dealing with texts that refer almost exclusively to non-human creation, such as Psalm 104, glosses over some of the implications of such texts for a creation theology.

Anderson takes issue with von Rad's stress on salvation history and warns of the dangers of imposing western philosophical

[104] Anderson, *From Creation to New Creation*, 3.
[105] Ibid.
[106] Ibid. 7.
[107] Ibid. 13.
[108] Ibid. 99, see also 2, 115.

dualisms—such as nature/history, mind/matter, and cosmic/existential—on the biblical texts.[109] Yet he asserts just a few pages later that it is not possible 'to avoid the distinction between history and nature or a Cartesian distinction between mind and matter... even though such distinctions are alien to the Old Testament'.[110] Although Anderson calls for a rediscovery and remodelling of the biblical creation traditions, the failure to have solved this basic tension suggests that he has not perhaps travelled very far along this road.

The challenge of the environmental crisis

As awareness of the need to take environmental issues seriously has grown, so too has the number of biblical scholars who have responded to the implications of attributing to the biblical traditions a world view that devalues nature and exalts human history. Some of these are in direct response to Lynn White's article, others arise from a questioning of prevailing currents of opinion, or more general concern about the environment.

James Barr discusses the concept of 'history' in the biblical traditions in his 1963 article 'Revelation through History'.[111] Barr highlights several problems with the commonly held belief that history is the primary means of YHWH's revelation to Israel, the most fundamental being the inability of scholars who hold this view to agree on what they mean by 'history'.[112] Furthermore he points out, a large part of the Old Testament, in particular the Wisdom literature, does not concern itself with history at all.[113] Barr concludes by suggesting that the Old Testament narrative is made up of a series of 'revelatory' events in which God acts, but which stretch the concept of 'history' beyond that meaning that the word normally bears.[114]

[109] Ibid. 106.
[110] Ibid. 115.
[111] Barr, 'Revelation through History'; see also Barr, 'Man and Nature'; Rogerson, 'Nature'.
[112] Barr, 'Revelation through History'.
[113] Ibid. 196–7.
[114] For example, the Creation and Flood narratives stretch the concept of history beyond that of the Exodus, but also the Exodus stretches the concept of history beyond that, say, of the destruction of Jerusalem (ibid. 198).

More specifically, Rolf Knierim addresses the issue of God's relationship to the world according to two perspectives—the aspect of history and the aspect of world-order.[115] He reverses the insistence of von Rad and others that YHWH is uniquely and primarily manifested in Israel's history.[116] Rather than subordinating Israel's creation theology to her theology of history, he maintains that 'creation provides the criterion under which the meaning and also the purpose of history can be determined, even and especially the purpose of Israel's election'.[117] Furthermore, YHWH's salvific action begins with creation out of chaos and not with Israel's history, hence: 'Yahweh is the liberating creator of Israel precisely because he is the liberating creator of the world. It is the creator who is at work in Israel.'[118] His sobering conclusion is that the ongoing existence of cosmic global order faces a very real threat from human history and should not be taken for granted, and he calls for human history to rediscover its 'rhythm' with the order of creation.

Challenging the nature—history dichotomy

Several more detailed studies have continued to address the prioritization of history over creation in biblical scholarship. These challenge the notion that contemporary categories of history and nature are appropriate ones for understanding the biblical world. Of particular note are a number of full-length monographs that deal with different texts of the Old Testament. Only a few will be examined in detail at this point, namely the exegetical studies of Theodore Hiebert and Ronald Simkins, and William Brown's analysis of culture and nature in the Old Testament.[119] Hiebert and Simkins each begin with an overview of the trends in Old Testament theology that have

[115] Knierim, 'Cosmos and History'.
[116] Ibid. 59–60.
[117] Ibid. 94.
[118] Ibid. 98.
[119] Simkins, *History and Nature in Joel*; Hiebert, *Yahwist's Landscape*; Brown, *Ethos of Cosmos*. Certain other studies that include discussion of these issues or at least awareness of them will be considered in subsequent chapters.

emphasized Israelite religion as a religion of history, before moving to in-depth analysis of the different texts—in Hiebert's case, the J narratives of Genesis, and for Simkins, the book of Joel.[120]

The Yahwist's perspective—Theodore Hiebert

Hiebert suggests that the perception of biblical religion found in much modern scholarship is based on two fundamental dichotomies, namely the distinction between nature and history already analysed and the geographical division between the desert and arable land—the desert and the sown.[121] The latter dichotomy is based on questionable assumptions about the categorization of ancient Near Eastern cultures into desert nomadism and agricultural settlement, and whether Israelite nomadic pastoralism 'represents a more primitive stage of societal development than sedentary agriculture'.[122] These assumptions, suggests Hiebert, are based on eighteenth- and nineteenth-century presuppositions which 'have serious if not fatal flaws as models for describing ancient societies'.[123]

Hiebert is rightly convinced that 'the kind of analysis needed to carry the discussion of nature in the Bible beyond the results of current work is the study of individual biblical authors in a comprehensive and systematic fashion', and proposes to re-examine the traditional view in the light of one biblical author—the Yahwist (henceforth J).[124] Rather than focusing on the perceived dichotomies between desert and sown, nature and history, found in much traditional scholarship, he investigates both the actual landscape

[120] Hiebert, *Yahwist's Landscape*, 4–12; Simkins, *History and Nature in Joel*, 3–30.

[121] Hiebert, *Yahwist's Landscape*, 5. He cites Alt, *History and Religion*, and de Vaux, *Ancient Israel*, as illustrative of the assertion that Israel's historical and religious consciousness was primarily shaped by its nomadic desert origins.

[122] Hiebert, *Yahwist's Landscape*, 12. The theory of a nomadic ideal is also challenged by Talmon, 'As early as patriarchal times the Israelite society bears the imprint of semi-settled life in which only occasional reflections of nomadic life may be discerned' (Talmon, 'The "Desert Motif"', 34).

[123] Hiebert, *Yahwist's Landscape*, 22.

[124] Ibid. 23. The Yahwist is generally regarded as the writer of substantial sections of the Pentateuch, particularly in Genesis and Exodus, including the second creation account of Genesis 2–3 (see Davies, 'Introduction to the Pentateuch').

presupposed by the narrative, and J's attitude toward that landscape.[125] In so doing, his aim is to formulate an understanding of J's ideology apart from these modern western dichotomies.

The bulk of Hiebert's study consists of detailed and often insightful exegesis of the J traditions, with particular attention given to the primeval narrative. The centre of J's world of thought is, suggests Hiebert, האדמה (the ground), from which the first human is formed and to which he returns. In his ensuing discussion of the ancient Israelite farmer's relationship with the arable landscape that sustained him, he observes that J's description of human agricultural endeavour is to serve (עבד) the land, in contrast to the Priestly writer's use of רדה (subdue) and כבשׁ (have dominion).[126] J's world is one without dualisms, a unified concept of reality shared, maintains Hiebert, by most of the Old Testament.[127]

Hiebert's conclusion that nature and society are viewed as part of a single reality by J, and cannot be discussed meaningfully in isolation from each other, comes as no surprise in light of his critique of traditional views. But Hiebert is equally concerned to stress that 'the Yahwist's landscape and point of orientation to the world is *the agrarian countryside and culture* in which biblical Israel originated' [italics added].[128] Although he is to be lauded for his desire to refute the dichotomies of traditional scholarship, his prioritization of agricultural concerns leads him to adopt uncritically a negative view of the desert as a lifeless place of 'stark solitude', a perception that is open to debate.[129] The reason for Hiebert's focus on agriculture becomes clearer in his chapter on modern environmental theologies, in which he endorses the view of a number of ecologists that agricultural concerns lie at the heart of the environmental agenda.[130] In

[125] Hiebert notes that these traditional dichotomies are present in the work of, among others, Wellhausen, *Prolegomena*; Ellis, *The Yahwist*; and, perhaps surprisingly, Westermann, *Genesis 1–11*.

[126] It should, however, be noted that the semantic range of עבד is broader than the 'service rendered to a superior... to a human master or to God' suggested by Hiebert (*Yahwist's Landscape*, 157).

[127] Ibid. 153. Only with the rise of apocalyptic thought was there a modification of the 'absolute valuation of earthly existence' (ibid.).

[128] Ibid. 146.

[129] Ibid. 142, 149; see the discussion on wilderness in Chapter 5 below.

[130] Ibid. 147–9.

the contemporary debate between ecocentric and anthropocentric ecology, Hiebert would seem to be firmly aligned with the latter.[131]

Nature and History in Joel—Ronald Simkins

The study of Joel by Ronald Simkins is also predicated on the need to refute the dichotomy between nature and history beloved of traditional scholarship. He begins by drawing on evidence compiled by Albrektson from other ancient Near Eastern religions to suggest that 'Israel was not unique in her acknowledgement of a deity who acts in the realm of historical events'.[132] He then explores the place of the natural world in Israel's religious belief, refuting von Rad's subsidiary view of creation by careful exegesis of a number of texts that describe YHWH's victory in the cosmological battle as grounds for hope in his salvific power in Israel's history (e.g. Psalm 74).[133] In such texts, suggests Simkins, it is 'God's creation, his victory over the sea dragon, [that] is the ground for his saving acts in human history, and thus serves for the psalmist as a source of hope'.[134]

In direct contrast to G. E. Wright, Simkins highlights the frequency with which biblical descriptions associate YHWH's theophany with natural locations or phenomena.[135] Furthermore, a number of texts portray the natural world as animate and conscious, participating in the cosmogonic battle (e.g. Psalms 96 and 114; Habakkuk 3): 'When God marches out to battle against the historical foes of Israel, nature is more than merely the arena in which the battle is fought, it engages in and is transformed by the cosmic drama.'[136] Simkins then states the relation between human and natural history in more specific terms: what happens in one arena has direct consequences in the other, both negative and positive.[137]

[131] See the discussion in Chapter 7 below.

[132] Simkins, *History and Nature in Joel*, 39; see Albrektson, *History and the Gods*.

[133] See also Ps 77; Isa. 51.

[134] Simkins, *History and Nature in Joel*, 53.

[135] The extent to which such language derives from Canaanite descriptions of the theophany of Baal is discussed in detail by Cross (*Canaanite Myth*, 113–63).

[136] Simkins, *History and Nature in Joel*, 63.

[137] A number of the texts cited to illustrate this, e.g. Hos. 4:1–3, Amos 9:13–14 and Isa. 34 and 35, will be considered in more detail later in this volume.

YHWH's work in sustaining the created order and blessing his people with agricultural abundance is not to be seen just as part of Israel's salvation history. Rather, 'God's actions in blessing transcend the dichotomy between history and nature, for they take place in the history of creation.'[138]

Having argued convincingly that 'human history and the history of nature are fused together in the history of creation', Simkins illustrates his thesis by means of a systematic exegesis of Joel.[139] The conclusions he reaches may be summed up as follows: in the book of Joel יום יהוה (the day of YHWH) is a multi-faceted event, described by both historical metaphors (the deliverance of the people from their enemies and the re-establishment of Jerusalem as YHWH's dwelling) and natural ones (the plague of locusts and its consequences). But these two perspectives should not be viewed in a linear time sequence or as independent unrelated descriptions. Rather, they have been fused by the author into 'one complex day of Yahweh that involves all creation'.[140] So, suggests Simkins, יום יהוה (the day of YHWH) has both a historical and a cosmological dimension as an event in the 'history of creation'.[141] It is only Simkins's failure to precisely define the latter phrase that mars an otherwise convincing argument. Nevertheless his work represents a thorough and successful attempt to refute the nature versus history dichotomy, as well as to make coherent sense of the book of Joel.

Nature and culture—William Brown

A somewhat different approach from the preceding two exegetical studies is that taken by William Brown in *The Ethos of the Cosmos.*[142] Like Hiebert and Simkins, his opening remarks highlight the negative effect of the separation between nature and history in traditional scholarship but he quickly moves on to talk of culture, rather than history, since human perception of the natural world is itself

[138] Simkins, *History and Nature in Joel*, 69. On the idea of blessing as a bridge between creation and history, see Westermann, *Blessing in the Bible.*

[139] Simkins, *History and Nature in Joel*, 75.

[140] Ibid. 277.

[141] Ibid. 278.

[142] Brown, *Ethos of Cosmos.*

culturally conditioned, and cannot be separated from the sense of history, the understanding of reality and the self-awareness that characterizes human societies.[143] Brown draws attention to Stephen Toulmin's account of the harmony between the order of creation and that of human affairs that existed prior to the Enlightenment, aptly described as a 'cosmopolis'.[144] The separation of nature and society into distinct independent realms brought about by the Enlightenment, and in particular Newtonian physics and Cartesian philosophy, is, suggests Brown, increasingly being challenged as the moral and theological implications of science are recognized. So, argues Brown, the scientific stress on the interdependence of entities within the biosphere 'naturally invites an ethic that values the integrity of all creation'.[145]

Whilst valuing the work of Simkins and Hiebert, Brown considers that their environmentally driven studies construe Israelite culture only in ecological terms.[146] For him, culture is more than that, comprising instead 'an interaction between a community's pre-existing traditions and codes and its current social contexts and practices', including its moral life as seen in 'its theological and symbolic discourse'.[147] Brown's self-confessed aim in his study is 'to show that the created world reflects certain discernible moral ethoses . . . in which the ancient community was to live by faith'.[148] He proposes to investigate the impact of Israel's varied understanding of her environment on her cultural and moral identity by examining five creation-orientated biblical texts to determine how they order the cosmos, and the reasons behind such ordering.[149]

Brown's study provided some illuminating insights into the biblical texts, although much of his writing is couched in terms of moral

[143] Ibid. 1–10.

[144] Ibid. 13, with reference to Toulmin, *Cosmopolis.*

[145] Brown, *Ethos of Cosmos*, 15.

[146] Ibid. 9.

[147] Ibid. 10.

[148] Ibid. 19.

[149] The Priestly creation account in Gen. 1:1–2:3 and subsequent P narratives; the Yahwist narratives in Genesis 2 and 3 and subsequent J texts; creation texts from Second Isaiah; Wisdom's creation hymn in Proverbs 8; and the book of Job (esp. chs. 3 and 38–41).

philosophy rather than biblical studies. The strength of his work lies in his refusal to separate nature from culture, and the conviction that there cannot be cosmology without morality—that human moral identity plays an important part in human perceptions of the world and vice versa. Indeed his criticism of the trend in current biblical studies to view creation texts as either texts of liberation or of oppression, and therefore to focus on power (or lack of it) rather than moral valuation, remains valid and are important in the development of this volume.

The work of each of these three scholars forms part of a necessary and ongoing corrective to readings of the Old Testament that have been both unbalanced and inherently costly, at least as far as Christian environmental ethics is concerned. Continuing to eschew the traditional, narrowly anthropocentric perspective of the Bible is, and will remain, crucial in the attempt to redress this imbalance. In the next chapter we examine some further ways in which this is already happening before proposing an alternative paradigm through which to read the biblical text in an ecologically sensitive manner.

3

Ecological Hermeneutics
Meaning and Method

> Hermeneutics seems to me to be animated by this double motivation: willingness to suspect, willingness to listen; vow of rigor, vow of obedience.
>
> Paul Ricoeur, *Freud and Philosophy*

INTRODUCTION

The analysis of the preceding two chapters suggests that interpretations of the Bible across the centuries have contributed in no small way to a functional view of the world that has at least tacitly endorsed, if not actively supported, the industrial and technological materialism of today with its negative environmental impacts. Although this volume is primarily concerned with biblical exegesis, and in particular with the emerging field of ecological hermeneutics, not all theological responses to environmental issues have focused on the biblical text. Indeed, the broader field of eco-theology, which explores the interface between religion and environmental concerns, has produced a wealth of diverse and creative theological reflection on the place of humanity within the world, some of which will be summarized here.[1]

[1] Although the term 'eco-theology' may be used broadly to refer to environmental concern in the context of religion in general or of a particular world religion or religions, the discussion here will focus on the Christian theological tradition.

ECO-THEOLOGIES

The field of eco-theology began to emerge in the early 1960s in the writings of Joseph Sittler and Richard Baer, and received new impetus with the publication of Lynn White's article.[2] Dieter Hessel identifies four emphases within the contemporary discipline: the recognition of the value of all creation; the need to explore the complex relation between cosmology, spirituality, and ethics; the bringing together of sacramental and covenantal commitments; and the connection between the plight of the earth and that of its poorest human inhabitants.[3]

In reality, however, Christian theological responses to environmental issues have been rather more diverse and piecemeal than Hessel implies, with no monolithic concept of what constitutes eco-theology.[4] They include those which propose a radical reorientation away from traditional theological concepts, such as the Gaia theology of Anne Primavesi or Thomas Berry's adoption of the process thought of Pierre Teilhard de Chardin.[5] For some, the conclusion that Christianity is very problematic from an ecological perspective is unavoidable. This is perhaps particularly true among feminist theologians, a number of whom suggest that the exploitation and abuse of nature both mirrors and is a consequence of patriarchal and exploitative attitudes to women in the Bible and in the Christian tradition since the time of Augustine.[6]

[2] Nash, *Rights of Nature*, 98–103.

[3] Hessel, *Christianity and Ecology*, xxxv–xxxvi.

[4] In this respect it is no different from, say, feminist theology and hermeneutics (see Gilfillan Upton, 'Feminist Theology', 97–104).

[5] Primavesi, *Sacred Gaia*; T. Berry, *New Story*; see also Teilhard de Chardin, *Phenomenon of Man*. In the realm of philosophy, close connections are drawn between the process thought of Heidegger, Spinoza, and Whitehead and the deep ecology of Naess and others, (see Palmer, *Environmental Ethics*, 164–7).

[6] On the rise of eco-feminism see Eaton, 'Ecofeminist Contributions', 55–7. Rosemary Radford Ruether suggests that the devalued view of nature that has characterized Christian theology from its earliest centuries has its roots in the cultural alienation of the late classical period which found particular expression in sexual dualism, that is, the alienation of the masculine from the feminine (Ruether, *Liberation Theology*). Sally McFague proposes that existing theological dualisms be challenged by restructuring traditional Judaeo-Christian values towards the liberation of

Other responses have sought to offer a more redemptive account of Christian theology that neither exonerates the abuses of the past nor totally repudiates the tradition or the Scriptures. Some of these are apologetic in tenor, defending the biblical text by explaining the command to subdue the earth in Genesis 1 as a call to responsible stewardship rather than selfish destruction and using other biblical texts, in particular certain Psalms and parts of Job, to support the theological premise of God as creator and sustainer of the earth, and human beings as his delegated representatives.[7] The covenantal aspect of the relationship between God and human beings, which is stressed in the Reformed tradition, becomes the basis for a retelling of the traditional Christian story of creation, fall, redemption in the context of new commitment to environmental as well as social justice.[8]

Approaches that are perhaps more characteristic of the Catholic and Orthodox traditions include the rediscovery of the sacred within creation.[9] These sacramental perspectives draw on contemplative traditions such as those of Celtic Christianity and early Christian mysticism. Interest has been rekindled in the writings of mystics such as Hildegard of Bingen, whose stress on divine immanence and the affinity between Wisdom and the creation drew her to celebrate creation as the 'lover' of the Creator.[10] Hildegard expressed the notion of the musicality of all creation—the sound of the word of God echoing in every creature.[11] The resurgence of a form of Benedictine spirituality that seeks to husband and nurture the land as a gift from God can be seen in the agrarian perspective of Wendell Berry and other American farmers.[12] Instead of the model of human

all the oppressed, including the earth (McFague, 'Earthly Theological Agenda'; see also McFague, *New Climate for Theology*).

[7] E.g. Nash, *Loving Nature*, 93–108; van Dyke et al., *Redeeming Creation*; see also C. J. H. Wright, *Old Testament Ethics*.

[8] See Nash, *Loving Nature*, 162–91; Ruether, 'Global Eco-Justice', 608–9.

[9] Rasmussen, 'Ecology and Morality', 271–2.

[10] On Celtic spirituality, see McDonagh, *Care for the Earth*, 204–9. On Hildegard of Bingen see ibid. 134–6; also Weeks, *German Mysticism*, 39–67; Newman, *Sister of Wisdom*, 64–71.

[11] Weeks, *German Mysticism*, 55.

[12] Wendell Berry writes 'To live we must daily break the body and shed the blood of creation. When we do this knowingly, lovingly, skillfully and reverently it is a

beings as stewards of the natural world, these mystical approaches emphasize human cooperation with the non-human, and the priestly function of human beings as co-creators alongside the divine.[13]

In the latter decades of the twentieth century, a resurgence of interest in the doctrine of the Trinity has led a number of theologians to explore Christian understanding of the world and God's relation to it from a trinitarian perspective. Most notable among these is Jürgen Moltmann, whose 1984 Gifford lectures (published in the following year as *God in Creation: An Ecological Doctrine of Creation*) set out to discuss the relevance and meaning of Christian faith, in particular the doctrine of the Holy Spirit, in the light of the irreversible ecological crisis.[14]

THE DEVELOPMENT OF ECOLOGICAL HERMENEUTICS

Although some of the eco-theologies referred to above include appeal to the Scriptures to support their perspectives, systematic and detailed exegesis of the biblical text is not usually a predominant feature. It is partly to address this perceived shortcoming that a number of biblical scholars have engaged in readings of the biblical text from the perspective of environmental issues.

The awareness that academic study of the Bible, hitherto primarily the province of white American and European males, needs to reflect the concerns of other population groups, has led to a welcome plurality in readings of the texts. This diversity includes feminist and womanist biblical studies, and political or ideological readings,

sacrament. When we do it ignorantly, greedily, clumsily and destructively it is a desecration. In such desecration we condemn ourselves to spiritual moral loneliness and others to want' (W. Berry, *Gift of Good Land*, 281).

[13] For an extensive discussion of the merits or otherwise of stewardship as a model for human relationship to the world see the essays in R. J. Berry, *Environmental Stewardship*, in particular those by Rasmussen ('Symbols to Live By') and Southgate ('Stewardship').

[14] Moltmann, *God in Creation*. See also the work of Colin Gunton (e.g. *Christ and Creation; One, Three and Many*).

including liberation approaches and, most recently, post-colonial exegesis. Such approaches are based on the premise that 'reading and interpretive strategies are socially, politically and institutionally situated'.[15] They attempt to read and understand the text from the perspective of marginalized and disempowered groups, often seeking to discover voices in biblical texts that have been ignored or hidden by centuries of monocultural exegesis.[16]

Increasingly the ideology of the biblical text itself has come under question—for many the Bible is seen as the product of a patriarchal and culturally elite society, and therefore itself warrants serious critique. This has been especially encapsulated in the hermeneutic of suspicion adopted by a number of interpreters, including some liberation theologians and those operating in the field of feminist biblical studies.[17] The Latin American liberation theologian Juan Luis Segundo proposes that the biblical text should be read in such a way as to 'acknowledge the hermeneutical privilege of the oppressed'.[18] Such readings should be preceded by profound and enriching questions and suspicions both about the reader's real situation, and about theological superstructures, since in many instances 'the prevailing interpretation of the Bible has not taken important pieces of data into account'.[19]

In her development of a feminist hermeneutic of suspicion, Elizabeth Schüssler Fiorenza takes as her starting point the assumption that 'all biblical texts are formulated in androcentric language and reflect patriarchal social structures'.[20] Such questioning of the text,

[15] Aichele, et al., *Postmodern Bible*, 267.

[16] To achieve this, a wide range of biblical studies methods are used, including historical-critical, sociological, and literary approaches. See Barton, *Reading the Old Testament.*

[17] The term 'hermeneutic of suspicion' was first coined by Ricoeur to describe the narrative suspicion of Marx, Nietsche, and Freud, all of whom articulated a distrust of the surface meaning of biblical narrative, and hence of all religion (Ricoeur, *Freud*, 32–6). For Ricoeur these atheistic philosophical stances highlighted the need to approach the text critically and suspiciously in order that the interpreter's pre-understandings and certainties would not mask its true meaning.

[18] Segundo, cited in Fiorenza, *Bread Not Stone*, 50.

[19] Segundo, *Liberation*, 9.

[20] Fiorenza, *Bread Not Stone*, 15. Fiorenza advocates careful selection of those texts which may be read from a feminist perspective and rejection of those that are sexist or patriarchal (ibid. 18). At a more extreme end of the spectrum feminist theologians

building on the methods of liberation, and especially feminist, hermeneutics, is a key principle in the ecological hermeneutics of the Earth Bible Project, which was established by Norman Habel of Flinders University, Australia. The work of the Project represents some of the most significant and sustained examples of ecologically sensitive readings of the biblical text, and has in many ways pioneered the developing field of ecological hermeneutics. In what follows, the Earth Bible hermeneutics are extensively analysed and reviewed, as befits a new interpretative method of such significance.

The Earth Bible Project

The publication in 2000 of the first volume in the Earth Bible series, entitled *Readings from the Perspective of Earth*, represented a unique and important contribution to the engagement between the biblical text and ecological concerns.[21] Since then, the Earth Bible Project has published a further four volumes, and been instrumental in bringing the topic of ecological hermeneutics to the attention of a wider academic audience, in particular through its inclusion since 2004 as a programme unit in the Society of Biblical Literature's Annual Meeting.[22]

The Earth Bible Project (hereafter EBP) has grown out of the participants' concern for the future of the planet in the light of the serious and often irreversible damage caused by human activity. It attempts to reverse the focus on the individual human being that has characterized Christian theology of the past 500 years, and to contribute to current interest in the theme of creation and ecological

such as Mary Daly (*For the Common Good*) and Daphne Hampson (*After Christianity*) totally reject both the biblical text and the Christian tradition on account of the inherent patriarchal and dualistic approaches to the world present in Scripture and in church traditions.

[21] Habel, *Readings*.

[22] Habel, *Psalms and Prophets*; Habel and Balabanski, *The Earth Story in the New Testament*; Habel and Wurst, *The Earth Story in Genesis* and *The Earth Story in Wisdom Traditions*. However, to what extent 'ecological hermeneutics' has yet achieved the status of a field of biblical studies in its own right is debatable, since, despite its profile at SBL, the recently published *Oxford Handbook of Biblical Studies* makes no mention of it (Rogerson, *Biblical Studies*).

issues in the Bible. By its own admission, however, the EBP is also critical of many recent theologies of creation which tend towards anthropocentrism, since the assumption that humans should be the central concern of biblical and theological reflection is itself considered suspect.[23]

In his introduction to the series in 2000, Habel briefly explores Lynn White's critique of Western Christianity, before considering whether the responses to White by many ecotheologians arguing for the ecological sensitivity of the biblical texts, are warranted.[24] He then explains that the principles of feminist hermeneutics will provide a framework for the EBP investigations of the biblical texts. This he explains as the interpreter standing with oppressed 'Earth' in a dialogue with the text, much as feminist interpreters stand with oppressed women as they read.[25]

Habel argues for a new perspective whereby interpreters read the text as members of 'the Earth community', and where they ask whether 'humans act *with and within* Earth, or... *upon* Earth' [Habel's italics].[26] This includes considering whether the earth is 'simply in the background of the text or whether it is actively being suppressed and hence devalued as secondary to the realm of history'.[27] For Habel, the assumption that the text, as well as most of its interpreters, is anthropocentric legitimizes adopting a hermeneutic of suspicion. Such an approach to the text does not, however, rule out a corresponding hermeneutic of retrieval, which looks for alternative readings that value the earth or its community in their own right.[28]

[23] Habel, *Readings*, 28.

[24] Ibid. 25–37. The question Habel asks, 'are contemporary ecological values genuinely supported by... the biblical texts?' is addressed in Chapter 7 below.

[25] Ibid. 34. Habel uses the capitalized, anarthrous Earth throughout his writing, although this convention is not followed by all contributors to the volumes.

[26] Ibid.

[27] Ibid. 35.

[28] Habel's hermeneutic was further developed and formalised in the guidelines issued to participants in the SBL programme consultation in the years 2004–6, into a set of three basic steps, a hermeneutic of suspicion, of identification and of retrieval. Each of the three years' consultation focussed on a different one of the three. A selection of the papers presented at these consultations has now been published as a series of essays (Habel and Trudinger, *Exploring Ecological Hermeneutics*).

Alongside these approaches to the text, the EBP has developed a series of eco-justice principles to function as a guide for the hermeneutical process and to relate their exegetical method specifically to the ecological context in which it operates.[29] These principles were drawn up in consultation with ecologists as well as theologians and draw on the work of those such as Thomas Berry who have articulated their own distinctive sets of ecological values.[30] The EBP's six eco-justice principles are set out in Figure 1.

It is notable that the wording of these principles consciously avoids the specific terms 'God' and 'creation'. According to the Earth Bible team, 'this formulation has been chosen to facilitate dialogue with biologists, ecologists, other religious traditions like Buddhism, and scientists who may not function with God or God's creation as an *a priori* assumption'.[31] The team suggests that it also allows the

1. *The Principle of Intrinsic Worth*
The universe, Earth and all its components have intrinsic worth/value.

2. *The Principle of Interconnectedness*
Earth is a community of interconnected living things that are mutually dependent on each other for life and survival.

3. *The Principle of Voice*
Earth is a subject capable of raising its voice in celebration and against injustice.

4. *The Principle of Purpose*
The universe, Earth and all its components are part of a dynamic cosmic design within which each piece has a place in the overall goal of that design.

5. *The Principle of Mutual Custodianship*
Earth is a balanced and diverse domain where responsible custodians can function as partners, rather than as rulers, to sustain a balanced and diverse earth community.

6. *The Principle of Resistance*
Earth and its components not only suffer from injustice at the hands of humans, but actively resist them in the struggle for justice.

Figure 1. The Earth Bible Project eco-principles

[29] Habel, *Readings*, 38–53.
[30] T. Berry, *Dream of the Earth.*
[31] Habel, *Readings*, 38.

interpreter to focus on the earth in its own right, rather than as an object of God's creation or ownership.[32]

The EBP has resulted in a welcome re-examination of some familiar biblical texts on the theme of creation, such as the Genesis creation accounts, as well as of those that are less well studied.[33] Both the series of volumes and the papers presented at the SBL consultations have included material that is thought-provoking and that challenges both traditional interpretations and current attitudes to the world we live in. Perhaps inevitably, since the approach is so innovative, other scholars have raised issues concerning the project's methodology to which Habel and his team have begun to respond.

A number of the subsequent volumes to *Readings from the Perspective of Earth* have sought to have dialogue with others writing in this field and to bring clarification to the EBP's aims. For example, Volume 2, *The Earth Story in Genesis*, begins with a chapter entitled 'Conversations with Gene Tucker and Other Writers'.[34] Likewise, Volume 4, *The Earth Story in the Psalms and the Prophets* includes a response to criticisms made by Tim Meadowcroft, some of which are included in the discussion on anthropomorphic language in Chapter 4 of this volume.[35] Nevertheless, the field of ecological hermeneutics is very much in its infancy, and relatively little space in each of the volumes is given over to discussion of methodological issues.[36]

Of the issues arising from the project which may benefit from further reflection, three can be singled out in particular for comment here: the inherent difficulties in using such a method-driven

[32] Ibid. One wonders whether their desire to create what one might call *neutral* ground effectively creates *secular* ground instead, and whether this is appropriate for dealing with religious texts. For an insightful explanation of the distinction between neutral and secular, see the work of David Ford, e.g. 'Public Life'.

[33] E.g. Ezek 6 (Stevenson, 'If Earth Could Speak'); Tobit (Urbrock, 'The Earth Story in Tobit'). However, comparatively little space is given to the pre-exilic prophets in the volumes of the EBP—only 1 essay in vol. 1(Habel, *Readings*) and three in vol. 4 (Habel, *Psalms and Prophets*).

[34] Habel and Wurst, *The Earth Story in Genesis*, 21–33.

[35] Habel, *Psalms and Prophets*, 23–8.

[36] The development of the EBP's eco-hermeneutic from the now well-established field of feminist methodology is in many respects not dissimilar from the rise of feminist hermeneutics which developed insights from the more established thought of liberation theology. Just as feminist hermeneutics has matured and 'come of age' over the past twenty years, so perhaps the same can be expected of eco-hermeneutics.

approach to the text, the lack of clarity with regard to terminology, and questions arising from the list of eco-justice principles. It is to these we now turn.

EBP method

The EBP's focus on method begs the question to what extent the hermeneutic task should be driven by such a systemic approach. There is a real danger that the method itself becomes a restrictive influence on the text, rather than bringing illumination. This is especially so in situations where a particular method is regarded as superior to other approaches to the text, as is often the case in ideological readings. Meadowcroft articulates this well in his response to Heather Eaton's chapter on ecofeminism in *Readings from the Perspective of Earth* when he states, 'Allowing that Eaton is right that the biblical text has been a dangerous ideology... any rigorously imposed interpretive paradigm may equally become a dangerous ideology.'[37]

The EBP Team recognize this danger and discuss their responses to this and other critical observations in volume 2 of the series, *The Earth Story in Genesis.* However, it is evident that the EBP sets great store by its method. This is perhaps summed up by the assertion that 'these [ecojustice] principles set the agenda for readings in this series'.[38] Under the EBP rubric, it is the method that determines not only how we *should* understand the text (and there is a definite sense of 'ought to' in the EBP rhetoric), but also how we conceive of the earth itself.

The application of feminist hermeneutical method to human relationship with the earth, although logical at first glance, presents significant difficulties. First, while the EBP alerts us to the influence of western dualisms and binary oppositions (human/nature, mind/matter, male/female) on much biblical interpretation, it is not clear that the relationship between humans and the created world can always be 'gendered' in the way that the team imply. Such gendering draws on the writings of eco-feminists such as Rosemary Radford

[37] Meadowcroft, 'Review of *Readings from the Perspective of Earth*'.
[38] Habel and Wurst, *The Earth Story in Genesis*, 23.

Ruether, who suggest that male domination of women and domination of nature are interconnected, both in cultural ideology and in social structures:

> Domination of women has provided a key link, both socially and symbolically, to the domination of earth, hence the tendency in patriarchal cultures to link women with earth, matter, and nature, while identifying males with sky, intellect and transcendent spirit.[39]

Ruether provides no data to substantiate such a claim, and one suspects that while veneration of the female, whether the earth itself or goddesses, forms part of many societies, there is no real evidence, either in the ancient world or in contemporary western society, that women have a closer or more empathetic relationship with nature than men.[40]

Secondly, the analogy between uncovering oppression of women and exploitation of earth's resources, between recovering female voices and those of the earth, is just that, an analogy, and if pushed too far breaks down and becomes meaningless. Indeed, as Eaton points out, the two may even be mutually exclusive, as is the case in some adherents of deep ecology, who notably lack critical analysis of feminist issues.[41]

Finally, and this is perhaps part of a wider critique of reader-response approaches in general, such an approach invites the dangers of ethnocentrism and anachronism. Ethnocentrism—interpreting texts on the basis of a particular (western) set of cultural values—may occur, insofar as the feminist hermeneutic outlined above is the product of white western feminists.[42] Likewise, anachronism—the judging of societies of the past according to standards of the present time—is a real danger, since suspicion for many contributors to the

[39] Ruether, *Gaia and God*, 3; see also Eaton, 'Ecofeminist Contributions'.

[40] This is not to denigrate the place of womanist theology in calling for a radical reorientation in our relationship with the earth (see Ruether, *Women Healing Earth*).

[41] Eaton, 'Ecofeminist Contributions', 64. Deep ecology is a form of ecological philosophy that was articulated by Arne Naess in the 1970s and that includes the claim that all living things have the same right to flourish as any other (Naess, *Outline of Ecosophy*).

[42] A refreshing example of an alternative interpretative matrix is that of Madipoane Masenya writing as an African South African woman in volume 4 of the series (Masenya, 'Eco*bosadi* Reading').

EBP involves reading the text critically and exclusively from the perspective of current ecological issues that were unknown in the biblical period.[43]

EBP Terminology

The second area of concern arises from the lack of precision and definition in the terminology used by the EBP, as illustrated by this introductory sentence:

> This *new Earth consciousness* invites us, as members of the Earth community, to return to the Bible, and in dialogue with the text, ascertain whether a similar kinship with Earth is reflected there. [Habel's emphasis][44]

The use of anarthrous, capitalized 'Earth' is never explained or justified by Habel, nor is the exact nature of Earth or Earth community specified in any but the vaguest terms.[45] Both the terminology and the convention bear resemblance to James Lovelock's Gaia hypothesis,[46] although the latter is only mentioned in passing.[47]

Some of the terminology adopted by the project is subjective and open to multifarious interpretations. For example, while 'kinship with Earth' has a warm, relational ring to it, more exact definition is difficult, especially for those operating in a western urban environment. The phrase is explained by the project in terms of indigenous, mainly Australasian, perspectives, for example Maori beliefs regarding an individual's spiritual connection with his or her birth-place.[48]

[43] See Simkins, *Creator and Creation*, 34–5.

[44] Habel, *Readings*, 26.

[45] Ibid. 27.

[46] Lovelock's hypothesis was originally formulated as a purely scientific theory in the 1970s and named 'Gaia' after the Greek earth goddess for convenience rather than through any religious convictions on the part of the author. He defines Gaia as 'a complex entity involving the Earth's biosphere, atmosphere, oceans, and soil; the totality constituting a feedback or cybernetic system which seeks an optimal physical and chemical environment for life on this planet' (Lovelock, *Gaia*, 10). The theory was almost immediately seized upon for its religious significance by advocates of New Age spirituality, and consequently has been regarded with suspicion by much of the scientific community.

[47] Habel, *Readings*, 46.

[48] As demonstrated in the Maori practice of burying human placenta at the place of birth and returning there to die; see also ibid. 30.

But this begs the question whether these perspectives can or should be fully embraced by those from other cultures. Can those who do not have a sense of kinship with their birthplace conceptualize this apart from just adopting the rhetoric of the phrase? Might it not even be offensive to a Maori for a westerner to talk in these terms when the experience is not part of the latter's lived reality? One wonders whether a more nuanced vocabulary would be preferable for the purposes of relating such a concept to western culture.

Eco-justice principles

The third area of concern lies with the wording of some of the eco-justice principles themselves. While most of these are easily understandable concepts, a number pose rather more questions than they answer. In particular the concept of the earth as 'a subject' and its capacity to 'actively resist' injustices (principles 3 and 6) introduces, in Eaton's words, 'notions of the subjectivity and agency of the Earth [that] are an intellectual minefield'.[49] Furthermore, the idea that the earth is capable not only of agency but of moral awareness (for example, of injustice) is, in the end, a construction and unlikely to promote the kind of dialogue with biologists and other scientists envisaged by Habel.[50] Interestingly, Meadowcroft notes when reviewing the first volume that none of the contributors succeed in presenting the earth as subject rather than topic, suggesting that the practical question of how this might be achieved has not been adequately addressed.[51]

The EBP's eco-justice principles are by no means unique. Indeed, apart from the two more controversial principles mentioned above, similar concepts can be found in the work of other authors, for example, that of Steven Bouma-Prediger.[52] His series of ecological virtues derived from the biblical texts, while couched in different terminology, reflect essentially the same underlying themes as those

49 Eaton, 'Ecofeminist Contributions', 66.

50 Habel, *Readings*, 38.

51 Meadowcroft, 'Review of *Readings from the Pespective of Earth*'.

52 Bouma-Prediger, 'Constructive Proposal', in response to van Wensveen, 'Virtue Ethics'; see also Nash, *Loving Nature*.

of the EBP, namely the intrinsic worth of the whole earth, mutual interdependence of living beings, the inherent purposefulness of the earth, and shared responsibility.[53] His approach, however, differs in one significant way: he writes from a Protestant confessional perspective, with the aim of proposing a Christian ecological virtue ethic. In so doing, Bouma-Prediger demonstrates that it is not necessary to eschew religious language as the EBP proposes.[54] Instead he outlines an environmental ethic that is unashamedly theocentric rather than ecocentric. Given the immense overlap between his approach and that of the EBP, between his virtues and the EBP's principles, it seems that the distinctive feature of the Earth Bible series is not so much its *method* but its *ideology.* But it is questionable whether such a strongly ideological agenda based on a hermeneutic of suspicion, can, in the end, lead to greater motivation for environmental responsibility.

The EBP, like Bouma-Prediger, seeks to examine the biblical text from a contemporary perspective, namely the state of the environment in the twenty-first century. The framework of principles together with the hermeneutic of suspicion is what drives the EBP's interpretative task, and influences its outcome. Whether this entails a positive or negative evaluation of the biblical text largely depends on the presuppositions of each contributing author, since this is a reader-led approach to the text. It is in this emphasis that one of the real dangers of the EBP lies, for such a reader-led focus has the potential for creating an ever greater distance between the world of the Bible and that of contemporary society. This may have the effect of inviting rejection of the biblical text by those who consider it to be irrelevant in today's world, but it may also encourage the rejection of concern for the environment by those for whom the Bible carries authority as sacred scripture. Moreover, the EBP's lack of concern to address practical ethical issues further limits the Project's capacity to provide the kind of moral imperative that is being called for by environmentalists.[55]

[53] His ideas are developed more fully in Bouma-Prediger, *Beauty of the Earth.*

[54] A proposal that is not carried through by the majority of contributors to the project.

[55] See Introduction to this volume.

Such a determinative and reader-centred hermeneutic is not the only way of investigating the potential for the Old Testament to inform contemporary ethical reflection. An alternative way forward would be to investigate how the biblical material portrays ancient Israelite understanding of the world, its world view, with the aim of determining a broader paradigm through which to explore the text—one that might be relevant for contemporary ecological ethics. Such an approach would focus rather more on the world of the text, while recognizing that it is being read through the lens of the twenty-first century. But to what extent can we talk meaningfully about the 'world of the text' or the 'Israelite world view'? Is there a single perspective on the world to be distilled from the biblical text? Unsurprisingly, such questions have provoked considerable debate.

IS THERE AN ANCIENT ISRAELITE WORLD VIEW?

Numerous attempts have been made to describe the understanding of the world held by ancient Israel and her neighbours. These range from descriptions of beliefs about the physical structure of the universe (including diagrams), gleaned from literary and iconographical evidence, to abstract articulations of 'the mind of early man'.[56] Such endeavours have been influenced and perhaps even complicated by the increasing popularity of the German concept *Weltanschauung* (world view) in modern western society. The term, first coined by Immanuel Kant in the eighteenth century, has become fundamental to a wide range of disciplines, from linguistics to cognitive philosophy. It became part of the vocabulary of German theologians such as Haeckel and Bultmann and, on the darker side, is a term applied to the distinctive outlook of German National Socialism.[57]

[56] Frankfort, et al., *Before Philosophy*, 19. For examples of the former, see Stadelmann, *Hebrew Conception*; and Cornelius, 'Visual Representation'; and, of the latter, Frankfort et al., *Before Philosophy*, esp. 241–8; and more recently Houtman, *Himmel im AT*.

[57] Pois, *National Socialism*, 6–17.

There are problems in both the understanding of the concept itself and in its application to ancient societies. The first is a certain terminological imprecision, due in part to the complexity of the overlapping expressions *Weltanschauung* and *Weltbild* (world-picture), and their English translations. In the biblical context Houtman distinguishes clearly between ancient Israel's *Weltbild* (the physical structure and functioning of the universe) and her *Weltanschauung* (the answer to the question of *who* is responsible for its foundation and continuing existence).[58] However, a blurring of the categories of *Weltbild* and *Weltanschauung* can be detected in the works of other scholars.[59] In a different context, Pois attempts to distinguish between the three terms, *Weltanschauung*, ideology, and religion, yet admits that the overlap in definition and usage of these terms found among leading writers will continue in his own work.[60]

A second problem is that the questions addressed by contemporary discussions of world view are not necessarily the same as those of the biblical texts. The Belgian philosopher Leo Apostel and his followers have suggested seven crucial components to an integrated world view.[61] Some of these entail concepts that may be applicable in a pre-modern context, in particular understanding of the nature, structure, and function of the world, and knowing how to act in, and have influence on, the world.[62] However, the majority are predicated on the assumptions and parameters of twentieth-century western thought and include factors such as a future and global orientation, the desirability of free choices, and complex information systems on which to base such choices. It would be anachronistic to expect coherent results from projecting such a complex set of components back on to the biblical texts.

The idea that a single determinative ancient Israelite world view can be discerned must also be treated with caution, since the diverse literary styles and dates of the biblical texts suggest, at very least, the

[58] Houtman, *Himmel im Alten Testament*, 299.

[59] E.g. Stock, 'Welt'.

[60] Pois, *National Socialism*, 8.

[61] Aerts, et al., *Worldviews*.

[62] The term 'world' is defined by Aerts as 'the broadest environment that is cognitively, practically and emotionally relevant ... the totality in which we live and to which we can relate ourselves in a meaningful way' (ibid. 7).

possibility of development and fluidity, and even of multiple world views.[63] Brown notes, 'it is difficult, if not impossible, . . . to construct a generalized monolithic *Weltanschauung* apart from the changing mores and historical vicissitudes a community faces throughout any given period of time.'[64] Furthermore, as Barton suggests, the attempt to discern the world view behind the text may result in the assertions of the text becoming tautological or vacuous.[65]

Is there then anything that can be said about the world view or views of ancient Israel? One of the broadest definitions of the term suggests that 'a worldview [*sic*] is a set of presuppositions (or assumptions) which we hold (consciously or subconsciously) about the basic makeup of our world'.[66] What then are the presuppositions of the biblical text? In the case of most Old Testament writers, belief in a divine being is the fundamental assumption. Though God may be questioned (e.g. Job and certain Psalms), his existence is not in doubt; theogony does not feature in the Old Testament creation accounts, unlike other ancient Near Eastern myths. The biblical concept of reality could be described as being predicated on a theocentric understanding of the world. But what does such a broad definition mean in practice for these ancient writers? How does a theocentric perspective influence human perception of the world, and how do we account for the way that this varies from book to book, and indeed, within individual books of the corpus? In particular, since the focus in this volume is on some of the prophets, is there any coherent sense of the way the world is, or ought to be,

[63] Knight's suggestion that such diversity is also reflected in Israel's cosmogonic traditions is to be preferred to those cited above who describe a single world picture (*Weltbild*) of the physical structure of the universe (Knight, 'Cosmogony', 136–40). Similarly, Houtman argues that the ancient Israelites had no single integrated concept of the heavenly realm, rather a series of complex images which articulated their awe for the cosmos (Houtman, *Himmel im Alten Testament*, 290–9; see also J. E. Wright, 'Heavenly Realm').

[64] Brown, *Ethos of Cosmos*, 9.

[65] Barton, 'Natural Law', 12. The wide range of possibilities suggested by scholars attempting to discern the 'organizing principle' of the Old Testament highlight the difficulty of identifying a central overarching theme in any but the broadest terms. See e.g. Brueggemann, *Theology*; Eichrodt, *Old Testament Theology 2*; Kaiser, *Old Testament Theology*; Zimmerli, *Old Testament Theology*.

[66] Sire, *Universe Next Door*, 17.

which undergirds the prophetic message of these books, and which could form the basis for an ecologically sensitive exegesis?

The influence of wisdom

Perhaps the most obvious place to begin the search for this is with the concept of wisdom in the Old Testament.[67] This is particularly appropriate since two themes commonly cited as important features of wisdom literature are the extent to which it refers to creation, and the idea of a fundamental moral order in the world. But how significant are these aspects of wisdom literature, and to what extent can they be found in the prophetic books? More importantly, do they provide useful criteria for ascertaining an Israelite understanding of the world?

Wisdom and creation

The suggestion that one of the key theological themes of the wisdom material is creation was first articulated by Zimmerli and has been developed by numerous scholars.[68] Perdue is among those who regard creation as the centre of wisdom theology, in that it 'integrates all other dimensions of God-talk, as well as anthropology, community, ethics, epistemology (both reason and revelation), and society'.[69] Although he illustrates this sweeping statement from

[67] The term 'wisdom' is used by scholars in a number of ways: to denote the corpus of biblical books dealing predominantly with wisdom material (i.e. Job, Proverbs, and Ecclesiastes); to describe an experiential outlook on reality; and to refer to a movement or school of ancient sages and teachers (Crenshaw, *Old Testament Wisdom*, 3–7). Overlap and imprecision in these uses of the word is evident in a number of secondary works, e.g. Westermann who, in the introduction to his monograph *Roots of Wisdom*, moves seamlessly and without explanation from talk of wisdom as a human characteristic to wisdom as a body of literature (Westermann, *Wisdom*, 1). For discussion of the marginalisation of wisdom literature in critical scholarship and its subsequent 'rediscovery'; and of the search for its theological centre see Dell, *Proverbs*, 1–17.

[68] Zimmerli, 'Place of Wisdom'; see also Murphy, 'Religious Dimensions'; Perdue, *Wisdom and Creation*; Westermann, *Wisdom*.

[69] Perdue, *Wisdom and Creation*, 35. Likewise in Bergant's liberation-critical study of the wisdom traditions, the integrity and intrinsic value of creation is the fundamental presupposition (Bergant, *Wisdom Literature*, 1–2).

selected texts, his work draws heavily on theological and sociological presuppositions and takes little account of the wealth of wisdom material that makes no reference to creation. The danger of this is that wisdom is viewed as a monolithic entity, when in fact scholars have suggested vast differences, even dissonance within wisdom literature.[70] Such a tendency to conflate wisdom with creation also brings the risk that references to creation in other parts of the Old Testament are automatically assumed to be wisdom texts.[71] In the discussion of the eighth-century prophets, it will be seen that the language of creation is a part and parcel of the prophetic understanding, rather than a 'wisdom' idea incorporated into the texts.

Wisdom and world order

The traditional view of wisdom is that it represents a 'practical knowledge of the laws of life and of the world, based on experience'.[72] Comparative studies have suggested that Egyptian and other ancient Near Eastern traditions lie behind the wisdom material, and parallels have been drawn to the Egyptian concept of *Ma'at*—the fundamental order in the world.[73] Wisdom has generally been regarded as distinct from, and perhaps inferior to, Israel's 'genuine' Yahwistic faith, being intrinsically anthropocentric, in comparison to the theocentric perspective of the law and prophets.[74] However, Murphy considers the idea that wisdom arose from a search for world order to be a modern retrospection that has resulted in the separation of wisdom and Yahwism outlined above. Rather, the essence of the Israelites' religion

[70] E.g. Dell, *Sceptical Literature*, 58–63; Morgan, 'Wisdom', 210–18.

[71] The tendency to 'overstate' the presence of wisdom material or influences in early prophetic texts is characteristic of, among others, Whedbee, *Isaiah and Wisdom*; and Wolff, *Amos the Prophet*.

[72] Von Rad, *Old Testament Theology 1*, 418. For similar thinking in contemporary scholarship see Bergant, *Wisdom Literature*, 12.

[73] Murphy, 'Wisdom', 928–9; see also Crenshaw, *Studies in Ancient Israelite Wisdom*, 205–6; Schmid, *Wesen Und Geschichte*, 17–22.

[74] E.g. Preuss, 'Weisheits Israels', 143–4; von Rad, *Wisdom in Israel*, 59–61. See also Lindblom who maintains this distinction despite arguing that wisdom and 'wise men' existed during the time of the early prophets ('Wisdom', 196–7).

as worshippers of YHWH is in the daily experience of life: 'The wisdom lessons and ideal were an essential expression of the Lord and of life.'[75] This integration is reflected in the rest of the Old Testament in which themes and motifs of wisdom teaching form 'an alternative mode of revelation through the everyday, through human experience of the world and of God'.[76]

In the prophetic books wisdom material is usually identified by form as much as by content, with particular emphasis on proverbial saying, parable, and numerical progression (e.g. 'For three . . . and for four', Amos 1:3, etc).[77] The volume of wisdom sayings or teaching varies from book to book, with Amos and Isaiah having demonstrably strong wisdom connections, and there being fewer in Hosea or Micah.[78] This variety is unsurprising since the work of each prophet is a unique response to a unique set of circumstances. Themes and motifs from wisdom traditions, if deployed, are only one element and are 'modified and transformed to find their place within a particular revelation'.[79] In the exegesis of the prophetic books in Chapters 4–6, wisdom elements in the text will be identified where relevant. However, the category of wisdom is at one both too broad and too restrictive to form a useful framework for the exegesis. It is too broad insofar as much of the ethical teaching of the wisdom books (particularly Proverbs) specifically concerns human society and is predominantly anthropocentric, and too narrow given that not all texts dealing with the non-human creation can be construed as wisdom material.[80]

[75] Murphy, 'Wisdom and Yahwism', 119.

[76] Dell, *Get Wisdom*, 77.

[77] There is however great variation in identifying wisdom material, with some scholars finding it at every turn (e.g. Morgan, *Wisdom*), others taking a more limited view (e.g. Crenshaw, *Old Testament Wisdom*). Lindblom's assumption that the presence of proverbial and metaphorical language in Isaiah is evidence of wisdom influence ('Wisdom', 201–3) is regarded as over-simplistic by Whedbee (*Isaiah and Wisdom*, 23–4).

[78] In the case of Amos, see Terrien, 'Amos and Wisdom'; Wolff, *Amos the Prophet*; for Isaiah, see Whedbee, *Isaiah and Wisdom*; Jensen, *Tôrâ in Isaiah*.

[79] Macintosh, 'Wisdom', 132.

[80] Habel, *Readings*, 29.

ORDERING THE WORLD: SOME ALTERNATIVE PROPOSALS

There are a number of other important themes easily identified in the Old Testament, which might provide a focus for an Israelite world view. Significantly, many of these are concerned with articulating a sense of order in the world, which, if breached, may result in disastrous consequences.

Land as inheritance

If wisdom literature and ideas suggest a particular creation-focused way of looking at the world, in the biblical narrative Israel's religious, economic, and political identity is very much tied up with the concept of the land as Israel's inheritance. The two defining events of her history, Exodus (Exod. 3:8) and Exile (2 Kgs 25:11; see also Jer. 24:1), are journeys into and out of the land, and much of what happens in between involves the struggle to maintain her boundaries in a hostile environment. Moreover, promises concerning the land which relate to the periods before and after these events form a crucial part of Israel's relationship with YHWH (e.g. Gen. 12:1; Ezek. 34:11–16).

Walter Brueggemann is one of a number of scholars who explore the biblical text as the story of God's people with God's land, suggesting that 'Israel's faith is essentially a journeying in and out of land, and its faith can be organised around these focuses'.[81] His study moves in a series of historical time frames—from promise of the land, through wilderness, entry into the land, monarchs and the land, exile from the land, and, finally, restoration to the land. As well as referring to the land as a source of fertility and blessing, he articulates a theology of the land in its political and social context, yet at the same time eschewing the antitheses of nature/history and space/time beloved of biblical interpretation.[82] For Brueggemann,

[81] Brueggemann, *The Land*, 13.
[82] Ibid. 197.

the 'landed' story of Israel leads away from the individualism and isolation of western society to a sense of rootedness and location within the community of faith.[83]

While land as Israel's story may be an important framing concept for the biblical accounts, such an approach carries the danger of harmonizing what are essentially different understandings of land in the Old Testament, and blurring important distinctions. Although land is a central or dominant image in the text, it functions in a variety of ways with a range of meanings, suggests Norman Habel. In his 1995 study of land and land rights, *The Land is Mine*, he identifies six clear land ideologies from a selection of texts, ideologies that are based on differing social and theological perspectives.[84] Like Brueggemann, Habel is primarily viewing land from the perspective of its human inhabitants and with their interests to the fore, a perspective that risks relegating land to a functional role as a resource for Israel's inhabitants.[85] However, Habel acknowledges this when he asks if any of the ideologies he has identified go beyond the right to control the land exercised by YHWH, Israel as a nation or the various social groups within her: 'Do any of these ideologies consider the rights of the land itself, even indirectly?'[86]

In the prophetic books, as elsewhere in the Old Testament, land is an important concept, both in terms of its social and political status but also as a literary and thematic feature of individual prophetic messages. Metaphors concerning the land form a key part of the figurative vocabulary of the prophets, a function that is heightened by the semantic range of הארץ (the land/earth). This fluidity is evident within the conceptual world of the prophets themselves, as we shall see; it is used to good effect by Chrisopher Wright in his move from a description of the ethical implications of Israel's relationship to YHWH and the land in *Living as the People of God* to his

[83] Ibid. 198.

[84] Habel, *The Land Is Mine.*

[85] See also Ellen Davis's reading of the Old Testament through agrarian eyes, which explores the interface between human society and the land in the Old Testament in the context of the serious ecological problems facing the US (Davis, *Scripture, Culture, Agriculture*).

[86] Habel, *The Land Is Mine*, 147. Only the hint of an answer is given but this is a question that is dealt with more fully in his work for the Earth Bible Project.

more theological account of Old Testament ethics applied to contemporary issues, including environmental ones, *Old Testament Ethics for the People of God*.[87]

The Cosmic Perspective

In the Old Testament the world is conceptualized not only in terms of the land, but also as cosmic space. The heavens and earth are appealed to together in a variety of contexts, often in parallelism—not least by the prophetic authors. The relationship between the order of the cosmos and harmony in land and society is evident in a number of texts, suggesting, according to Robert Murray, the notion of a cosmic covenant between YHWH and his world.[88] Murray identifies in the Old Testament fragments of creation myths in which the forces of nature are personified and ascribed supernatural powers, and which depict God imposing his rule on these cosmic elements and establishing boundaries for them (e.g. Ps. 104:5–9; Job 38:8–9).[89] This cosmic rule (also spoken of in terms of a covenant, Jer. 33:20–6) can be broken by the inhabitants (or rulers) of the earth, whose transgression of the law violates the order of the world (e.g. Isa. 24:1–3, 33:7–9).[90] The resultant disorders in society, the land, and the cosmos are the consequences of that broken covenant (e.g. Isa. 24:7–13).

However, a number of texts also describe the reversal of this disorder and the renewal of a covenant with creation, a covenantal tradition which according to Murray predates the traditional 'mythical history' sequence of the Priestly narratives—creation followed by disorder punished by the Flood, culminating in the Noachic covenant.[91] Murray suggests that texts such as Hosea 2, Isaiah 55, and Ezekiel 34 'present the vision of harmony restored between heaven

[87] C. J. H. Wright, *People of God* and *Old Testament Ethics*. Wright's work is discussed further below and in Chapter 7.

[88] Murray, *Cosmic Covenant*.

[89] Ibid. 1–13.

[90] See also Jer. 4:23–4.

[91] It is somewhat unclear whether Murray considers this a precursor of the Noachic covenant, or synonymous with it.

and earth, humankind and other creatures, sometimes by what is referred to as a covenant, eternal or peaceful'.[92]

Murray's study draws on a range of textual material and clearly demonstrates the fundamental interconnection between the order of the cosmos and human behaviour. However, whether the cosmic covenant represents the overarching world view of the Old Testament is by no means clear.[93] The references to cosmic order and disorder are fragmentary and scattered and attempting to determine a systematic theory from them is fraught with difficulty. Nevertheless, it remains the case that a clear link between covenant, human transgression, and disorder in society and earth can be seen in a number of texts, including prophetic ones.

Justice and righteousness

Another possible approach is via the idea of justice and righteousness in the Old Testament, which is represented in the text by the Hebrew hendiadys משפט וצדקה 'justice and righteousness' or a variation thereof, and also by various combinations of the words used in parallelism.[94] While it is the concept of social justice in ancient Israel that is generally assumed to be represented by these words, a number of texts link this motif with the well-being and flourishing of the earth.[95] When the king's wise rule ensures that justice and righteousness prevail in society, the land yields fruitfulness and peace reigns (e.g. Ps. 72:1–4; see also Isaiah 11; Isaiah 32). Conversely, the abuses of social justice and exploitation of the poor which some of the classical prophets so roundly condemn result in famine, flood and cosmic disturbance (e.g. Amos 5:6–8).

92 Murray, *Cosmic Covenant*, 43.

93 Watson highlights the difficulties in imposing a monolithic concept (the different, yet related notion of '*Chaoskampf*') on diverse biblical material (Watson, *Chaos Uncreated*, 1–5).

94 Weinfeld, 'Justice and Righteousness', 228–9; see also Houston, *Contending for Justice*; Miranda, *Marx and the Bible*. Weinfeld notes that similar word pairs are found in Ugaritic and other ancient Near Eastern literature ('Justice and Righteousness', 229).

95 See Marlow, 'Justice for Whom?'.

The idea that justice (צדקה) is concerned with world order is developed by H. H. Schmid in his monograph *Gerechtigkeit als Weltordnung*.[96] This study analyses the use of the Semitic root צדק (just, justice, judge) in other ancient Near Eastern literature as well as in the Old Testament and concludes that the term indeed denotes a comprehensive world order, akin to that of the Egyptian concept *Ma'at*. Central to this order, at least as far as the Old Testament is concerned, is the idea of one creator—of the world and of other gods—who maintains the order of the world, with the king as his earthly representative.[97]

Schmid pays no particular attention to the pairing of justice and righteousness, and draws no specific conclusions concerning a unique prophetic world view.[98] His study of the root צדק in the text leads him to conclude that its meaning developed over time and in specific response to Israel's particular historical circumstances.[99] The infrequency of the root in Hosea, coupled with the fact that it primarily occurs as part of the word pair 'justice and righteousness' in First Isaiah and Amos, means that this word alone is insufficient for articulating the world view of the prophetic texts under consideration in this volume. Moreover, like the notion of a cosmic covenant, it is difficult to see how ideas of justice and righteousness, whether taken together or as separate concepts, can provide a comprehensive understanding of ancient Israelite world views.

Natural Law

John Barton's studies of ethics and the prophetic texts address the question from a slightly different perspective, namely that of natural

[96] Schmid, *Gerechtigkeit*, 66. His conclusions are supported by Seifrid ('Righteousness Language', 422). Gossai's study on justice and righteousness in the 8th-century prophets makes only passing reference to Schmid's study (Gossai, *Eighth-Century Prophets*).

[97] Schmid, *Gerechtigkeit*, 65, 25, 167.

[98] Ibid. 111–18, 37. His tendency to rely on statistical data on word use and to read texts outside their contexts results in a work which, according to Krašovec, is based on 'abstract suppositions' and hence unconvincing (Krašovec, *La Justice*, 16; see also Reventlow, *Justice and Righteousness*).

[99] Schmid, *Gerechtigkeit*, 167.

law.[100] In 'Natural Law and Poetic Justice in the Old Testament' Barton seeks to establish whether the Old Testament contains any moral norms that are common to all humanity or even built into the very nature of things (i.e. not explicitly predicated on God's revelation in law and/or covenant).

Barton draws on the work of Horst in the book of Job and the priestly narratives to conclude that certain texts carry a sense of 'the rights of human beings *qua* human'.[101] In particular, he cites the oracles against the nations in Amos 1–2, in which, he suggests, the foreign nations around Israel were condemned because they infringed a commonly held moral obligation, obvious to all.[102] With respect to First Isaiah, Barton suggests that the prophet's condemnation of the people for infringements that lie beyond the articles of Torah, such as excessive luxury, political allegiances and pride, exemplify a kind of '"cosmic nonsense", a reversal of the sane way of looking at the world'.[103] In Barton's view, both Amos and Isaiah exhibit belief in a 'cosmic order' which places natural law more in the mainstream of Israelite thought than previously maintained.[104] This is further elaborated in 'Ethics in Isaiah of Jerusalem' where Barton states that Isaiah presents an early example of an ethical approach that 'begins with a hierarchically ordered universe whose moral pattern ought to be apparent to all . . . and derives all particular moral offences from the one great sin, a disregard for natural law'.[105]

[100] Barton defines 'natural law' according to the *Dictionary of Christian Ethics* as 'the view that there are certain precepts or norms of right conduct, discernible by all men' (Barton, 'Natural Law', 1). The phrase itself is not unproblematic since it is so saturated with Graeco-Roman concepts as to be potentially misleading in the Old Testament context. However, a number of scholars have identified the concept of natural law in the Old Testament, including Gehman, 'Natural Law'; Weber, *Ancient Judaism*; and Jones, *Oracles against Foreign Nations*—as Barton notes (Barton, *Oracles against the Nations*).

[101] Horst, 'Naturrecht'; Barton, 'Natural Law', 4.

[102] This is developed in his monograph on Amos's oracles against the nations, in particular the assumption that these ethical standards would be evident to his Israelite audience (Barton, *Oracles against the Nations*).

[103] Barton, 'Natural Law', 7. He cites Amos 6:12 as another prime example of 'cosmic nonsense'.

[104] E.g. by Horst, 'Naturrecht'; see Barton, 'Natural Law', 8.

[105] Barton, 'Ethics in Isaiah', 13.

Israelite understanding of a fundamental 'natural law' may be indicated by texts that stress the appropriateness of a divine judgement to a particular sin.[106] Rather than adopting Koch's mechanistic understanding of poetic justice, Barton suggests that the prophets who used such a notion were 'implicitly appealing to a human consensus about what sort of acts are just and unjust, which ... rests on ideas about ethics formed by reason'.[107]

Although predominantly concerned with human relationships with God and within society, Barton's analysis of natural law and poetic justice highlights a hitherto unnoticed aspect of the ethical basis of the prophets Amos and Isaiah.[108] Like Murray and Schmid, he highlights a natural order, an ethos, which may explain the way the Old Testament writers viewed their world. However, the textual evidence is insufficient to conclude that natural law is the predominant motif by which the prophetic texts articulate an overlying sense of cosmic or societal order.

THE RELATION BETWEEN HUMAN AND NON-HUMAN CREATION

If none of the four possibilities outlined in the preceding pages—land as inheritance, cosmic covenant, justice and righteousness, and natural law—provide an adequate framework around which biblical views of the world may be organized, what does? While all these themes provide a valuable contribution to the overall picture, each one offers a narrow focus that is dependent upon certain specific texts. Taking full account of a greater proportion of the biblical material, or even of prophetic texts, must entail viewing the material from a wider perspective. In recent scholarship, in particular in the context of environmental issues, this has happened as the focus has

[106] Barton, 'Natural Law', 9.

[107] Ibid. 13; see Koch, 'Doctrine of Retribution'.

[108] Barton's work on ethics, which will be discussed further in Chapter 7, provides a helpful basis for discussion of ethical responses to environmental issues.

turned towards understanding ancient Israelite attitudes to, and connections with, the natural world.

The idea that the Old Testament assumes a reciprocal relationship between humans and the natural world forms the basis for Ronald Simkins's monograph, *Creator and Creation.*[109] He uses a cross-cultural sociological model to identify a range of attitudes towards nature in ancient Israel, which he proposes to integrate into a single Israelite world view.[110] Simkins's study suggests that the Bible presents a world view that recognizes both the intrinsic worth of the natural world and the special place of humans within it.[111] Although he devotes a large portion of the book to discussion of biblical texts and theological concepts (such as covenant), his detailed analysis is based on sociological modelling, and in the end, remains a sociological model, despite his concerns to avoid ethnocentrism and anachronism.

If Simkins is concerned about Israelite attitudes to the natural world, Terence Fretheim's starting point in his theological study of creation in the Old Testament is with the close connection between God and the world.[112] His discussion is predicated upon the conviction that 'Israel's understanding about God has decisively shaped its reflection about creation.... God and creation must be considered together, because again and again the texts keep them together'.[113] In his chapter on the prophets, Fretheim discusses the 'created moral order' as an agent of God's judgement. By this he means the principle of act/consequence that operates in the created world (as a direct and deliberate result of God's creative agency). Like Barton, he is keen to stress that 'this moral order does not function in any mechanistic, precise, or inevitable way'.[114]

[109] Simkins, *Creator and Creation.*
[110] Ibid. 39–40.
[111] Ibid. 162.
[112] Fretheim, *God and World.*
[113] Ibid. xvi.
[114] Ibid. 165.

AN ECOLOGICAL FRAMEWORK FOR EXPLORING THE TEXTS

Both Simkins and Fretheim offer a broad and useful basis for consideration of the ethical implications of human interaction with the non-human creation. A more specifically ecological framework within which to consider the Old Testament view of creation is provided by Christopher Wright's chapter on 'Ecology and the Earth' in *Old Testament Ethics for the People of God.*[115] Wright builds on an articulation of the theocentric perspective of the Old Testament to propose a paradigmatic ethic by which to reflect on the 'ecological dimension' of Old Testament ethics.[116] This represents a development of his earlier work on the ethical triangle as a model for Old Testament ethics, which connects the theological aspect of ethics (God) with the social one (Israel) and the economic one (the land) in a triangular relationship.[117] His discussion is based on two affirmations concerning the earth: that of divine ownership and of divine gift:

> This double claim (that God owns the earth and that God has given the earth to humanity) must therefore be the foundation for our reflection on the *ecological dimension* of Old Testament ethics. [Wright's italics][118]

He suggests expanding the 'inner redemptive triangle' of God, Israel, and the land, into a 'creation triangle' of God, humanity, and the earth, and it is this which forms the basis for his theological environmental ethic.[119]

Wright's study, like that of Fretheim, is fundamentally theological rather than exegetical in character, although both draw extensively on

[115] C. J. H. Wright, *Old Testament Ethics.*

[116] Ibid. 103–5. To what extent the biblical text can be normative for, rather than merely descriptive of, ethics will be discussed in Chapter 7.

[117] C. J. H. Wright, *People of God* and *God's People*; see also Block, who also portrays the complexities of the interrelationship between deity, people and land using a triangular model. Having established this as a reasonable portrayal of the Israelite perception of their national territory, he then discusses to what extent this perception was shared by the surrounding peoples (Block, *Gods of the Nations*).

[118] C. J. H. Wright, *Old Testament Ethics*, 103.

[119] Ibid.

textual exegesis. Because the whole Old Testament is under consideration, a broad overview emerges, rather than detailed engagement with specific texts. The strength in both Wright's and Fretheim's work lies in the fact that they highlight the impossibility of detaching human beings from the rest of the creation. In the biblical world, as in modern society, people cannot be viewed in isolation from the environment they inhabit, either physically or morally. Furthermore, both authors clearly suggest in different ways that in the Old Testament God's dealings with the whole creation, not just with human society, are presented in relational terms.

It is this concept of interrelationship that will be adopted in the following three chapters of this volume. But unlike the broad brush approach adopted by Fretheim and Wright, the focus in this study is the exegesis of a particular section of the biblical corpus. This is an attempt to avoid the pitfalls of studies that apply a list of principles to the text, such as those of Habel and Bouma-Prediger, or that derive theological concepts from texts that differ widely in genre, date, and context, such as that of Murray. Limiting the range of material studied will not result in an overarching framework for an Old Testament *Weltanschauung* as Schmid's study might be said to do, nor does it encompass the breadth of theological reflection such as that provoked by Brueggemann or Fretheim. Rather it provides a window into some key sections of Israel's religious tradition, from which there is the potential to derive paradigms for a contemporary ecological ethic.

The ecological triangle

The 'creation triangle' of God, humanity and the earth that Wright has proposed provides a helpful lens through which to explore the biblical text, and for the purposes of this exegesis has been slightly modified to an 'ecological triangle'. This triangular model seeks to identify ways in which the selected Old Testament texts exhibit interrelationship—between God and the earth as well as between God and human beings, and also between humanity and the non-human creation. By undertaking a close reading of the texts through the lens of this relational matrix we will uncover hitherto neglected

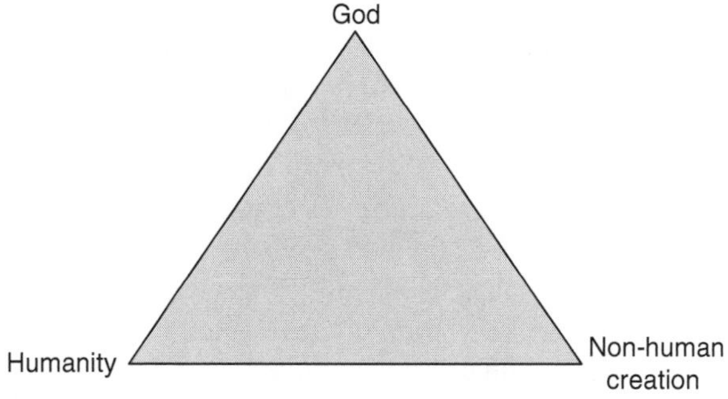

Figure 2. The ecological triangle

ideas and motifs—the unnoticed involvement of the non-human creation in the story of Israel.

There are a number of questions that can be posed to guide the exploration of individual texts within this framework:

1. What understanding of the non-human creation (whether cosmic or local) does the text present?
2. What assumptions are made about YHWH's relationship to the created world and how he acts within it?
3. What effect do the actions and choices of human beings have on the non-human creation and vice versa?

It should be stressed that these questions form the background to the exegetical process. They are not a formal grid that will be applied over the texts—this would be little different from, say, using the eco-justice principles of the Earth Bible Project. Rather, it is important to let the texts speak for themselves, and in so doing to discover the differences in emphasis between books and indeed the tensions inherent within individual texts.

Selection of texts

The books chosen for this exegetical process are the prophetic texts of Amos, Hosea, and First Isaiah. Why the prophets, and why this particular combination that spans neither the whole of the prophetic corpus nor one particular section of it (such as the whole of Isaiah or the Book of the Twelve)? In the first place, the decision to study texts in depth rather than give a broad overview has necessitated a drastic limitation on the range of material studied. It simply would not be possible to do justice to, say, all the prophets with this approach. Secondly, it has been important to select parts of the Old Testament that have not already been the focus of substantial scholarly discussion as far as the concept of creation is concerned. On these grounds, the creation and flood accounts of Genesis are excluded, as are the Psalter and Wisdom literature. A number of studies (including Wright's *God's People in God's Land*) have included a focus on material from the Pentateuch.[120] Studies on creation themes in the prophetic texts of Jeremiah and Second Isaiah have already been undertaken by Habel and Stuhlmueller, among others, and on Joel by Simkins.[121] Thirdly, the selected texts needed to have potential—in terms of the extent to which they refer to the natural world and the presence of themes and ideas that could provide insights into the interrelationship between God and his human and non-human creation. An initial survey suggested that the books of Amos, Hosea, and First Isaiah fitted this criterion; furthermore none of these books have hitherto been extensively mined for creation themes nor been the focus of much 'ecological attention'.[122]

This study is not primarily concerned with historical-critical matters, preferring to take a synchronic approach rather than a diachronic one (while recognizing that an absolute polarization is both artificial and misleading).[123] However, the fact that these books by

[120] The Exeter University project on the Uses of the Bible in Environmental Ethics includes a doctoral student working specifically on ecological ethics in Leviticus (see http://www.huss.ex.ac.uk/theology/research/ubee.htm).

[121] Habel, *The Land Is Mine*; Stuhlmueller, *Deutero-Isaiah*; Simkins, *History and Nature in Joel*.

[122] At the time of selecting texts the newly published work of Paas on the 8th-century prophets had not yet come to my attention (Paas, *Creation and Judgement*). Despite the title, his work has a significantly different focus from this study, and will be further discussed at the end of this chapter.

[123] Frolov, *Turn of the Cycle*, 29; see also Möller, *Prophet in Debate*, 9–10. Sherwood suggests that 'the 'axiomatic' dichotomy between the 'old' literary criticism, with its emphasis on fragmentation, and the 'new' literary criticism, with its stress on unity and coherence, ultimately breaks down' since both are concerned to explain and thus 'to

virtue of their opening statements are all attributed to prophetic activity in the eighth century BCE, and are regarded by traditional scholarship as containing significant amounts of material from the pre-exilic period places them within a coherent sub-group, a factor that may be instructive when it comes to intertextual comparison.[124]

On this basis it would seem that the book of Micah should be included since, like the other three, its self-designated context is that of the eighth century BCE. However, Micah provides a greater challenge in terms of the exegetical framework outlined above. Most of the references to the created world are brief and passing, and the non-human creation functions within the context of the book's indictment of social injustice. There are only passing references to suggest Micah is aware of interconnectedness within the created world. Furthermore, most of the references or allusions that touch on the creation are also found in the other three prophetic texts. For example, the theophany of Mic. 1:2–3 echoes that of Amos 4:13 and 9:5, and the poetic justice of Mic. 6:14–15 calls to mind Hos. 4:10 (cf. Amos 5:11). Comparison with First Isaiah shows a number of thematic and verbal parallels (e.g. 'heap of ruins' Mic. 1:6 cf. Isa. 17:1; 'desolation of the land' Mic. 7:13 cf. Isa. 24:1–4).[125] For these

attempt to repair the damaged text' (Sherwood, *Prostitute and Prophet*, 325). Rather, both diachronic and synchronic frames of references are valid and may be viewed in relation to each other along a continuum between two extremes (Frolov, *Turn of the Cycle*, 29). Likewise Clines notes that in exegesis and literary theory everything he wants to do is neither synchronic nor diachronic, but 'an indeterminate mixture of the two'. He suggests it might be better to think of synchronic and diachronic as 'names for segments of a spectrum, rather than labels on the only two pigeon holes . . . of biblical scholarship' (Clines, 'Beyond Synchronic/Diachronic', 52; see also Barr, 'Synchronic, Diachronic, Historical'; and Barton, *Biblical Criticism*, 187–8).

[124] In the three exegetical chapters that follow, the sequence Amos, Hosea, First Isaiah has been followed, rather than the canonical one. The decision to place Amos at the start is governed by the fact that it marginally precedes the other two chronologically. Moreover, according to the book's superscription, Amos's prophetic utterances span a relatively short period of time and the prophet may have been active for less than a year (Jeremias, *Amos*, 13). Hosea belongs most logically alongside Amos, since both are prophets to the Northern Kingdom, followed by First Isaiah, which spans the same monarchs as Hosea does, yet is firmly placed within the Jerusalem context.

[125] The most substantial example of intertextuality is Mic. 4:1–3 which almost exactly repeats Isa. 2:2–4. Since space precludes treatment of the theme of the mountain of YHWH, it is not included in the discussion.

reasons Micah has not been accorded a chapter in its own right, but, wherever relevant, will be referenced in each of the other exegetical chapters.

Identifying common themes

While the aim is not to undertake a comparative study of these prophetic books, certain broad areas of investigation or themes have provided guidance for the exegetical process. The aim is to explore how the non-human creation functions with respect to each area or theme. These include:

1. The use of figurative language.
2. The appeal to natural order/poetic justice.
3. The presence of other wisdom-type material (e.g. parable).
4. The extent to which cosmic themes are found.
5. The language of judgement/blessing.

These themes are not rigid categories through which to examine the material. Rather they provide some common ground for exploring the rich diversity of these prophets. Not all themes are specifically explored with respect to each prophet and there is enormous variety in the amount of material on any one area. For example, while extensive use of figurative language is found in all the texts, cosmic themes are present in Amos and Isaiah but virtually absent from Hosea, and Isaiah stands out as being particularly rich in parabolic material. In each of these three books certain aspects of the inter-relationship between God, human beings and the non-human creation come to the fore, and form the focus for that particular prophetic book.

Diachronic or synchronic readings?

As already noted, this exegetical study tends towards the synchronic end of the continuum, and prioritizes reading the final form of the text. However, it takes account of the fact that the prophetic oracles were originally addressed to certain specific historical and cultural situations. Much of the core material of Amos, Hosea, First Isaiah, and Micah can reasonably be said to have originated as a response to situations or events in the world of the eighth century—whether cultural (religious, political, social) or natural (such as earthquake or drought). The written form of this material has been subject to a process of revision and editing before reaching its present shape. The need for the word of YHWH to come fresh and new to each succeeding generation undoubtedly prompted the reapplication of earlier prophecies into different historical situations and guided the redactors' hands. However, in addition to, and perhaps preceding, the more formal activity of redactors, the material both drew upon and contributed to a pool of prophetic ideas, motifs, and phrases that were reused and adapted to new situations and new audiences, time and time again. As Davies puts it, the prophetic word 'not only retained its validity outside the situation in which it was originally delivered, but was capable of being adapted to new situations and of inspiring fresh oracles modelled on it'.[126] It is this reuse that helps account for the repetition of themes and idioms and the prevalence of intertextuality which are a notable feature of this prophetic literature.[127]

CREATION THEMES IN THE PROPHETS

Scholarly lack of interest in the theme of creation in the supposedly 'early' prophetic texts of Amos, Hosea, and First Isaiah is predicated upon a number of tendencies in Old Testament scholarship over the past hundred years. Most significant of these are the suggestion that the doctrine of creation is a 'late' development, coupled with the focus on vocabulary, in particular the root ברא (to create), as the determining factor in establishing whether a particular text is concerned with creation. Allied to these considerations is the propensity to view creation as a single one-time divine action concerning the

[126] G. I. Davies, 'Destiny of the Nations', 108.
[127] See the discussion on biblical intertextuality in Eslinger, 'Inner-Biblical Exegesis'.

origin of the world rather than God's involvement in its continuing existence, a distinction foreign to biblical thought.[128]

Creation as a 'late' idea

As discussed in Chapter 2, the desire to distinguish Israelite religion from the 'primitive' nature religions of her neighbours, coupled with an anthropocentric focus on salvation history, has characterized scholarship of the past century or more. Although von Rad is by no means the only proponent of these ideas, his thesis of the late emergence and subsidiary nature of the doctrine of creation has proved extremely influential.[129] Of particular significance is his reading of parts of Second Isaiah which led him to conclude that the doctrine of creation is subordinate to that of redemption. His analysis of texts such as Isa. 42:5, 44:24–8, and 51:9–10 (among others) correctly shows the juxtaposition of ideas of YHWH as creator and redeemer, but prejudges the issue of which is more important, to the extent that he can state that 'the doctrine of creation has been fully absorbed into the complex of soteriological belief'.[130] For von Rad, the frequent references to creation in Second Isaiah merely provide a foundation for faith in God's power in history.

A number of scholars have subsequently defended and amplified this stress on soteriology with its consequential relegation of creation faith to a secondary position.[131] But such interpretations are often based on preconceptions about the theological message of the Old Testament in general, and a misreading of selected texts in particular. For example, Stuhlmueller's study begins from the assumption that creation in Second Isaiah is 'an aspect or characteristic subordinate to the work of redemption'.[132] From this he develops the idea of 'creative redemption' by redefining creation as the

[128] See Schmid, 'Creation', 103–4, for a critique of this view of creation as a single event.

[129] Von Rad, *Old Testament Theology* 1, 136–9.

[130] Von Rad, 'Old Testament World View', 136.

[131] For an extensive survey of this literature, see Reventlow, *Problems of Old Testament Theology*, 134–54; and Clifford, 'Unity of Isaiah', 5–8.

[132] Stuhlmueller, *Deutero-Isaiah*, 1.

exceptionally wondrous redemptive act of Yahweh bringing to Israel a *new* national existence and a *new* prosperity of *unprecedented* scope, with 'creative' repercussions upon all the elements of Israel's existence, even upon the cosmos. [Stuhlmueller's italics][133]

Stuhlmueller's argument is based on a number of factors, including Second Isaiah's use of creation ideas as the introduction or conclusion to oracles of salvation or judgement, the use of traditional doctrinal motifs such as exodus and election to articulate the new 'creative redemption' and syntactical issues concerning Second Isaiah's use of participles which give a 'spirit of contemporaneous activity' emphasizing 'Yahweh's (re-)creating as he redeems Israel'.[134] However, while his textual observations may be valid, his interpretation of them is governed by his presuppositions. Although he correctly notes that a number of texts have creation ideas framing those of redemption, it is not necessary to infer from this, as he does, that creation is secondary to redemption. Indeed Rentdorff suggests that the opposite may be true: 'Faith in God the Creator was perceived and experienced as the all-embracing framework, as the fundamental, all-underlying premise for any talk about God, the world, Israel, and the individual.'[135]

Other scholars disagree with the conclusions of von Rad and Stuhlmueller. Westermann strongly refutes von Rad's attempt to give a soteriological relevance to all creation statements in Second Isaiah.[136] For Westermann creation is not a subset of redemption; it has a universal dimension of its own, which originated in early traditions handed down through the generations and which essentially precedes Israelite recognition of YHWH as saviour.[137] Schmid suggests that in the ancient Near East 'creation faith... [is] concerned above all with the present world and the natural environment

[133] Ibid. 9.

[134] Ibid. 55.

[135] Rendtorff, *Canon and Theology*, 107–8; see also the discussion in Fretheim, *God and World*, 189–94.

[136] Westermann, 'Schöpfer Und Schöpfung'. In a subsequent volume he counters von Rad's position by contrasting God's acts of blessing with his redemptive action (Westermann, *Theology*).

[137] For a brief comparison of the views of Westermann and von Rad, see Paas, *Creation and Judgement*, 1–10.

of humanity now'.[138] The connection between legal offence and political or natural disaster and 'the connection of act and consequence' indicate that 'law, nature and politics are only aspects of one comprehensive order of creation'.[139] These perspectives are to be welcomed as paving the way for the re-evaluation in contemporary scholarship of the importance of creation themes in the Old Testament.

The root ברא (to create)

Part of the justification by von Rad and others for adducing a post-exilic date for the understanding of YHWH as creator is derived from the absence of the verb ברא (to create) in earlier texts. Studies of the usage of this root conclude that it denotes exclusively the creative activity of YHWH and is found infrequently in the pre-exilic prophetic texts.[140] Of the 47 occurrences of this verbal root in the Old Testament, 20 are in Second and Third Isaiah and a further 11 in the P texts of early Genesis (Gen chs. 1, 5, and 6), leading von Rad to conclude that it is 'a technical term in the vocabulary of the priests'.[141] The only use of ברא in First Isaiah is the vision of the restoration of Mount Zion in 4:5, which is regarded by many commentators as a post-exilic addition.[142] A similar case is made for the only instance of this root in Amos (4:13) by Crenshaw and others, although there is less scholarly consensus surrounding the origin of this text.[143]

The suspicion that circular arguments are operating in such discussions means that their confident conclusions may be open to question. The use of ברא (to create) in so-called 'late' texts may indeed suggest the word was not in common use in the pre-exilic period. However,

[138] Schmid, 'Creation', 103.
[139] Ibid.
[140] See especially Humbert, 'Emploi et Portée'.
[141] Von Rad, *Old Testament Theology 1*, 142.
[142] E.g. Kaiser, *Isaiah 1–12*, 85; Wildberger, *Isaiah 1–12*, 165; Williamson, *Isaiah 1–5*, 306. Humbert supports the LXX reading (*καὶ ἥξει καὶ ἔσται* 'And he will come and be') on the grounds that the passage is describing a theophany rather than an act of creation (Humbert, 'Emploi et Portée', 402).
[143] Crenshaw, *Hymnic Affirmations*, 62–3.

allowing the argument for or against pre-exilic belief in YHWH as creator to be determined by one specific verbal root places a restriction that takes no account of the variety and scope of Hebrew language and understanding.[144] That there are other terms used to denote the creative activity of YHWH is made clear in Stefan Paas's detailed study of Amos, Hosea, and First Isaiah, *Creation and Judgement*.[145] His discussion of creation terminology centres on a number of Hebrew roots used in these prophetic books to refer to the creational activity of YHWH, as well as several wider concepts, metaphors, and motifs that are, in his opinion, connected to God's creative power, whether explicitly or implicitly.[146] His conclusion suggests that in the Old Testament the scope of YHWH's creative activity is broader than that suggested by the modern term 'creation', and includes God's ongoing creative work in nature and history.[147]

Interesting as Paas's study is, it is concerned with only one aspect of creation—that of God as creative agent. Unlike the present volume, it is not especially concerned with relationships within the created order or, despite his conclusion, with the ongoing interaction between God and the world. The exegetical chapters which follow will explore just such considerations—by looking at ways in which the natural world is described in the text and determining how this connects with the authors' experiences of human society and their understanding of God and his interaction with the created order.

[144] A number of scholars suggest that an Israelite concept of creation is not confined to the post-exilic period. Wolff, following Humbert, argues that the use of ברא in the Amos text as well as in Ezek 28:13 and 28:15 supports the idea that the word belongs to 'pre-exilic Canaanite cultic language' (Wolff, *Joel and Amos*, 223; Humbert, 'Emploi et Portée'). Following an extensive discussion of the issue, Crenshaw lists six reasons 'that almost demand an early belief in creation' (*Hymnic Affirmations*, 93–4).

[145] Paas, *Creation and Judgement*.

[146] ibid. These include God as father, and God as king.

[147] This is broader than his own initial definition of creation as 'the making of something new in the sphere of nature, with God as Actor' (ibid. 58). Paas's claim to have discovered in the texts 'hidden metaphors... in which there may have been a clear place for YHWH as Creator' (p. 60), together with his choice of root words with a broad semantic range, means that he explores texts that are of marginal relevance for the discussion God's interaction with his creation.

4

Who Can But Prophesy?
Creation Dialogue in the Book of Amos

First in his East the glorious Lamp was seen,
Regent of Day, and all th' Horizon round
Invested with bright Rayes, jocond to run
His Longitude through Heav'ns high rode: the gray
Dawn, and the PLEIADES before him danc'd
Shedding sweet influence: less bright the Moon,
But opposite in leveld West was set
His mirror, with full face borrowing her Light
From him, for other light she needed none

(Milton, *Paradise Lost*, Book VII)

INTRODUCTION

The close reading of Amos, Hosea, and First Isaiah which follows in the next three chapters will demonstrate that the interconnection between human and non-human creation, and between God and the world, is a significant feature of these books. How exactly this interrelationship is portrayed varies from text to text, as will be seen. However, an important feature common to all three books is the use they make of figurative language to portray the natural world as well as human beings and God. In view of this, the first part of this chapter will examine the nature and function of metaphor in the Old Testament and particularly the prophetic books, before moving to a detailed discussion of imagery of the non-human world.

FIGURATIVE LANGUAGE IN THE OLD TESTAMENT

A number of studies of the Old Testament in recent years have been concerned, either wholly or in part, with the subject of imagery, and in particular, metaphor.[1] These have drawn on and developed metaphor theories from the world of literature and philosophy to articulate the meaning and function of metaphor in the Old Testament, including the relation between speaker and audience, author and reader.[2] Only a brief overview of the extensive work in this subject can be given here and more comprehensive accounts can be found in the footnoted sources. An initial difficulty is establishing exactly what is meant by 'metaphor' and related terminology since, as Janet Soskice notes, what serves as a useful explanation in one discipline is inadequate in another.[3] Soskice herself gives a broad definition of metaphor as 'that figure of speech whereby we speak about one thing in terms which are seen to be suggestive of another'.[4]

Metaphor theory

Discussions of metaphor theory as it relates to theology and biblical studies draw on the work of a number of key figures, in particular the 1930s literary theorist Ivor Richards and, twenty years later, Max Black. Richards's somewhat unsystematic discussion suggests that the metaphorical process comprises an 'interaction' between 'two thoughts of

[1] The broader term imagery is taken to include simile, allegory and parable as well as metaphor. For an overview of different forms of speech closely allied to metaphor, see Soskice, *Metaphor*, 54–66.

[2] E.g. Nielsen, *Hope for a Tree*; Eidevall, *Grapes in the Desert*; Shields, *Circumscribing the Prostitute*; Moughtin-Mumby, *Sexual and Marital Metaphors*.

[3] Soskice, *Metaphor*, 15.

[4] Ibid. Soskice notes that a metaphor forms part of a discrete figure of speech or trope and thus is to be distinguished from allegory or parable which comprise a longer textual unit. Certain types of simile, whilst differing grammatically, perform a function similar to metaphor, but are somewhat more limited in scope (Soskice, *Metaphor*, 54–5). In particular similes are limited by their inability to perform the function of catachresis—the deliberate misuse of a term to supply one which is lacking in vocabulary, e.g. in English, calling the lower part of a mountain 'the foot' (Soskice, *Metaphor*, 61).

different things', and he introduces the terms 'tenor' (the reality being described) and 'vehicle' (the terms in which it is described), which have become standard terminology.[5] Black's treatment is more methodical; he identifies two broad views of metaphor which he terms 'substitution' and 'interaction'.[6] The substitution view holds that the metaphorical 'focus' of a phrase or sentence 'is used to communicate a meaning that might have been expressed literally'.[7] The interaction view, according to Black, involves an extension of meaning beyond the literal in which the metaphor evokes a 'system of associated commonplaces' related to the literal, and from which the hearer can construct 'a corresponding system of implications about the principal subject'.[8] In this understanding, metaphor creates interaction between two initially disparate realms, bringing them into 'cognitive and emotional relation by using language directly appropriate to the one as a lens for seeing the other'.[9]

Closer to the subject matter of this volume, Kirsten Nielsen's study of the tree as metaphor in First Isaiah explores the brief history of research into the function of imagery with respect to the Old Testament.[10] She draws on Black's dual theory of substitution and interaction to discuss the dynamic nature of metaphor, in particular with regard to prophetic texts, and its possibility of reuse and reinterpretation as prophetic oracles are reapplied in new historical contexts.[11] This fluidity of metaphor gives it a function beyond the replacement of one expression with another in order to communicate information. In Nielsen's view, imagery therefore has two functions that cannot be separated: an 'informative' one and a 'performative' one.[12] The informative function

[5] Richards, *Rhetoric*, 93.

[6] Black, 'Metaphor'; see also Ricoeur, *Metaphor*. Some studies adopt the term 'cognitive' in preference to 'interaction' (e.g. Moughtin-Mumby, *Sexual and Marital Metaphors*).

[7] Black, 'Metaphor', 280.

[8] Ibid. 288.

[9] Ibid. 237. This view accounts for the fact that metaphors that work in one culture may seem inappropriate or ridiculous in another (ibid. 40).

[10] Nielsen, *Hope for a Tree*.

[11] Ibid. 42–47. Nielsen finds Black's view of metaphor insufficient, because it deals only with language at one point in history (ibid. 50).

[12] Ibid. 47. Although Nielsen initially apparently rejects Black's diachronic model of language as insufficient, she then seems instead to expand it in a way that is consistent with a synchronic reading of the texts.

(in Nielsen's case of the tree metaphors in First Isaiah) provides information about a particular historical situation, whilst the performative capacity involves 'that aspect of imagery whose purpose is to involve the hearer in the image's world, so that the hearer participates in it'.[13]

In his examination of metaphor in Hos. 4–13, Gören Eidevall highlights a number of issues that pertain to the understanding of biblical imagery. In particular he draws attention to the importance of time-frame and context for identifying and understanding metaphors.[14] His study identifies the presence of underlying 'root-metaphors' or 'themes', which 'recur in a conspicuous manner' and thus exert influence on the text.[15] The understanding of metaphor suggested by both Nielsen and Eidevall provide an important basis for the discussion of imagery of the non-human creation in this chapter and those that follow.[16] In particular, the flexibility of interpretation which the 'performative' function of metaphor implies facilitates a polyvalent understanding of biblical motifs and thus the ability of prophecy to speak into new situations.[17] The capacity of metaphor to create conceptual meaning, and thus to offer a new perspective on reality contributes to the possibility that the biblical texts may have something significant to contribute to contemporary perceptions of the world we live in.

Metaphors of the non-human creation

The Old Testament authors, in particular in prophetic and poetic texts, make extensive use of imagery of the natural world, both in relation to God and to human situations. As a number of scholars

[13] Ibid. 57. Her study suffers from a lack of precision in her definitions, an observation made to me by Alison Gray in a private conversation.

[14] Eidevall, *Grapes in the Desert*, 27–8.

[15] Ibid. 40; see also Eidevall, *Grapes in the Desert*, 48.

[16] At the present time, two decades since Nielsen's study, most biblical scholars working in this area consider metaphors to have a conceptual function, i.e. to make meaningful assertions about their tenor, although there is a range of opinions on how metaphors create such meaning, as exemplified by the essays in Hecke, *Metaphor*.

[17] See the discussion on the polyvalence of figurative language in Chapter 5.

note, almost all language used of God is, of necessity, metaphorical.[18] Whilst many of these metaphors of the divine are drawn from the sphere of human life, a significant proportion feature the non-human creation, such as God as rock (e.g. Ps. 18:3 [2], Isa. 17:10) or God as lion (e.g. Isa. 31:4, Jer. 4:7).[19] Terence Fretheim notes that

> [the] use of natural metaphors serves to temper a certain anthropocentricity in our talk about God. In fact... it could be said that God's transcendence is given a special lift by the use of such natural metaphors, for among other things they evoke wonder and awe in human beings.[20]

Natural world imagery also functions to describe human beings or their circumstances, including humans as grass (e.g. Job 5:25, Ps. 103:15) and as sheep (e.g. Ps. 95:7, Isa. 53:6). These metaphors can be positive or negative, with the vehicle functioning in both capacities. In the last example, the comparison of the people with sheep is a positive one in the pastoral imagery of Ps. 95, but negative in depicting human propensity to waywardness in Isa. 53.

In the current climate of sensitivity in biblical scholarship towards anthropocentric, as well as patriarchal, biases in the biblical texts, some have asked whether it is problematic to use metaphors of nature to describe human situations. In their discussion of metaphor in Amos as part of the Earth Bible Project, Jobling and Loewen consider this to be so, maintaining that 'the world, rather than sharing in human reality, becomes merely an instrument for thinking about human reality'.[21] However, this statement implies that the vehicle in a metaphor is necessarily of secondary importance to the tenor, which undermines the whole thrust of metaphorical language. Indeed in metaphor, it is the mental image conjured up by the vehicle that gives the metaphor focus and substance.[22] As Nielsen explains,

[18] Brettler, *God Is King*, 18; Caird, *Language and Imagery*, 18; Eidevall, *Grapes in the Desert*, 35; Fretheim, *Suffering of God*, 5–6.

[19] The metaphor God as rock is primarily found in the Psalter (17 times), once in Gen. (29:24) and a further four times in the prophetic books (Isa. 26:4, 30:29, 44:8; Hab. 1:12). For discussion of God as lion see Chapter 5.

[20] Fretheim, *God and World*, 257.

[21] Jobling and Loewen, 'Earth Reading of Amos', 84.

[22] The opposite understanding is provided by the Earth Bible team's suggestion that the metaphor of earth having a voice is more than just a rhetorical device; it functions as 'another hermeneutical tool to enable us... to begin relating to Earth as

the object of such imagery 'is to involve the hearers in such a way that by entering into the interpretation they take it over as their own perception of reality'.[23]

Jobling and Loewen fail to acknowledge that using images of the non-human to describe human life is not substantially different from the frequent use of anthropomorphic language to describe nature, a fact that is not seen as demeaning to human beings. Moreover, removing all metaphors of the non-human world from speech and writing (assuming it were possible) would result in a greater alienation between human and non-human, as well as the impoverishment of human literature and conversation.

Rather, as will be seen in each of the exegesis chapters, imagery of all kinds enriches and enlivens the language, and gives colour and immediacy to the pronouncements of the prophet. Furthermore, the non-human creation is a reference point, a yardstick, at times even an ideal, against which human experience is measured. Metaphor becomes a means through which humanity and the earth either connect or are contrasted. As Claus Westermann maintains in his discussion of metaphor in proverbial wisdom:

> In the comparisons, what has been created—the creature—joins in communicating the overall message of the proverbs. The human is a part of the whole to which his thought life and sense world are linked. He discovers things that correspond to him, since everything that he observes and ponders belongs to the whole.[24]

METAPHOR IN AMOS

In the book of Amos examples drawn from the natural world provide both the vehicle of metaphors and the substance of visions. In Amos 2, the size and strength of the Amorites is likened to that of cedar and oak trees (v. 9), but this physical advantage does not

kin rather than commodity, as partner and co-creator rather than property'. Habel, *Psalms and Prophets*, 28.

[23] Nielsen, *Hope for a Tree*, 65.

[24] Westermann, *Wisdom*, 120.

prevent their destruction at the hands of YHWH, just as even the mightiest trees can be felled or burned down. The totality of this destruction is expressed in the second half of the verse 'I destroyed his fruit from above [the ground] and his root from below' (2:9b).[25] Is this imagery simply depicting the downfall of a great nation? Or does it also imply a negative or instrumental view of the trees themselves?[26]

Nielsen's explanation is helpful here and is applicable to other metaphors of the natural world. She draws attention to what she calls the 'material status' of the tree and its 'ideological status'.[27] The strength of the image 'lies in its evident accuracy'—it reflects what is observable and known by everybody.[28] However, she suggests, the view of the tree as sacred by virtue of its association with fertility myths in the ancient world also informs the metaphorical use. In two of the examples from Isaiah that Nielsen cites, Isa. 10:33–4, and 2:13–17 (both, she suggests, original to Isaiah of Jerusalem), as well as a number of other places in the prophetic books, the Hebrew root רום normally referring to a spatial characteristic—i.e. 'to be high'—is used in a figurative sense signifying 'to be proud'. If these two factors are brought to bear on Amos 2:9, the tree metaphor can be seen implicitly to indict the Amorites for their pride and their religious practices, as well as their military power. However, there is no suggestion that the trees are themselves intrinsically proud or hostile to YHWH, and indeed elsewhere in the Old Testament the tree metaphor is used in both a positive and a negative sense.[29]

In other texts the imagery is drawn from pastoral rather than agricultural life. In Amos 3:12 the deliverance of Israel is likened to snatching part of a domestic animal from the jaws of a lion, whilst in 5:19 the dangers of the natural world (lions, bears, and snakes) are used as metaphors for the danger about to come upon the Israelites. As Jobling and Loewen point out, it is not that these animals are

[25] A similar phrase emphasising completeness is used in Isa. 37:31—in this case to describe the restoration of Judah's fortunes.

[26] Jobling and Loewen, 'Earth Reading of Amos', 84.

[27] Nielsen, *Hope for a Tree*, 85.

[28] Ibid. 140.

[29] For positive tree metaphors see Ps. 92:12; Isa. 29:17, 36:16; Hos. 14:6, and compare with negative ones in Ps. 37:35; Isa. 1:30, 2:13, 34:4.

dangerous *because* God uses them as a means of punishment, rather that the people's 'experience' of nature precedes their experience of God.[30] These similes and metaphors invoke the audience's understanding of the natural order of the world as it applies to them by alluding to what happens in the rest of creation; such an understanding is an important prerequisite for understanding the prophet's message of condemnation or hope. Moreover, part of the powerful impact of Amos' message lies in the potential reversal of apparently known and secure elements of life.[31]

Amos 3:4–5 and 6:12 both use metaphors that suggest 'unnatural behaviour'. In each case the rhetorical question draws on observable animal behaviour and begs the answer 'No, of course not!' So, for example, in 6:12 the reader is asked 'Do horses run on the crags or does one plough the sea with an ox?'[32] The force of the image lies in what Wolff calls 'the antithetical relationship between the similes and that to which they are compared'.[33] It contrasts the natural wisdom of a horse, whose hooves are unsuited to mountaineering, with the foolishness (and danger) of setting justice aside, and compares the absurdity of an ox ploughing the sea with the stupidity of neglecting righteousness. A similar contrast is found in Isa. 1:2, 'An ox knows its owner, a donkey its master's feeding trough, but Israel does not know, my people do not understand', and here too Israel's stupidity is linked to a failure of justice and righteousness (v. 17).[34]

[30] Jobling and Loewen, 'Earth Reading of Amos', 83.

[31] Gillingham notes that in Amos 4 the presumption that Israel's God enjoys sacrifices and offerings is turned on its head; the following verses subvert the confident hope in his natural providence as provider of harvests and sustainer of the seasons' cycles (Gillingham, 'God and Creation', 168–87).

[32] Based on the BHS suggested emendation בבקר ים for בבקרים in the second part of the question. The MT reading, 'Does one plough with the oxen?' has little weight as a rhetorical question. Interestingly the LXX is completely different, 'Do horses run on rocks, or pass by females in silence?' This is arguably an appeal to one of the most basic 'natural laws'!

[33] Wolff, *Joel and Amos*, 284.

[34] See the works by Barton (e.g. Barton, 'Natural Law'), and discussion below, Chapter 6.

The visions of Amos

In addition to the use of metaphors and similes drawn from nature, three of the five visions of Amos involve images of the natural world. Two describe the devastation of the land by YHWH's judgement in terms of a locust plague on the spring crop (7:1–2) and a raging fire (7:4). Commentators suggest that the spring crop in 7:1 refers to non-grain crops sown in March and April, by which time the grain crop would be well advanced.[35] The locusts would therefore destroy both the grain and the newly sprouted spring crop—a double disaster. Judgement by fire (7:4) is already firmly established as a prerogative of YHWH (cf. 1:2 – 2:5), although here the connection with תהום רבה, 'the great deep', suggests a wider disruption than the effect of military action. In both of these visions the prophet pleads with YHWH on account of the people, 'How will Jacob stand, for he is small?' (7:2, 5), and the judgement is rescinded. The implied contrast between divine strength and human weakness involves the non-human creation as a means by which YHWH's power is displayed.

Amos' fourth vision in 8:2, the third with natural world imagery, adopts a word play between קיץ (summer fruit), and הקץ (the end, or reaping time).[36] Like the other visions, Amos sees something that symbolizes punishment, rather than the punishment itself.[37] The strength and meaning of the vision lies in the prophet's verbal reply to YHWH's question 'What do you see, Amos?' Visionary description is here combined with a rhetorical device to great effect. In each of these visions as well as most of the metaphors, the outcome is a negative one for the Israelites, although in many cases, the vehicles provided by the non-human creation are not themselves intrinsically negative. Rather, the natural environment itself has provided the material that the prophet shapes into his oracles and that inspires his visionary experiences.

[35] See Paul, *Amos*, 227.

[36] Although phonetically similar, these Hebrew words are not related etymologically, see Hammershaimb, 'Ethics', 120.

[37] Ibid. 118.

RHETORICAL STRUCTURE OF AMOS

Important as these metaphors and visions are, Amos uses relatively little figurative language of the natural world in comparison to Hosea and First Isaiah. Rather, the book relies significantly on rhetoric to communicate its vivid message. One instance of this—the rhetorical questioning of 3:3–4 and 6:12—has already been noted above; the remainder of this chapter will explore the rhetorical structure of the book, in particular its distinctive use of the vocabulary of speech and dialogue to depict relationships between the participants in the text, including the non-human creation. The focus of investigation will be on features in the text that suggest the presence of dialogue, whether explicit or implicit, between God and the non-human creation, and between humanity and the earth. Four concepts are particularly noteworthy: the earth responding to God's voice; creation revealing YHWH; the earth's role in judgement and restoration; the voice of the people in contrast with that of the earth. Together these features form part of a rhetorical structure that highlights the importance of the natural world and its relationship with God and humanity.

Speech in Amos

The book of Amos is characterized by speech of many kinds—proclamation, dialogue, interrogative, woe oracle, each used to enhance the message of the text. Not only is YHWH portrayed as the one who speaks, and Amos the prophet as his spokesman, as one might expect in a prophetic book, but the work features a number of other literary or rhetorical devices, that stress the communicative elements of the book:

1. The format of direct speech is used to set up the tension between the prophet Amos and the priest Amaziah (7:10–15), and to put words into the people's mouths that highlight their failings (e.g. 4:1, 8:5).
2. Although by no means unique to Amos, the frequent insertion by the redactor of the prophetic formulation נאם־יהוה,

'a declaration of YHWH' (16 times), emphasizes the divine nature of the pronouncements.[38] The book also concludes, uniquely among the prophetic books, with the editorial insertion אמר יהוה אלהך 'says YHWH your God'.[39]

3. The disputation in Amos 3:3–8 suggests that not only does YHWH choose to reveal his plans to the prophets (v. 7) but he does so in such a way as to compel prophecy: 'YHWH speaks and who can but prophesy' (v. 8). The sense of urgency about delivering his own message is passed on to his audience in 3:9—'proclaim . . . and say'—as the prophet calls them to public speech 'with the language of herald instruction'.[40]
4. The other side of the exhortation to Amos to prophesy is the command to the people to listen (3:1, see also v. 13, 4:1, 5:1). Not only does YHWH speak, both to Amos and to the people, but his voice must also be responded to. If not, the terrible consequence will be a 'famine' of hearing his word (8:11–12). This dire warning contrasts with the emphatic nature of the prophetic pronouncement of YHWH's voice and suggests a future too awful to contemplate. Whether the people recognize it as such is another matter.
5. In the visions sequence, YHWH enters into extended dialogue with Amos, twice agreeing to suspend judgement at Amos' request (7:1–6), and twice asking Amos to describe what he sees (7: 8, 8:2). The use of direct speech, here and elsewhere, personalizes and intensifies the interaction between YHWH and the prophet, and among the human players in the drama.

Such a focus on speech has been noted in the secondary literature, with various commentators drawing attention to the rhetorical and

[38] This expression occurs a total of 253 times in the Old Testament, most frequently in Jeremiah (162 times). It is relatively infrequent in the other 8th-century prophets (First Isaiah 11 times, Hosea 4 times, and Micah twice). The more usual translation is 'word' or 'declaration' of YHWH, however Gesenius-Kautzsch points out that its literal rendering is the 'whispering' of YHWH (GK 50a n.1). The fuller form נאם יהוה צבאות is found 25 times, all in the prophets (Isaiah 4 times; Jeremiah 4 times; Nahum twice; Zephaniah once; Haggai 5 times; Zechariah 9 times).

[39] Zephaniah ends with the simple phrase אמר יהוה, and Haggai with the fuller prophetic statement נאם יהוה צבאות.

[40] Jeremias, *Amos*, 57.

didactic skills exhibited by the book—whether of the eighth-century prophet or of his redactor/redactors.[41] Such studies focus primarily on aspects of human and divine speech in the text. But is there another participant in the conversation? As seen in Chapter 3, the Earth Bible Project's eco-justice principles have encouraged the identification of non-human voices in the biblical text. Although some of the EBP's methods have been questioned, in the light of the emphasis on communication in Amos it seems reasonable to ask whether the non-human creation might be said to 'speak' in the text, and with what effect.

Anthropomorphic language

The use of the terminology of speech with regard to the non-human, especially to the non-sentient, raises questions concerning the use of anthropomorphic language. Some commentators consider it problematic to attribute such a uniquely human attribute to inanimate objects. Tim Meadowcroft raises such an objection to the use of the phrase, 'the voice of the earth', by the Earth Bible Project, asking whether this is not itself a human creation—'a thoroughly anthropocentric device', and therefore counter to the Project's own eco-justice principles.[42] However, the Earth Bible team explain it in these terms: 'By the voice of Earth we mean the many languages of Earth, be they gesture, sign, image or sound, that send a message—whether to humans, to other members of the Earth community or to God.'[43] They go on to suggest that it is no less problematic to speak of the voice of earth than of the voice of God—both are metaphors that

[41] E.g. Paul, *Amos*; Wolff, *Joel and Amos*. On application of classical rhetorical theory to biblical prophetic texts, see Möller's detailed analysis of rhetorical structure and strategy in Amos (Möller, *Prophet in Debate*). He stresses the importance of rhetoric for written work that would be primarily received orally, not in writing. See also Wendland, 'Organisation of Amos'; Wood, *Amos in Song*; Shields, *Circumscribing the Prostitute*.

[42] Meadowcroft, 'Some Questions for the Earth Bible', cited in Habel, *Psalms and Prophets*, 24.

[43] Habel, *Wisdom Traditions*, 23.

enable humankind 'to...appreciate the reality of communication with a 'thou' other than ourselves'.[44]

The Old Testament itself frequently uses anthropomorphic language to describe the non-human creation. The heavens and the earth are summoned as God's witnesses (e.g. Deut 30:19; Isa. 1:2), they rejoice at his coming (e.g. Ps. 98:7–8; Isa. 55:12), and declare his glory (Ps. 19). The latter text is particularly interesting, since not only is the capacity for speech specifically attributed to cosmic phenomena: 'The heavens recount the glory of God...day to day pours forth speech (אמר)' (v. 2 [1]), but the Psalmist recognizes that this is perhaps an anomaly: 'there is no speech (אמר); there are no words' (v. 4 [3]). However, he still maintains that by their very existence these cosmic events speak: 'through all the earth their voice has gone out, and their utterances to the end of the world' (v. 5 [4]).[45]

Traditional scholarship has described such language in terms of 'a figure of speech' and 'rhetorical personification'.[46] Implicit in this is the concern not to attribute any hint of divinity to the natural world, and to preserve the distinction between humanity and the rest of creation. But such interpretations take insufficient account of the volume of biblical material that seems to articulate the interconnection between YHWH and the non-human creation in personal terms.[47] In other Psalms, the call to worship God is issued to all creatures (Ps. 150: 6) and to all creation, animate and inanimate (Ps. 148:3, 7–10). For these psalmists the capacity to worship God is something that human beings share with the rest of creation, not something that distinguishes them from it. Moreover the inclusion of sun, moon, and stars in Ps. 148's list of those participating in the praise of YHWH suggests a corrective to any tendency to worship these heavenly bodies.

In Amos, the rhetorical structure of the book includes the natural world as part of a cosmic dialogue between Creator and creation.

44 Habel, *Psalms and Prophets*, 24.

45 Based on the LXX ὁ φθόγγος αὐτῶν, which is to be preferred [LXX Ps. 18: 5].

46 C. J. H. Wright, *OT Ethics*, 110; and, with regard to Ps. 148, Allen, *Psalms 101–150*, 316.

47 Fretheim, *God and World*, 249–66.

There are a number of ways in which this voice of the earth may be heard, both explicitly and implicitly. Rather than a direct attribution of speech to the cosmos, the non-human creation is portrayed as responding to God's voice, and acting in cooperation with him both to reveal his power and to enact his judgement.

GOD SPEAKS AND EARTH RESPONDS

A number of texts in the Old Testament refer to speech acts by God in the context of the created world. The most obvious is the creation account of Genesis 1 in which the voice of God results in both the separation of various elements of the universe (vv. 1–10) and the filling of the world (vv. 11–27).[48] In Ps. 148:5 the cosmos is exhorted to praise YHWH because 'he commanded and they were created'. In Ps. 104:6–9 YHWH's control over the force of the waters is expressed in terms of speech—they are responsive to his command and flee at his rebuke. Likewise, in Amos, the vocabulary of God speaking and earth responding is used in several significant places.

Amos 1: 2

The book begins with an account of the voice of YHWH and its effect on the natural world. Amos 1:2 reads:

> YHWH roars from Zion, from Jerusalem he utters his voice, the grazing pastures mourn and the top of Carmel dries up.

The placing of this theophany 'as a motto summarising the message of the prophet' sets the tone for the whole book.[49] The first half of the verse is repeated in exactly the same format in Joel 4:16 [3:16] and a variation of it occurs in Jer. 25:30. Whether or not this indicates that each reference drew independently on a traditional source or that there is a relationship of dependence between them is subject to

[48] Echoed in Ps. 33:6.
[49] Wolff, *Joel and Amos*, 119, 25.

debate.[50] Intriguingly, in Joel the second half of the sentence is less specific than in Amos, referring in general terms to the heavens and earth shaking. Such a reaction is in keeping with the allusions to earthquake in Amos 8:8 and 9:5 (cf. also 1:1), but in Amos 1:2 the reaction of the natural world to YHWH's voice is described in more concrete terms.[51] The language used of YHWH in 1:2 is that of the divine warrior (roaring), and of the storm God (thundering) and both suggest divine anger, an understanding that is supported by the judgement oracles which follow immediately after this pronouncement.[52]

The second half of Amos 1:2 describes the reaction of the natural world to the proclamation of divine power and anger—the landscape undergoes a significant and visible change. If this verse implies that God's anger is directed at the natural world, it begs the question: why should it be the focus of his rage? Does this verse not imply wanton destruction of the earth's landscape by YHWH? A number of factors in the text suggest that a subtle process is at work whereby the non-human creation acts as a channel for YHWH's message, rather than itself being the recipient of divine displeasure. Four observations highlight this process:

1. The author has chosen the root אבל with its ambiguous meaning (primarily 'to mourn' but possibly a secondary nuance meaning 'to dry up') to describe the response of the pastures to YHWH's voice.[53] The motif of the earth (or parts of it) mourning is found

[50] See Hayes, *The Earth Mourns*, 20.

[51] Although YHWH is not specifically identified as a lion, the verbs used of him, שׁאג, 'to roar' and נתן קולו, 'to give his call' recur in 3:4, 8 as part of the leonine imagery. This, together with the extensive use by Hosea of the metaphor of YHWH as lion, may, according to Hayes, suggest an early pre-exilic origin to Amos 1:2 (ibid. 21, see also Paul, *Amos*, 36). Jeremias and Wolff take the opposite view—that this verse is the work of an exilic redactor (Jeremias, *Amos*, 8; Wolff, *Joel and Amos*, 122).

[52] Other refs in Old Testament to נתן קולו associate it with thunder, e.g. Ps. 18:14 [13], Ps. 68:34 [33]. See Hayes, *The Earth Mourns*, 22; Cross, *Canaanite Myth*, 174. The apparent contradiction between storm language (which implies rainfall) and the drought that follows is addressed by Weiss, 'Behandlung Der Metapher'. Hayes discusses other biblical texts in which rain and drought are mentioned concurrently (*The Earth Mourns*, 23–7).

[53] Hayes, *The Earth Mourns*, 12–18; Houtman, *Himmel im AT*; Clines, '"Be Dry" in Classical Hebrew'.

in nine prophetic passages of the Old Testament, spanning a wide range of dates.[54] The significance of this recurrence, according to Hayes, lies in the linking of the earth mourning to the state of human communities, whether local or global: 'Here the earth assumes a persona, responding to human distress or transgression (or to both)'.[55] In Amos, the motif acts as a prelude to the repeated theme of wickedness and punishment that characterizes the book, and in particular the oracles against the nations.[56] Such personification of the natural world suggests that the non-human creation is somehow involved in YHWH's theophany, not as a passive victim, but actively responding to God's call for action.

2. Two ideas found here are repeated in the final chapter of Amos: the 'mourning' of the pastures (9:5) and 'the top of Carmel' (9:3). This provides an emphatic reminder of the 'enduring validity' of the message of Amos.[57] The shift of subject from non-human in 1:2 to human in Amos 9 suggests that the relationship between YHWH and the natural world is more subtle than first appears. In 9:5 it is the inhabitants of the earth, implicitly its human population, who mourn, and in 9:3 Carmel, part of the non-human creation, works against the people, by providing no hiding place for those who attempt to flee God's wrath.
3. The mourning of the earth parallels the forthcoming judgement by fire on the foreign nations, and defeat of Israel in the succeeding oracles (1:3 – 2:16). The juxtaposition of 1:2 with the following sections establishes a connection between the devastation of the earth and that of human political landscapes. More specifically, suggests Hayes, 'the Earth responds to the punishment YHWH will inflict because of the sins of the community'.[58]
4. On a more local level, it is notably the shepherds' pastures that are affected by the drought, with the inherent possibility that their

[54] Isa. 24:1–20, 33: 7–9; Jer. 4:23–8, 12:1–4, 7–13, 23:9–13; Hos. 4:1–3; Joel 1: 5–20; Amos 1:2. See Hayes, *The Earth Mourns.*

[55] Ibid. 2.

[56] According to Hayes, the use of the qal form of the stative verb יבשׁ, 'conveys a response on the part of the earth rather than simply narrating an effect brought about by the agency of YHWH, as a passive form would do' (ibid. 26).

[57] Jeremias, *Amos*, 14.

[58] Hayes, *The Earth Mourns*, 30.

> flocks will lack food.[59] In other words the earth's response to YHWH affects the economic well-being of the people, and as we shall see, this is part of his judgement on them. This is given further weight if the suggestion of some commentators is adopted, that ראש הכרמל, 'head of Carmel', refers to the political head, i.e. the king of Israel, rather than a geographical location.[60]

But why does the pastureland mourn? Is it in anticipation of its own ravaging at the hand of YHWH, as an inevitable consequence of the judgement against the nations? Or is the earth responding to the revelation of YHWH's intentions and mourning in sympathy with the people? The semantic range of אבל suggests that both may be true. As Hayes notes, 'The . . . motif combines the two possibilities: the earth mourns for its own death as well as for the nation's and experiences both mourning and dying in the act of drying up.'[61] From the outset the book is setting up a three-way connection—between the voice of YHWH, the response of the earth and the fate of human beings.

YHWH summons creation

It is not only the pastures and top of Carmel that are responsive to God's voice. In three places in Amos, YHWH summons (קרא) parts of his creation to act in judgement against the people—the waters of the sea in 5:8 and 9:6, and fire in 7:4. Whilst the Hebrew root קרא occurs frequently in the Old Testament, its use with YHWH as subject is relatively unusual, apart from the naming of creation (Genesis 1) and of characters in narrative texts (e.g. 1 Sam. 3:4). In particular the combination of YHWH (as subject) calling to some

[59] Other biblical references that join together 'mountains' and 'pastures' suggest that the parallelism of this phrase conveys a representative totality (e.g. Jer. 9:9).

[60] Kapelrud, 'Central Ideas', 19. Wolff rejects this idea (Wolff, *Joel and Amos*, 125) but cf. Soggin who suggests Carmel has significance to the Jerusalem cult (Soggin, *Amos*, 84).

[61] Hayes, *The Earth Mourns*, 32.

aspect of the non-human creation (as object) is rare and almost always denotes the summoning of the natural world against the human population.

In Isa. 48:13, the context of God calling heaven and earth is that of his creative power over the world as well as over its human inhabitants. The judgement theophany of Psalm 50:1–4 proclaims that God 'has spoken and summoned (קרא) the earth' (v. 1). Verse 4 indicates that this is in order to judge his people, implicitly by means of the 'devouring fire' and 'mighty tempest' (v. 3) that accompany God's coming. In three other texts the specific form of the judgement is given: YHWH is twice portrayed as summoning a famine (2 Kgs 8:1; Ps. 105:16) and once a drought (Hag. 1:11). Behind each of these texts, as well as the ones in Amos, is the implication that such natural disasters are the prerogative of YHWH and can be summoned to do his bidding.[62]

In Amos 5:8 and 9:6 a contrast is made between the waters of the sea which respond in obedience to YHWH's summons, and the people who have not heeded his warning (5:6), or who have left it too late to escape (9:2–3). In 7:4, in the second of Amos' visions, YHWH is portrayed as calling forth fire, using the same vocabulary as Ps. 50:3.[63] The fire initially has a cosmic impact, first consuming את־תהום רבה, 'the great deep', and only then the terrain (החלק).[64] Amos's vision of the destruction of the primeval waters as well as tracts of human settlement depicts the full scope of YHWH's power—over the whole cosmos as well as over the affairs of human beings.

COOPERATING WITH YHWH

The texts already discussed have demonstrated ways in which the non-human creation responds to YHWH's voice: by undergoing a physical change (the mourning of the pastures, 1:2), and by being

[62] A similar inference is made in Jer. 25:29, in this case in respect of a political/military disaster.

[63] For discussion of the difficulties surrounding לרב באש see Andersen and Freedman, *Amos*, 746–7; Paul, *Amos*, 230–1.

[64] Wolff, *Joel and Amos*, 298.

summoned to do his bidding (the fire, 7:4, and the waters, 5:8, 9:6). In these verses the communication is verbal—at least on God's part: YHWH speaks and the earth responds. Other texts in Amos suggest that the interconnection between YHWH and the non-human creation may also be demonstrated non-verbally. In these cases the earth exhibits the capacity for dialogue, implicitly rather than explicitly, by means of 'gesture, sign, image or sound'.[65]

One example of this is the partnership between the natural world and YHWH whereby the non-human creation cooperates with the deity against the human population. This is most clearly seen in the fifth and final vision of the prophet (9:1–4), which describes the futility of trying to escape God's hand of judgement. The vision is almost certainly of the main altar in the Bethel shrine and, according to some commentators, represents a special judgement against religious or political institutions.[66] Whether verse 1 suggests an actual earthquake (Soggin, Wolff) or a supernatural intervention by YHWH to destroy the sanctuary (Andersen) remains a matter for debate.[67] Whichever the case, it represents a catastrophic judgement, and those escapees who seek shelter in remote parts of the cosmos that might hide them from YHWH will not find refuge. Perhaps this suggests an attitude among the people that the rest of creation exists to do their bidding, including sheltering them from God's wrath. If so, their assumptions are sorely misguided.

Verse 2 describes the futility of hiding from YHWH in the mythical extremes of the world (the depths of Sheol and heights of heaven). In verse 3 the physical limits—the top of Carmel, (renowned for its dense forest) and the depths of the sea (impenetrably dark)—will not shelter them. Carmel has already responded to YHWH's voice (1:2); now it, and the other extremities of the world, work along with him to expose those who are attempting to flee his judgement.[68]

[65] Habel, *Wisdom Traditions*, 23.

[66] Andersen and Freedman, *Amos*, 841; Jeremias, *Amos*, 155. On the question of who the 2nd person singular imperatives הַךְ and בצע (v.1) are addressed to, see Hammershaimb, *Amos*, 131; Paul, *Amos*, 274; Soggin, *Amos*, 120.

[67] Soggin, *Amos*, 120; Wolff, *Joel and Amos*, 339; Andersen and Freedman, *Amos*, 839.

[68] A similar description of the extremities of the universe depicting the inability of humans to hide from God (in an ambiguous, rather than purely negative sense) is

The whole cosmos, physical and mythical, appears to be in cooperation with YHWH against humanity.

The second and more significant of these non-verbal communications between YHWH and the earth comes in the three 'creation hymns' (4:13, 5:8–9, 9:5–6), which will now be examined in some detail. In these, the author depicts YHWH primarily in terms of his interaction with the natural world and only secondarily with humanity. Implicit in these texts' portrayals of God's creative power is the understanding that natural phenomena and the rhythms of the created world reveal the name, and therefore the character, of YHWH.

THE CREATION HYMNS

The creation hymns or doxologies have been the subject of extensive discussion in the secondary literature, in particular with regard to form and redaction-critical issues, resulting in a range of suggestions concerning their origin and purpose.[69] Each hymn takes the form of a number of participial phrases, describing YHWH almost exclusively in term of his creation of and control of the cosmos. Each one affirms that the attributes of YHWH to which they refer are part of his essential and unalterable character, his 'name', and in each of them YHWH is depicted as the God who communicates—to humankind in 4:13, and to the non-human creation in 5:8 and 9:6. The fragments each exhibit close links with the preceding or subsequent material, and together with these contexts, play a significant role in the text as we have it.

found in Ps. 139:7–12. Likewise in Job 28:12–22, the human search for wisdom takes him to the ends of the earth, but to no avail.

[69] The issues debated include the extent to which the hymns interrupt the flow of the texts (so Crenshaw), whether they comprise three different hymns (Crüsemann) or are taken from the same one (Horst, Mays) and when and why they were inserted into the Amos speeches at these points (Crenshaw, Brueggemann). See the extensive discussion in Crenshaw, *Hymnic Affirmations*; Crüsemann, *Hymnus Und Danklied*; Horst, 'Doxologien' as well as in the commentaries (Jeremias, *Amos*, 76–9; Mays, *Amos*, 83–4; Paul, *Amos*, 152–3; Wolff, *Joel and Amos*, 215–17).

Amos 4:13

The context of this hymn is provided in 4:6–12 in a series of reminders of the judgements that YHWH has already employed to recall the people to himself, and their failure to respond (vv. 6–11), followed by a intimation of further judgement (v. 12).[70] YHWH's previous actions against the people include 'natural' disasters such as erratic rainfall and blighted crops resulting in famine (vv. 6–9), and 'supernatural' plagues and military defeat (vv. 10–11). What the future holds is unspecified: the threat 'thus shall I do to you' is uttered twice in verse 12, followed by the imperative 'prepare to meet your God, O Israel'.

The creation hymn inserts into the text a reminder of key qualities of Israel's deity, as an answer to the unspoken question, 'who is this God?'[71] The first two participles highlight the cosmic power of YHWH as Creator: 'he who formed the mountains and created the wind', and the final two talk of his activity in maintaining the diurnal rhythms of the earth: 'making the dawn darkness', and of his presence within the world: 'treading on the high places of the earth'—perhaps referring to divine theophanies.[72] Micah 1:2–4 weaves this phrase into a more specific theophanic description, in which YHWH descends from his holy temple (מהיכל קדשו) in order to judge the peoples, resulting in catastrophic upheaval of mountains and valleys.[73]

In Amos 4:13 these descriptions are designed to provoke a response of awe and dread at the name of YHWH. If mountains, wind, and sea are powerful, unpredictable, and dangerous, how much more so their creator. If changing days and seasons, and the movement of the night sky are mysterious and unfathomable, how much more so the one who causes them. Yet it is precisely because YHWH is the

[70] Discussed later in this chapter.

[71] Cf. Ps. 24:7–10 describing an encounter between Israel and the king of glory.

[72] Andersen and Freedman, *Amos*. Whilst most commentators see in this phrase a reference to the natural world, i.e. mountains or hills, Wolff briefly alludes to the possibility that 'the high places' is a reference to Bethel, and derives from Canaanite traditions (Wolff, *Joel and Amos*, 224). The possibility that a deliberate ambiguity is intended by the author should not be ruled out.

[73] Comparison with Ps. 97:4 suggests that it is the fire that accompanies theophany that causes the mountains to melt.

all-powerful creator and sustainer of the world that drought and crop failure are at his disposal as a means of judgement.

In 4:13, in the middle participial phrase of five, YHWH is described as ומגיד לאדם מה־שׂחו 'declaring to humans his thoughts'.[74] Commentators differ over whether the pronominal suffix in the phrase מה־שׂחו, '*his* thoughts', should be taken as referring to אדם, 'humanity', or to YHWH.[75] In the light of the forthcoming 'meeting' between Israel and her God which 4:12 warns of, and the proclamatory nature of the whole hymn, it seems most likely that God's thoughts or plans are in view. This is supported by Mic 6:8, which uses similar terminology to refer to YHWH's standards: הגיד לך אדם מה־טוב, 'He declares to you, O human, what is good.'

That this phrase in Amos is the middle one of the five participles and occupies the central position of the verse serves to stress the smallness and insignificance of humanity (or possibly of the author himself) in comparison with the might and grandeur of creation, and, ultimately, with the power of the creator. However, it also highlights the fact that YHWH enters into communication with humanity, choosing to reveal something of himself, not just through the wonders of the created world, to which attention has been drawn, but also by revelation of his plans and intentions. That YHWH should do so comes as no surprise, since 3:7 has already suggested that communicating his intentions is a natural consequence of who he is.

The final phrase of the hymn ends with the statement יהוה אלהי צבאות שׁמו 'YHWH God of Hosts (is) his name', a truncated form of which, יהוה שׁמו 'YHWH is his name' is repeated at the end of

[74] The whole phrase is given a messianic slant by LXX as *ἀπαγγέλλων εἰς ἀνθρώπους τὸν χριστὸν αὐτοῦ*. See discussion in Lust, *Messianism*, 13; and Ehrlich, *Randglossen*, 239.

[75] The former is proposed by Cripps, who links the *hapax legomenon* שׂח with the similar שׂיח of 1 Sam. 1:16 and Job 7:13 (Cripps, *Amos*, 177; see also Hammershaimb, *Amos*, 73; and Laetsch, *Minor Prophets*, 158). Of those who think that the phrase refers to God's thoughts, Jeremias and Andersen see a link with God's revelation to his prophets in 3:7 (Andersen and Freedman, *Amos*, 456; Jeremias, *Amos*, 79); Ehrlich suggests the context of God's power and omniscience is decisive (Ehrlich, *Randglossen*, 239) whilst Wolff bases his decision on the use of the *hapax* together with the hiphil of נגד (Wolff, *Amos the Prophet*, 224).

the other two hymns in 5:8 and 9:6.[76] The only two Old Testament references to the extended form of the phrase are here in 4:13 and in Amos 5:27; the shorter form יהוה צבאות שמו features predominantly in Second Isaiah and Jeremiah, in the context of both salvation and judgement oracles.[77]

According to several scholars, the title יהוה צבאות, 'YHWH of hosts' was probably first used in association with the ark at Shiloh (1 Sam. 4:4) suggesting, maintains C. L. Seow, a military connotation. However, Old Testament uses of the plural noun צבאות, 'hosts' are varied and include reference to Israel's armies (e.g. 'the hosts of YHWH' Exod. 12:41), and the heavenly bodies created by YHWH (Ps. 33:6, 148:2).[78] Robert de Vaux notes that 'whatever be the exact meaning of Sabaoth, the word certainly includes the idea of power'.[79] The suggestion of Frank Cross that the phrase encompasses a creation formula—YHWH as creator as well as warrior—is dismissed as being too arbitrary by H. J. Zobel.[80] Nevertheless the expression 'YHWH of Hosts (is) his name' frequently occurs in prophetic texts in the context of YHWH in relation to the created world. Of particular note is Jer. 31:35, which uses participial phrases and cosmic themes to formulate a creation hymn reminiscent of those in Amos, and Isa. 51:15, which echoes the Jeremiah hymn.[81] In a similar manner, the extended phrase in Amos 4:13, יהוה אלהי־צבאות שמו 'YHWH God of Hosts is his name', emphasizes

[76] The simple form יהוה שמו is also found in Jeremiah 33:2 and Exodus 15:3. In all three creation hymns in Amos the LXX has ὁ θεὸς ὁ παντοκράτωρ; various other manuscripts also add the equivalent of צבאות to 5:8 and 9:6 (see BHS textual apparatus on these verses).

[77] A total of twelve times—four in Second Isaiah and eight in Jeremiah (Isa. 47:4, 48:2, 51:15, 54:5, Jer 10:16, 31:35, 32:18, 46:18, 48:15, 50:34, 51:19, 51:57).

[78] Seow, 'Hosts', 304, see also Crenshaw, *Hymnic Affirmations*, 110.

[79] De Vaux, *Ancient Israel*, 304.

[80] Cross, 'Yahweh', 256; *TDOT XII*, 219.

[81] The likelihood that both the Amos and Jeremiah occurrences of 'YHWH of Hosts is his name' represent exilic or post-exilic redactional activity leads Zobel to conclude that 'this formula reflects the faith of the exilic-postexilic community' (*TDOT XII*, 228). It should be noted however that the association between the name of YHWH and his hosts is established in David's proclamation to Goliath (1 Sam. 17:45)—the only Old Testament passage that appears to offer an explanation of צבאות (see *TDOT XII*, 218).

the hymn's proclamation of God's power over the natural world as well as over the destinies of his people and the nations of the world.

Amos 5:8–9

The whole of Amos 5 has been described by Barstad as 'belonging within the same ideological context'—words of one prophet, delivered to one audience (although not necessarily all on the same occasion).[82] Nevertheless, the chapter has been the focus of various attempts to identify material 'original' to Amos and subsequent layers of interpretation.[83] Many commentators suggest that the creation hymn of 5:8 [9] is out of place because it interrupts the prophet's indictment of Israel (vv. 7 and 10).[84] However, more recent scholarship has suggested that Amos 5:1–17 is deliberately structured in a consistently artistic arrangement of concentric circles around a hymnic core.[85] Jan de Waard has identified a chiastic structure in verses 1–17, in which the declaration at the end of verse 8, יהוה שׁמו, 'YHWH is his name', forms the pivotal point on which the verses hinge.[86] In his analysis, as in that of Jeremias, verse 9 becomes part of the hymn along with verse 8, and it is this structure that will be followed here.

The hymn expands the description of YHWH's cosmic power found in the first hymn to include the creation of the constellations: 'the one who made Pleiades and Orion', and reiterates God's role as the one who maintains the rhythms of night and day.[87] Some

[82] Barstad, *Religious Polemics*, 76.

[83] E.g. Jacob, et al., *Amos*, 211–12; Wolff, *Joel and Amos*, 231–4.

[84] Paul, *Amos*, 169. In particular it is maintained that the difficult and fragmentary nature of v. 9 suggest it is a later addition, and not part of the original hymn. Others adduce that its hymnic style means it should be included as part of this doxology, and propose either transposing vv. 8 and 9 or relocating Amos 5:7 to the end of v. 9 (e.g. Wolff, *Joel and Amos*, 241). Even Barstad admits that these verses appear to break up the unity of the text (Barstad, *Religious Polemics*, 80).

[85] Jeremias, *Amos*, 84–5; de Waard, 'Chiastic Structure'.

[86] De Waard, 'Chiastic Structure', 174–7.

[87] The Hebrew words כסיל and כימה, whose meaning is much debated, also occur with the verb עשׂה in the creation hymn of Job 9:5–10 and commentators have drawn attention to the close affinities between the two hymns (Andersen and Freedman, *Amos*, 490; Paul, *Amos*, 168, fn. 88, 89; Crenshaw, 'Influence of Wise').

scholars also suggest that, since Pleiades and Orion are associated with the alternation of seasons from winter to summer, YHWH is being praised as the one who maintains the annual rhythms of the earth as well as the diurnal ones.[88] The verse is semantically linked to the preceding one by the antithetical repetition of the root הפך, thus contrasting the Israelites' negative 'turning' of justice into its opposite with the actions of YHWH who 'turns' darkness to dawn.

In this fragment, as in 9:6, the voice of YHWH is heard as הקורא למי הים, 'the one calling to the waters of the sea', in order to pour them out on the earth. This may be looking forward to a local inundation yet to come, perhaps as a result of the earthquake, or harking back to an ancient flood tradition (cf. Gen. 6–9).[89] But perhaps it could also be seen as signifying God's ability to reverse his own acts of creation—in particular the separation of dry land from water as described in the priestly creation account (Gen. 1:6–10). The use of the language of speech here invokes the sense that God is in dialogue with his creation, as already noted, with the implied result that the waters hear and obey his call.

Most scholars read verse 9 as a depiction of the destruction of war or invasion, in contrast to the heavenly realm of verse 8.[90] As Mays puts it, 'Verse 9 turns from the heavens to earth, from creation to history, and celebrates Yahweh's exercise of his power as a God of war.'[91] The two verses of the hymn, sandwiched together by the declaration יהוה

כסיל and כימה also occur in Job 38, a chapter that contains a number of other linguistic parallels with the Amos hymns (vv. 4, 7, 12, 17, 18).

[88] E.g. Paul, *Amos*, 168; and Wolff, *Joel and Amos*, 241. Jeremias's suggestion that the phrase is a religious polemic against the Babylonian astral cults reads rather too much into the text (Jeremias, *Amos*, 91).

[89] The latter possibility is held by rabbinic traditions (*b. Ber 59a)* and a few other commentators. See Paul, *Amos*, 168. Jeremias considers the prediction a prelude to 9: 6 which, he maintains, alludes more directly to the Flood (Jeremias, *Amos*, 91). De Waard makes the suggestion that this phrase is deliberately ambiguous, since one of its meanings, rain, relates to the preceding list of regular activities of YHWH, whilst the sense of flood or inundation links with the destruction of v. 9 (de Waard, 'Chiastic Structure', 174).

[90] Contra de Waard's suggestion that v. 9 describes the destructive power of the inundation, and G. R. Driver's proposal, followed by the NEB translation, that three more constellations as referred to here (G. R. Driver, 'Two Astronomical Passages'; see also discussion in Paul, *Amos*, 170, fn.111).

[91] Mays, *Amos*, 96.

שְׁמוֹ, 'YHWH is his name', encompass the breadth of YHWH's power—over the constellations and the elements, and over the affairs of human history.

Amos 9:5–6

The stark warning of 9:1–4 that YHWH will search out the people to destroy them is given credence in the third hymn, which again depicts the all-encompassing nature of God's power. However, the difference in chapter 9, as Jeremias points out, is that the hymn follows a harsh pronouncement of judgement, rather than the exhortation to seek God and live in 5:6.[92] Perhaps this explains the more catastrophic nature of the description of YHWH as 'the one who touches the earth and it melts'. (v. 5a) The verse is generally regarded as describing the effects of the earthquake, alluded to in verse 1 (and specifically mentioned in 1:1). The description of the Nile rising and falling (also in 8:8) signifies a sudden change in levels, rather than the gentler annual inundation upon which Egyptian agriculture depended.[93] As already noted, the effect on the earth's inhabitants, ואבלו, 'and they will mourn', is the same as the impact of YHWH's roaring on the earth in 1:2. Although most commentators assume that the phrase כל־יוֹשׁב בהּ, 'all who dwell in it' refers to human inhabitants, this is not necessarily so, as the parallelism of Ps. 24:1 suggests.[94] However, the context provided by the preceding verses places the focus on humans as recipients of divine displeasure. In verse 6, God's might is seen to extend from the 'heights of the heavens' to 'the vaults of earth', and to include power over the sea, the latter phrase being identical with 5:6b. The proclamation echoes some of the places of refuge to which people were trying in vain to flee in the verses immediately preceding: 'to the heavens' (v. 2); 'to the height of Carmel' and 'to the bottom of the sea' (v. 3).

[92] Jeremias, *Amos*, 159.

[93] Hammershaimb, *Amos*, 133; Mays, *Amos*, 155; see also Marlow, 'River Nile', 235–6. The other two occurrences of the verb נגע in conjunction with the natural world, Pss. 104:32 and 144:5, are also suggestive of catastrophic natural disaster, in both cases resulting in the mountains 'smoking', so perhaps suggestive of a volcanic eruption.

[94] See also Hos. 4:3.

In each of these creation hymns, whatever their origin and dating, the character and power of God are articulated by appealing to the mysteries and splendour of the cosmos. The God of creation is able to summon the elements to do his bidding. The earth's response is that of obedience and cooperation, in contrast to the people with their lack of response to YHWH and their vain attempts to escape judgement. But YHWH is presented also, at least initially, as one who offers the possibility of transformation and who chooses to reveal himself to human beings. His activity in the world involves all creation, human and non-human, and impacts not just his own people, but those of surrounding nations, whether for good or ill.[95] In Kapelrud's words: 'Yahweh is painted as overwhelmingly great, as the one who has power all over the earth and under the earth, who leads nature and history, who fixes the stars and destines the fate of nations.'[96]

The voice of the earth in this context then is its ability to reveal something of God and his power as creator and sustainer of the universe. Much of the rest of the book of Amos is concerned with the ways in which both Israel and the nations have failed to respond to this revelation, and the consequences of that failure. But, more than that, the evoking of the created world in the context of YHWH's judgement against the people suggests a moral order built into the very structure of creation. It is to this reality that the cosmos testifies.

THE EARTH AS A MEANS OF JUDGEMENT

C. S. Lewis wrote, 'God whispers to us in our pleasures, speaks in our conscience, but shouts in our pains: it is His megaphone to rouse a deaf world.'[97] If this is so, in Amos the natural world operates the megaphone! In numerous instances in the book the non-human creation functions as the means of YHWH's warning and

[95] E.g. the Oracles against the Nations (1:3–2, 5) and the universalism of 9:7.
[96] Kapelrud, 'Central Ideas', 39.
[97] Lewis, *Pain*, 81.

punishment. A wide range of natural elements act as YHWH's agents and are available to him to direct at those who have warranted his judgement. This agency sends a clear message that the world does not revolve around the anthropocentric concerns of its human inhabitants, but that they are at the mercy of the natural world and, ultimately, of its creator.

Fire on the nations

In the oracles against the nations, YHWH threatens to send fire on each of the nations indicted (1:3 – 2:5), suggesting, according to most commentators, the reality of ancient warfare, 'in which conflagration accompanies the capture and destruction of enemy cities and citadels'.[98] But the first person singular assertion, ושלחתי אש, 'I will send fire', suggests also the status of YHWH as divine warrior executing judgement on the nations.[99] It is this aspect that is presaged in the second of Amos's visions, as already noted (7:4), and is echoed by Hosea's repetition of the entire refrain: 'I will send a fire upon his cities and it shall devour his strongholds' (Hos. 8:14, with reference to Israel and Judah). Anderson and Freedman note the 'mythic' element of fire as YHWH's agent, not dissimilar from fire gods of the surrounding nations, and draw attention to the use of both inanimate and animate objects to execute YHWH's punishment in 9:3–4.[100] The root שלח, 'to send' also occurs in 4:10 to depict plague as God's punishment of the Israelites, and in 8:11 to denote YHWH as the one who sends famine.[101] Such usage suggests that these other catastrophes, plague and famine, are, like fire, part of YHWH's entourage.[102]

[98] Paul, *Amos*, 49. This is particularly supported by the references to other warlike activities in 1:14 and 2:2.

[99] Wolff, *Joel and Amos*, 154–5; see also Paul, *Amos*, 49–50.

[100] Andersen and Freedman, *Amos*, 239.

[101] Plague as threatened or actual punishment is a feature of the accounts of early Israelite history—see Exod. 32:35, Lev. 26:25, Num. 11:33, 14:12, etc.

[102] Andersen and Freedman, *Amos*, 442.

Famine and disease

In a number of other instances, the book describes natural disasters that either have been, or will be, brought upon the people by YHWH. In these events the non-human creation participates in the process whereby God first warns and then executes his judgement. In Amos 4 the prophet proclaims the people's unwillingness to repent in the face of God's judgement by describing a series of five calamities already inflicted by him (vv. 6–11). The content of these bears resemblance to the covenant blessings and curses enumerated in Leviticus 26 and Deuteronomy 28, and also in Solomon's temple dedication prayer in 1 Kings 8 (2 Chronicles 6).[103]

The first three disasters of Amos 4 concern the dependence of Israel on her agricultural productivity. In verse 6 it is famine that strikes, the ambiguous expression נקיון שׁנים, 'cleanness of teeth' being explained by the parallel statement וחסר לחם, 'lack of bread'. The reason for the famine is elucidated in the following verses which describe the drought in great detail (vv. 7–8).[104] In verses 9 and 10, when famine fails to galvanize the people to return to YHWH, pests and diseases attack the crops. The word pair used in v. 9a, בשׁדפון ובירקון, 'with blight and mildew' forms 'a stereotyped pair in the topos of a catalogue of calamities'.[105] It occurs in Deuteronomy 28 and 1 Kings 8 (2 Chronicles 6) as already mentioned and also in Hag. 2:17, where it is followed by the same formulaic 'yet you did not [return] to me', as is repeated five times in Amos 4.[106] Each disaster is prefaced with a verb in the first person (as in the oracles against the nations), denoting YHWH not only as the initiator of these

[103] See comparison table in Wolff, *Joel and Amos*, 213.

[104] According to several commentators the timescale cited places the failure of the rains in the winter period—a most unusual time for such an occurrence (Hammershaimb, *Amos*, 71; Paul, *Amos*, 144; Soggin, *Amos*, 74; Wolff, *Joel and Amos*, 220).

[105] *TDOT VI*, 366. Most commentators interpret these as the parching and subsequent withering to a pale yellow of the grain crops (e.g. Paul, *Amos*, 146; Wolff, *Joel and Amos*, 221). However, Redditt suggests that they represent two climatic extremes of drought (blight) and excessive moisture (mildew) and as such depict a series of crop failures (Redditt, *Haggai*, 30; see also Soggin, *Amos*, 74).

[106] The MT lacks the verb שׁוב, which is supplied by LXX (ἐπιστρέφω).

particular disasters, but as the one on whose providence the Israelites depend.

In verse 10 the destruction moves to the arena of the battlefield, and concerns punishment by plague and by the mass slaughter of war. The exact nature of the plague (דבר) is unspecified, but its linking with the death of Israel's young men evokes the slaughter of the first-born inflicted on the Egyptians.[107] Finally and climactically, in verse 11 a mighty upheaval akin to the destruction of Sodom and Gomorrah is described.[108] The analogy drawn in the Old Testament between the punishment of other nations, including Israel and that of Sodom and Gomorrah suggest that the expression is paradigmatic for total and complete destruction.[109] Most commentators therefore conclude that the disaster takes the form of a catastrophic earthquake, as referred to in 1:1.[110]

Each of the calamities enumerated is intended to provoke a change of heart but to no avail, as suggested by the repetition of the phrase, ולא שׁבתם עדי, 'Yet you did not return to me' (4:6, 8, 9, 10, 11). The use of the same root שׁוב, 'to turn/return', deliberately evokes the oracles against the nations in which YHWH repeatedly proclaims לא אשׁיבנו, 'I will not turn it back'.[111] Soggin notes that although the transgressions of the people in Amos 4 are apparently connected with the cult (vv. 4–5) their exact nature is by no means certain, unlike the oracles against the nations.[112] It is ostensibly simply the people's failure to 'return' that prevents God from holding back their

[107] Wolff notes that דבר is used of the epidemic that befell the Egyptian livestock (Exod. 9:3–7) but that elsewhere it 'appropriately denotes pestilence that afflicts humanity' (Wolff, *Joel and Amos*, 221).

[108] The same verb הפך occurs in the Genesis account (Gen. 19:25, 29).

[109] E.g. Deut. 29:23; Isa. 1:9–10, 13:19, 34:19; Jer. 23:14, 49:18, 50:40; Zeph. 2:9. See discussion on Isaiah 34 in Chapter 6. On the relationship between the destruction of Sodom and Gomorrah and social justice in Amos and Isaiah see Marlow, 'Justice for Whom?'.

[110] Hammershaimb, *Amos*, 73; Paul, *Amos*, 148. However, Wolff considers that the analogy with Sodom and Gomorrah is used merely to denote destruction of political entities (Wolff, *Joel and Amos*, 221), whilst Jeremias links it specifically to the fall of Jerusalem and the temple in 586 BCE (Jeremias, *Amos*, 73).

[111] Andersen and Freedman, *Amos*, 445.

[112] Soggin, *Amos*, 78.

punishment, with the implication that repentance and restoration is an option, though one the people have not chosen.

Who suffers most?

It is notable that the judgement described here is not directed just at political leaders (as in the oracles against the nations), or at the ruling elite (cf. 5:7, 11). Famine, drought, and disease affect all levels of society, with the poorest arguably suffering the most. The prophetic indictment of injustices by the rich and powerful against the vulnerable in society (8:4–6), and its call for the restoration of justice and righteousness (5:24) seem at variance with such comprehensive disasters.[113] How can this apparent discrepancy be explained?

Some scholars have attempted to explain it in terms of theodicy: the need to justify God's actions in the world.[114] Barton suggests that the prophets employ rhetorical techniques to intimate that the predicted judgement is only what could have been expected in the light of the nation's sins against God.[115] In Amos 4, the implied abuse of the cult is imprecise enough to implicate not just the rich, but all levels of society in transgression against YHWH. As Kapelrud notes, this chapter counters any misplaced ideas that the Israelites' relationship with YHWH is unshaken and unshakeable so long as they adhere to their sacrificial observance.[116]

However, such an explanation is less certain with regard to Amos 8, in which a comprehensive national disaster (v. 8) follows a specific indictment of the ruling classes (vv. 4–6). An alternative possibility for both texts is predicated upon the nature of the social exploitation condemned by the texts. Gossai and others suggest that it is the

[113] A similar problem is evident in Isa. 1:12–20 and 5:7–17. In both cases an indictment of the rich or powerful for exploitation of the poor is followed by warning of disaster that will impact all levels of society (destruction by sword (1:20), and exile and abasement (5:13, 25).

[114] Barton suggests that this is the chief concern of the classical prophets (Barton, 'History and Rhetoric', 52; see also Koch, 'Doctrine of Retribution').

[115] Barton, 'History and Rhetoric', 61.

[116] Kapelrud, 'Central Ideas', 47.

dispossession of the poor from their lands that Amos denounces (2: 7; 8:4; see also Isa. 5:8):

> Now, the 'fruitful earth' is no longer providing for the poor, the 'people of the land', but is taken over by the powerful. . . . The land, as a gift from Yahweh and as an element which is the right of every Israelite, now becomes the exclusive property of the rich.[117]

The failure of crops and inundation of the land are thus forms of judgement intended specifically to reduce the rich and powerful to the level of the poor whom they have dispossessed: namely, lacking any means of economic support. This is more explicit in Mic. 6:11–15, which cites failure of crops and the attendant hunger and poverty as YHWH's punishment for 'commercial trickery'.[118] The prophet employs the rhetorical tool of hyperbole to make his point, contrasting wealth and poverty, gain and loss, in an indictment which is addressed to those who have illegitimately acquired land and who will be deprived of it.[119]

There is an interesting link between such a failure of social justice and the prophet's sarcastic denunciation of the people's cultic practices at Bethel and Gilgal in the earlier part of Amos 4 (vv. 4–5). In the patriarchal narratives, traditions surrounding the gift of the land are associated with Bethel. It is the place where Jacob first builds an altar following YHWH's promise to him and his descendants in a dream (Gen. 28:10–19, cf. 35:9–15).[120] The importance of Bethel as the place of meeting with, and worship of, YHWH is, in these texts, closely linked with the promise of the land.[121] If this is applied to Amos 4:1–10, the prophet is not only indicting the Israelites for breaching a code associated with the inalienable right of all to an inherited

[117] Gossai, *Eighth Century Prophets*, 249. Cf. the story of Naboth's vineyard (1 Kings 21) as illustrative of this tradition.

[118] Allen, *Micah*, 378.

[119] Koch, *Prophets*, 1:46–47.

[120] See also Gen. 12:7, 13:3–4.

[121] Before this event, Isaac's blessing of his two sons bestows the elder son's blessing on Jacob, which includes 'the fatness of the earth, and plenty of grain and wine' (Gen. 27:28). These blessings are precisely those that are reversed in Amos 4:6–10.

portion of land, but castigating the hypocrisy of their worship at the Bethel sanctuary. Social justice and the cult are in this text inextricably linked.[122]

The litany of disaster upon disaster, first famine, drought, and crop failure, then plague and warfare, followed by the turmoil of verse 11, culminates in verses 12 and 13 in the unspecified warning and reaffirmation of YHWH's cosmic power which has already been discussed. His providence over the weather and crop cycles, over human affairs and politics and over the earth's movement is fully in line with his cosmic sovereignty.

Future devastation

Elsewhere in Amos we find the threat of catastrophes which are yet to be experienced by the people. These include floods (5:8, 9:6), earthquake (8:8, 9:5; see also 1:1), and disruption of the cosmic rhythms, which as already noted, demonstrate the all-powerful name and character of YHWH: 'I will make the sun go down at noon ... and the earth dark in broad daylight' (8:9).[123] These judgements are a consequence of human action, and confirm the interconnection between YHWH's voice, the non-human creation and human society set out at the beginning of the book (1:2). In 8:8 the mourning of the earth and its inhabitants again utters YHWH's verdict on Israel's sin: 'On account of this [Jacob's deeds], will not the land quake and all who dwell in her mourn?' Rather than declaring God's glory as in Psalm 19, the non-human creation proclaims his anger—and so is part of the 'dialogue' between YHWH and Israel. Since the people have not listened to warnings mediated through God's *human* agent, the prophet, God chooses to speak through his *cosmic* one.

[122] See Marlow, 'Justice for Whom?'.
[123] Pfeifer, 'Jahwe Als Schöpfer'.

THE VOICE OF THE PEOPLE

If the connection between YHWH and the earth as portrayed in Amos can be described in terms of a speech-act, in which the non-human creation responds to YHWH, reveals his power and acts as his agent of judgement, what can be said of the part that the people play? Do those to whom God's words of indictment are addressed have a voice, and if so, how do they speak? The next section of this chapter is a brief consideration of the ways in which the author of the book articulates the relationship between God and the people, in particular with respect to the use of speech.

The prophetic pronouncements of Amos describe a number of instances in which the people of Israel are vocal, but almost always in ways that set them against YHWH and his word.[124] In the context of social injustice, the voices of the rich and elite are raised to flaunt their status (4:1), and to oppress the poor (8:5). By such use of direct speech the author brings these characters to life and highlights their unacceptable attitude and behaviour. The use of the verb אמר, 'to speak' on each occasion, in participle form in 4:1 (האמרת), and infinitive construct in 8:5 (לאמר), sets up a contrast with the many occasions in the book in which YHWH is said to speak (e.g. כה אמר יהוה, 'thus says YHWH' repeated in the oracles against the nations, and in 3:12, 5:4, etc.), and demonstrates that it is out of their own mouths that they stand condemned.

In the cultic sphere the prophet parodies the voices of the priests in their summons to worship (4:4)—not in itself a negative thing, but in the context apparently a hollow and meaningless ritual.[125] The voices of the people can also be heard in the singing and religious chanting that they so delight in (6:5, see also 8:3); again, this is not wrong *per se*, but in the light of their indulgent and unrestrained lifestyles (6:4–6), it is condemned as shallow and hypocritical. In two further passages, again using direct speech, the people are indicted

[124] Interestingly, in the Oracles Against the Nations (1:3 – 2:5) there are no instances of nations or individuals speaking—only YHWH's voice is heard.

[125] See also Pss. 95:6, 100:2. Begrich notes the use of imperative and jussive to create 'eine Parodie einer Priestertora' (Begrich, 'Priesterliche Tora', 73–7).

for denying YHWH's sovereignty by swearing on the Asherah of Samaria[126] and invoking other gods (8:14), as well as for arrogantly denying the approaching judgement (9:10).

However, one intriguing contrast to all the spoken words attributed to the people is the use of the motif of silence. Just as serious as her social and religious hypocrisy, is Israel's desire throughout her history to silence the voice of YHWH. In 2:12 she is condemned for ordering the prophets whom YHWH had raised up not to prophesy.[127] This historical tendency is illustrated by the description of Amaziah's current attempt to silence Amos by sending him back to Judah in 7:10–17—again making use of direct speech to paint a sharp and vivid picture.

In three other places in Amos, the silence of the people is noted. In 5:13 the prophet suggests that in the forthcoming evil times (most probably alluding to the coming of YHWH mentioned in 5:9 and 5: 16, 17), the wise will remain silent. Although the origin and interpretation of this verse has been the subject of much discussion, it stands in great contrast to the 'foolish' talk of the people already outlined above.[128]

In the final destruction of 8:3, survivors will act in silence: 'In every place they will throw [the corpses] out [saying] hush.' The Hebrew injunction הס is used in other texts (e.g. Neh. 8:11; Hab. 2:20; Zeph. 1:7; Zech. 2:17 [13]) to promote silence in response to YHWH's immanent presence, and here too it is not just the silence of the defeated dealing with their dead, but that of awe and fear at the presence of YHWH 'passing through [their] midst' (see 5:17). Similarly, in 6:10 the fear of YHWH engenders silence among those burying the dead. In these verses, whether through wisdom or fear, the people of Israel who were once so vocal in flaunting their wealth and observing cultic ritual are reduced to silence.

[126] Following the emendation proposed by BHS.

[127] A similar indictment against Israel is found in Isa. 30:9–11.

[128] See Paul, *Amos*, 175, 329.

THE HOPE OF RESTORATION

In all the texts discussed so far, the earth, acting on YHWH's behalf, has spoken entirely with a negative voice. But the other side of the picture of devastation and natural disaster is the hope of restoration and renewal. This is a theme that occurs frequently in other prophetic texts, but in Amos only a few verses right at the end of the book touch on it (9:11–15).[129] The absence of other restoration texts in Amos has contributed to the widely accepted view that the eighth-century prophet is exclusively a prophet of doom offering nothing by way of hope.[130] It is for this reason, among others, that these verses in chapter 9 are regarded by numerous commentators as a later addition. Whether or not this is the case, compelling arguments can be made for their inclusion as an integral part of the book, not to be read in isolation from the rest.[131]

The oracle of restoration of 9:11–15 is in stark contrast to the opening 'hymn' of Amos 1:2, which, as has been seen, depicts the negative effect that YHWH's voice has on the earth, both in terms of the economic infrastructure and the land's productivity. Yet the inclusio formed by these verses (1:2 and 9:13–15) provides the context for the whole book—that this is indeed the word of YHWH, but his words may be those of judgement or of salvation. In contrast to the devastation of the natural world at the start of Amos, the end of the book presents a vision of the renewal of the fertility of the natural world (9:13) as well as of human social and political institutions (9:11–12, 14). Although YHWH does not speak or call in this final section (apart

[129] Particularly in Isaiah, e.g. 30:23–26, 35:1–9, 41:18–21, but see also Ezek. 34: 25–27; Hos. 2:20–25[18–23]. In Amos, hints of hope are also found in 3: 12 and 5: 6, 14, both in the context of hope for the remnant.

[130] First enunciated by Wellhausen (*Kleinen Propheten*), see discussion in Paul, *Amos*, 288–9; Wolff, *Joel and Amos*, 113, 352–3. Countering this, Barstad argues convincingly that hope is implicit throughout the prophet's indictment, although his conclusion that Amos is a 'missionary' prophet calling the people to turn for the first time to YHWH rather than Baal is less certain (Barstad, *Religious Polemics*, 60, 78–9).

[131] E.g. Williamson, who suggests they were composed specifically for their present setting (Williamson, *Book Called Isaiah*, 114).

from the repetition of נאם יהוה), he is clearly the cause and initiator of the promised restoration.

Two complementary images are used to depict the reversal of fortunes, namely the rebuilding of את־סכת דויד, 'the booth of David' (v. 11), and the replanting of the crops (v. 13), symbolising both the restoration of political stability and the renewal of YHWH's gift of the land.[132] In both images, the result is more comprehensive than might be expected by the normal reversal of misfortune, hinting at an ideal, eschatological future. In verse 12 the promise of universal allegiance to YHWH creeps in alongside the hope of restoration of the Davidic city and temple, whilst verse 13 alludes to the restoration of an edenic landscape, flowing with wine. It is, however, with the descriptions of the non-human creation in the latter image that we are primarily concerned.

In 9:13–15 the author juxtaposes the natural productivity of the earth (v. 13) with the agricultural endeavours of the people (v. 14). The sense of extraordinary abundance in verse 13 in which 'the ploughman will catch up with the reaper and the grape-treader with the one who sows seed' is similar to a lengthier vision of hope for the land articulated in the Holiness Code (Lev. 26:3–6). Verse 13 continues with the statement 'the mountains will drip sweet [or fresh] wine', which invites a supernatural interpretation, implying that this is YHWH's doing, achieved without human agency.[133] The book of Joel ends in a similar way (Joel 4:18 [3:18]); in Joel the promise is preceded by announcement of YHWH's theophany couched in the same language as Amos 1:2, 'YHWH roars from Zion, and from Jerusalem he utters voice' (Joel 4:16 [3:16], cf. Hos. 14:4–8). In Joel as in Amos, the non-human creation acts as a mediating voice between YHWH and the people; in both texts the earth is a conduit for the blessings of fertility or the sorrow of famine.

The predominant metaphor of Amos 9:14 is that of grapes and wine, frequently found in prophetic texts (in particular First Isaiah,

[132] Mays, *Amos*, 166.

[133] The root מוג, 'melts', can denote a negative reaction—of fear or disaster, as earlier in the chapter (9:5, cf. Isa. 14:31). However, here it signifies 'the gentle falling rain (or even dew) that softens the ground and makes it dissolve' (*TDOT VII*, 150).

who uses it in antithesis to 'thorns and briars') to depict the ideal of fruitfulness and fertility.[134] The abundance of natural fertility, both on the mountainside (v. 13) and in the restored city gardens (v. 14), speaks of the restoration of harmony between the natural world and humanity as well as between YHWH and his people (v. 15).[135] The last two verses of Amos 9 are characterized by a strong degree of assonance, and are linked by virtue of the wordplay on נטע, 'to plant'. These rhetorical devices with which the book of Amos ends provide a compelling illustration of the interplay between the different 'voices' in the book—those of YHWH, of the human population and of the non-human creation.

SUMMARY

Within the rhetorical structure of Amos, the non-human creation performs a significant role in demonstrating the powerful and all-encompassing nature of God. Both in response to YHWH's voice and by revealing his character and attributes by virtue of its very existence, the natural world engages in a 'dialogue' with its creator. In the context of act–consequence, aspects of the non-human world, in particular disasters such as drought, earthquake, flood, are used as the means by which YHWH first warns and then judges his people, who are characterized both by their inappropriate speech and by their silence in the face of God's coming. The restoration of Israel's fortunes is expressed both in terms of urban regeneration and supernatural abundance of fertility in the natural world. The text of Amos invites an understanding of the world that sets the cooperation of the non-human world with its creator against the rebellion of its human inhabitants. Within a reading of the text through the framework of the ecological triangle, it is the relationship between God and the non-human creation which comes to the fore.

[134] The figurative use of vines and vineyards is discussed in Chapter 6.
[135] Cf. Joel 4:18 [3:18].

5

The People Do Not Know
Covenantal Failure in the Book of Hosea

> Gentlemen . . . look around you at the gifts of God, the clear sky, the pure air, the tender grass, the birds; nature is beautiful and sinless, and we, only we, are godless and foolish, and we don't understand that life is a paradise, for we have only to understand that and it will at once be fulfilled in all its beauty, we shall embrace each other and weep.
>
> (Fyodor Dostoevsky, *The Brothers Karamazov*)

INTRODUCTION

In Hosea the interaction between God, humanity, and non-human creation does not permeate the whole book as thoroughly as in Amos. Nevertheless, the instances where such interaction is clearly articulated form a significant part of the whole book. These are the poetic oracle sandwiched between Hosea's two sign-act 'marriages' (Hosea 2), and the accusation against priest and people in Hosea 4. Discussion of these texts will form the major part of this chapter, along with exploration of Hosea's extensive use of figurative language, in particular imagery of the natural world.

Before moving to these topics, one significant feature of Hosea should be noted: the nearly total absence of cosmic language. The book of Amos depicts YHWH in terms of his cosmic power as creator and judge of the world (e.g. Amos 4:13, 5:8–9, 8:9, 9:5–6), as well as in his agricultural providence.[1] Likewise, as we shall see, in Isaiah 1–39 YHWH's judgement is depicted in terms of its cosmic, as well as its agricultural impact.[2] In contrast, reference to the non-human creation in Hosea is almost exclusively concerned with the land and its produce. There are no descriptions of cosmic powers or global disorder. In virtually every instance of the ambiguous term הארץ, the context requires the translation 'the land' or 'the ground'.[3] Possible exceptions to this are the disruption to the land/earth described in 4:3 and the effect of the covenant in 2:23–4 [21–2], both of which will be the subject of more extensive discussion later in the chapter.[4]

FIGURATIVE LANGUAGE IN HOSEA

A number of scholars draw attention to the frequent use of metaphorical language in Hosea, particularly of similes.[5] While a few of these are extended metaphors, developed over several verses (or in the case of the marriage metaphor over several chapters), in many instances Hosea 'clothes the thoughts of each succeeding sentence in new imagery'.[6] Apart from the family metaphors of husband/wife and parent/child that are used to describe the relationship between God and Israel, the book draws extensively on imagery of the natural world to portray both YHWH and his people.[7] As Fretheim notes, these natural metaphors 'demonstrate an integral relationship

[1] See also Mic. 1:3–4, 6:1–2.

[2] See Chapter 6.

[3] Twelve of these references are clearly geographical—whether to Egypt (ארץ מצרים 6 times), to Assyria (ארץ אשור once) or to Israel (5 times). A further two may be considered synonymous with the people (1:2, 4:1), while four are descriptive of the ground or soil.

[4] The latter is the only instance in which השמים 'the heavens' is paired with הארץ. The other three occurrences are in the phrase עוף השמים 'the birds of the air' (2:20 [18], 4:3, 7:12).

[5] E.g. Eidevall, *Grapes in the Desert*, 5–6; Moughtin-Mumby, *Sexual and Marital Metaphors*, 49–51; Wolff, *Hosea*, xxiv.

[6] Wolff, *Hosea*, xxiv.

[7] The exception is 7:4, 6–8 which uses the language of the bakehouse to describe Ephraim.

between God and the nonhuman created order, with continuities seen between God and that world'.[8]

Imagery describing YHWH

Hosea's use of imagery of the natural world to describe God centres on images connected with the interface between the natural world and human society. These include natural phenomena such as rainfall, as well as metaphors of animals (both wild and domesticated). Like Amos, Micah, and First Isaiah, Hosea employs a number of pastoral and hunting metaphors: YHWH is depicted as a shepherd/herdsman with recalcitrant herds in 4:16, and as a fowler netting a bird in 7:12.[9]

Rather more unusual than such pastoral imagery is the simile of 5:12, 'But I will surely be like a moth to Ephraim and like decay to the house of Judah.' Although at first reading עָשׁ, 'moth' and רקב, 'decay' seem an unusual pairing, this is perhaps due to Hosea's succinct style rather than anything else, since these nouns occur together (in reverse order) in Job 13:28, which expands (and explains) the simile.[10] Some commentators interpret Hosea 5:12 in the light of 13a, which speaks of Ephraim's sickness (חלי) and Judah's wound (מזור).[11] However, in the light of Hosea's fondness for employing multiple metaphors in close succession, there is no reason to assume that the same imagery is intended in both verses. Taken individually, the images of moth and decay each convey the 'slow and unseen deterioration' that will be the result of YHWH's action in undermining and punishing his people.[12] Read together and in conjunction with the more familiar sickness metaphors of the next verse, these metaphors of seemingly insignificant aspects of the natural world communicate a powerful warning.

[8] Fretheim, *Suffering of God*, 6.
[9] E.g. Amos 3:5 (netting birds); Isa. 14:30 and Mic. 2:12 (pastoral imagery).
[10] See also Isa. 50:9, 51:8.
[11] E.g. Macintosh, *Hosea*, 207; Andersen and Freedman, *Hosea*, 412.
[12] Sweeney, *Twelve Prophets*, 67.

Rainfall images

There are four separate instances where Hosea makes use of images of rain or dew, with meanings that differ significantly from one another (6:3, 6:4, 13:3, and 14:6 [5]). In 6:3 YHWH's appearance is described with confidence, 'as certain as the dawn', and as eagerly anticipated refreshment, 'he will come to us like the rain, like the spring rain watering the earth'. The preceding sentences comprise an exhortation to return to YHWH (vv. 1–3a), who will restore and heal Israel. Whether this represents the prophet's own call to repentance or is part of a cultic community lament is not explicit in the MT, although debated by commentators.[13] However, both the change of speaker and the rhetorical nature of the first person question in the next verse (v. 4) suggest that the latter verse is a response by YHWH to the priests' (and hence the people's) vacuous declaration of intent in verse 3.

A number of commentators maintain that this section, and verse 3 in particular, reflects the language of Canaanite religion in which the gods, particularly Baal, were responsible for weather and the seasons.[14] The imagery of death and resurrection in 5:12 – 6:3, according to Day, 'appears to reapply the imagery of a dying and rising fertility god'.[15] In contrast, Oestreich argues strongly against this conclusion, adducing that 'images of nature are not necessarily a sign of Canaanite religion'.[16] The assumption that nature imagery signals the influence of 'foreign' religious beliefs or practices is a classic example of the tendency within older scholarship, which has already been discussed, to draw a distinction between the historical religion of ancient Israel and the nature religion of her neighbours.

[13] LXX links these verses with the preceding chapter by means of *ὀρθριοῦσι πρός με λέγοντες* 'They will come early to me, saying'; see also Tg. and Syr. Wolff suggests that vv. 1–3 form a penitential song sung by the priests at times of danger (Wolff, *Hosea*, 117–18), while Davies favours Hosea as the speaker, noting that by his use of the first person plural he identifies himself with his people (G. I. Davies, *Hosea*, 160).

[14] Macintosh, *Hosea*, 119; Mays, *Hosea*, 95–6. Davies sees a distinction between the two parts of the verse; while the coming of dawn might be certain, the Palestinian rains certainly were not, so the point of the latter simile is to stress the fertility and prosperity that the rains guaranteed (G. I. Davies, *Hosea*, 163).

[15] Day, 'Baal', 549.

[16] Oestreich, *Metaphors and Similes*, 161.

That distinction is not at all sustainable as far as the book of Hosea is concerned. As we shall see in our discussion of Hosea 2, it is not that nature is regarded as subsidiary to history, rather that the prophet subverts the popular belief in Baal as god of fertility and reassigns this prerogative to YHWH.

Hos. 6:3 is followed immediately by the reuse of similar imagery to describe another reality—Israel's apostasy. YHWH's words to Israel in verse 4 draw on a similar metaphorical field, yet are in stark contrast to the positive image conveyed by the simile in verse 3. Initially the comparison is ambiguous: וחסדכם כענן־בקר, 'your [Ephraim/Judah's] loyalty is like a morning cloud'. However, the parallel phrase, וכטל מַשׁכים הלך, 'like the dew which goes away early', makes the sense explicit. The transitory and fickle nature of the Israelites' professed return to YHWH is highlighted in contrast to certainty concerning YHWH. Hosea's use here of טל (dew) as a metaphor for human inconstancy is interesting and unusual in the Old Testament, although appropriate to describe Israel's fleeting and changeable allegiance.[17] So too is its reuse in 13:3 to describe the negative outcome of YHWH's judgement, in which Israel will be dispersed like the morning dew 'which goes away early', like chaff that is scattered and like smoke that blows away. In contrast, Micah 5 likens the remnant of Jacob to dew and rainfall (v. 6 [7]), the context suggesting that this denotes Israel's 'beneficent effect' on the nations.[18]

Many of the other instances of טל (dew) in the Old Testament are concerned with YHWH as giver or withholder of rain and thereby of fertility (e.g. Gen. 27:28; Deut. 33:28; Hag. 1:10; Zech. 8:12), and of his wider provision and blessing (e.g. manna in Exodus 16). It is with this sense of YHWH as provider that Hosea uses טל in 14:6 [5] where he is described as 'like the dew' (כטל) to Israel, enabling abundant growth (v. 6b [5b]). Here an identical phrase to that found in 6:4 and 13:3 is invested with a totally different meaning by the metaphor of flowering and growth which follows. The imagery is similar to that of 6:3—denoting YHWH as provider of the means

[17] Wolff, *Hosea*, 119. Oestreich suggests such a negative use of the dew metaphor may have already existed. However, the Akkadian reference he cites is rather more ambiguous (Oestreich, *Metaphors and Similes*, 165).

[18] Allen, *Joel, Obadiah, Jonah, and Micah*, 354.

for Israel's flourishing. In this verse, as in 6:3, some of the attributes generally associated with Baal—producer of rain and guarantor of fertility—are here reapplied to YHWH, in a manner reminiscent of 2:10 [8] and 2:18 [16].

In these four instances of rainfall imagery, YHWH is likened to rain in 6:3 and to the dew in 14:6 [5], drawing on the positive characteristics of rain and dew which water the ground and ensure fruitfulness. Israel is compared to the early dew and a morning cloud in 6:4 and 13:3, reflecting the transient and temporary features of these natural occurrences. The prophet's use of the semantic field of rain/dew/moisture to describe two virtually opposite realities serve to highlight the polyvalent and consequently open-ended nature of figurative language.

YHWH as lion

The most frequent imagery used to denote YHWH in Hosea likens him to a wild animal, in particular a lion (see 5:14, 11:10, 13:7–8).[19] The variety of Hebrew words which appear to denote 'lion' suggest that this is a rich field of imagery, although care must be taken regarding the exact meaning and significance of each term.[20] Both Isaiah and Amos refer to YHWH as a lion (Isa. 31:4, 38:13; Amos 3:8), while in Micah it is Jacob that is so described (5:6[7]).[21] In the Old Testament, lion imagery used of YHWH always 'bespeaks power and threat, even and especially fear' and Hosea's use of this metaphor is no exception.[22]

In Hosea 5:14 and 13:7–8, YHWH's dealings with Israel are compared to a wild animal with its prey. One of the more unusual

[19] Strawn draws attention to the large number of references or allusions to lions in the Old Testament (over 200) and to the ubiquitous and varied nature of lion symbolism and metaphor throughout the ancient world (*Stronger Than a Lion*, 11).

[20] For a detailed analysis of each of the Hebrew terms, including Semitic cognates and translations in the Versions, see ibid. 293–326.

[21] Cf. Isa. 5:29, denoting a foreign nation (Williamson, *Isaiah 1–5*, 408).

[22] Strawn, *Stronger Than a Lion*, 66. This is in contrast to the rest of the ANE in which the lion is used frequently to represent the king or mighty one, especially in art and literature. (See Strawn's extensive appendix of lion 'figures', *Stronger Than a Lion*, 377–498).

words for lion (שחל) is paired with כפיר, generally translated 'young lion' in 5:14, and with נמר, 'leopard' in 13:7. In 13:8 the imagery is expanded with the introduction of further animal similes: דב שכול, 'a bear separated from its cubs', a second lion term, לביא, and the generic חית השדה, 'beasts of the fields', i.e. wild animals.[23] In both texts YHWH's reaction to Israel's 'reckless ingratitude and consequent disregard of him' is analogous to the behaviour of a wild animal, which comes upon its prey with sudden and devastating consequences.[24] In 5:14 he is like a lion tearing (טרף) and carrying off his people; in 13:7–8 he is depicted as ripping them apart (קרע) and devouring them. Such imagery draws on various known attributes of wild animals—as fierce, unpredictable killers, silent in approach and liable to attack unexpectedly, and paints a picture of a God who is not to be trifled with.

The other reference to YHWH as a lion, in 11:10, evokes a different aspect of this magnificent animal's behaviour. The context is an impassioned expression of YHWH's compassion towards Israel, followed by a reaffirmation of his presence among his people (vv. 8–9a). Verse 10 describes God's call and their response to him: 'After YHWH they will go, he who roars like a lion; when he roars, [his] sons come trembling from the sea', and Israel's response is elaborated in the succeeding verse.

The portrayal of YHWH as one who roars is also a significant feature of the beginning of Amos (1:2), as noted above, Chapter 4, as well as of Joel 4:16 [3:16], although in neither instance is YHWH specifically identified as a lion. In all three cases (Hosea, Joel, and Amos) the verb שאג (to roar) is used of YHWH's call, and on each occasion a response is elicited—from the hill tops and pastures in Amos, from the cosmos in Joel and from the people in Hosea. The effect of YHWH's voice is to disturb and disrupt, yet here in Hosea, as in Amos and Joel, the result is at the very least ambivalent. On the one hand, the preceding verses have expressed YHWH's deep and passionate commitment to Israel: 'My heart has been overturned within me and my compassions grow tender together' (11:8b). On the other hand, the choice of the lion imagery, together with the

[23] For discussion re לביא as the female 'lioness' see ibid. 311–19.
[24] Macintosh, *Hosea*, 534.

trembling and fearful response of the sons of Israel in 10b and 11, suggest YHWH's supremacy, power, and capacity to destroy.[25] The two aspects of God's character are summed up by the prophet in the description of Israel's God as 'holy in your midst' (v. 9), which draws together divine mercy and justice. As Macintosh puts it,

> He is ineffably majestic, characterised by absolute moral purity, isolated from all sin and the destroyer of all that is sinful (so Rudolph). Further, the essentially moral character of his holiness embraces the quality of love and compassion and it is in him, and in him alone, that such loving compassion finds expression in the face of his people's sinfulness.[26]

Imagery of people

Within the extensive range of figurative language which Hosea uses to depict Israel, many images are taken from the natural world. As with descriptions of YHWH, in many cases these are fragmentary, and at times elusive, comparisons. Israel's pride and independence are likened to the stubbornness of a heifer (4:16, cf. 10:11) and a wild ass (8:9), and her transience is described in terms of a bird flying away (9:11) and of chaff or smoke being dispersed by the wind (13:3). Bird metaphors are also used to describe Ephraim's senselessness in 7:11, and her fear in 11:11. The language of sowing and reaping is applied to Israel's dubious religious and moral practices in 8:7 and 10:12–13, while other images from plant cultivation are used positively to convey her beauty (9:13) and fruitfulness (9:10, 10:1, 14:7–8 [6–7]).[27] As has already been noted, these are often only phrases or single sentences that convey a glimpse of the prophetic imagination at work. Far more pervasive and developed is the imagery arising from Hosea's marriage and children, to which we now turn.

[25] Even Strawn's discussion of Hos. 11:10 as the only possible instance in the Old Testament of an unambiguously positive use of lion imagery is forced to conclude that '[the] presentation of God's love... [is] tempered by the steel of... YHWH's ability to judge and destroy' (*Stronger Than a Lion*, 64).

[26] Macintosh, *Hosea*, 465.

[27] Although in the interpretations of these images the major commentaries have been followed, it should be noted that alternative interpretations have been proposed, e.g. with respect to 10:1, see ibid. 383.

RELATIONAL IMAGERY IN HOSEA

In Hosea 11 it is the sons of Israel who are at the receiving end of YHWH's roaring like a lion, in contrast to the books of Amos and Joel in which it is natural world that responds. This highlights an important feature of the book of Hosea—the emphasis on human relationship with the divine. This is especially evident in the depiction of the relationship between God and his people in terms of husband and wife and of parent and child. Such relational language is not at all unexpected, since the relationship between God and his people is at the heart of the Old Testament story. What is significant in Hosea is the fact that this relationship is not portrayed in isolation from the rest of the created order, but in terms of the overall understanding of the interconnection between God, the people, and the non-human creation.

HOSEA 2

The relational imagery of the book of Hosea begins in its opening verses with the prophet's dramatic enactment of the word of YHWH. Obeying YHWH's command to take a wife and children 'of whoredom' (זנונים) provides Hosea with the language and categories for his depiction of the broken relationship between Israel and YHWH in Hosea 1–3. However, this is more than just the language of human personal relationships. Interwoven with the marriage/childbearing imagery is the theme of the land and its fruitfulness. The explanation for YHWH's command to Hosea states 'for the land is surely committing whoredom in turning from YHWH' (1:2). This reference to the land is taken by many commentators to be a shorthand for the people of the land i.e. Israel.[28] But although Israel and the land may be synonymous in this verse, an important distinction is blurred if

[28] E.g. Andersen and Freedman, *Hosea*; G. I. Davies, *Hosea*; Mays, *Hosea*; Wolff, *Hosea*. The suggestion by Wolff and others that this parodies the Baal fertility cult is rejected by Davies (G. I. Davies, *Hosea*, 52).

the two are equated throughout Hosea 1–3. Rather than collapsing these two categories, land and Israel, into one, how might the text read if we regard them as two separate, but linked participants in the drama?[29] The weaving together of these twin themes (of the land and of Israel) can be displayed diagrammatically as shown in Figure 3.

Hosea's symbolic marriage and the naming of his children provide the starting point for a drama which depicts the cycle of cause and effect in terms of human experience and that of the natural world, and which highlights the mutual interdependence of people and land, Israel and ארץ. There are three critical stages in the interplay

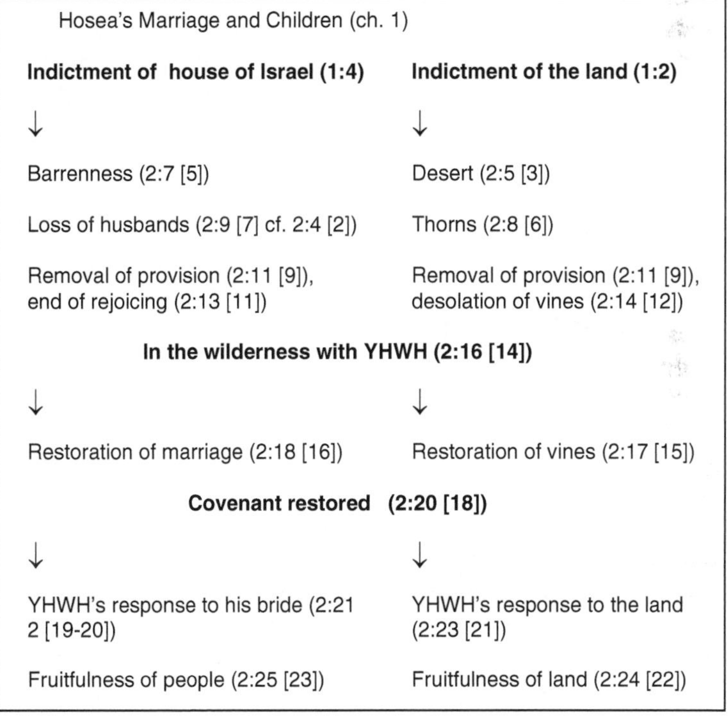

Hosea's Marriage and Children (ch. 1)
Indictment of house of Israel (1:4)
Indictment of the land (1:2)
↓
↓
Barrenness (2:7 [5])
Desert (2:5 [3])
Loss of husbands (2:9 [7] cf. 2:4 [2])
Thorns (2:8 [6])
Removal of provision (2:11 [9]), end of rejoicing (2:13 [11])
Removal of provision (2:11 [9]), desolation of vines (2:14 [12])
In the wilderness with YHWH (2:16 [14])
↓
↓
Restoration of marriage (2:18 [16])
Restoration of vines (2:17 [15])
Covenant restored (2:20 [18])
↓
↓
YHWH's response to his bride (2:21 2 [19-20])
YHWH's response to the land (2:23 [21])
Fruitfulness of people (2:25 [23])
Fruitfulness of land (2:24 [22])

Figure 3. The interrelation of themes of land and people in Hos. 2

[29] See Braaten, 'Hosea 2'.

between YHWH and his creation: the initial condemnation and its consequences (1:2, 4; 2:7–14 [5–12]), the wilderness encounter (2:16 [14]), and the (re)-making of the covenant (2:20 [18]). The first of these is, of course, wholly negative and the last unequivocally positive. However, the wilderness encounter is a deliberately ambiguous place for Israel, as will be seen, and as such acts as the fulcrum of Hosea 2 and the bridge between negative and positive outcomes.

Israel's condemnation 2:5–14 [3–12]

The indictment of the land in 1:2 is paralleled by YHWH's verdict upon the house of Israel in 1:4, 6. The result of this judgement is described figuratively in Hosea 2 in terms of fertility. In a metaphor from the land, YHWH will make her 'like a wilderness' (כמדבר in verse 5 [3] and 'hedge her way with thorns' (בסירים verse 8 [6]), and in a metaphor from family life, she will suffer a barren womb (2:7 [5]) and abandonment by her husband (2:9 [7]). These powerful images intersect with reality in verses 10–11 [8–9], which speak of YHWH as the provider, and withholder, of all good things. Because YHWH has withdrawn from the house of Israel, so that they are now לא־עמי 'not my people' (1:9 [7]), his provision for their daily needs comes to an end (2:11 [9]).[30]

Israel's primary offence against YHWH is to pursue her 'lovers', in the mistaken belief that they provide grain, oil, and wine for her needs (v. 7 [5]). The reference is undoubtedly to the Canaanite fertility gods whose role as guarantors of rain, fertility, and successful harvests is well attested in various ancient texts. There seems little doubt that the polytheistic religions of the land of Canaan form the backdrop to Hosea's oracles and inform his polemic against Israel. Constructing a picture of Canaanite mythology from the Old Testament polemic against Baal worship is potentially difficult, since there is no means of knowing whether the polemic is based on accurate evidence or real practices. However, the points of connection between the biblical record and Canaanite myths suggest that Baal

[30] The devastating failure of Israel's crops is echoed in Hos. 8:7 and 9:2.

worship in the eighth century, at least in the Northern kingdom, followed in the ancient Canaanite mythological tradition.[31]

The Baal myths

The primary source of information about Baal worship in Canaan comes from the archaeological discoveries made in the early twentieth century at the city of Ugarit/Ras Shamra.[32] These included a number of cuneiform tablets inscribed with ancient religious myths, which identify a number of deities under the overall rule of the high god El (*Il*), including Baal (*Ba'lu*), Yam (*Yammu*), and Mot (*Môtu*), who have jurisdiction over, respectively, the earth, the sea, and the underworld (or place of the dead), and are in perpetual conflict with each other. One of the characteristics of Baal, as depicted in the Baal–Mot cycle of the Ras Shamra Tablets, is as the god of rain, cloud, and storm.[33] Since in the Ugarit region fertility is dependent upon reliable and regular rainfall (unlike Mesopotamia or Egypt, which rely on flooding of their great rivers), Baal is often said to represent agricultural fertility, although this is inferred from the texts rather than explicitly stated.[34] Indeed, many commentators consider that the Baal–Mot myth depicts the alternation of the seasons in the Syro-Palestinian year—and hence refers to the annual agricultural cycle.[35]

[31] Koch notes that Baal is not mentioned in connection with the Southern Kingdom until the time of Manasseh (2 Kgs. 21), suggesting that anti-Baal polemic occurred first in the Northern Kingdom (Koch, 'Ba'al Sapon', 166–74). He surmises that this time gap may indicate that a different deity is being opposed in each place. While his discussion highlights the possibility of development in Canaanite as well as Israelite religion, his argument is somewhat speculative.

[32] See G. I. Davies, *Hosea*, 91–4, and the Introduction to Gibson's translation of the texts (Gibson, *Canaanite Myths*, 1–33).

[33] E.g. CTA 4.v.68–71, CTA 16.iii.4–11 (Gibson, *Canaanite Myths*).

[34] Day, 'Baal'; Kapelrud, *Baal*. Statuettes have been found depicting Baal with a stylized thunderbolt in his hand (i.e. as the rain and storm god) and wearing a horned helmet (i.e. as the bull-god, symbolizing fertility).

[35] Kapelrud, *Baal*, 128; see also Green, *Storm God*. More specifically, van Zijl suggests that underlying this conflict myth is the idea that Baal represents the winter season with its rainfall, and Mot represents heat and the dry summer season. When Mot overpowers Baal, everything withers—it is summer and everything has died. As soon as the first showers of autumn fall, Baal is resurrected, heat is ended by the rain,

Cyrus Gordon suggests that the extended nature of Baal's fight with Mot along with references to the passing of seven years indicates that a seven-year cycle—of famine followed by plenty—rather than an annual one is in mind.[36] However, as Mark Smith notes, such interpretations are in danger of reading the texts within too narrow a framework and engaging in undue speculation about them.[37] A similar caution is expressed by Gibson, who considers that Mot with his 'voracious appetite for human flesh' represents far more than the disruption of fertility and is simply the personification of death itself, the ultimate enemy.[38]

Although Baal's role as storm god and bringer of rain implies responsibility for the success of the harvest, this is of marginal interest in the Ugarit texts themselves, which are primarily concerned with activity among the gods. In this respect, biblical texts such as Hosea 2 perhaps make a clearer link between Baal and earth's fertility than the Baal–Mot cycle itself. Moreover, the Old Testament seems to be much more explicit than the Ugarit texts in attributing to YHWH the role of guarantor of fertility as well as storm god, although not necessarily both at the same time (e.g. Amos 4:7–8; Joel 2:23).[39]

YHWH as God of fertility

In the context of the book of Hosea, the prophet's repudiation of Baal as the giver of fertility can be clearly seen. Throughout Hosea 2

which also softens the earth for ploughing, and fertility returns to the earth (van Zijl, *Baal*, 157).

[36] C. H. Gordon, 'Poetic Legends', 5.

[37] Smith, 'Kinship and Covenant', 61–2. Smith provides an extensive analysis of various interpretations of the Baal–Mot cycle (ibid. 58–114).

[38] Gibson, *Canaanite Myths*, 18.

[39] Whether this is due to the paucity and fragmentary nature of the material from Ugarit or represents a development of traditions is open to question. Similarly, Greenfield notes that the designation of the Baal Cycle as a cosmogony by a number of scholars assumes an association between defeat of Yam and creation which is present in Old Testament texts such as Ps. 74:12–17 (and as a similar association in the Babylonian myth *Enuma Elish*) but not in the Ugarit texts themselves (Greenfield, 'Canaanite Literature', 557).

YHWH is identified as Israel's lord, including his role as the provider of agricultural fertility. This is evident both implicitly, for example in the number of first person verbs with YHWH as subject, and explicitly in verse 10 [8] (see also 14:8).[40] The overturning of Ugarit myths may also be detected in the mourning of the land in 4:3, which Hillers traces back to the mourning of the goddess Anat over Baal's death at the hands of Mot.[41] Hillers notes the twist given to this by Hosea, namely that the cause of mourning is Israel's lack of faithfulness, not the death of their God.[42]

The text of Hosea 2 subverts the Baal myths in one further and highly significant way. As already noted, the language is relational, using the imagery of marriage to express both Israel's wanton rejection of YHWH and also, towards the end of the chapter, a restoration of the relationship between them. It is on the basis of this relationship that YHWH has provided grain, wine, and oil for her. By contrast in the Baal myths, the notion of the gods acting for the well-being of humans is notably absent. The gods are preoccupied with their own affairs and battles, and have limited contact with the world of human beings and only incidental interest in them and their welfare.

[40] In contrast to the Old Testament, the Ugarit texts contain few references to love affairs or marriage between deities and humans, although love among deities is expressed in explicit and graphic scenes denoting sexual pleasure and prowess. Korpel suggests that this is because in biblical religion, monotheism meant that there was no longer room for female deities and sexuality in the sphere of the divine. Hence the relationship between God and his people became the focus of language of love as seen in the startling metaphors of Hosea and Ezekiel (Korpel, *Rift in the Clouds*, 211–25).

[41] Hillers, 'Zion'. See also Hayes, *The Earth Mourns*, 9–10.

[42] A further example is seen in the LXX of 13:14 (and other versions) adopted by various English translations (AV, NIV, etc.), which suggests the overcoming of death and Sheol by YHWH—a direct allusion to, and subversion of, Baal's vanquishing of Mot in the Baal–Mot myth (Day, 'Ugarit and the Bible', 42). It is this interpretation which the apostle Paul cites in 1 Cor. 15:55, but in Hosea the context of the verse, both preceded and followed by hopelessness, seems to imply that it is YHWH who summons the plagues of death to act as his agents of destruction—much as he does with earthquake and flood in Amos (see G. I. Davies, *Hosea*, 295–6).

The cessation of joy

The picture of YHWH's abandonment is expressed in two phrases which are symbolic of Israel's future prospects outside of YHWH's protection: he will bring about the end of rejoicing (2:13 [11]), and the desolation of the vineyards (2:14 [12]). These two concepts are also brought together in Isaiah 24, in which the mourning and languishing of the vineyard (24:7) is followed by the cessation of joy (24:8).[43] In Isa. 24:8 as in Hos. 2:13 the same unusual word combination is found (שׁבת 'to cease' with משׂושׂה 'rejoicing'), which, apart from these two prophetic texts, occurs only in Lam. 5:15.[44] In Hos. 2:14 [12] the Hebrew root שׁמם 'to be desolate' is used to describe the desolation of the vineyard (גפן), while the Isaianic author prefers אבל, 'to mourn' and אמל, 'to languish' (24:7). All three roots are part of the rich and graphic vocabulary used by these prophets to describe the impact of YHWH's judgement on the land.[45] Likewise the references to vineyards and wine in this section of Hosea, as elsewhere in the prophetic books, serve a double purpose. While they refer in a specific way to a key feature of the economic wellbeing of Israel, at the same time they have a metonymic function, representative of Israel itself. Such polyvalence is particularly evident in Isaiah 1–39 and is explored more fully in Chapter 6.

The walk in the wilderness 2:16–18 [14–16]

Following the description of the relentless and all-embracing effect of YHWH's displeasure, the opening phrase of Hos. 2:16 [14] appears to deliver the final blow: Israel will be brought into the wilderness. Commentators differ over whether this is a reference to forthcoming exile or an allusion back to the wilderness wanderings of Israel's past; either way, the previous reference to wilderness (מדבר) in verse 5 [3]

[43] See discussion in Chapter 6.

[44] Such lexical similarity adds to the stock of intertextual allusions between the 8th-century prophets, but whether it contributes to Day's argument for the literary dependence of parts of Isaiah 24–7 on the final chapters of Hosea is open to question (Day, 'Inner Scriptural Interpretation').

[45] See also Jer. 12:10–13; Joel 1:8–18.

suggests that this will be an entirely negative experience.[46] However, as the verse unfolds, a more nuanced perspective emerges. Although it begins similarly to verses 8 [6] and 11 [9] with the particle of consequence, לכן 'therefore' followed by the emphatic הנה אנכי, 'behold, I', it does not continue in the uncompromising way that might be expected from such an opening. The verse goes on to state that YHWH will 'entice' (מפתיה) Israel into the wilderness to speak to her.

The piel of פתה 'to entice' does not necessarily bear the sexual or romantic connotations some translators and commentators have accorded it.[47] Mosis suggests that the wilderness allusion, with all it conjures up of testing and trial, provides the interpretive key: 'Yahweh...leads Israel, who is now as stubborn as a stubborn heifer (Hos. 4:16) back into a condition in which she can be shaped and tutored.'[48] For some commentators the sexual interpretation of this verb is influenced in part by the last phrase of the verse ודברתי על-לבה, 'and I will speak to her heart'. However, Fischer strongly refutes the idea that this phrase constitutes 'Liebessprache', and suggests that in Hos. 2:16 [14] לב, 'heart' should simply take the sense of the personal pronoun and the phrase be translated 'to speak to her'.[49] It is possible that neither extreme is to be welcomed as the primary sense of the phrase. In the Old Testament, לב, 'heart' is generally regarded as the seat of the will, of decision-making, rather than of the emotions. As Wolff puts it, 'The essential characteristic that, broadly speaking, dominates the concept of לב is that the heart is called to reason, and especially to hear the word of God.'[50] With this understanding, the verse concerns an appeal to Israel to hear and respond to her God as a matter of choice, rather than emotion.

[46] Wolff, *Hosea*, 41–2. For discussion on whether the references to מדבר, 'wilderness' in Hosea constitute an appeal to a wilderness wanderings tradition see Dozeman, 'Wilderness Wandering'.

[47] E.g. Mays, *Hosea*; Macintosh, *Hosea*; Stuart, *Hosea-Jonah*. Clines and Gunn express caution over allowing the contextually determined interpretation of piel פתה in a passage such as Exod. 22:15 [16] to influence other usages (Clines and Gunn, 'Jeremiah XX 7–8'). Such renderings represent an example of what Barr terms 'illegitimate identity transfer' (Barr, *Semantics*, 218).

[48] *TDOT XII*, 172.

[49] 'Und ihr zureden' (Fischer, 'דבר על-לבה im AT', 249).

[50] Wolff, *Anthropology*, 55.

The ambiguity of wilderness

The nature of 'wilderness' as a concept in the Old Testament has been much debated. Some earlier commentators advocated the nomadic 'ideal': that it was easier for the Israelites to be wholeheartedly devoted to YHWH in the wilderness than in the settled land.[51] Others have viewed it essentially as a hostile and threatening place, as is reflected in those translations which render 'desert' for מדבר.[52] The latter perception probably has more to do with medieval and Enlightenment notions of wilderness than the biblical text itself, and conjures up images of vast featureless sand wastes.[53]

In reality the portrayal of wilderness in the Old Testament is much more nuanced than extremes of primitive idyll or hostile desert.[54] For Moses, the wilderness is first of all a place of divine encounter and commissioning (Exodus 3). For the Israelites, the wilderness is where they experience shortage of food and water, but also YHWH's dramatic provision (Exodus 16–19, see also the patriarchal traditions, e.g. Genesis 16 and 21). The wilderness at Sinai is the location both of God's election of Israel (Exodus 19), and of their rebellion and punishment (Exodus 32).[55] Within the prophetic material, the following broad categories of meaning can be detected, although it should be stressed that these semantic fields overlap and in some instances are ambiguous or interchangeable.

1. The term מדבר, 'wilderness' is used to denote a geographical location/geophysical description (e.g. Isa. 16:1), with its attendant

[51] Flight, 'Nomadic Idea', drawing on the work of Budde, 'Nomadic Ideal'. See also Leal, *Wilderness* and Mauser, *Christ in the Wilderness*. This theory is rebutted by, among others, Talmon, 'The "Desert Motif"'. However, such an idealistic understanding of wilderness is not without support in the biblical texts, e.g. Jer. 2:2.

[52] מדבר is one of a number of words which denote wilderness in the broadest sense of the word, although it is by far the most common (271 times). Others include ערבה(61 times) listed by BDB as 'desert-plain, steppe' (BDB 787), and the rarer ישׁימון, 'wasteland' (13 times).

[53] Leal, *Wilderness*, 41–5. Modern ecology has demonstrated that deserts have varied and rich eco-systems supporting a wide range of flora and fauna.

[54] Philip Davies sees evidence of this ambivalence within the book of Hosea itself, maintaining that the two references to wilderness in 2:5 [3] and 2:16 [14] represent a debate between the different understandings of wilderness (P. R. Davies, 'Wilderness Years').

[55] See Brueggemann, *The Land*, 27–41.

privations and dangers. In particular the expression 'pastures of the wilderness' (נאות המדבר suggests wilderness as a place for grazing flocks and herds, not just the habitat of wild animals (e.g. Jer. 9:9; Joel 1:19, 20).[56]

2. It is used figuratively, drawing on wilderness characteristics of dryness and lack of vegetation, in particular in antithesis to the language of agricultural plenitude and fruitfulness (e.g. Hos. 2:5 [3]; Isa. 32:15, 16).
3. It is a theological construct, often harking back to events in Israel's history (e.g. Hos. 13:5; Amos 2:10, 5:25). As such, wilderness becomes a shorthand for God's dealings with Israel, and Israel's response to him. The overall theme embraces such concepts as God's deliverance and leading, his testing of his people and his provision for their needs, and on the part of the Israelites, fickleness and disobedience, resulting in God's punishment.

The use of wilderness in 2:16 [14] is an example of how the three senses of the word can be combined to give a multilayered and complex meaning. At one level, the wilderness conjures up for Hosea's audience the immediate surroundings of their cultivated environment, its hardships a daily reality faced by herdsmen and travellers. At another level, in the light of the language of fertility and barrenness which characterizes this chapter of Hosea, the figurative use of the term can be clearly seen. In addition and perhaps most significantly, is the theological sense with its deliberate ambiguity. The emphatic first person singular pronoun אנכי, together with the hiphil והלכתיה, 'I will bring her', places YHWH firmly as the agent of the prophesied wilderness experience, with all that might involve of trial and hardship, yet it is there also that YHWH will speak to them. Israel's walk in the wilderness, like the wilderness wandering tradition, will be a time of pain and trouble, but also of incredible encounter with her God.

The ambivalence of the wilderness walk is quickly clarified in the verses that follow. The result of YHWH's conversation with Israel is a twofold restoration—of vineyards (v. 17a [15a]) and of marriage (v. 18 [16]). This deliberately overturns the negative consequences

[56] See Hillel, *Natural History*, 27–31.

of God's judgement expressed, as has already been seen, in the desolation of the vines and the loss of husband in the preceding verses. Verse 17 [15] goes on to draw on two historical memories: the Valley of Achor and the deliverance from Egypt. The former is a reference to the story of Achan's sin in Joshua 7 where Achor (עכור) is the name given to the valley in which Achan and his family are stoned (from the root עכר 'to trouble').

In Hos. 2:17 [15] the prophet speaks of a reversal of that former setback, which perhaps functions in a metonymic fashion to denote all Israel's hardships.[57] The valley of trouble will be exchanged for a doorway of hope (פתח תקוה).[58] If, as some commentators suggest, there is evidence of substantial editorial activity in this section (2: 17–22 [15–20]), this verse may be an allusion to the return from exile. As Davies suggests, 'The new entry into the land will surpass the earlier one by being free from disobedience and the "trouble" which it brought.'[59] There is no explicit mention of Israel's repentance following YHWH's judgement, such as characterized her wilderness wanderings, (e.g. Num. 14:21). Nevertheless she is described as 'responding' or 'singing' to YHWH (ענה, BDB I and IV) as she did when God brought her out from Egypt (17b [15b]).[60]

Although most commentators prefer to translate ענה as 'to respond', and it certainly conveys the reciprocal nature of Israel's relationship with YHWH, there are two possible reasons why 'to sing' might be just as appropriate. First is the possibility that it alludes to the song which the Israelites sang to YHWH following the crossing of the Sea of Reeds (Exodus 15).[61] In Miriam's song (vv. 20–1), ענה is used alongside שׁיר in the exhortation to proclaim YHWH's victory. Earlier in the chapter, Moses' song (שׁיר) describes

[57] Davies notes Hosea's fondness for using place names to recall Israel's history (G. I. Davies, *Hosea*, 79–80).

[58] See also the reference to the Valley of Achor in Isa. 65:10.

[59] G. I. Davies, *Hosea*, 80.

[60] The derivation and meaning of ענה is not without difficulty and BDB lists four roots that are attested in Hebrew (see discussion on Isa. 27:2–5 in Chapter 6, below). LXX *καὶ ταπεινωθήσεται* and Syr. ܘܬܬܡܟܟ follow ענה III 'to be bowed down' or 'to be humbled', while Vg. *et canet* follows root IV.

[61] Macintosh, *Hosea*, 72, cites Jerome, ibn Ezra and Kimchi who draw on Exod. 15: 21 to conclude that ענה in Hos. 2:18 [16] means 'to sing'.

the election of Israel in terms of their being 'planted' by YHWH on his mountain (v. 17). The agricultural motif of planting as a symbol for Israel's restoration, which is picked up elsewhere in the prophets (and which I discuss further in Chapter 6), features in that early song of victory; here in Hosea 2 the replanting of the vineyards will also cause a 'song' to burst from the earth and its produce (v. 24 [22]).

A second connection between the restoration of vineyards and singing is found in Isa. 27:2, in the second vineyard parable.[62] In this case, ענה is almost certainly deliberately chosen for its multi-faceted interpretation and a similar multivalent intention can be seen in Hosea's use of this root. Like the Isaiah parable, in Hosea 2:17 [15] Israel's response to YHWH includes a song of gratitude and joy—the reversal of verse 14 [12] in which YHWH brought to an end her celebrations and festivals. The verse harks back to the Exodus, apparently an idyllic age in the memory of the community, and suggests a rejuvenation of Israel and her relationship with YHWH (see also Hos. 11:1).

The result of Israel's wilderness encounter with YHWH is described not just in terms of restoration of vineyards with all their social and economic symbolism. Alongside this agricultural motif, Hosea continues to weave the thread of a marriage metaphor drawn from his own symbolic marriage. In Hos. 2:18 [16], YHWH's relationship with Israel will be changed from that of a master to that of a husband. In a deliberate wordplay on the name of the Canaanite god בעל 'Baal' or 'Lord', Hosea reaffirms YHWH as the one to whom Israel is committed in intimate relationship and sweeps aside her previous 'dalliances'. Both this imagery and the reminder of the deliverance from Egypt portray the ideal relationship of love, trust and obedience between YHWH and his people.[63]

Remaking the covenant 2:20–5 [18–23]

We have seen how the results of YHWH's judgement on Israel are expressed in terms of failing harvests and a broken, barren family

[62] Discussed in detail in Chapter 6.
[63] Macintosh, *Hosea*, 76.

(2:5–14 [3–12]), and how the ambivalent nature of her wilderness encounter with YHWH brings restoration of both her vineyards and her marriage (2:16–18 [14–16]). It remains now to examine the renewal of YHWH's covenant with Israel and the three-way interchange which results from it (2:20–5 [18–23]).

The book of Hosea is redolent in covenantal language or allusions, which has been extensively discussed in the secondary literature.[64] The present example begins with a covenant initiated by YHWH which is enacted on Israel's behalf or 'for their benefit' (v. 20 [18]).[65] This covenant is neither with YHWH nor other nations but is 'with the creatures of the field, with the birds of the air and the creeping things of the ground'. Restoration of harmony between human beings and animals in verse 20 [18] is followed by the removal of war within human society (v. 21 [19]), resulting in peace and security for the Israelites. A few commentators suggest that verse 20 [18] has eschatological connotations, and represents a cosmic return to the primeval, edenic ideal.[66] This is supported by its resemblance to the collective description of the animal kingdom in Gen. 1:30 as 'all the creatures of the earth, and... all the birds of the air and... all the creeping things of the earth' (see also the similar list in Gen. 8:19, 9: 2). Other scholars see rather a more limited reversal of the prophesied desolation of 2:14 [12] in which חית השׂדה 'animals of the field' consume the vines and figs.[67]

The latter interpretation fits more closely with the removal of conflict from Israel's territory in the second half of the covenant promise (v. 20b [18b]), in particular since the aftermath of warfare undoubtedly includes damage to crops and property (e.g. Isa. 7:23–5).[68] Nevertheless, the formulaic language of the covenant

[64] See e.g. Daniels, *Hosea and Salvation History*; Holt, *Prophesying the Past*; McCarthy, *Treaty and Covenant*; Nicholson, 'Israelite Religion'; Perlitt, *Bundestheologie*; Smith, 'Kinship and Covenant'.

[65] Macintosh, *Hosea*, 81.

[66] Andersen and Freedman, *Amos*, 281. Although Wolff describes it as the establishment of 'a paradisiacal harmony between man and animals', he goes on to suggest that the context places it firmly as a tangible act of redemption within Israel's historical consciousness (Wolff, *Hosea*, 51). Davies suggests an affinity with the Noachic covenant (G. I. Davies, *Hosea*, 84).

[67] E.g. Tucker, 'Peaceable Kingdom', 222; see also Mays, *Hosea*, 49.

[68] See Macintosh, *Hosea*, 82.

declaration in 2:20 [18], which goes beyond the simple statement of 2:14 [12], suggests a broader outlook than Israel's immediate political landscape. This perspective is developed in the verses that follow, which speak of a new beginning for Israel as YHWH's betrothed, and of renewal of the fertility of the land. In this final section of Hosea 2 the twin themes of Israel and the land are again intertwined by means of carefully constructed interplay of the imagery of marriage and of agricultural fecundity.

A series of key words and phrases is employed in vv. 21–5 [19–23] to suggest the all-embracing, radical nature of the new relationship between Israel and her God. These include a four-part stipulation of ethical attributes: righteousness (צדק), justice (מִשְׁפט), kindness (חסד), and compassion (רחמים) in 2:22 [20], followed by the declaration that Israel will 'know YHWH' (וידעת את־יהוה), a theme which will be explored further later in this chapter.[69] These attributes both govern YHWH's conduct towards Israel, and are requirements for his people as they enter into a new reciprocal relationship with him.[70] Elsewhere in the prophets such characteristics describe the ideal ruler of Isa. 11:3–5, and the pardoning God of Mic. 7:18–20. They are also frequently stipulated as the standards of behaviour YHWH demands of his people (e.g. Amos 5:15, 23–4; Mic. 6:8; Isa. 5:7).[71] Justice and righteousness and the like are not just ethical qualities which affect—for good or ill—the relationship between YHWH and his people. In a number of prophetic texts, in particular in Isaiah, they are a reflection of the fundamental world order established by YHWH, which includes the well-being of the natural world (e.g. Isa. 11:3–9, 32:15–17).

In a similar vein, Hosea presents the effect of YHWH's righteousness, justice, kindness and compassion in terms of the whole earth, not just its human inhabitants.[72] The results of the radical

[69] Three of these qualities are repeated in Jer. 9:23 [24] (חסד, מִשְׁפט, צדקה), again in the context of knowing YHWH.

[70] For discussion of the meaning(s) of the Hebrew word חסד see Clark, *Hesed*; Sakenfeld, *Meaning of Hesed*.

[71] Such a concern also permeates the rest of Hosea—each of the words used in 2:20 [18], or some cognate of them, reappears in Hosea 4–14 (see Morris, *Hosea*, 112).

[72] Sakenfeld notes that in the Mosaic traditions, when חסד is used to refer to God, it may encompass notions of divine forgiveness, often expressed in terms of

reorientation in Israel's relationship with God are outlined in the final verses of the chapter (23–5 [21–3]); verses 23–4 [21–2] comprise a repetitive pattern as follows:

YHWH	answers	the heavens
the heavens/sky	answer	the earth/land (הארץ)
the land/earth (הארץ)	answers	the produce (grain, new wine, oil)
the produce	answers	Jezreel

These verses form two groups of interactions—each with three participants. The first describes the interrelationship between YHWH, the heavens and the world—the cosmic sphere (v. 23 [21])—and the second that between the land, its produce and the enigmatic 'Jezreel' in the earthly sphere (v. 24 [22]). As well as this rhythmic repetition, the literary quality of these two verses is enhanced by means of an exceptional number of wordplays and use of terms with multiple or ambiguous meanings.[73]

As has already been discussed with respect to v. 17 [15], ענה carries a double meaning—'to answer' and 'to sing'. In vv. 23–4 [21–2] the repetition of the verb (five times in two verses) conveys a sense of dialogue, or even antiphonal response.[74] The progression establishes YHWH's pre-eminence as the source of all blessing and provision, and demonstrates the prophet's understanding of 'the route of human nutrition'.[75] It also includes a movement from the cosmic realm to the earthly one by means of the dual sense of השמים and הארץ in v. 23 [21].[76] The former term signifies both the heavens as the dwelling place of God, and also the sky, which gives rain for the crops; the latter suggests the global earth in parallel to the heavens, but also the land which receives the rain. In v. 24 [22] the sense of הארץ as the land which yields produce is re-established.

deliverance (Sakenfeld, *Meaning of Hesed*, 237). Similar implications may be behind the use here in Hosea 2.

[73] See Morris for a discussion of Hosea's distinctive use of wordplay and verbal repetition (Morris, *Hosea*, 133–4 and throughout).

[74] Macintosh suggests these verses may even originate in 'an incantation of rogation' (*Hosea*, 88).

[75] Wolff, *Hosea*, 53.

[76] As already mentioned, the only place in Hosea in which these words are paired.

The deliberate use of the ambiguity contained within this Hebrew term ('land' or 'earth') at the intersection of the heavenly and earthly realms serves to emphasize God's initiative in the restoration of Israel's land and its well-being.

The final wordplay of verses 24 [22], יזרעאל, 'God sows', echoes 'the ominous naming of Hosea's first son' in 1:4.[77] Here, according to Wolff, the term does not refer to the geographical location of the valley of Jezreel as does 1:5; rather, it denotes the people of Israel.[78] There is however another important aspect which Wolff's suggestion fails to note. In this wordplay based on זרע, 'to sow', Hosea is deliberately alluding to the completion of the cycle of nature, the sowing of seed which will yield the crops, but is establishing it as YHWH's doing, rather than merely a human activity (cf. Isa. 28: 23–9). In the following and final verse (25 [23]), he develops the wordplay and brings it round again to Israel's relationship with YHWH and with the land וזרעתיה לי בארץ, 'I will sow her for myself in the land'. Here the figurative 'sowing' of Israel parallels the use of planting as a metaphor for settlement in the land elsewhere in the Old Testament (e.g. Exod. 15:17, Ps. 80:9 [8]).

In this section, as indeed throughout Hosea 2, the interplay of figurative language and reality provides a rich depiction of the relationship between YHWH, his people Israel, and the natural realm. Both the motifs of marriage and agriculture are developed throughout the chapter as metaphors for the mutual interdependence of people and land, and of their utter dependence upon YHWH. Each of the motifs also picks up on aspects of reality—the prophet's disastrous marriage, and, implicitly at least, the effect of invasion or warfare on the agricultural infrastructure. The themes are woven together in a complex arrangement which, at times, defies attempts to separate figurative from non-figurative language, or to delineate precisely the structure of individual metaphors. The resulting composition demonstrates the interrelational nature of Hosea's thought, whereby YHWH, Israel and her surrounding environment interact for good or ill, to Israel's benefit or detriment.

[77] Macintosh, *Hosea*, 88.
[78] Wolff, *Hosea*, 54.

It is notable that this model of interrelationship concerns primarily the economic and social well-being of the Israelites. In the light of the current study it might therefore be construed as presenting a utilitarian perspective on the relationship between human and non-human, in which both the earth's resources and YHWH's generous provision function purely to meet Israel's needs. Even the wild animals are tamed in order to give safety to the human population (2:20 [18]). Such a focus on human welfare receives a severe jolt in Hosea 4, which indicts the people, not just for failure to keep the covenant, but for the consequent devastation of the whole of the natural world.

HOSEA 4

Chapter 4 of Hosea commences the prophetic oracles which comprise the bulk of the book (chs. 4–14) and is marked by the introductory formula, 'Hear the word of YHWH, sons of Israel'. (v.la).[79] Of particular interest is the first half of the chapter (vv. 1–11), which details the failures of two categories of people—the inhabitants of the land (vv. 1–3) and the priests (vv. 4–8), before pronouncing judgement on them both (vv. 9–11).[80]

Against priests and people

The indictments against people and priests (in vv. 1–2 and 6–8, respectively), although different in content, have a number of common points. In particular, YHWH's charge against both groups takes the form of a ריב; an 'accusation' (vv. 1 and 4), one of the key components of which is the lack of knowledge of God (vv. 1 and 6).

[79] In the view of a number of commentators this is undoubtedly the work of a redactor (G. I. Davies, *Hosea*, 110; Wolff, *Hosea*, 66). For examples of a similar introductory imperative, see Joel 1:2; Amos 3:1, 4:1, 5:1, Mic. 1:2.

[80] Some commentators treat the whole of Hosea 4 in its entirety (e.g. G. I. Davies, *Hosea*; Macintosh, *Hosea*), others regard vv. 1–3 as a separate, self-contained unit (e.g. Wolff, *Hosea*).

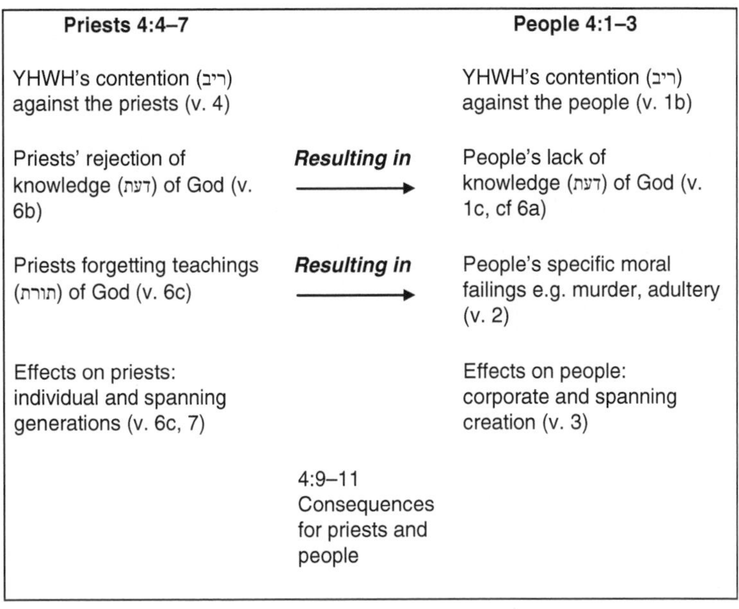

Figure 4. The interconnection between priests and people in Hos. 4

But the connection is more than that of common word usage, since the failures for which the inhabitants of the land are indicted in verses 1–2 are, at least in part, due to the failures of the priests in verses 4–6.[81] The implicit connection between the two groups is one of cause and effect, in which failings in the priesthood contribute to the moral and religious deficiency of the people, an interconnection which is portrayed diagrammatically in Figure 4.

As Figure 4 suggests, the twin charges against the priests in verse 6 form a key component of the indictment against them and are pivotal in 4:1–11 as a whole.[82] These two accusations and their consequences are expressed in parallel formation as follows:

81 Although 'priest' is singular in 4:4, the translation of Macintosh who regards כהן as a collective singular is followed here (Macintosh, *Hosea*, 135). His reading is supported by the fact that Hosea 5 begins with a plural summons to the priests to hear the word of YHWH.

82 The post-exilic prophet Malachi gives a comparable diatribe against the priests of his day (Mal. 2:1–9). Although his language is drawn from Deuteronomic sources,

Because you have rejected knowledge, I will reject you from being my priest,
You have forgotten the teachings of your God (תורת אלהיך),
even so I will forget your sons. (v. 6)

The parallelism of this verse sets דעת 'knowledge' and הורת 'teachings' alongside each other as at least mutually interdependent, if not synonymous, ideas, and each is reflected in the indictment against the people in 4:1–2. Moreover, the extent to which the priests are implicated in the people's sin is clear, since the destruction of God's people in verse 6a, 'My people are being destroyed for lack of knowledge', is attributed to the priests' rejection of knowledge in verse 6b.

The peoples' responsibility

The opening stanza of 4:1 makes clear, however, that the people cannot abdicate their own responsibility—like the priests in verse 4 they are liable to YHWH's condemnation.[83] The use of ריב in prophetic texts has been taken by many scholars to indicate the genre of 'prophetic lawsuit' (*Gerichtsrede*) first identified by Hermann Gunkel, who argued that the language, imagery, and form of certain speeches depicting YHWH's contention against Israel were drawn from the arena of civil lawsuit.[84] However, the use of ריב does not always imply legal connotations but may carry the broader sense of a quarrel or controversy of any kind.[85] As with the use of ריב in 2:4 [2], there is nothing in this verse *per se* that indicates a legal framework to the charges.[86] The denunciation which follows

his emphasis on moral integrity and divine knowledge and instruction reflect that of his pre-exilic predecessor.

[83] A similar point is made in v. 9—both priest and people will receive YHWH's recompense for their actions.

[84] Gunkel and Begrich, *Psalms*, 277–80.

[85] *TDOT XIII*, 473–9. The tendency among some commentators (e.g. Mays, *Hosea*, 61; Wolff, *Hosea*, 67) to read 4:1, as well as 2:4 [2] as an example of prophetic lawsuit fails to take account of this broader meaning, as noted by Williamson, 'Isaiah 1'.

[86] DeRoche helpfully distinguishes between ריב as lawsuit and as quarrel in his article on Hosea 4:1–3 (DeRoche, 'Reversal of Creation').

encompasses a wide spectrum of attitudes and behaviour, which takes it beyond the boundaries of a law court.[87]

In 4:1 YHWH's contention is directed at the inhabitants of the land—emphasized by the reiteration of בארץ 'in the land' at the end of the verse. The first two qualities that are lacking, אמת 'truth' and חסד 'goodness', signify according to Macintosh moral integrity and common decency respectively and the absence of such attributes is due to their failure to recognize God's character and accept his demands.[88] In the Deuteronomist's account of the entry into Canaan the connection between obedience to God, ethical behaviour towards others and the well-being of the land is clearly affirmed (Deut. 11:8–15). The stress on the Israelites' identity as people of the land (twice in Hos. 4:1) in the context of their ethical and religious failure is perhaps evidence of the importance of this connection in the early prophetic traditions.

The precise meaning of the word חסד has been the subject of many Old Testament studies, with scholarship now moving away from giving it an exclusively covenantal or quasi-legal meaning.[89] In Hosea the word is used in a variety of senses—to refer to the ethical responsibilities of human beings towards one another (10:12, 12:7 [6]), to denote YHWH's love for his people (2:21[19]) and describe human relationship with YHWH (6:4, 6). The latter text (6:6) pairs חסד with דעת אלהים 'knowledge of God' in the context of the true worship acceptable to God. The conjunction of the selfsame two phrases in 4:1 suggests that חסד here denotes more than merely kindness between human beings. As Davies explains, 'It seems most likely that it [חסד] embraced for Hosea living up to one's responsibilities both to Yahweh and to fellow members of the community'.[90] Both אמת and חסד, whether directed towards God or other people,

[87] Whether the presence of the word pair יכח/ריב in Hos. 4:4 indicates a forensic context is in view depends on the meaning attributed to יכח, variously translated as 'reprimand' (Macintosh, *Hosea*, 134), 'debate' (Andersen and Freedman, *Hosea*, 342) and 'accuse' (G. I. Davies, *Hosea*, 117).

[88] Macintosh, *Hosea*, 128.

[89] See discussion and references on the meaning of חסד in G. I. Davies, *Hosea*, 94–7.

[90] Ibid. 96.

are, for Hosea, an outworking of the third phrase in the list, דעת אלהים.

Like חסד the usage and meaning of the expression דעת אלהים 'knowledge of God' in the book of Hosea has been subject to much discussion.[91] Earlier commentators interpreted the verb ידע 'to know' against the background of the marriage metaphor in Hosea 1–3, but the emotional and ethical connotations of such an understanding have been queried by Wolff.[92] He suggests that this root in Hosea has more to do with intellectual understanding of God, which the priests were responsible for disseminating: 'Hosea's usage of the word undoubtedly indicates more the cognitive knowledge of facts and people than it signifies subjective character attributes'.[93] While Wolff's exegetical reasoning makes sense, the categories he uses—'cognitive' and 'subjective character attributes'—are the product of modern rationalism, and it is doubtful whether an ancient Israelite would have drawn such a distinction between head knowledge and moral action.[94]

Wolff's ideas are developed in Holt's study on the connection between דעת אלהים and חסד in Hosea in the wider context of the concepts of תורה 'teaching' and ברית 'covenant'.[95] She concludes that דעת אלהים refers to an understanding of YHWH, both his actions in Israel's history, and his provision for daily needs, which is a prerequisite for a right relationship with him.[96] This relationship

[91] The theme of knowledge of God (or the lack of it) is popular with the prophet Hosea, as can be seen from a survey of the root ידע. There are 14 occurrences of this root in Hosea, as follows: verbal forms: 2:10 [8], 2:22 [20], 5:3, 4, 6:3, 7:9, 8:2, 11:3, 13:4, 14:10, nominal forms 4:1, 4:6, 6:6, 8:4. All except one (7:9) are concerned to some degree or other with Israel's relationship with YHWH.

[92] Wolff, 'Wissen Um Gott'.

[93] '[D]as Wort im allgemeinen hoseanischen Gebrauch fraglos mehr auf die kognitive Erfahrung von Fakten und Personen hindeutet und nicht so sehr subjektive Verhaltungsweisen charakterisiert' (ibid. 537).

[94] This point is made by Vriezen, who maintains that knowledge of God in the Old Testament is existential, not ontological, and denotes 'an immediate spiritual communion between the God, the Holy One and man and the world' (Vriezen, *Old Testament Theology*, 157).

[95] Holt, 'Buche Hosea'.

[96] Ibid. 102–3.

between deity and people, suggests Holt, is expressed by use of the term חסד in 6:6.[97]

Even Holt's analysis does not fully capture the emphasis found in Hosea's use of ידע. For example, in 11:3, where the people lack knowledge of God as their healer, the context is that of parent/child relationship. In 13:4–5, in which, like 11:1–4, YHWH's deliverance from Egypt is followed by his sustenance in the wilderness, the emphasis created by the first person pronoun אנכי followed by two prepositions זולתי 'apart from me' and בלתי 'besides me' sets a personal and relational tone. In 2:10[8] God is to be known as the provider of the agricultural abundance which Israel needs to sustain life. For Hosea then, knowledge of God encompasses relationship with God as well as knowledge about him. Davies has noted with regard to Hos. 2:22 [20] that 'to "know" Yahweh is . . . to recognise his action in nature and history . . . and to submit to his law'.[98] In Hosea 4 as we shall now see, the opposite is true—their failure to submit to God's law results in societal breakdown and devastation of the natural world.

Israel's failings

In 4:1 the people of Israel are charged by the prophet for their inability to live in right relationship with YHWH—implicitly at least a result of the priests' failure to disseminate a proper understanding of what that entails (4:6). The results of their shortcomings are itemized in 4:2, which comprises a catalogue of crimes against fellow human beings, culminating in the prophet's pessimistic verdict on his own society: ודמים בדמים נגעו, 'and bloodshed follows bloodshed'. If the priests' rejection of knowledge has resulted in lack of knowledge of God in the land, so too the moral lapses of 4:2 can be attributed to the parallel charge that the priests 'have forgotten the

[97] Holt regards חסד in 4:1 as referring to relations among human beings. However, as already stated, its juxtaposition with knowledge of God suggests the inextricable link in the prophet's mind between responsibilities towards God and those towards fellow human beings.

[98] G. I. Davies, *Hosea*, 88.

teaching of your God' (תשכח תורת אלהיך, v. 6c).[99] Implicit in the phrasing of this verse is the expectation that the content of such teaching should be already known by those responsible for disseminating it. Hosea is therefore undoubtedly drawing upon an established tradition of teaching, known by priests and people alike, rather than articulating his own new code of conduct, as some suggest.[100]

The list of offences in 4:2a has been compared with the two versions of the Decalogue (Exod. 20:2–17 and Deut. 5:6–21) by numerous commentators, with differing views expressed over the extent and direction of the literary dependence.[101] The offences listed by Hosea take the form of five infinite absolutes, three of which (רצח 'murder', גנב 'theft', and נאף 'adultery') use the same Hebrew roots as in the sixth, seventh, and eighth commandments in both versions of the Decalogue, albeit in a different order.[102] The other two offences, אלה 'swearing' and כחש 'lying' while not using the same verbal roots as the Decalogue, are regarded by a number of commentators as equivalent to the third and ninth commandments respectively.[103] However the connection between Hosea and the Decalogue is conceptualized, both texts have in common the following factors:

1. Human attitudes towards God and towards fellow human beings are inextricably linked, by virtue of being included within the same body of material in each case.

[99] Here as in 4:4 the singular subject כֹּהֵן is to be regarded as a collective singular (Macintosh, *Hosea*, 135).

[100] E.g. Holt who regards him as a 'reformer of the cult' rather than a 'restoration prophet' (Holt, *Prophesying the Past*, 115). For outline of the debate over dating and origin of the Decalogue see Stamm and Andrew, *Ten Commandments*.

[101] Andersen and Freedman, *Hosea*, 337; Cassuto, *Biblical and Oriental Studies*, 1: 89–91; G. I. Davies, *Hosea*, 115; Macintosh, *Hosea*, 130–1.

[102] This is perhaps as Cassuto suggests, Hosea's own alteration, in order to draw attention to the sin of adultery with which the earlier chapters of the book have been concerned, metaphorically if not literally (*Biblical and Oriental Studies*, 1:89). According to the traditional Catholic numbering these commandments are the 5th, 6th, and 7th ones respectively (see Freedman's table showing the numbering of the commandments in the various traditions: Freedman, *Nine Commandments*, 15–16). Weiss concludes that these differences suggest variant traditions in existence at different stages of Israel's history (Weiss, 'Decalogue', 67–72).

[103] Andersen and Freedman, *Hosea*, 337; Macintosh, *Hosea*, 129–30; G. I. Davies, *Hosea*, 115.

2. A right understanding of God and relationship to him is a precursor and prerequisite for the ethical qualities demanded by the law (or 'teachings'). In the Decalogue, the exclusive demands of YHWH worship and the injunction to love him (Exod. 20:6, Deut. 5:10) precede obligations towards other human beings. In Hosea 4, as has been seen, when knowledge of God, faithfulness and love fail, human moral behaviour suffers.
3. The conditional nature of the divine stipulations is made clear in both cases—in the Decalogue this is in the form of promises for obedience (Exod. 20:6, 12; Deut. 5:10, 16), while in Hosea 4 it is the consequences of failure that are elaborated (Hos. 4:3, 6).
4. In both the Decalogue and Hosea 4 the people's relationship to the land is involved as part of the call to ethical living. The commandment to 'honour your father and mother' is accompanied in both Exodus and Deuteronomy by the condition 'that your days may be long in the land the Lord your God is giving you' (Exod. 20:12; Deut. 5:16). The idea that covenantal obedience brings blessing in the land is articulated in more detail later in Deuteronomy 28 in the language of the blessings and cursings which accompany the Israelite settlement in the land. This presents both the positive and the negative conditions associated with the gift of the land: obedience to YHWH's commandments will result in agricultural and pastoral fertility (cf. Hos. 2:18 [20]); drought, crop failure, and disease will be the consequences of disobedience.

Act and consequence

It is this same sequence of act and consequence that we find articulated in Hosea 4, albeit with a wider scope than the well-being of Israelite field and flocks. The shortcomings of the priests with regard to their responsibilities for the religious well-being of Israel rebound on them in a devastating way in verse 6. As they have rejected knowledge, YHWH will reject them as priests; since they have forgotten תורה 'the teaching', their own descendants will be forgotten. The parallel breakdown in relationship between Israel and her deity and the resulting transgression of this teaching by the people in 4:1–2 has an equally dramatic effect in verse 3:

Therefore the land mourns, and all its inhabitants languish,
with the animals of the fields, and with the birds of the air,
and even the fish of the sea are taken away.

The preposition עַל־כֵּן 'therefore' establishes a clear causal link between the indictment of the people in verses 1 and 2 and the devastation of verse 3. As already noted, the verb אבל 'to mourn' is used throughout the prophetic texts to describe the reaction of the natural world to the actions of YHWH or of human beings—in this case breakdown of societal order.[104] In Hosea 4, unlike Amos 1:2, YHWH is not explicitly named as the agent; rather, the sequence of cause and effect which began with the priests' abdication of responsibility reaches its climax here in verse 3. Thus the priests' neglect of תּוֹרָה results in the failings of the people, which in turn results in the mourning of the land.

Brueggemann suggests that עַל־כֵּן 'for this reason' at the start of verse 3 deliberately leaves the relation between verses 2 and 3, and hence between Decalogue and creation, unspecified.[105] This may be because his twenty-first-century sensibilities are less comfortable with such a clearly articulated connection of cause and effect than was the ancient world.[106] As Koch has demonstrated, the perspective that there is a close connection between human actions and consequences is an underlying premise in much of the Old Testament material, including Hosea.[107] He cites Hos. 4:9b as an example of the way in which YHWH is involved in this—as the one who sets in motion and brings to completion the act-consequence process.[108] This parallel, together with the accusations of verses 1 and 4, clearly establishes that it is YHWH who is calling both priests and people to account, not some spontaneous and unrelated event.

[104] See the discussion on the meaning of אבל with regard to Amos 1:2 (above, Chapter 4) and Isa. 24:4, 7 (below, Chapter 6).

[105] Brueggemann, 'Hosea 4:1–3'.

[106] His view seems to take insufficient account of the fact that the Hebrew phrase עַל־כֵּן usually conveys the notion of causal sequence whether or not it is regarded as heralding a statement of fact rather than a declaration as BDB suggests (BDB 487, col 1 f; see discussion in Macintosh, *Hosea*, 132–3).

[107] Koch, 'Doctrine of Retribution', 67–8.

[108] Ibid. 67.

Repercussions in creation

The consequences of Israel's sins of omission and commission are described in terms of their effect on various categories of living things. The verb אמלל 'to languish' includes the sense of loss of fertility and life-bearing capacity.[109] It is used of the natural world in a number of texts, particularly in First Isaiah (e.g. Isa. 16:8; 19:8; 24: 4, 7; 33:9), and in parallel with אבל on seven other occasions throughout the Old Testament—almost always in oracles of lament or judgement describing mourning and woe.[110] The subjects of the two verbs—הארץ 'the land' and כל־יושב בה 'all who live in it' pick up on references to the land and its inhabitants in 4:1. The repetition focuses attention on the concrete physical situation, although, as Hayes points out, Hosea does not always clearly distinguish between physical and political senses of 'land'.[111] Whereas the accusation in verse 1 was addressed to the human population, in the culmination to YHWH's accusation of verse 3 it is the wider natural world that is affected by devastation and loss of fertility suggested by the word pair 'mourn'/'languish' (אבל/אמלל).[112]

The sequence used to describe the natural world evokes similar ones in Genesis 1–9 as well as echoing the language of the covenant of Hos. 2:20 [18], suggesting the existence of set collective phrases to denote the creation.[113] The specific phraseology used in these lists is subject to variation and in fact differs from list to list—even within Hosea itself.[114] DeRoche notes that the order in which the creatures

[109] E.g. 1 Sam. 2:5; Jer. 15:9. See Hayes, *The Earth Mourns*, 42.

[110] Isa. 19:8, 24:4,7, 33:9, Jer. 14:2; Lam. 2:8; Joel 1:10.

[111] Hayes, *The Earth Mourns*, 42.

[112] The inseparable preposition ב, which accompanies each of the categories of animal life, gives according to Gesenius—Kautzsch the explicatory sense 'consisting of' (GK 119i).

[113] This is by no means unique to the Old Testament—see ANE texts cited by DeRoche ('Reversal of Creation', 404–5). Within the Old Testament such collective phrases can be found in Gen. 1:26, 28, 30, 2:19, 20, 9:2. The list in Ps. 8:8–9 [7–8] is more focused on domestic animals—'flocks and herds' in the first instance.

[114] No two lists are exactly the same, with 'birds of the air' being the only species common to all lists. The order of species varies and a fourth category, 'things that crawl' (רמש) is present in a number of lists, either alongside the other species (Gen. 1:26, 9:2), or substituted for one of them (Gen. 1:30; Hos. 2:20[18]). The first items

are cited in Hos. 4:3—animals, birds, fish—represents a reversal of the order in which Genesis 1 records the creation of these species: fish (v. 20a), then birds (v. 20b), and then animals (v. 24), as well as that in which humans are given responsibilities over the rest of creation (Gen. 1:28).[115] This, he suggests, indicates that 'Hosea is not merely employing the imagery of a drought to illustrate Israel's punishment; he is announcing the reversal of creation'.[116]

The undoing of creation is hinted at in Amos 1:2 and 5:8 (see above, Chapter 4, p. 152). It is also present in other prophetic texts, including Isaiah 24 and 34, to be discussed in Chapter 6. It is depicted *par excellence* in the flood narrative of Genesis 6–9, in which the entire range of animal species apart from fish is destroyed: 'People together with animals and creeping things and birds of the air' (Gen. 6:7, cf. 7:23). The flood narrative is preceded by two other instances where human beings have engendered God's displeasure and the non-human creation has been included in the consequences. The first is the act of disobedience by Adam and Eve in the garden which results in the ground being cursed. Only with difficulty will it yield fruitfulness (Gen. 3:17–19). Likewise in Genesis 4, the murder of Abel by Cain results not only in the cursing of Cain himself but also in a reduction in the capacity of the ground to support his needs (Gen. 4:10–12). In each of these instances, as in Hosea 4, human failure results in widespread disruption to the natural order.

The final phrase of Hos. 4:3, וגם־דגי הים יאספו 'and even the fish of the sea are perishing' is, in Landy's words, 'metonymic for the whole of creation' and adds an emphatic note to the picture depicted by the prophet.[117] The passive form of the verb אסף in the sense 'to perish' is repeated three times in the reversal of creation of Zeph. 1:

on the two Hosea lists are identical ('birds of the air' and 'beasts of the field'), but the last of the triad differs: דגי־הים, 'fish of the sea' in 4:3 compared with רמש האדמה, 'creeping things of the ground' in 2:20 [18].

[115] DeRoche, 'Reversal of Creation', 404.

[116] Ibid. He notes a similar sequence in Zeph. 1:2–3 for which see DeRoche, 'Zephaniah I 2–3'.

[117] Landy, 'Hosea 2:4–17', 54.

2–3.[118] The verb is used with reference to the natural world in a number of other prophetic texts, in each case within the context of God's judgement, as is the case here.[119] Such a dramatic and out of the ordinary event as the extinction of fish populations suggests that Hosea is describing something 'out of prophetic expectation rather than present experience'.[120]

In these verses of Hosea 4, the inextricable link between human behaviour towards God and other humans and the well-being of the created order is clearly established. This interplay has already been depicted in the poetic oracle of Hosea 2, which, as has been seen, interweaves the language of human marriage and fecundity with that of agricultural fruitfulness. In Hosea 4 the scope has been extended beyond a utilitarian perspective of the land as source of provision for human sustenance. The people's unfaithfulness to YHWH has repercussions, not just on their own land and its fertility, but on the whole created order. In Landy's synchronic reading of Hosea he notes that Hos. 4:3 does not just echo the reversal of creation but introduces the motif of the breaking of the covenant with all creatures of 2:20 [18].[121] Moreover, a new dimension has been added by the appeal to the knowledge of God and his תורה and, by implication, to Israel's covenantal obligations towards YHWH.

In this section of Hosea the people of Israel are charged with 'covenantal unfaithfulness' and the priests with failure as guardians of this crucial commitment in Israel's religious life. The combined lack of moral and religious leadership and of communal responsibility produces an outcome which has far reaching and devastating consequences. Not only have both priests and people abrogated their obligations towards YHWH and allowed moral degradation to become rampant, their actions have set off a reaction which has repercussions far beyond the boundaries of their own society. The chain of act and consequence in these verses suggests an inextricable connection, not just between YHWH and his people, but also between

[118] More commonly used with the sense 'to gather', whether of people (e.g. Exod. 4:29; Josh 24:1), or of the harvest (e.g. Lev. 23:39), but also in the metaphor for death: 'gathered to his peoples' (e.g. Gen. 25:29).

[119] Notably Isa. 10:14, 16:10; Jer. 48:33; Joel 2:10, 4:15 [3: 15]; Zeph. 1:2–3.

[120] G. I. Davies, *Hosea*, 117.

[121] Landy, *Hosea*, 54.

covenant and creation, law and land. Both the covenant with creation in 2:20 [18] and the fracturing of that covenant and the reversal of creation in 4:3 are interwoven with, and contingent upon, the relationship of Israel with her God.

SUMMARY

In the book of Hosea the non-human creation does not play such a pivotal role, either structurally or thematically, as it does in Amos. In terms of the ecological triangle, the overall shape of the book focuses most clearly on the relationship between God and humanity. Hosea's concern to stress the relational nature of YHWH's dealings with Israel is expressed in the context of Israel's cultic traditions, using the imagery of marriage and family life. This relationship is articulated by means of the deliberate interweaving of the themes of land and people in Hosea 2. The indictment against priests and people in Hosea 4 establishes the connection between knowledge of God and ethical behaviour within the community and presents the failure to maintain this relationship with YHWH in terms of the devastation of the natural world. By means of an appeal to cause and effect, act and consequence, the book's dual presentation of warning and hope suggests to its readers that there is a choice to be made—between the reversal or the restoration of the created order.

6

The Vineyard of the Lord of Hosts
YHWH, the People and the Land in Isaiah 1–39

What are the roots that clutch, what branches grow
Out of this stony rubbish? Son of man,
You cannot say, or guess, for you know only
A heap of broken images, where the sun beats,
And the dead tree gives no shelter, the cricket no relief,
And the dry stone no sound of water.

T. S. Eliot, *The Waste Land*

INTRODUCTION

Studies of the book of Isaiah now tend to regard it as a carefully constructed redactional unity instead of two or three separate and independently constructed works brought together under one heading.[1] Numerous scholars have explored the way in which themes from earlier in the book are reused in later sections, and the contribution of such studies to an understanding of the book as a whole is wholeheartedly acknowledged.[2] It might therefore seem to be

[1] See Melugin and Sweeney, *New Visions*, and discussion in G. I. Davies, 'Destiny of the Nations', 107–14.

[2] E.g. Clements, 'Beyond Tradition History'; Conrad, *Isaiah*; G. I. Davies, 'Destiny of the Nations'; Williamson, *Book Called Isaiah*. See also Rendtorff, *Old Testament Introduction*, 198–200.

flying in the face of contemporary scholarship to focus solely on First Isaiah, as this volume does. The reason is simple: far more attention has been given to Second Isaiah's understanding of creation, to the neglect of some important and very different texts in the earlier chapters of Isaiah. Despite the fact that numerous scholars have questioned von Rad's suppositions concerning the 'late' date of Israel's creation ideas, it would still be true to say that First Isaiah has not received the attention it deserves with regard to its creation language and imagery. Even Paas, whose study is specifically concerned with creation in the eighth-century prophets (as noted in Chapter 4), gives far less attention to First Isaiah compared with his treatment of Amos.[3] However, a cursory reading of First Isaiah reveals that it too contains much material about the created world, ranging from passing allusions to rich and detailed descriptions.[4] Motifs of creation play a significant and prominent part, and the reuse of themes, imagery, and vocabulary of the natural world, both within chapters 1–39 and in the whole of Isaiah, suggests that there is a common pool of prophetic material drawn upon by redactors and reused or reapplied to new situations. A detailed examination of some of these natural images and themes in Isaiah 1–39 will enable a better understanding of how such motifs function in the book as a whole.[5]

[3] Paas, *Creation and Judgement.* Most of the Isaiah texts containing 'creation terminology' cited by Paas are concerned either with humans as the object of creation or with YHWH's activity in history, although he does discuss some broader texts under the heading 'motifs of creation'.

[4] For example, in First Isaiah only two chapters make no mention at all of the non-human creation (Isaiah 20 and 39) and a further five have only brief references (Isaiah 3, 21, 22, 26, and 36). This compares positively with the rest of Isaiah—in Isaiah 40–66 there are only two chapters that contain no natural world material (Isaiah 52 and 63) and seven with a negligible amount (Isaiah 46, 47, 48, 54, 57, 62, and 64).

[5] Although all the significant texts concerning the created order will be discussed in this chapter, since First Isaiah is considerably longer than Amos and Hosea not all passing allusions to the natural world will be referred to. First Isaiah perhaps more than Amos or Hosea bears evidence of multiple hands from different periods in Judah's history in its composition and arrangement. As noted in Chapter 4, this exegesis prioritizes a synchronic approach over a diachronic one, whilst noting that some texts clearly reflect a particular historical context, or are reused in new situations. For further discussions, see e.g. Clements, *Isaiah 1–39*, 2–23; Blenkinsopp, *Isaiah 1–39*, 74–92.

The study begins by discussing the few texts in First Isaiah that adopt a cosmological perspective, with a particular focus on Isaiah 24.[6] Then, since First Isaiah gives far greater attention to individual plant and animal species than to cosmic language, the remainder of this chapter will focus on specific texts that reflect tension or harmony between Israel's agricultural and pastoral life and the flora and fauna of the surrounding country. These will include texts that express ideas of natural order in proverbial format (Isa. 1:2–3 and Isa. 28:23–9), the two vineyard parables (Isa. 5:1–7, 27:2–6), and three texts that speak of the devastation and restoration of human society and the natural world (Isa. 34, 35, 11:1–10).

COSMIC UPHEAVAL IN ISAIAH 1–39

The book of Isaiah begins with reference to the cosmos in the appeal to the heavens and the earth in 1:2. Apart from this and Hezekiah's prayer to YHWH as maker of heaven and earth in 37:16, there are only three other significant references to השׁמים 'the heavens' (14: 12–15, 13:9–13, and 34:2–5), each describing some aspect of the heavenly realm and, in the latter two texts, the response of cosmic elements to human activity.

Isaiah 14:12–15

The context of Isa. 14:12–15 is a poetic description of the downfall of a tyrannical ruler (identified as king of Babylon by the superscription of v. 4a), which ridicules his pretentious behaviour and aspirations to divinity (v. 13).[7] Verses 12–19 present a view of the world in which the heights of heaven are contrasted with the deepest recesses of

[6] The cosmic perspective is more characteristic of Second than First Isaiah, (e.g. Isa. 40:21–3, 42:5, 45:7, 12, 18, 48:12–13). It is probably no coincidence that all of the cosmological texts discussed below are in chapters generally not attributed to the 8th-century prophet.

[7] Commentators are generally agreed in suggesting that this text alludes to an ancient myth of the banishment of a divine being from heaven, but are less united in

Sheol, both in terms of spatial location (heights and depths, vv.12–15) and also the relative merits of the two locations: one the place where God dwells (v. 14), the other to be feared far more than the normal process of death and burial (see v. 19).[8] The description does not strictly speaking deal with disturbance in the heavens. Rather, the cosmic references serve to illustrate the hubris of earthly rulers who presume to act like gods, and who will be reduced to nothing, both in the eyes of their contemporaries, and in terms of their legacy (see 14: 16–21).

Isaiah 13:9–13 and 34:2–5

In both 13:9–13 and 34:2–5 the coming judgement of YHWH is described in terms of upheaval in the heavens as well as punishment of the earth's inhabitants.[9] The failed relationship between YHWH and his people, and the consequent drama enacted on the earth is reflected in what happens to the heavenly bodies. In Isaiah 34 the scope of YHWH's judgement is presented as being universal rather than specific to Israel or another nation (על־כל־הגוים 'against all the nations' v. 2), whilst Isaiah 13 is directed at Babylon (as indicated by the superscription 13:1 and vv. 17–19).[10] Although the descriptions of judgement in the two texts are different, a number of broad areas of correspondence can be found.[11]

identifying the meaning of הילל בן־שחר in v. 12. See esp. Watts, *Isaiah 1–33*, 209–11; Wildberger, *Isaiah 13–27*, 62–8.

[8] As was noted in Chapter 4, the contrast between heights of heaven and deepest Sheol is one that features in the final vision of Amos (9:2).

[9] Other similarities between Isaiah 13 and 34 will be discussed later in the chapter, in particular the description of wild animals in 13:20–2 and 34:13–15.

[10] However, the actual description of the day of YHWH in Isa. 13:2–16 is without identification markers, unlike other oracles against named nations which have numerous internal references to the particular nation (e.g. Isaiah 15 and 19). This suggests that, like Isaiah 34, the text of 13:2–16 may have been re-applied to new situations in Israel's history.

[11] See also the discussion on these texts later in the chapter.

1. Both texts are introduced by a series of imperatives calling the people to attention, which establish the proclamatory nature of the succeeding verses (13:2 and 34:1).
2. Both texts speak of the coming day of YHWH, יום יהוה which will be characterized by his fierce anger and destruction (13:9, 34: 8, cf. v.5).[12]
3. Both suggest that the day of YHWH will include darkness. This is explicit in 13:10, and implicit in 34:4 in the description of the heavens rolled up and the withering of their hosts, particularly if כל צבא השמים 'all the hosts of the heavens' is taken as referring to the stars.[13] A similar interplay between darkness and the day of YHWH is found in other prophetic texts (e.g. Joel 2:2, 4:14–15 [3:14–15], Amos 5:18–20 and Zeph. 1:15). The more general concept of darkness accompanying a theophany occurs, among other places, in Mic. 3:6.[14]
4. In both texts, YHWH clearly executes judgement on human behaviour (13:9, 11, 34:2–3), and the effect in the heavens is portrayed as a reflection of this (13:10, 34:4). The heavens are not punished by YHWH for the sins of the people, but his anger disrupts the whole world order: 'All creation is affected by the sins of nations and the necessary divine reaction'.[15]

[12] For discussion of the meaning and origin of the phrase יום יהוה see Bourke, 'Le Jour De Yahvé'; Brin, *Concept of Time*; Čern', *Day of Yahweh*; Hoffmann, 'Day of the Lord'; Munch, *Bajjôm Hāhū*'; Stuart, 'Day of Conquest'; Wilch, *Time and Event*; von Rad, 'Day of Yahweh'; and excursus in Wolff, *Joel and Amos*.

[13] See Leupold, *Isaiah*, 527; Watts, *Isaiah 34–66*, 9; Wildberger, *Isaiah 28–39*, 330. Although the heavens are likened to a curtain in Isa. 40:22, Ps. 104:2 and Zech. 12:1, this is the only instance where they are described as a scroll, an image that is picked up in Rev. 6:14.

[14] See also Sinai theophany in Exod. 19:18–25 and Deut. 4:11; and other theophanies in 2 Sam. 22:10–12 (Ps. 18:11); Ps. 97:2; Ezek. 30:3.

[15] Watts, *Isaiah 34–66*, 9. Houtman also stresses the interconnection between YHWH, people and the cosmos in this text (Houtman, *Himmel im Alten Testament*, 144–5). He notes 'Beim Aufruhr des Kosmos wird deutlich, dass eine tiefe Einheit hinsichtlich des Schicksals und der Bestimmung zwischen dem Menschen und dem Kosmos besteht. Nicht nur der Mensch ist das Opfer des göttlichen Gerichtes, sonder der ganze Kosmos ist von der Manifestation des göttlichen Zornes zutiefst betroffen' (Houtman, *Himmel im Alten Testament*, 145).

ISAIAH 24

A number of other texts in First Isaiah allude to devastation of the earth or parts of it, rather than the heavens, in the context of divine theophany or judgement.[16] The most graphic and extensive description of this is Isa. 24, in particular verses 1–13, which will now be considered in detail.

Isaiah 24–7 is generally regarded as forming a distinct unit, and differs from oracles against named nations in the preceding chapters by the absence of specific geographical and historical markers. This, and the perceived eschatological character of the material, has led to Isaiah 24–7 being viewed by many commentators as a later, exilic or post-exilic addition to predominantly pre-exilic material, and even to its being dubbed the 'Isaiah Apocalypse'.[17] The latter designation is undoubtedly misleading since, as Kissane has observed with regard to these chapters, 'the only characteristics of an apocalypse . . . are the descriptions of a world-judgement and the veiled manner in which the victims of God's wrath are mentioned'—hardly strong enough criteria to merit the title apocalypse.[18] Support is given to Kissane's point if the suggestion of Watts is adopted, namely that הארץ is translated as 'the land' rather than 'the earth'.[19] Doyle also prefers this

[16] E.g. Isa. 2:19, 21, 5:25. The latter may reflect knowledge of the earthquake of *c.*760 BCE, see Paul, *Amos*, 45.

[17] For detailed discussion of issues surrounding the dating, authorship and unity of these chapters see the commentators, especially Kaiser, *Isaiah 13–39*, 173–9; Oswalt, *Isaiah 1–39*, 440–3; Watts, *Isaiah 1–33*, 367–71; Wildberger, *Isaiah 13–27*, 447–51. Despite the variety of opinion among scholars, there is growing consensus that Isaiah 24–7 must also be understood in the context of the preceding chapters (Isaiah 13–23) and vice versa (see Clements, *Isaiah 1–39*; Delitzsch, *Isaiah Vol I*; Vermeylen, *Prophète Isaïe*; Wildberger, *Isaiah 13–27*). Although many scholars now doubt whether any of this material can properly be labelled apocalyptic, many still refer to these chapters as the 'Isaiah Apocalypse'.

[18] Kissane, *Isaiah*, 259; see also G. W. Anderson, 'Isaiah XXIV–XXVII', 118–26.

[19] Watts, *Isaiah 1–33*, 313–17. He suggests that it is the prior interpretive judgement that these chapters are apocalyptic in nature which determines most commentators' choice of 'the earth' in Isaiah 24–7. A number of older commentaries translate ארץ as 'land' in 24:1–13 (e.g. Gesenius, *Jesaia*, 761–3; Lowth, *Isaiah*, 261). Interestingly 1QIsa[a] has האדמה in place of הארץ in 24:1, although it follows the MT on every other occasion.

translation and maintains that the obvious presence of hyperbole (especially in 24:1–13) indicates that these verses are to be understood metaphorically rather than literally, and therefore as referring to real and imminent events rather than apocalyptic or eschatological ones.[20] Whether this necessarily implies an earlier date for these chapters is open to question, and a number of features of this section suggest otherwise, including the pairing of הארץ 'earth/land' with תבל 'world' in 24:4, the latter noun according to *TDOT* being 'almost without exception . . . found in late OT lyric poetry'.[21]

If the majority view of a late date for much of chapters 24–7 is accepted, it is nevertheless evident that significant use has been made of earlier prophetic material. Within Isa. 24:1–13, for example, the description of the land or earth 'mourning' echoes similar vocabulary in Hos. 4:3 and Amos 1:2. Likewise, verses 7–12 comprise a lament or dirge over the failure of the grape harvest which may well have originated separately from a tradition of vineyard songs and laments and has been incorporated here (see also 16:8–10 and Amos 5:16–17).[22] The composition reflects the power of the prophetic oracle, where by virtue of a few changes in emphasis a message originally directed at the people of Israel is reconstructed to encompass the whole world and a powerful Israelite concept concerning the well-being of the land is universalized.

The structure and repetition of key words and phrases in this whole section suggest a poetic and rhythmic account of the interplay between human behaviour and the welfare of the land or earth.[23] The verses follow a structure that is broadly chiastic in form and is centred around verses 3–6 as depicted in Figure 5. Within the central verses 3–6 the interrelationship between YHWH, the inhabitants and

[20] Doyle, *Apocalypse*, 155; see also Johnson, who suggests that the writer is viewing the fall of Jerusalem and exile as a return to chaos and so 'limned his prediction in the cosmic language of the chaos myth' (Johnson, *Chaos to Restoration*, 16).

[21] *TDOT XV*, 561. *TDOT* also notes that the word is primarily associated with cosmological and mythological themes and, with regard to Isa. 24:3–4, concludes that 'the synonymous parallelisms in this paronomastically structured poem address the whole universe'.

[22] Within chapters 24–7 as a whole this dirge is balanced by the vineyard 'song' of 27:2–5 to be discussed later in this chapter.

[23] This is another example of a prophetic text that is open to multiple reapplication in new situations.

A	Opening summary of forthcoming judgment (v. 1)
B	Details of who is affected—all groups of society (v. 2)
C	Emphatic and repetitious description of judgement—its causes and effects (vv. 3–6)
B′	Details of how effect is felt in society (vv. 7–12)
A′	Closing summary of effects of judgement (v. 13)

Figure 5. The chiastic pattern of Isa. 24:1–13

the earth can be clearly seen, with the emphasis on the interaction between people and the landscape they inhabit.

3. The earth will be utterly emptied and
   utterly despoiled, for
   YHWH has spoken this word.
4. The earth mourns and withers,
   the world languishes and withers,
   the heights languish with the earth.[24]
5. The earth is polluted beneath its inhabitants for
   they have passed over the teachings and
   transgressed the statute and
   broken the everlasting covenant.
6. Therefore
   a curse consumes the earth
   its inhabitants are held guilty.
   Therefore
   the inhabitants of the earth are burned up
   and few remain.

Emphasis is provided by the tricola in verse 4 describing the desolation of the earth, followed by the threefold indictment of its inhabitants (v. 5).[25] This culminates in the enigmatic phrase 'broken

[24] Based on BHS proposed emendation.

[25] The root שׁמם to denote specifically the desolation of the natural landscape is found in Isa. 1:7, 5:9, 6:11, 13:9; Hos. 2:14 [12]; and Mic. 7:13.

the everlasting covenant' (הפרו ברית עולם), generally assumed by scholars to refer to either the Noachic or the Mosaic covenant.[26] The term 'everlasting covenant' occurs sixteen times in the Old Testament, yet is never actually used of the covenant with Moses.[27] Nevertheless, as Kissane and Wildberger both point out, the Mosaic covenant is the only biblical one that involves obligations on both sides, and therefore is capable of being broken by the people.[28]

Here in Isaiah 24, as in Hosea 4, failure to adhere to the 'teaching' has serious effects on the physical world, in this case depicted in terms of its pollution and cursing (vv. 5, 6). Pollution of the land in the Old Testament is seen as a result of the shedding of innocent blood (Num. 35:33; Ps. 106:28) and of apostasy (Jer. 3:2–3). In either case it is the direct consequence of human moral and religious failing. Unlike Hosea 4 there is little in Isaiah 24 to indicate what specific transgressions of the people are in view, but the link between these and the disruption of the physical environment is clear. Moreover the laws and statutes are not even identified as those of YHWH, as one might expect. Is this, as Wildberger suggests, evidence of 'a general knowledge of basic rules about how life is to be lived, which have no other outcome than to put one under a curse if ignored'?[29] If so it supports John Barton's notion of an concept of natural law or natural order operating in Israel (or at least in the mind of the author of these verses).[30]

[26] On the one hand, the perceived global aspect of the text, together with the allusion to the flood later in the chapter (v. 18b), is taken as indicative that the covenant with Noah of Gen. 9:12 is in view. See, with varying degrees of certainty, Hayes, *The Earth Mourns*, 150; Kaiser, *Isaiah 13–39*, 527; Oswalt, *Isaiah 1–39*, 446; Vermeylen, *Prophète Isaïe*, 353. On the other hand, the reference to 'the teachings' and 'the statutes' (v. 3) is, for some scholars, more suggestive of the Sinai covenant. See Johnson, *Chaos to Restoration*, 27–9; Kissane, *Isaiah*, 272 and, to a limited extent, Wildberger, *Isaiah 13–27*, 479–80.

[27] The phrase is used to describe the covenants with Noah (Gen. 9:16), with Abraham (Gen. 17:7, 13, 19; 2 Chr. 16:15–16; Ps. 105:10) and with David (2 Sam. 23:5; Isa. 55:3; Ezek. 37:26). It also is found in the context of the Sabbath (Exod. 31:16; Lev. 24:8), and of Levitical rights (Num. 18:19), and in a number of unspecific contexts, mostly eschatological. (Ps. 111:5, 9 in the form לעולם בריתו; Isa. 61:8; Jer. 32:40, 50:5; Ezek. 16:60).

[28] Kissane, *Isaiah*, 271; Wildberger, *Isaiah 13–27*, 480.

[29] Wildberger, *Isaiah 13–27*, 480.

[30] See Barton, *Oracles against the Nations*; and discussion in Chapter 3 of this volume.

Both a curse on the fertility of the land and dispossession or depopulation (Isa. 24:6) form part of the Deuteronomic blessings and cursings.[31] As Deuteronomy 28 makes clear, the productivity of the land is directly dependent on the covenantal obedience of the people, resulting in either the blessings of fruitfulness (vv. 4–5, 8, 11–12), or curses on land and people (vv. 17–18, 23–4, and 38–42). Likewise in Jer. 23:10, in the context of the fall of Jerusalem, the effect of human wickedness is a curse on the land (אלה), leading to mourning (אבל) and drought (יבשׁ). Here both prophets and priests are singled out as polluted in v. 11 (חנף—the same word as is used of the land in Isa. 24:5).[32]

The following section (Isa. 24:7–13) elaborates the effects of this disruption in terms of the failure of the grape harvest and consequent lack of wine (v. 7), resulting in the cessation of harvest celebration (v. 8), and ultimately leading to devastation in the city (v. 10) and uproar among the people (v. 11). The categories of disobedience to the teachings (v. 5) and the ensuing curse provide the framework to explain both the failure of the harvest and the wider disaster, whether in the first instance the national catastrophe of the destruction of Jerusalem, or reapplied later in a more eschatological sense. In either context, the reality of cause and effect is clear: failure to live by YHWH's standards results in disruption of the agricultural rhythms of the land as well as its very infrastructure, both geological and political.

The connection between agricultural failure and urban disruption follows the same pattern as the effect of the Nile drought in Isa. 19:5–10, with both texts using the language of mourning and languishing, אבל, and אמללה.[33] In Isaiah 19 as in Isaiah 24 human dependence on the produce of the land is emphasized and the interconnection between YHWH's standards, human failure to adhere to them and the well-being of the land is clearly established.

[31] Although Deut. 11, 28, and 30 use different vocabulary for 'to curse' (ארר and קלל), אלה occurs five times in Deut. 29, two of which specifically refer back to the curses of Deut. 28 (vv. 19, 20 [ET 20, 21]).

[32] Further descriptions of the physical disruption of the land in Jeremiah can be found in Jer. 4:23–8, 9:10, 12:4, 10–11, and 14:2–6, each attributed to human transgressions, whether implicitly or explicitly.

[33] Also in Isa. 33:9; see Marlow, 'River Nile' and discussion on Amos and Hosea in this volume.

THE LANGUAGE AND IMAGERY OF FLORA AND FAUNA IN ISAIAH 1–39

The majority of references to the created world in First Isaiah are not concerned with cosmological events or descriptions, but with the flora and fauna that formed part of everyday life in ancient Israel. Plants and animals feature in figurative language, such as similes, metaphors, and parables, as well as in descriptions of actual and prophesied disaster or restoration. The importance of agriculture and livestock to Israelite religion and economy, and the constant threat posed by wild animals and encroaching weeds, ensure that such language would be understood even by urban dwellers. In what follows we shall consider some of the imagery that is used to depict the relationship between YHWH, people, and their environment, before looking at oracles of judgement and restoration that also include such interrelationship.

Like Amos and Hosea, First Isaiah is rich in metaphorical language which draws on the author's understanding of the natural world to describe activity or attitudes in the human sphere. Human populations, whether of Judah or of other nations, are likened to plants that can wither, be pruned or threshed (e.g. 1:30, 2:12–17, 5:24, 15:6, 17:13, 18:5–6, 27:11–12, 33:9–11), or to fields that can be overrun by animals or destroyed by fire or other means (e.g. 9:17–18 [18–19], 10:17–18, 17:2). At times the agent is clearly identified as YHWH (e.g. 18:5–6, 9:18–19, 33:9–11), but more often the comparison is phrased in the passive voice, so that only the object affected is identified. However, the context of YHWH's punishment following violation of his laws establishes him as the implicit agent in a number of cases (e.g. 1:30, 5:24). The corollary of these metaphors and similes of punishment is the language of sprouting and regrowth used to describe God's restoration (e.g. 4:2, 11:1, 27:17). On occasions the imagery can bear a double meaning, e.g. the frequent use of the metaphor of a tree to describe Judah. Since a tree may be cut down but can also sprout again, this image is deliberately chosen, as Nielsen explains, to express the ambiguity of YHWH's plans—which include both judgement and salvation for his people.[34]

[34] Nielsen, *Hope for a Tree*, 71–4; see Job 14:7–9.

The fragility of human life is also depicted using animal imagery, which reflects the reality of life in the ancient world. The downfall of nations is couched in terms of danger from wild animals (e.g. 15:6, 18:6). The Assyrian army is likened to a roaring lion (5:29) and a plague of insects (7:18–19) and, in the only animal metaphor in which YHWH is the tenor, he too is described as a roaring lion (31:4). The vulnerability of the people is conveyed by likening them to scattered and terrified animals and birds at the mercy of a predator (10:14, 13:14, 16:2), whilst just a few texts use images of pastoral harmony to indicate God's restoration (e.g. 5:17). In all these images, as in a number of texts we shall consider in more detail, the metaphor is rooted in known species and observable behaviour, which suggest that the author was familiar with the flora and fauna of his day.

APPEAL TO THE NATURAL ORDER—ISA. 1:2–3 AND 28:23–9

But is there anything in First Isaiah to suggest that its authors' understanding goes further than the ability to illustrate their messages from the world of nature? How do they construe the working of the world and the relation between its human and non-human populations? Two texts make specific reference to divinely instituted order in the world of farming and agriculture to illustrate their point. The first, the proverbial saying of Isa. 1:2–3, describes the unvaryingly predictable behaviour of domestic livestock, while the parable of the wise farmer in 28:23–9 is concerned with the rhythm of sowing and harvesting crops.

Isaiah 1:2–3

Like Amos, the book of Isaiah incorporates language of the natural world in its opening verses.[35] These set the tone for what follows,

[35] For discussion of how Isaiah 1 functions in relation to the rest of First Isaiah and the book as a whole see Ackroyd, 'Isaiah I–XII'; Carr, 'Reading Isaiah'; Fohrer, 'Jesaja 1'; Melugin, 'Reading Isaiah 1'; Williamson, 'Relocating Isaiah 1:2–9'.

introducing the created realm as a sphere of action and as a player in the drama. Just as Amos 1:2 speaks of the effects of YHWH's roar of judgement, firstly on a grand scale (the mountains of Carmel), then on pastoral life (the shepherds' pastures), so in Isa. 1:2–3 the language is initially cosmic, then moves into the more 'earthy' sphere of domestic animals. As in Amos the appeal to the cosmos is rhetorical. The Isaiah passage, however, portrays a contrast rather than a sequence of events, establishing an unfavourable comparison between the behaviour of human beings, specifically the people of Judah, and that of their livestock. Both Amos 1:2 and Isa. 1:2–3 are concerned with moral failure, the former as a prelude to YHWH's indictment of foreign nations for war crimes and of Judah and Israel for religious and social sins, the latter with the failure of Judah to recognize and acknowledge YHWH's sovereignty and its implications for her way of life.

Numerous scholars regard the appeal to heaven and earth (Isa. 1: 2) as an example of a prophetic or covenantal lawsuit.[36] However, the use of the plural imperatives from שׁמע 'to hear' and אזן (Hiphil) 'to give ear', both elsewhere in Isaiah and in other prophetic texts, is not at all restricted to legal contexts.[37] Similarly, in Isa. 1:2, the address to heaven and earth is not a legal one.[38] Rather, according to Oswalt, it is an appeal to 'a pattern of living, without which life cannot be sustained'.[39] Houtman takes this one step further when he asks, 'Who better to express a verdict over the breaking of a natural relationship, a creation order, than the creation itself?'[40]

[36] E.g. Clements, *Isaiah 1–39*; Sweeney, *Isaiah 1–39*, 286–7; Watts, *Isaiah 1–33*, 15; Sawyer, *Isaiah*, 8; Wildberger, *Isaiah 1–12*, 9–11. The existence of the 'prophetic lawsuit' as a genre is assumed by certain other works, e.g. Nielsen, *Prophetic Lawsuit*. Although in some cases, use of the imperative plus the presence of terminology such as המשׁפט and ריב would seem to suggest 'lawsuit' material, in practice there is variation and fluidity in the definitions proposed by different commentators. See discussion in Wolff, *Hosea*, 97–8; and Williamson, *Isaiah 1–5*, 26–7.

[37] E.g. Isa. 1:10, 28:23, 32:9, Jer. 13:15.

[38] The suggestion that this represents a lawsuit is comprehensively rebutted by Williamson, 'Isaiah 1 and the Covenant Lawsuit'.

[39] Oswalt, *Isaiah 1–39*, 85.

[40] 'Wer ist mehr imstande, ein Urteil über das Zerbrechen einer natürlichen Beziehung, einer 'Schöpfungsordnung' auszusprechen, als die Schöpfung selbst?' (Houtman, *Himmel im Alten Testament*, 125).

In verse 3 the breakdown of creation order is brought down to earth in the comparison between God's people and the livestock they tend.[41] The wisdom characteristics of this verse have long been noted by scholars.[42] What is significant is the juxtaposition of the appeal to heaven and earth in verse 2a with the family allusion in verse 2b and the proverbial saying (מָשָׁל) in verse 3. The call to 'hear... give ear' in Isa. 28:23 is similarly followed by wisdom material in the parable of the farmer (vv. 24–9), and there are examples of similar encouragement in introductions to instruction material in Proverbs.[43] In Isa. 1:2–3 a number of characteristics of the wisdom traditions can be discerned, in particular the tension between a cosmological perspective and an anthropological one, and the comparison between humans beings and animals.[44]

The latter is illustrated in verses 2b–3, where domestic animals are held up as a model of behaviour and an example of the natural order of life.[45] Comparisons with animals are frequent in the wisdom literature, where animals function as both examples and warnings. Dell's analysis of references to animals in the Psalms and wisdom literature draws attention to the rich variety and broad scope of the language used, which includes descriptions of the limitations of human understanding in comparison with that of animals.[46] It is this contrast that is presented in Isa. 1:3. A number of commentators have suggested that the proverbial stupidity and stubbornness of the ass and ox are implied in this verse and constitute an *a fortiori* argument in favour of the people's stupidity.[47] Whether such

[41] First Isaiah is specifically addressed to the southern kingdom, Judah (1:1). However, the designation 'Israel' is frequently used, including here in 1:3, for either the southern kingdom or both kingdoms (see Kratz, 'Israel in Isaiah', 103–5).

[42] Isa. 1:3 forms a significant part of Whedbee's argument for the presence of wisdom influences in the book of Isaiah (Whedbee, *Isaiah and Wisdom*, 26–43). The extent of wisdom motifs in First Isaiah is questioned by Williamson, *Isaiah 1–5*, 27–8; see also discussion on Isa. 28:25–9 later in this chapter.

[43] E.g. Prov. 4:1, 5:1.

[44] See Dell, 'Animal Imagery'; Perdue, *Wisdom and Creation.*

[45] According to the infancy narrative of the *Gospel of Pseudo-Matthew* (6th-century CE), this verse in Isaiah was fulfilled when an ox and ass worshipped at the manger of newborn Jesus (Schneemelcher, *Apocrypha*, 462).

[46] Dell, 'Animal Imagery', 275–91.

[47] Delitzsch, *Prophecies of Isaiah*, 1:59; Whedbee, *Isaiah and Wisdom*, 40–1.

commentators are right is open to question; Whedbee, for example, draws on scant and inconclusive evidence from biblical texts and ancient Near Eastern parallels to make this point.[48]

On the contrary, in the wider biblical context, the ass and ox are regarded as valued domestic animals, often cited together, and perhaps typifying a settled agricultural prosperity. Various stipulations in the law (in particular the Book of the Covenant and Deuteronomy) concern responsible ownership, including compensation for theft or death of a domestic animal.[49] In Job 24:3 the wickedness of those who seize asses and oxen from orphans and widows is described. Most striking, perhaps, is the story of Balaam's ass in Num. 22, in which the donkey both recognizes the angel of YHWH and is enabled to speak, in contrast to Balaam's apparent obduracy.

The power of the imagery in Isa. 1:2–3 is constituted by the contrast, not between supposedly intelligent human beings and senseless beasts, but rather between those of God's creatures who act according to their God-given instincts and those who deliberately shun the divinely instituted moral order.[50] The animals of the field not only recognize their owner's dwelling, but know that they will find shelter, food, and water there at the end of a day's work. It is part of their way of life. Yet Israel has failed to show even this degree of understanding: 'Israel does not know (ידע), my people do not understand' (v. 3) and has therefore acted in a way contrary to God's order and command.[51] A similar comparison is found in Jer. 8:7, 'Even the stork in the sky knows (ידע) her appointed times; the turtle dove, the swallow and the crane keep the time of their coming [ie migration], but my people do not know (ידע) the justice of YHWH'.[52]

[48] Whedbee, *Isaiah and Wisdom*, 40. In the Sumerian proverbial collection he refers to, both the restoration and translation of some of the proverbs is uncertain, casting doubt on their meaning (cf. E. Gordon, *Sumerian Proverbs*, 230–44).

[49] E.g. Exod. 21:33–6, 22:1–4, Deut. 22:1–4.

[50] Barton, 'Ethics in Isaiah', 11.

[51] One of several occasions in Isaiah 1–39 where 'Israel' appears to be a generic term for God's people, rather than the northern Kingdom in contrast to the southern Kingdom, Judah. See Eichrodt, 'Prophet and Covenant', 170–2.

[52] מועדיה 'her times' and עת באנה 'time of their coming' presumably refer to migratory seasons; each of the birds named is well known for its annual migration.

As already noted with respect to Hosea, the failure of knowledge and understanding—of YHWH and his ways—results in devastation and desolation, and it is this scenario that plays out in Isa. 1:4–9.[53] The two metaphorical fields employed in these verses encapsulate the interrelational nature of the prophet's thought. First, Israel's plight is depicted in terms of a badly beaten and bruised body (vv. 5–6), with the suggestion that the nation's trauma is self-inflicted (v. 5). Secondly, the desolation encompasses the land, with both city and countryside destroyed (vv. 7–8). Here, as in the description of Hosea's marriage in Hos. 2, reality and metaphor merge, as the devastation of verse 7, which may indeed refer to the actual effect of enemy invasion, elides into the remnant simile of verse 8.[54]

The rest of Isaiah 1 gives further details of the scope of Israel's lack of knowledge: God's people are charged with 'rebellion' (v. 4), 'futile offerings' (v. 12), 'evil-doing' (v. 16), but above all with the failure of the powerful to exercise justice and righteousness towards the needy (vv. 17 and 21). The chapter also spells out other consequences of their rebellion in addition to the desolation of war in verses 7–9, namely the ineffectiveness of their sacrifices and prayers (vv. 12–15) and destruction of those who persist in rebellion (v. 28).

These opening verses of First Isaiah serve to highlight several important aspects of the book. First, as in Amos, YHWH's intention to speak demands a response on the part of the cosmos, and of its inhabitants, a response that is amplified in the succeeding verses. Secondly, the inclusion of both cosmological elements, 'heavens and earth' and some more earthy aspects of creation, namely ox and ass, establishes the scope of YHWH's authority over his creation. Thirdly, the contrast set up between the behaviour of the animals and that of God's people indicates an understanding of the divinely ordained world order, which Israel has chosen to ignore. Finally, verse 3 suggests a parallel between a farmer's relationship with his animals, and that between YHWH and his people. In response to the hard work and obedience of his animals, the farmer provides food and

[53] The concept of knowledge and understanding is used elsewhere in First Isaiah as a synonym for following the ways and teaching (תורה) of YHWH or even for his presence itself, e.g. 5:13, 6:9–10, 11:2, 9, 27:11, 28:9, 29:24. See Rignell, 'Isaiah 1', 142.

[54] See discussion on vineyard imagery later in this chapter.

shelter. This mirrors YHWH's care for Israel, which has to all intents and purposes been thrown back in his face.

Isaiah 28:23–9

Like Isa. 1:2–3, this passage is regarded by many commentators as following the pattern of a משׁל or wisdom instruction, and is described by Whedbee as 'swarming with wisdom characteristics'.[55] The significance of what is, at face value, a simple statement of farming activity has puzzled interpreters, for neither the addressees nor the point of the poem are specified. Indeed Kaiser observes that it is only its location within a prophetic text rather than a wisdom collection that leads one to look for hidden meaning or even regard it as a משׁל.[56]

The MT is not without lexical and linguistic difficulties, including identification of the crops enumerated in verse 25, but according to Whedbee, 'not in a way that would cripple an interpretative effort'.[57] In verse 28, instead of the MT: 'he surely will not thresh it forever; the wheel of his cart and his horses move noisily but do not crush it', the LXX has a significant difference: 'for I will not always be angry with you, nor will my voice of bitterness trample you underfoot'.[58] The interpretive note introduced by the LXX translator perhaps helps explain the tendency among older commentators to read the poem allegorically, with the language of threshing denoting YHWH's judgement. Just as the farmer does not perpetually thresh his crops, so too God's judgement will eventually be replaced by his salvation.[59]

[55] Whedbee, *Isaiah and Wisdom*, 54. Other commentators who emphasize its wisdom connections include Beuken, *Isaiah 28–39*, 60; Kaiser, *Isaiah 13–39*, 258; Watts, *Isaiah 1–33*, 375–6; Wildberger, *Isaiah 28–39*, 51–3. Clements regards it as a parable (Clements, *Isaiah 1–39*, 232) and Sweeney as an allegory (Sweeney, *Isaiah 1–39*, 264).

[56] Kaiser, *Isaiah 13–39*, 259.

[57] Whedbee, *Isaiah and Wisdom*, 51. See also Beuken, *Isaiah 28–39*, 64.

[58] *οὐ γὰρ εἰς τὸν αἰῶνα ἐγὼ ὑμῖν ὀργισθήσομαι οὐδὲ φωνὴ τῆς πικρίας μου καταπατήσει ὑμᾶς.*

[59] Delitzsch, *Prophecies of Isaiah*, vol. 1; Kissane, *Isaiah* and more recently Sweeney, *Isaiah 1–39*. The LXX translation of the enigmatic צו לצו 'command to

Whedbee rejects this and other similar interpretations and instead suggests that the parable (as he designates it) has a disputational function; it is the prophet's response to the scoffing of his hearers. In this Whedbee follows Begrich's identification of disputational speeches in other prophetic texts such as Amos 3:3–7, in which the prophet supposedly uses the techniques of question and answer, assertion and counter-assertion, to defend his viewpoint and counter opponents. Whether or not Begrich's analysis is correct, Whedbee does not explain satisfactorily how Isaiah 28 fits that model, since he can find no specific evidence of the prophet's message being attacked (in contrast to Amos 3:7). He concludes that the parable affirms the wisdom of YHWH, since 'YHWH's actions, like the farmer's, bear one of the hallmarks of wisdom—namely, the ability to match the proper method with the proper time'.[60]

Whedbee's perspective undoubtedly reflects his desire to identify wisdom traditions in the book of Isaiah as is suggested by his translation of verse 29b: 'he [YHWH] is wonderful in counsel and great in wisdom'.[61] Although תושׁיה is found primarily in the wisdom books of the Hebrew Bible (Job 6 times, Prov. 4 times) it does not always convey the sense of 'wisdom' in the way that Whedbee intends.[62] Here in Isa. 28:29 a better rendering in the context is 'he causes success to be great' indicating the agricultural productivity to be expected from those who follow God's instructions (v. 26).[63] A similar intention may be behind the use of the same word, תושׁיה in Mic. 6:9, which is followed by the failure of crops as the consequence of iniquity.

Although Whedbee cites other Isaiah oracles to demonstrate the prophet's confrontation with his opponents (e.g. 5:19–21), these are

command' and קו לקו 'line to line' in v. 10 of this chapter as respectively θλῖψις 'suffering', and ἐλπίς 'hope', may also support this interpretation.

[60] Whedbee, *Isaiah and Wisdom*, 62.

[61] Ibid. 52.

[62] It occurs twice in parallel with חכמה, 'wisdom' (Job 11:6, 26:3) and once paralleling עצה 'counsel' (Prov. 8:14), but in other places the meaning is less specific (in parallel with עזרה 'help' in Job 6:13, with עז 'strength' in Job 12:16 and with מזמה 'purpose' in Prov. 3:21), and it is better translated 'success' in Job 5:12.

[63] This is supported by Syr. of 28:29 with ܐܘܪܒ ܬܪܒܝܬܐ 'he causes growth to increase' (Leiden Critical Edition). Both LXX and Tg. differ significantly from MT (see Driver and Gray, *Job*, part II, 30–1).

fragmentary and do not necessarily provide the clearest interpretive key.[64] A more satisfactory explanation can be found if the parable is read in its immediate context.[65] The preceding verses (vv. 14–22) have highlighted the attempt by political leaders in Jerusalem to bring security by alliance with Assyria—couched in heavily satirical terms as a 'covenant with death' (v. 15). But the prophet reminds them that it is YHWH who has established Zion on a sure foundation (v. 16), and that he will re-establish his standards of justice and righteousness in it (v. 17).[66]

This description of divine order and rule in the city has its parallel in the agricultural sphere, as verses 24–8 illustrate. That God is the provider of order in the world is demonstrated by the fact that, in the agricultural setting, living in harmony with the rhythms of the seasons and using farming methods appropriate to the type of crop are what ensures successful harvests (vv. 24–5, 27–8).[67] Moreover it is from YHWH that a farmer receives the knowledge and understanding to farm correctly in this way (v. 26) and to enjoy success. So the poem becomes a parable of how to live in the world—by acknowledging YHWH as the creator and guarantor of order and by working in harmony with him and the principles he has established.

A further possibility presents itself if the poem is read in tandem with Isa. 1:2–3, which may be warranted by the opening instruction to listen, common to both passages (1:2, 28:23). Just as the children of God were compared unfavourably with livestock in 1:3, perhaps here the 'sophisticated' rulers of Jerusalem, with perceived wisdom and understanding (v. 9), are being contrasted with a 'humble' farmer, faithfully and wisely tending his land, in harmony with the

[64] Whedbee, *Isaiah and Wisdom*, 62–3.

[65] Although many commentators regard the chapter as composite (e.g. Clements, *Isaiah 1–39*; Kaiser, *Isaiah 13–39*; Wildberger, *Isaiah 28–39*), Sweeney argues convincingly for reading it as a whole, in particular drawing attention to the call to instruction in v. 14 which parallels that in v. 23, and the summary-appraisal in v. 22b (see also v. 29), as well as the overall theme of the threat of Assyria (Sweeney, *Isaiah 1–39*, 361).

[66] Although יסד (v. 16) is in participle form in 1QIsa[a] (piel) and 1QIsa[b] (qal) instead of 3 m s piel, and LXX has the future ἐμβαλῶ, the MT is to be preferred as the more difficult reading. See Irwin, *Isaiah 28–33*, 30–1.

[67] That the seasonal rhythms derive from YHWH, and are a sign of his blessing, is echoed by the J account of the Noachic covenant (Gen. 8:21–2).

divinely appointed methods and seasons.[68] YHWH's response to such faithfulness is to grant success, demonstrated in the size of the harvest (v. 29).

In both 1:2–3 and 28:23–9 the idea of divine order in the world is not an abstract impersonal quality, but is associated with the relationship between YHWH, his people and the world around them. In Isa. 1 this is indicated both by the language of parent/children in verse 2, and also in the reference to animals' relationship with their owners. In Isaiah 28 the farmer's sensitive understanding and working of his land is the fruit of the teaching of his God (v. 26) and rewarded by YHWH with abundance (v. 29).

THE VINEYARD PARABLES

The idea that the relationship between a farmer and his crops illustrates the principles of divine order in the world is echoed in a very different fashion in the two vineyard parables (5:1–7, 27:2–6). These texts demonstrate the interrelationship between YHWH and his people using the imagery of viticulture, part of the agricultural mainstay of Israelite economy.[69]

Isaiah 5:1–7

This short text, identified as original to Isaiah of Jerusalem by most commentators, has been the subject of much study, not least because of its reuse and reinterpretation in both Jewish and Christian traditions, including the reworking of the vineyard motif in Isa. 27:2–6.[70] In *Tg. Isa.* the translation of 5:1–7 into Aramaic is, as usual, very free and gives a strongly allegorical interpretation undoubtedly

[68] See Oswalt, *Isaiah 1–39*, 522.

[69] Walsh, *Viticulture*, 27.

[70] For the most extensive recent discussion of Isaiah's vineyard parable, see Williamson, *Isaiah 1–5*, 316–44.

influenced by later historical events.[71] The New Testament parable of the vineyard (Matt 21:33–46; Mark 12:1–12) draws on the traditions behind the Targum and other sources to reinterpret Isa. 5:1–7 as an attack on the Jewish leaders of the day.[72]

Much of the secondary literature has been concerned with identifying the form and function of the text. In his article 'The Genre of Isaiah 5:1–7', Willis suggests twelve possibilities before concluding that the text represents 'a parabolic song of a disappointed husbandman'.[73] Gale Yee is one of a number who note the similarities with the juridical parable of the poor man's lamb in 2 Samuel 12. She also compares Isa. 5:1–7 with Deuteronomy 32 before suggesting that the passage is composed of 'two similar but also functionally different literary forms', namely a song and a juridical parable.[74]

Probably the most helpful observation on the interpretation of 5:1–7 is Gary Williams' suggestion that the parable be understood dynamically as it unfolds.[75] The strength of it as a communicative device lies in the fact that audiences continually have to revise their interpretation of it. So, although the poem is initially addressed to the poet's friend, the addition of לכרמו 'for his vineyard' to the opening song suggests a figurative reinterpretation as a lover's song (v. 1), the care of the vineyard symbolizing a husband's provision for his wife (v. 2).[76] But this interpretation is frustrated by the lack of

[71] Chilton, *Isaiah Targum*, 10–11. According to Weren, the Targumic interpretation is probably inspired by the destruction of the Second Temple in 70 CE (Weren, 'Isaiah 5, 1–7', 14).

[72] Including *I Enoch 83–90* and 4Q500. See G. Brooke, '4Q500 1', 268–94; Evans, *Jesus and His Contemporaries*, 394–403.

[73] Willis, 'Isaiah 5:1–7', 359.

[74] Yee, 'Isaiah 5:1–7'. Her analysis is critiqued by Sheppard ('Anti-Assyrian Redaction', 206–7).

[75] G. R. Williams, 'Isaiah V 1–7'.

[76] Williams is not alone in suggesting that the use of דוד 'beloved' in conjunction with כרם can have erotic connotations (Nielsen, *Hope for a Tree*, 94–7; Watts, *Isaiah 1–33*, 53–4). However, Song of Solomon is the only biblical example of such a juxtaposition, although similar examples can be found in Egyptian and Akkadian literature (Willis, 'Isaiah 5:1–7', 345–6), perhaps indicating that a sexual interpretation is not necessarily what Isaiah had in mind. Indeed Williams himself points out that דוד can also mean friend (G. R. Williams, 'Isaiah V 1–7', 460 fn. 6; see also Wildberger, *Isaiah 1–12*, 179–80). Furthermore, Isa. 5:1 uses the variant form ידיד, which nowhere in the OT carries an erotic meaning and is used primarily to describe the relationship between YHWH and Israel (Deut. 33:12; Ps. 60:7 [5]; Ps. 108:7 [6];

good grapes (perhaps signifying children), and the 'song' becomes a matrimonial complaint (v. 3). The change of person in verse 3 invites the audience to further adjust their understanding and identify not with some unknown third party, but with the singer himself. It is only in verse 7 that the final reinterpretation takes place, in which the audience are confronted with their own role as the fruitless vineyard, and the wild grapes are identified as the social abuses of their day.[77] Reading the parable dynamically in this way highlights the repeated frustration of the interpreter's expectations and, according to Williams, 'this hermeneutical frustration is a literary device which strengthens the main message of the song: Yahweh's frustrated expectations concerning Judah'.[78]

The observations of Laurence Boadt on the oral and rhetorical qualities of the poem fit well with Williams' suggestion.[79] Boadt observes that the structure has two parts or stanzas, one positive (vv. 1–4) and the other negative (vv. 5–7). Within each one are two smaller strophes, representing an element of the parable (v. 1–2, v. 5–6) followed by commentary/judgement (v. 3–4, v. 7), in an A B : A′ B′ format. The whole makes for an oral presentation of maximum dramatic impact. Other features which, he suggests, enhance the oral impact are the delay in revealing the protagonists until the very end, the repetition of key phrases, the direct addressing of questions to the audience, and the wordplay of the final line.

Both the choice of imagery used to depict God's people, and the way in which the metaphor develops in the text give a valuable insight into the relational dynamic as well as the principles of divine order. The figurative use of vineyard language is particularly significant in the light of the importance of viticulture in ancient Israel and the frequency with which the prophetic books refer to vines and vineyards.

Ps. 127:2). The only other usages are in address to the King (Ps. 45:1 [title]) and describing the courts of YHWH (Ps. 84:2 [1]).

[77] Alter suggests that this is a characteristic of prophetic poetry: '[It] is thus very often constructed as a *rhetoric of entrapment*, whether in the sequence of a few lines or on the larger scale of a whole prophecy' (Alter, *Biblical Poetry*, 144; author's italics).

[78] G. R. Williams, 'Isaiah V 1–7', 465.

[79] Boadt, 'Prophetic Persuasion', 12–16.

Vineyards and viticulture in the biblical text

The prevalence and importance of vineyards in the ancient Near East from as far back as the Early Bronze Age has been well documented in archaeological and epigraphical records.[80] According to Walsh, although there is some evidence of viticulture in ancient Egypt and Mesopotamia, the large amount of silt produced by their rivers in flood would not provide the well-drained soil required by vines.[81] Hence viticulture was minimal and wine remained a rare luxury commodity centred round the royal court. However, the ecological conditions of ancient Israel—water resources, soil composition, and long hot dry summers meant that viticulture flourished in Palestine and was a crucial part of the economy.[82]

Both Borowski and Frick draw attention to the importance attributed to other crops such as grain, olives, and figs in the ancient world.[83] However, it is noticeable that the poetic and prophetic books of the Old Testament make far more reference to vines and vineyards than to other agricultural commodities. Whilst there are approximately forty-five references to vineyards (כרם) and vines (גפן) in these books, the fig tree (תאנה) occurs in only twenty-one contexts, of which sixteen are in parallel with vine. There are even fewer references to grain and olives.[84]

An explanation for this preference is partly due to the aptness of vines as a metaphorical description, as suggested by both Nielsen and Walsh.[85] The constant attention required by a vineyard compared with the hardy olive tree, combined with the appearance of a deciduous vine—apparently dead in winter, but sprouting vigorously with new growth in the spring—make it a good source of imagery for

[80] Borowski, *Agriculture*, 102–14; Broshi, 'Bread', 144–55; Hopkins, 'Bare Bones', 132–4; Matthews, 'Treading the Winepress', 19–31; Walsh, *Viticulture*.

[81] Walsh, *Viticulture*, 22–7.

[82] Ibid. 21–32; see also Matthews, 'Treading the Winepress', 21.

[83] Borowski, *Agriculture*, 114–17; Frick, 'Olive Cultivation', 3–5.

[84] References to fig and olive in the prophets comprise both figurative use and actual descriptions, as is the case with vineyard/vines references. The approximate proportions are: תאנה 'fig': figurative (metaphor/simile/parable) 7 times, literal 14 times; זית 'olive': figurative 11 times, literal 4 times.

[85] Nielsen, *Hope for a Tree*, 76–8; Walsh, *Viticulture*, 250.

biblical writers. However, a large number of vineyard references in the prophetic books appear to denote actual rather than metaphorical descriptions (e.g. Isa. 7:23; Jer. 31:5; Joel 1:7).[86] How might this literal usage of vine and vineyard language be explained?

In the prophetic texts, the literal use of such terminology is often accompanied by the verb נטע, 'to plant'. Two such references are couched in the negative, describing the failure of planted vineyards to produce wine (Amos 5:11, which is echoed in Zeph. 1:13). The others represent a more optimistic view in which the future restoration and stability of Israel is characterized, among other things, by planting of vineyards (Isa. 37:30, 65:21; Jer. 31:5; Ezek. 28:26; Amos 9:14). Although in these verses the notion of planting a vineyard is not used figuratively in the sense that the vineyard itself refers to the people of God, the concept does function as a metonymy to describe an ideal future or the lack of it. Encapsulated in that single agricultural task is the prophetic understanding of the blessing of YHWH and the settled and fertile life represented by living under his favour. This is highlighted by Ezek. 28:26, 'and they shall plant vineyards and live in security', a verse that culminates with the prophetic refrain 'and they will know that I am YHWH their God'.

In Amos 9:14–15, a wordplay emphasizes the connection between the restoration of physical fruitfulness and YHWH's concern for his people, as the metonymic use of the phrase 'they will plant vineyards' in verse 14 is followed in verse 15 by the use of the same verb (נטע) to describe YHWH re-establishing Judah in its land. In contrast, in Amos 5:11 the failure to live by YHWH's standards is exemplified by the lack of social justice, which results in the failure of the vines. In both positive and negative references, the prophets use the concept of planting vineyards to symbolize the profound and enduring interconnection between obedience to YHWH and well-being, failure to obey and ruin.

An understanding of the significance of vineyards can be clearly seen in First Isaiah who, of all the prophets, makes most frequent reference to vines and vineyards.[87] Apart from the second vineyard

[86] Excluding Song of Solomon where the blurring of the distinction between figurative and literal usage of words leads to ambiguity of meaning.

[87] A total of 20 times, using two words: כרם (15 uses in 8 texts) and גפן (5 uses). This includes the false promises of the King of Assyria in Isa. 36:16–17. There are no

parable in Isaiah 27, which carries an ambivalent interpretation, and the promises of restoration of vineyards as an indication of peace in the narrative of Isaiah 36–7, all the references to vineyards in Isaiah 1–39 are in the context of destruction or loss, only one of which (apart from the two parables) is clearly figurative.[88] On other occasions the reference is to a real situation, e.g. the failure of the grape harvest (16:8–10) or the destructive force of an invading army (7:23–5). Each conveys an underlying sense of the connection between YHWH's favour and the well-being of the land and the people.

Moreover, the metonymic nature of this terminology is given further emphasis in a number of Isaiah texts, including the two vineyard parables, by the use of שׁמיר ושׁית 'thorns and briers' to describe the opposite of fruitfulness and well-being. In addition to the parables, it is found in opposition to vines in 7:23–5 (three times) to denote the outcome of the threatened destruction of Jerusalem. Isaiah 32:13 uses שׁמיר with קוץ 'thorn bush' to signify a similar idea, again in contrast to the fertile vineyards.[89] Behind these literal descriptions of the reversion of fertile vineyards to thorny scrubland lies a symbolic understanding. Just as fruitful vines epitomize the blessings of YHWH, so too the presence of thorns and briers denotes removal of those blessings, and the downfall and degradation of the nation, not just its physical environment.[90]

Returning now to Isa. 5:1–7, it can be seen that the vineyard imagery operates on two levels. The first is the parabolic nature

references in Second Isaiah and only two in Third Isaiah. The next closest is Jeremiah with 13 references, then Ezekiel (eight references), Hosea, Joel, Amos (four each), Micah and Zechariah with two each and the remainder of the prophets one each.

[88] The simile in 1:8. In other prophetic texts, restoration of Israel's fortunes is epitomized by the success of the vines, e.g. Mic. 4:4, which adds this promise to its reiteration of Isa. 2:2–4.

[89] Whether Nielsen is correct that this latter usage represents a departure from an established metaphor, which indicates that the destruction is to be understood as an actual event, is debatable, since 7:23–5 is just as much concerned with the literal destruction of the vineyards (Nielsen, *Hope for a Tree*, 105).

[90] In 9:17 [18] and 10:17, שׁמיר ושׁית is used on its own (i.e. without reference to vineyards) in what Nielsen describes as a figurative sense (ibid. 104–5). But the imagery in these verses is somewhat different, since, as she suggests, 'thorns and briers' is used alongside 'thickets of the forest' (9:17) and 'glory of the forest' (10:17) to signify the bottom and top of the social hierarchy, whether of Israel (Isaiah 9) or Assyria (Isaiah 10).

of the text, in which the gradual revealing of the identity of the participants heightens the dramatic impact. Once the denouement has been reached, the high degree of preparation and care needed for successful vine growing can be understood as an epitome of the lavish attention YHWH has bestowed on his beloved people (v. 2). Since this has not produced the expected result (v. 4), YHWH's response is the undoing of what had been done before—the removal of protection, and the cessation of nurture (vv. 5–6). This will leave the nation open to being overrun by other forces—perhaps an invading army as many commentators suggest. The cultivated settled people of God, his 'vineyard', will be replaced by overgrown, arid wasteland.[91]

The second level of figurative language is encapsulated in the contrast between vines and 'thorns and briers' (v. 6a). Besides the identification of the vineyard with the nation, the use of these opposites constructs a picture of barrenness replacing fertility, poverty replacing fruitfulness, disaster replacing security.[92] The withholding of rain, itself a sign of God's blessing, further enhances this symbolism (v. 6b). But it is a picture rooted in the economic and social reality of pre-exilic Judah, communicating to an audience who knew how quickly unfenced vineyards could be trampled or overrun by weeds, who recognized their dependence on the seasonal rains to ensure a good harvest, and who in their cultic life (in theory at least) acknowledged the role of YHWH as giver and sustainer of life, including agricultural fecundity.

The final verse does more than simply identify the characters in the parable and bring the message of condemnation home to roost. It suggests that the threatened downfall of the vineyard is rooted in the nation's failure to produce justice and righteousness—the fruit expected by YHWH. But to whom exactly is the parable addressed? The

[91] The philosopher and ecologist Bernard Callicott observes that 'thorns and thistles attend disturbed, eroded, and exhausted soil' ('Genesis', 139 fn. 83).

[92] In the LXX where *ἄκανθος* 'thorn bushes' translates both באשׁים (v. 2, 4) and שׁמיר (v. 6), the comparison is perhaps more emphatically presented, and is heightened in v. 6 when YHWH 'deserts' his vineyard (*ἀνήσω τὸν ἀμπελῶνά μου*) rather than appoints it for destruction (ואשׁיתהו בתה).

meaning of 'inhabitant of Jerusalem, man of Judah' in verse 3 and 'house of Israel, man of Judah' in verse 7 has been the subject of much debate, in particular whether the condemnation applies to both kingdoms, or whether the two designations in verse 7 are used synonymously.[93] The prevailing tendency is to regard them as collectives for the general population—either of both kingdoms, or, if the parallelism here is that of greater precision (where the second line of the couplet further defines the first), of Judah.[94]

The following verses (vv. 8–10) condemn the selfish accumulation of wealth and property by a ruling minority—the same group as is also censured in 3:14–15 for robbing the poor of their vineyards. If, as most commentators maintain, the parable is addressed to the entire Judean population, v. 8 with its focus upon a subsection of Jerusalem society represents a significant shift in emphasis, as is also signalled by the introductory formula הוי 'woe' (v. 8 and five further times in this chapter). An alternative suggestion is the social scientific perspective of Chaney who argues that the addressees of verses 3 and 7, all morphologically singular, denote the ruling elite and dynastic powers of both kingdoms.[95] Verses 8–10 further condemn their actions and prophesy actual fruitlessness for their immorally acquired vineyards.[96] So the parable, with rich irony, condemns those who have stolen vineyards by using the very same vineyard imagery to describe their downfall. The powerful wordplay in Hebrew in verse 7 between מִשְׁפט 'justice' and מִשְׂפח 'bloodshed', and צדקה 'righteousness' and צעקה 'a cry' (not reproduced in the LXX and impossible to render in English), provides a resounding rhetorical ending to a parable that is remarkable for its succinct literary and artistic quality.

[93] Yee argues that the northern kingdom as well as the southern is included in the indictment (Yee, 'Isaiah 5:1–7', 37–39), whilst Nielsen takes the opposite view (Nielsen, *Hope for a Tree*, 108–14).

[94] Williamson, *Isaiah 1–5*, 342–44. On this form of parallelism see Clines, 'Parallelism of Greater Precision'.

[95] Chaney, 'Whose Sour Grapes'.

[96] See also Mic. 2:2.

Isaiah 27:2–6

This second vineyard parable is regarded by many as a positive reinterpretation of the first song in 5:1–7.[97] Presumed to date from the post-exilic period, against the background of Jewish/Samaritan discord, its message is generally understood as one of comfort and encouragement to the returnees, whilst also inviting Samaritans to find refuge with YHWH.[98] But both the late dating and the unequivocally positive interpretation of the text can be called into question. The fragmentary and often difficult nature of the Hebrew in this section has caused problems for both translation and interpretation, and led to a number of suggested emendations by scholars.[99]

In that day, a delightful vineyard, sing of it;
It is I, the Lord who watches over her,
at every moment I water her.
Lest someone attacks [lit: visits] her,
day and night I watch over her.
I have no rage—yet who has given me thorns and briers?
Let me march out against her in battle; let me set fire to her, all at once.
Or, let him grow strong in my protection,
let him make peace for me, peace let him make for me.
In days to come, Jacob will take root, Israel will blossom and sprout forth,
They will fill the surface of the world with produce.

[97] Commentators differ over whether the section ends at v. 5 or v. 6., or even, as Lindblom suggests, at v. 11 (Lindblom, *Jesaja-Apokalypse*, 53–60), a proposal that has been vigorously refuted by Johnson (*Chaos to Restoration*, 86). The debate generally hinges around whether the first word of v. 6, הבאים, represents an introductory formula similar to ביום ההוא (v. 2), or a closing one, (see Oswalt, *Isaiah 1–39*, 224; Wildberger, *Isaiah 13–27*, 583). A number of scholars recognize that v. 6, whilst having continuity with the subject matter of the preceding verses, is most likely a later addition and constitutes an additional explanatory note—a 'postscript to the song' as Kaiser terms it (Kaiser, *Isaiah 13–39*, 583).

[98] See Jacob, 'Esaïe 27, 2–5'; Nielsen, *Hope for a Tree*, 116–17; Vermeylen, *Prophète Isaïe*.

[99] Both the LXX and the Targum differ greatly from the Hebrew, the latter in particular in vv. 4–6.

Neither the juxtaposition of 27:2–5 to the strongly mythical element of 27:1, nor the prefacing of the parable with ביום ההוא (undoubtedly the work of a redactor) in themselves necessitate that the core of the material should be categorized as of post-exilic origin, since it contains nothing that is specifically eschatological.[100] There are no historical markers within the section itself, so attempts to give it a particular setting are at best speculative.

Indeed, given the apparent predilection for vines and vineyard imagery shown by Isaiah of Jerusalem, together with the use in 27:4 of one of his stock phrases, 'thorns and briers', one cannot but ask whether there is any reason why these verses could not originate from the eighth-century prophet himself. Could this be a reworking of his own highly successful imagery emanating perhaps from a later period of his life at a time when there were signs of hope and restoration (under Hezekiah's reign for instance), which has been incorporated into later material and hence reapplied to a post-exilic context?

If so this would help explain the subtle and often neglected correspondences between 5:1–7 and 27:2–5. The imagery in these two songs is not antithetical as many suggest but complementary, in that one fills in the gaps left by the other. So the two descriptions give details of different aspects of viticulture. In Isa. 5 the preparation of the ground and planting of the vines is described; that such preparation has been undertaken is assumed from the start of 27:2, otherwise how could the vineyard be described as חמד 'delightful'?[101] The protection of the vineyard that is directly ascribed to YHWH in 27:3 is implicit in 5:2, which describes the building of a watch tower in the vineyard. Similarly, the fact that the vineyard is watered (27:3) is also implied by the threat of the withholding of rain in 5:6?

There are however also some notable differences. The opening verb of 27:2 is ענה (compared with שׁיר in 5:1), one root of which signifies 'to respond' (BDB I), another 'to sing' (BDB IV), and there is some suggestion that these two roots overlap or even originally coincided.[102]

[100] As Jacob points out, the chapter is better read as 'une série de petits appendices' (Jacob, 'Esaïe 27, 2–5', 326) *contra* Wildberger who maintains that the context places vv. 2–5 within an apocalyptic framework (Wildberger, *Isaiah 13–27*, 583). For discussion on the possible Ugaritic background to 27:1, see Barker, *Isaiah 24–27*, 133–4.

[101] Or, following the MT textual variant, חמר 'of wine'.

[102] See Stendebach, ' ענה ' in *TDOT XI*, 215–16.

This invites an understanding of 27:2–5 as a response to 5:1–7—one addressed to the same audience as the first, and one that fills in the gaps and suggests an alternative to the total destruction of the earlier parable. Further contrasting elements between the two texts include the fact that in Isaiah 5 YHWH is the agent of destruction (v. 6), whilst in Isaiah 27 he protects against destruction by others (v. 3).

An interesting difference is the choice of שׁלום, 'peace' rather than justice and righteousness to describe the desired outcome (27:5 cf. 5:7). Most commentators assume that this represents restoration of the relationship between YHWH and his enemies, and indeed the text can be read in this way. However, verse 5 may also be rendered as 'let him make peace for me', and since שׁלום encompasses a breadth of meaning not conveyed by the English term, this verse suggests a responsibility on those to whom it is addressed to act in a way that promotes well-being in society, including the justice and righteousness so conspicuously absent in 5:7.[103] The final verse, 27:6, which completes this section, but perhaps was added as part of a later redaction, emphasizes the full extent of the harmony, and reinterprets it in another, more eschatological context—the re-establishment of the nation, described in terms of the vineyard flourishing, accompanied by abundance of produce that benefits the whole world.

The picture painted by 27:2–5 is not unequivocally positive, as demonstrated by YHWH's strongly worded intention to contend with those who produce thorns and briers (v. 4). Conditionality is implied in verse 5—YHWH's protection is not guaranteed, but dependent on human choice.[104] Despite the differences between this and the first parable, the imagery conveys the same message: that YHWH's care and protection for his people is conditional upon their willingness to uphold his divine order in the world, as summed up in the concepts of peace, justice, and righteousness.

Isaiah's use of such vivid agricultural imagery to describe the failure and then the restoration of the people of God may have its

[103] Peace, justice, and righteousness are also closely linked in the restoration oracle of Isa. 32:15–17 and in this case they are hallmarks of wilderness as well as cultivated land (v. 16) (Porteous, 'Jerusalem-Zion', 243–4).

[104] The LXX presents an even more ambivalent reading, from the perspective of a besieged city (v. 3), suggesting that the capture of the city is inevitable (v. 4) and only then will be followed by a restoration of peace (v. 5) and the blossoming of Israel.

roots in the tradition of the land as a gift from YHWH, as detailed in the Exodus and conquest narratives (e.g. Exod. 13:11; Deut. 8:1). Explicit references to the Exodus are scarce in First Isaiah (11:16 being the only clear example), but it is notable that these vineyard parables have certain resonances with Ps. 80:9–17 [8–16] which also uses the metaphor of a vine for Israel and describes YHWH's action in bringing her out from Egypt and planting her (נטע v. 9 [8], cf. Isa. 5:2) in the land.[105] In this psalm are details of the land being cleared and the vine taking root (שׁרשׁ v. 10 [9], cf. Isa. 27:6), the extent of Israel's spread in the land (vv. 10b–11 [9b–10], cf. Isa. 27:6), and her walls being broken by YHWH (פרצת גדריה v. 13 [12], cf. 5:5).

In the Isaiah parables, the planting, destruction and replanting of the vineyard describes the fate and future hope of Israel, using graphic and accessible imagery, based upon a vine grower's care for his vineyard. The destruction of the vines and their subsequent flourishing also function metonymically, as a representation of the agricultural fertility and hence the economic, social and political stability (or lack of it), of the whole land.

THE PHYSICAL ENVIRONMENT AND YHWH'S JUDGEMENT AND BLESSING

Alongside the figurative language employed in First Isaiah, a number of texts involving more literal descriptions also highlight the link between divine order and well-being in the land. These include depictions of the relationship between human and animal populations, and between YHWH's actions of judgement or blessing and the physical environment. The most graphic descriptions of the effects of judgement and blessing are found in the oracles of Isaiah 34 and 35. These two chapters present contrasting pictures and operate antithetically to one another, drawing on material and

[105] If, as Davies suggests, Ps. 80 originated in the Northern Kingdom, then three possibilities suggest themselves namely that (*a*) the similarities between Ps. 80 and the Isaianic vineyard metaphor is coincidental; (*b*) Isaiah was aware of this Northern Psalm; (*c*) the motif predates the division of the kingdoms (G. I. Davies, *Hosea*, 32).

ideas from elsewhere in First Isaiah. A further expression of God's future blessing is the ideal age described in 11:1–10. Here too the interrelationship between the restoration of harmony in society and that in the non-human creation is clear. Although none of these texts uses figurative language in the same way as the ones already discussed above, their message is also rich in symbolism.

Chapters 34 and 35 form the end of the prophetic material of First Isaiah. The exact relationship between them and the preceding chapters has been subject of much debate, as has the relation of Isaiah 35 with the remainder of the book of Isaiah.[106] Many commentators view Isaiah 34 and 35 as forming a distinct unit from the same author, even dubbing them the 'little apocalypse'.[107] The many thematic and linguistic connections between the two chapters have been analysed in a number of recent studies, in particular those by Mathews and Miscall.[108]

In the context of the relationship between human and non-human creation, the connection between these two chapters is one of broad concepts rather than that of closely intertwined texts. As will be seen, Isaiah 34 depicts a process of environmental degradation and change in both the rural and urban landscapes. Isaiah 35, which by no means has such a clear sequence, presents the reversal of some, but not all of these elements, using different themes and terminology.

[106] See Beuken, *Isaiah 28–39*, 283–8; Steck, *Bereitete Heimkehr, passim*; Williamson, *Book Called Isaiah*, 211–21. Of these, Beuken in particular sees Isaiah 35 as a bridge between the prophetic sections immediately before and after it (Isaiah 32–4 and Isaiah 40), rather than between the main parts of the book. Such issues are connected with the wider debate on the relationship between the 'parts' of Isaiah, and its formation, which has already been referred to.

[107] 'La petite apocalypse' (Vermeylen, *Prophète Isaïe*, 440); see also Kaiser, *Isaiah 13–39*, 353. Clements is among those who suggest a 'proto-apocalyptic character', similar to that of Isaiah 24–7, to these chapters (Clements, *Isaiah 1–39*, 271). The designation 'apocalyptic' is strongly rebutted by Wildberger (Wildberger, *Isaiah 28–39*, 317–18).

[108] As with Isaiah 24–7 the designation 'apocalypse' here is misleading since there is little that is truly apocalyptic (rather than eschatological). Mathews draws attention to a number of linguistic and stylistic points that suggest the two poems have been intentionally brought into relation with each other (Mathews, *Defending Zion*). Miscall reads the two chapters as a single poem from the very outset, and develops a reading of the text based on his study of the 'fantastic' in biblical narrative (Miscall, *Isaiah 34–35*).

ISAIAH 34 AND DESOLATION OF THE CITY

Isaiah 34 describes the effect of YHWH's judgement on an international scale (vv. 1–3), on a cosmic one (v. 4) and on an individual nation or nations (vv. 5–17), with the identity of the addressee in verses 8–17 being much debated by commentators.[109] However, it is unnecessary and perhaps unhelpful to stipulate a specific nation, since the recurrence of the themes and vocabulary of these verses in a range of other prophetic texts, addressed both to the people of God and to a variety of foreign nations, suggests a common pool of ideas and language of judgement upon which prophetic authors were able to draw.[110]

The cosmic language of verses 2–5 has already been discussed, so attention here will focus on the effect of YHWH's judgement on the land in verses 9–15. Like verses 2–5, this section has numerous features in common with Isaiah 13, leading Vermeylen to suggest that Isaiah 34 follows an identical outline to Isa. 13 and is self-consciously modelled on it.[111] The section also finds echoes in Jer. 50:38–40, which, like Isaiah 13, prophesies the downfall of Babylon. In the discussion that follows, Isaiah 34 will be the main focus, but parallels with the other two texts will be drawn where appropriate.

Ecology in Isaiah 34

It is interesting that 34:9–17 presents a scenario that is not unfamiliar in contemporary ecology. Although there is little in the text of this section to suggest a clear chronological progression, the

[109] Discussed in Wildberger, *Isaiah 28–39*, 322–9; see also Jeppesen, 'Isaiah 13–14'; Kissane, *Isaiah*, 369; Young, *Isaiah*, 433. Lust suggests that the bulk of the oracle is directed at Judah (Lust, 'Isaiah 34', 281).

[110] In addition to texts in Isaiah, see Jer. 10:22, 49:33, 50:39, 51:37; Mic. 3:12; Zeph 2:14, 15. Although the vocabulary is different, Isa. 1:7, 5:8–9, and 6:11–12 also speak of the threat of desolation of the land and depopulation of cities as part of YHWH's judgement against Judah. See discussion concerning re-use of these themes in Second Isaiah in Williamson, *Book Called Isaiah*, 51–3; and Clements, 'Beyond Tradition History', 95–113.

[111] Vermeylen, *Prophète Isaïe*, 440.

v. 9	burning of the land degradation of the soil
v. 10	desertification depopulation of rural landscape
v. 11a	alternative ecology develops
v. 11b, 12	destabilisation of society urban depopulation
v. 13	encroachment of vegetation
vv. 13,14	species colonisation
vv. 16,17	permanent habitat change

Figure 6. Environmental degradation in Isa. 34

description in these verses encompasses a series of stages that reflect ecologists' observation of environmental disturbance (see Figure 6).[112] In verse 9, the streams and soil are described as being turned into זפת 'pitch' and גפרית 'brimstone'. This echoes the description of the devastation inflicted on Sodom and Gomorrah in Genesis 19 and is undoubtedly an allusion to the totality of the destruction.[113] Indeed, in Isa. 13:19 and Jer. 50:40 the overthrow of Babylon is specifically likened to that of Sodom and Gomorrah, although in these instances the terms pitch and brimstone are not used. It is notable that only in Isaiah 34 is this terminology used to describe devastation in the natural environment, including degradation of the soil (עפר, v. 9) rather than destruction of people or cities. However, fresh water and fertile soil are, of course, prerequisite for agriculture and the survival of human populations.

The text stresses the continued and permanent aspect of the destruction. The landscape will burn 'night and day' and smoulder

112 Not all of which is necessarily ecologically damaging (P. White, 'Disturbance').
113 See discussion in Chapter 4.

'forever' (עד־עולם v. 10a), both expressions used poetically to denote continuous action. The second half of the verse parallels the first:

From generation to generation (מדור לדור) it will be dried up,
There will be no-one passing through it forever (לנצח).

From the perspective of the human population, the permanent duration of such devastation is a further blow. The same parallel terminology is also used of the destruction in Isa. 13:20 and Jer. 50:29 (לנצח and לדור עד דור in both verses).[114] However, in Isa. 34:17b, this phraseology takes on a more positive slant, at least for the wildlife who have begun to inhabit the ruined buildings:

They will take possession of it forever (עד־עולם),
From generation to generation (לדור ודור) they will settle down in it.

The context (vv. 16b–17a) suggests that this is YHWH's deliberate provision for these animals. It is only for the human population, not the animal one, that the outcome is disastrous.

Alongside the degradation of the soil and decimation of the physical landscape in Isa. 34:9–10, and perhaps even a consequence of it, is the depopulation of human settlements. This is implied by the lack of king or rulers in verse 12, and by verse 13a which describes the fortifications of the city overgrown with thorns and brambles. Depopulation is explicit in Jer. 50:40, and assumed in Isa. 13:20b, the latter suggesting that not even nomadic peoples or wandering shepherds will take up temporary lodging there.[115]

The use of תהו 'formlessness' and the rare בהו 'emptiness' in 34:11b emphasizes the desolate nature of the landscape, devoid of pasture, agriculture, domestic animals and people. The fact that these two words are also used in Gen. 1:2 to describe the pre-creation state may at first glance suggest that here, the unmaking of the created order is being described, as was discussed with regard to

[114] Joel 4:20 [3:20] also uses לדור ודור with לעולם, but to describe the restoration and repopulation of Judah and Jerusalem.

[115] See also Isa. 24:10.

Hos. 4:3.[116] However, the devastation here is not that of the whole created order, but only a part of it, namely human civilization and society. Such desolation provides scope for the development of an alternative ecology as wild animals and birds take up residence (vv. 11a and 13b–15). Five of the species named in these verses are also found in Isa. 13:21–2.[117]

Animal names in Isaiah 34

Here, as elsewhere in the Old Testament, it is often unclear which animal species are intended by the Hebrew animal names, leading to a wide variation in translations and commentaries.[118] However, with respect to First Isaiah, a number of observations may be made. First, on occasions the suggested identification offered by the translator or commentator is inconsistent with the known habits of the species described in the text and therefore cannot be correct. For example ינשׁוף (34:11) is translated 'ibis' by the earliest versions (LXX, Vg.), yet this bird would be unlikely to frequent uninhabited buildings, particularly in an arid upland area such as that around Jerusalem, since it is primarily a water bird of lowland coastal or riverine marshland.[119] NRSV chooses 'hedgehog' for קפוד in 34:11 and 14:23, but 'screech owl' for the same Hebrew word in Zeph. 2:14. The verb קפד 'to gather together' 'to roll up' is only attested once in

[116] Apart from Genesis 1, the only other occurrence of בהו in the Old Testament is in Jer. 4:23, where it is used in conjunction with תהו to describe a similar desolation and 'unmaking'. תהו on its own is found frequently in a variety of contexts.

[117] These are איים, ציים, תנים, שׂעיר, and בנות יענה. Jer. 50:39 has ציים, איים, and בנות יענה.

[118] Various surveys of early versions and reviews of English or German translations have been undertaken, in an attempt to provide a definitive list. However, the secondary literature as well as the translations demonstrate a great diversity (e.g. G. R. Driver, 'Birds I'; G. R. Driver, 'Birds II'; Janowski et al., *Gefährten Und Feinde*; Tristram, *Natural History*). For more general surveys, see Borowski, *Every Living Thing*; Cansdale, *Animals*; Feliks, *Animal World*; Grigson, 'Plough and Pasture'; Pangritz, *Das Tier*; Parmalee, *Birds*.

[119] LXX ἴβεις, Vg. Ibis. Driver considers that the LXX choice suggests an Egyptian translator, since the ibis was the sacred bird of ancient Egypt (G. R. Driver, 'Birds I', 15 fn. 79). For current distribution of *Threskiornis aethiopicus*, Sacred Ibis, see Snow and Perrins, *Birds of the Western Palearctic*, 148.

the Old Testament (Isa. 38:12), and these are the only instances of the noun derived from this root. Translating the noun as a species of owl in Zephaniah is undoubtedly prompted by the context—a description of the creature settling on the tops of pillars. It also seems unlikely that such a small, timid animal as the hedgehog, not normally found in derelict buildings, would naturally characterize the depictions of desolation in Isaiah 14 and 34. The owl, however, does so precisely. The NASB's choice of 'tree snake' in 34:15 for the *hapax legomenon* קפוז (from the unattested Hebrew root קפז 'to leap or spring') is also misleading.[120] In biological terms, the description that follows—'lays eggs there'—indicates that this translation may be inaccurate since tree snakes, like most snakes, are viviparous.

Secondly, the mere fact that so many species are mentioned, coupled with the detailed description characteristic of Isaiah, suggest that the inspiration behind this prophetic utterance is born out of observation of desolate landscape and ruined buildings.[121] It is reasonable to suppose that, although the creatures named are not easily identifiable from the Hebrew, they represent a range of birds and animals known to the author. Moreover, since the prophet's purpose is to convey a fearful and terrible judgement, he deliberately names species that contribute to this, namely scavengers (e.g. ערב 'raven' v. 11) and various kinds of raptors, especially owls. As Feliks points out, owls are ideally suited to 'exemplify the horrors of destruction', since they typically frequent deserted buildings, and their appearance, i.e. large head with forward facing eyes, and behaviour, i.e. silent flight and chilling call, contribute to the sense of terror.[122]

Thirdly, if the author is basing his description on observable wildlife, the question arises whether the obscure terms לילית (*lîlît*) and שׂעיר (*śāʿîr*) could refer to real species, rather than mythological

[120] Derived from the Arabic (BDB 891).

[121] The same may be said of the descriptions of viticulture in the two parables. Such detail suggests a knowledge of the processes or at very least, a keen eye for observation on the part of the prophet.

[122] Feliks, *Nature and Man*, 102. He undoubtedly pushes it too far when he suggests that all the species listed are members of the owl family. איים, ציים, and תנים all more likely refer to scavenging wild animals (hyena, jackal, etc.); see also Feliks, *Animal World*, 72–81.

creatures as many commentators suggest.[123] As Clements notes, the context does not support 'the idea of an uncanny and powerful supernatural figure'.[124] According to Feliks, these names more likely represent members of the owl family and should perhaps be translated as tawny owl and scops owl respectively.[125] With regard to לילית (*lîlît*), although the names of Mesopotamian demons derived from the term *líl* in Sumerian and Akkadian literature may indeed be influential, the possibility that the name is connected by popular etymology to לילה 'night' should not be discounted.[126] In reality the two are probably not mutually exclusive since the distinction between real and mythological creatures is somewhat blurred in the ancient world, and the appearance and sounds made by a nocturnal bird such as an owl are sufficient to explain its subsequent association with demonic or evil forces.[127]

It is notable that the descriptions of the activity of these various creatures in Isaiah 34 are typical of bird and animal behaviour, supporting the idea that the author was a careful observer of the world around him. These activities also contribute to the idea of permanence suggested by verse 17b. In verse 11 they will 'take possession of' (ירשׁ) and 'settle in' (שׁכן) the ruined land, both terms that are used more often to describe the activity of humans.[128] The nouns נוה 'abode' and חציר 'habitation' in verse 13 convey the sense of permanent occupation as does the description of a bird

[123] Kaiser, *Isaiah 13–39*, 20; Wildberger, *Isaiah 28–39*, 225. Similarly, Geyer argues that Isaiah 13 shows a dependency on mythological traditions (Geyer, 'Desolation and Cosmos').

[124] Clements, *Isaiah 1–39*, 274. His tentative suggestion of 'nightjar', for לילית seems less plausible than Feliks' proposed 'owl'. Wildberger counsels against trying to distinguish too closely between known animals and demons: 'One cannot draw sharp distinctions between animals that are sinister, but recognizable, over against demons.' Nevertheless, he still conceives of לילית in demonic terms (Wildberger, *Isaiah 28–39*, 335).

[125] שׁעיר is the Modern Hebrew word for Scops Owl.

[126] See Gadd, 'Gilgamesh XII', 135–6; Lachenbacher, 'L' *ardat-Lilî*', 148–52; Seow, 'Lilith', 973–6.

[127] The tendency towards 'mythologization' can be seen in the development of Talmudic legends concerning the demon Lilith right up until the Medieval period (Seow, 'Lilith', 975).

[128] ירשׁ is used by OT writers particularly in the context of the Israelite possession or inheritance of the land.

nesting and raising young in verse 15. In verse 14 the שׂעיר(*sā'îr*) calls to its mate and the לילית (*lîlît*) finds a roost (מנוח), both typical bird activities that suggest a level of security and lack of disturbance necessary for breeding. It is hard to see how anything other than the natural world is being described.

However individual animal terms are translated, the power of the description lies in the contrast between the human and the wild animal populations, set at variance with one another. Implicit in this portrayal is the idea that part of YHWH's punishment is the disruption of the natural order. Here, as elsewhere in First Isaiah, the boundary between human populations and animals, always a place of tension, has been breached, and animals are invading human 'space'. Also part of this destabilization of society is the uncontrolled encroachment of vegetation into urban areas, with buildings becoming choked with thorns, thistles, and brambles (סיר, קמושׂ, חוח, v. 13).[129] The power of the natural world, whereby settled land reverts to wilderness, and is colonized by wild animals is a reminder, then as now, that human settlement and cultivation is not the default mode of the physical environment.

A number of other texts in First Isaiah exhibit similar tension between animal and human populations. As already discussed, this is true of 13:20–2, where not only will human habitation come to an end, but the land will not even supply pasturage for domestic animals (v. 20b). However, elsewhere the tension seems to be between agricultural and pastoral activity, reflecting perhaps the perceived superiority of cultivated land over pasture.[130] One outcome of the Assyrian invasion prophesied in 7:18–25 is that the vines will be ruined and the land become grazing land for cattle and sheep (v. 25), a destruction also implicit in the vineyard parable (5:5). Likewise the abandoned city of Jerusalem will become a place for flocks and wild donkeys in 32:14, whilst in 17:2 Damascus will suffer the same fate, and, according to LXX, her towns will be deserted forever.[131]

[129] Like animal names, exact translation of קמושׂ and חוח is uncertain.

[130] However, Hillel notes that the assumption that the 'land flowing with milk and honey' of the Exodus traditions signifies a particularly fertile agricultural land (Exod. 3:8, 13:5, etc.), is misplaced, since milk is more typically the produce of herdsmen (Hillel, *Natural History*, 293 n.32.

[131] See also Isa. 1:7–8 and Mic. 1:6.

It is not that these animals are in themselves hostile to human beings, merely that in the wrong place their capacity to wreak destruction is emphasized. If YHWH is the guarantor of order in the world, then it is entirely appropriate that his judgement on human beings should be characterized, at least in part, by the breaking and crossing of boundaries, so that fertile fields and vineyard become trampled by livestock, and cities are taken over by wild animals.

ISAIAH 35 AND OTHER RESTORATION TEXTS

In Isaiah 35, the desolation of Judah's land, which was epitomized in the preceding chapter by its city becoming a ruined habitat for wild creatures, is reversed, powerfully depicted as the flowering of the desert. The juxtaposition of these two chapters inevitably invites comparison, but there are even stronger thematic links between Isaiah 35 and an number of other texts in Isaiah 28–35. Of these, one is an oracle of desolation (33:7–9); the others, namely 29:17–21, 30:18–26 and 32:9–20 depict aspects of YHWH's restoration and its effects on both human and non-human creation.

The connection between Isaiah 35 and the desolation oracle of 33: 7–9 is established by the repetition of the triad of names, Lebanon, Carmel, and Sharon (35:2, cf. 33:9).[132] Isaiah 35 depicts a specific reversal of several themes in Isaiah 33, including the coming of joy (35:2, 6) instead of weeping and crying (33:7), the holy way (35:8) instead of desolate highways (33:8), and rejuvenation of the land (35:1, 7) instead of its desiccation and withering (33:9).[133]

The thematic links between Isaiah 35 and the restoration texts cited above can be grouped under four broad headings as shown in Figure 7.

[132] The only two instances in the Old Testament. Like Isa. 35:1, Isaiah 33 also uses the description ערבה 'arid plain' of Sharon (v. 9).

[133] The language of safety in travelling is far more meaningful in the context of the ancient world than the modern one.

Restoration of non-human creation	29:17 30:23–25 32:15–6 35:1, 7
Healing of human beings	29:18 30:26 35:5–6
Coming of joy, peace	29:19 30:19 32:17–18 35:6, 10
Absence of evil, trouble	29:20 30:22 32:19 35:8–9

Figure 7. Restoration themes in Isa. 28–35

Restoration of non-human creation

Three of the four texts use the ambivalent term כרמל (signifying both 'a fruitful field' and the place name Carmel) in their descriptions of the restoration of the non-human creation.[134] In 35:1–2 and 6b–7 the splendour of the wilderness in full flower will even exceed that of Lebanon, Sharon, and Carmel, and is, by implication, a reflection of YHWH's glory and splendour (v. 2). This restoration is echoed in the more muted language of 29:17. In this verse the repetition of כרמל is surely a deliberate word play, depicting the revitalization of Lebanon and Carmel in terms of, respectively, a fruitful field (כרמל), and a wooded grove (יער).[135] A similar pattern in 32:15 describes the restoration of the wilderness and of Carmel, in

[134] On the symbolic use of Lebanon, Sharon and Carmel to denote fertility and abundance see Nielsen, *Hope for a Tree*, 126–8.

[135] See Kaiser, *Isaiah 13–39*, 277, and Wildberger, *Isaiah 28–39*, 109, but few other commentators.

response to an outpouring of רוח ממרום 'a spirit from on high'.[136] In Isaiah 30, it is the provision of rain and the consequent agricultural productivity that is a sign of YHWH's favour (vv. 23–4). This fertility of the land is a direct consequence of the people turning to YHWH (מוריך, 'your teacher', v. 20) and renouncing their idols (vv. 21, 22).[137]

Healing of human beings

The renewal of the wilderness in Isaiah 35 is followed by the healing of people from physical disabilities (vv. 5, 6). The dramatic outpouring of water in verse 6 is pivotal, linked not only with the rejuvenation of the parched and thirsty ground (v. 7), but also causally (by the use of כי) with the healing and joyful response of the lame and deaf.

As in Isaiah 35, in Isaiah 29 and 30 the descriptions of the restoration of fertility to the land are followed by healing of the human population. In particular, Isa. 29:18 echoes the theme of the restoration of sight and hearing of 35:5 (but makes no mention of the lame and the dumb referred to in 35:6). Isaiah 30 is more general, referring to YHWH's healing of the wounds he has inflicted on his people, implicitly as a result of judgement on their sin (v. 26). Commentators differ over whether all these afflictions are physical in nature or are intended to symbolize moral and spiritual deficiencies. In particular, the Isaianic motif of seeing and hearing as metonymy for spiritual obedience should be taken into account (see Isa. 6: 9–10).[138] Yet it is possible that both the literal and figurative

[136] This phrase is unique in the MT as is the use of ערה in the Niphal. *Tg. Isa.* adds a reference to the 'Shekhinah in the heavens' to make it clear that this spirit is from YHWH (Chilton, *Isaiah Targum*, 64).

[137] Most commentators suggest that the plural of מורה is a plural of majesty. Since YHWH is agent in the first clause of v. 20, it is likely that the teacher also refers to YHWH, although the use of the plural personal pronoun in the first clause (2 m. pl.) as opposed to the singular (2 m. s.) in the second produces a certain separation between the two clauses, and may indicate an intermediary teacher (see discussion in Witmer, 'Taught by God', 18).

[138] Clements ('Beyond Tradition History', 101–4) argues that the removal of deafness and blindness in Isaiah 29 and 30 should be taken in the literal sense, as part of a 'new creation' (see also Clements, *Isaiah 1–39*, 241), whilst Kaiser, Kissane,

understandings are intended, since, as already noted, the connection between ethical or religious failure and physical disaster, whether in respect of the land or its inhabitants, is a close one in First Isaiah. The restoration of relationship with YHWH involves the removal not only of moral imperfections, but of physical ones too.

Joy and cessation of evil

The results of this restoration are exuberant and animated. Not only do the lame leap and the mute burst into song (35:6), but the non-human creation rejoices for joy (v. 2). The reason given in verse 2b is the bestowal of glory (כבוד) and splendour (הדר) which will result in the revelation of the glory and splendour of YHWH. In the Psalter, this word pair are attributes of YHWH and his kingdom (Pss. 29:2; 145:5, 12), and are imparted by YHWH to the earthly king (Ps. 21:6 [5]), and to human beings (Ps. 8:6 [5]). Here, uniquely, these qualities are bestowed on the non-human realm, although it is notable that in Isaiah's temple vision, the angels proclaim of YHWH that 'the fullness of all the earth (i.e. the creation) is his glory (כבודו)' (Isa. 6: 3).[139]

Likewise, in 29:19 the renewal of creation, human and non-human, results in an outpouring of joy in YHWH, the holy one of Israel.[140] Rejoicing is also implied by the cessation of weeping in 30: 19, and the use of אשרי 'blessed' in 30:18 and 32:20. The rejoicing in YHWH as holy is specifically linked with the abrogation of wickedness in 29:20, and this characterizes the holy pathway of 35:8. In 30:21 the input from the teacher is depicted as instructions for walking a 'straight' path.[141]

and Wildberger opt for a figurative interpretation (Kaiser, *Isaiah 13–39*, 279; Kissane, *Isaiah*, 320; Wildberger, *Isaiah 28–39*, 111–12.

[139] The noun מלא 'fullness' is often used in poetic and prophetic texts to denote the entirety of the creation, e.g. 'The earth is YHWH's and all that is in it' (Ps. 24:1); 'Let the earth hear and all that fills it' (Isa. 34:1).

[140] The title קדוש ישראל for YHWH occurs 30 times in Isaiah, out of a total of 40 in the OT as a whole, and is more or less equally divided between First Isaiah (14 times) and Second Isaiah (13 times), with only three occurrences in Third Isaiah (see Kratz, 'Israel in Isaiah', 105–11).

[141] Cf. 35:9.

Each of these texts from Isaiah 28–35 uses similar themes and motifs to demonstrate a fundamental interconnectedness within the created order. Abundant regrowth and rejuvenation of the physical world is accompanied by the physical and moral healing of its human population, and both result in rejoicing and renewed relationship with YHWH.

ISAIAH 11:1–10

The final text for consideration in this chapter is one that is very well known yet raises interesting interpretive questions. Isaiah 11's portrayal of harmony in the created order differs significantly from that of Isaiah 35, and offers a unique vision of the reign of the coming ideal ruler. The dating and the delineation of the various sections of Isaiah 11 has been greatly debated.[142] For present purposes, verses 1–10 will be treated as a unit on the grounds that the reference to שֹׁרֶשׁ יִשַׁי 'root of Jesse' in verses 1 and 10 forms an *inclusio* and acts as a bridge between the description of paradise in verses 2–9 and the historically specific oracle of verses 11–18.[143] The verses can be grouped according to the chiastic pattern shown in Figure 8. This passage presents a picture of idyllic harmony, in which a Davidic ruler ushers in a reign of justice and righteousness for the poor and judgement for the wicked (vv. 1–5), and where predatory and poisonous wild animals no longer pose a threat to human beings or their livestock (vv. 6–8). The knowledge of YHWH is both the prerequisite for, and the end result of, the reign of this ideal king (vv. 2–3a, 9).[144] Under his reign of justice and righteousness, not only will the wrongs in society be righted, but changes will occur even in the non-human creation.

[142] For a detailed discussion see Wildberger, *Isaiah 1–12*, 465–9.

[143] According to Gitay, the function of ביום ההוא 'on that day' (v. 10) is not to introduce new speech, but rather represents 'a certain syntactical dependence on the previous text' (Gitay, *Isaiah 1–12*, 2143).

[144] See discussion on 'knowledge of YHWH' in Hosea in Chapter 5.

A	A shoot from the stem of Jesse/a branch from his root will go forth (v. 1)
B	The knowledge of YHWH will rest on him (v. 2)
C	The ideal age: justice in society restored and evil judged (vv. 3–5)
C′	The ideal age: harmony in nature initiated and evil removed (vv.6–9a)
B′	The knowledge of YHWH will fill the land (v. 9b)
A′	A root of Jesse will stand as a signal, to which nations will come (v.10)

Figure 8. Chiastic symmetry in Isa. 11:1–10

The theme of a reversal of the whole natural order, including the establishment of harmony between wild and domestic animals, and with human beings, is unique to Isaiah 11 and its reuse in Isa. 65: 25.[145] In most other instances, YHWH's redemption is restricted to the removal of wild animals e.g. Isa. 35:9 (see also Ezek. 34:25; Lev. 26:6b). There are, however, other parallels for the idea of a primordial golden age of peace with animals, in ancient Near Eastern texts such as the Sumerian myth *Enki and Ninhursag* (*ANET* 38).[146] This particular characteristic of the golden age is implicit rather than explicit in the primeval stories of Genesis—in the description of Adam naming the animals in Gen. 2:19–20 and in the flood narrative (Gen. 7:14–15), as well as the Genesis 1 tradition that both animals and human beings were vegetarians (Gen. 1:30).[147]

Unlike Isaiah 13 and 34, which contain animal names that are hard to identify, this picture of harmony in the natural world deals mostly

[145] Apart from the elusive and much debated reference in Job to 'the wild animals at peace with you' (Job 5:23). For the relationship between Isaiah 11 and 65, see Van Ruiten, 'Intertextual Relationship'.

[146] Nwaoru correctly notes that this motif is absent from Egyptian literature, but it is doubtful whether the examples he cites from Graeco-Roman poetry depict an unequivocal harmony between animal species, rather than a more general period of social well-being (Nwaoru, 'Isaiah 11:6–9', 132–4).

[147] Although the latter can in no way be classed as a 'golden age', the description of the animals entering Noah's ark implies a certain harmony between species, and between humans and animals.

with unambiguously recognisable species.[148] The named creatures are linked with great artistry in a series of contrasting pairs and triads, and are intended to depict the scope of the harmony rather than provide a definitive list.[149] The predator (זאב 'wolf' and נמר 'leopard') is set alongside its helpless and frail prey (כבשׂ 'lamb' and גדי 'kid', v. 6); the wild untamed strength of a lion (אריה) contrasts with the harnessed might of an ox (בקר, v. 7b), the unpredictability of a snake with the innocence of a small child (v. 8).

The description of a peaceful idyll in which wild animals are apparently tamed poses a number of questions concerning the ancient Israelite understanding of the world, as well as interpretation of the text in the light of modern ecological understanding. Does it not present a picture at odds with the violent judgement of v. 4?[150] Does it imply cessation of the 'natural' order of creation, articulated elsewhere in the Old Testament, in which some animals are dependent upon others for food?[151] What are we to make of the biological impossibility of a carnivore eating grass?

Some of those who are uncomfortable with a purely mythological interpretation avoid these problems by suggesting that the wild animals represent individual nations, and the passage is symbolic of peace among enemy peoples.[152] But, as Wildberger points out, such an allegorical reading does not explain the references to children alongside animals.[153] The minimalist view expressed by Kaiser may avoid the problems: 'in the end the present text merely expresses the longing for a life with no danger', but this is rather an oversimplification.[154] Clements's suggestion that the Old Testament presents an ambivalent attitude to the natural world is undoubtedly partly correct, although he is careful to suggest that the existence of a divinely

[148] See Olley, 'Earth Community in Isaiah', 219–21. The exception is פתן (perhaps cobra) and צפעוני (perhaps adder or viper—from the onomatopoeic root צפע), since the precise identification of venomous snakes throughout Isaiah is, like bird species, open to question.

[149] It is not however necessary to follow Gray's example and emend the Hebrew to provide a metrical list of pairs (Gray, *Isaiah I–XXVII*, 219–20).

[150] See Vermeylen, *Prophète Isaïe*, 275.

[151] E.g. Ps. 104:21. See Clements, 'Reading Isaiah'.

[152] See Wildberger, *Isaiah 1–12*, 481.

[153] Ibid.

[154] Kaiser, *Isaiah 1–12*, 260.

ordained world order was a *sine qua non* for the ancient Israelites.[155] His conclusion that in Isa. 11:6–9, as also in Hos. 2:20 [18], *human* violence is the primary evil to be removed may represent an over-interpretation of the text.[156]

It is not easy to answer all the questions raised by verses 6–9, but a few comments may be made, in particular in the context of 11:1–10 as a whole. First, the passage is grounded (one might say rooted!) in Judah's understanding of her identity as God's chosen people as epitomized by the Davidic line (vv. 1, 10).[157] What follows is an articulation of the longed-for ideal of Davidic kingship.[158]

Secondly, the initiative is God's, since YHWH's spirit will be the empowering force behind the ideal ruler, who will act from a spirit of the knowledge and fear of YHWH (v. 2–3) to bring about justice and righteousness for the poor (v. 3–5). The word רוח is used elsewhere in First Isaiah in the context of an attribute of or blessing from YHWH. As already noted, in 32:15 the spirit from on high results not only in literal fruitfulness but also in justice and righteousness. In 28:6 it is YHWH himself who will be a spirit of justice (לרוח משׁפט) to the remnant of his people, and in 34:16 the spirit of YHWH gathers the wild animals into the ruined city. In Isa. 11:2 the attributes of wisdom (חכמה), understanding (בינה), and strength (גבורה) upon the appointed ruler which result from the spirit of YHWH convey a sense of divine intentionality. The fulfilment of divine purpose and the consequent restoration of the fear of YHWH (vv. 2, 9) brackets the reconstruction of society (vv. 4–5) and of the natural world (vv. 6–8).

Thirdly, in contrast to Isaiah 13 and 34, which describe the consequences when the boundaries between wild animals and human populations are broken, 11:6–9 describes the removal of these boundaries. What had hitherto been impossible will now become possible. This depiction of perfection is not intended to negate the

[155] Clements, 'Reading Isaiah'.

[156] Ibid. 99.

[157] See 1 Sam. 16:1; 2 Sam. 7:8–11.

[158] Whether this was understood as a restoration of the Davidic monarchy or an ideal of kingship according to the Davidic pattern is open to question. Either way, the point stands.

natural biological processes of the world, but rather to paint a wide picture of the potentiality of YHWH's ideal reign.

Finally, the passage moves outwards from a local to a global context, from dealing with the social and political struggles of Judah (vv. 2–5), to suggest a future in which the knowledge of YHWH is as widespread 'as the waters covering the sea' (v. 9), and in which the nations all turn to YHWH (v. 10). Both the advent of justice and righteousness within Judean society, and the promise of the nations coming to YHWH represent an incredible overturning of the status quo, a reversal of order in society and in world politics. It is perhaps in that context that the description of peace in the animal kingdom should be read: as poetic hyperbole depicting a radical and astonishing change in the world, initiated and maintained by YHWH himself.

SUMMARY

The theme of disaster as a consequence of disobedience to YHWH and his order is woven throughout First Isaiah, in historical narrative, prophetic oracles, and metaphorical descriptions. As has been demonstrated, in a number of texts this theme is set forth in terms of the relationship between human beings and the rest of creation, whether animate or inanimate. This relationship is one of tension (e.g. Isaiah 13 and 34), and of disruption (e.g. Isaiah 24). It is also one characterized by joy and renewal (e.g. Isaiah 35). In First Isaiah it is this stress on the interrelationship between human and non-human creation, the third side of the ecological triangle, that forms a powerful part of the prophetic message.

In many instances Israel's fractured relationship with YHWH is depicted by reference to parables and metaphors of the natural world. Likewise the restoration of God's people is expressed in terms of the renewal of the created order, including return to an idyllic world free from cruelty, disease, and pain. In other parts of First Isaiah, not only is human society described in juxtaposition or contrast to the non-human creation, but there is also an strong suggestion of cause and effect. The consequences of human disobedience and God's judgement are felt, not only by the breakdown of society, but also in the fragmentation of relationship between people and land and the disruption of the natural world. The divine order of the world is characterized by the three key terms, justice, righteousness, and peace; these are the hallmarks not only of societal harmony, but also of the revitalization of the natural world and the restoration of relationship between human and non-human creation.

7

The Old Testament Prophets and Environmental Ethics
A Dialogue

All things by immortal power
near and far
hiddenly
to each other linked are.
Thou canst not stir a flower
without troubling a star.

Francis Thompson

Homo Sapiens putters no more under his own vine and fig tree; he has poured into his gas tank the stored motivity of countless creatures aspiring through the ages to wiggle their way to pastures new.

Aldo Leopold, *A Sand County Almanac*

INTRODUCTION

The preceding three chapters on Amos, Hosea, and First Isaiah, respectively, have explored in some detail the ways in which these biblical books conceived of the world, both human and non-human, and of the interrelationship between the created world and YHWH. This exegetical task has been undertaken with an awareness of the serious nature of current global developments that represent a threat to the survival of the planet and its inhabitants—human and non-human. As such it offers a way of exploring the biblical texts through the lens of contemporary environmental concerns—an ecological hermeneutic—that yields interesting, and sometimes surprising, results. The study thus far has also sought to address some of the assumptions of previous generations of biblical scholarship concerning the priority, even exclusivity, of the human story within the Old Testament.

This is fine so far as it goes, but is there anything further that the biblical text can contribute to current ecological issues? In order to do more than just suggest a new model for reading the texts, albeit an eco-friendly one, the task of the current chapter is to consider how such an ecological hermeneutic might interact with and inform the concerns of contemporary environmental ethics. It begins with a discussion of the issues and problems arising from attempting to derive twenty-first-century ethics from the biblical texts. It then focuses on the specific questions that are raised by environmental ethics, both from the perspective of biblical scholarship and in contemporary secular ecology, in the latter case giving a brief overview of ethical theory and how this applies to ethical decision-making within the world of species conservation. The final part of the chapter explores areas of continuity and discontinuity between the biblical texts and contemporary issues, and suggests ways for establishing a dialogue between the texts and current environmental ethics theory and practice.

USING THE BIBLE IN ETHICS

Interest in Old Testament ethics has until recently been at a very low ebb. However, the past few decades have seen a significant change in this situation, with the publication of numerous articles and several full length monographs on the subject—so much so that Chris Wright notes that of the 400 titles in his 2004 bibliographical survey of Old Testament ethics, over 75 per cent were written since 1983.[1] In

[1] C. J. H. Wright, *Old Testament Ethics*, 14.

this chapter discussion will be limited to the most relevant full-length studies, each of which provides bibliographies and/or extensive summaries of preceding and shorter discussions.[2] It will be seen that there is a wide variety in approaches to the biblical text and also to the all important questions concerning the nature of the ethics of the Old Testament and its applicability to the modern world.

Descriptive or normative ethics?

Broadly speaking, studies on Old Testament ethics fall into two categories: those that seek to articulate the ethical principles and practices of ancient Israel, and those that attempt to go beyond such descriptions to derive contemporary ethical guidance from the biblical text.[3] In his exploration of the sociological and community basis for ancient Israelite ethics, Andrew Mein names these respectively 'descriptive ethics' and 'normative ethics'.[4] Probably the most thorough examples of studies in the latter part of the twentieth century that are primarily concerned with descriptive ethics are those by Eckart Otto and Cyril Rodd.[5] Otto provides a detailed analysis of the relationship between law and ethics in the Book of the Covenant and related traditions, and in the work of the Deu-

[2] Priority has been given to studies that focus on the Old Testament as a whole, rather than those concerned with a particular biblical book or books, and to those that specifically address ecological issues. For a detailed bibliographical essay, see ibid. 415–40.

[3] As Wright observes, a distinction should be made between the ethical principles and the actual Israelite practices described by the text (ibid. 442–3).

[4] Mein, *Ezekiel*, 6. His study is a prime example of a descriptive approach. As the title suggests it is exclusively based on the exilic community that the book of Ezekiel addresses, and therefore outside the remit of this study.

[5] Otto, *Theologische Ethik*; Rodd, *Glimpses of a Strange Land*. Prior to this, only two full length studies worthy of serious consideration were published, namely that by Johannnes Hempel and the major section of Eichrodt's *Theology of the Old Testament* devoted to Old Testament ethics (Hempel, *Ethos Des Alten Testaments*; Eichrodt, *Theology of the Old Testament*, vol. 2; see Barton, *Understanding Ethics*, 162).

teronomic and Priestly laws, as well as exploring the ethics of the wisdom literature.[6] Rodd's study is more thematic, dealing with motivations for ethical behaviour as well as specific moral issues and categories suggested by the Old Testament. He describes it as a series of windows, 'through which glimpses of occasional features of the Old Testament may be obtained'.[7]

Both Otto and Rodd confront the problems of using the Old Testament for contemporary ethics. For Otto, both the time distance between ancient Israel and modern society and the increasing secularisation generated by the Enlightenment prevent 'the normative application of Old Testament codes of behaviour to today's society'.[8] Although he does occasionally make observations on the impact of Israelite law in shaping western culture, this is not his main focus.[9] Rodd is more explicit in his rejection of the Old Testament as a basis for contemporary morality. He examines attempts by Rogerson and a number of other scholars to apply Old Testament ethics to modern society, before concluding that such an undertaking is 'fraught with risk and uncertainty', and inevitably leads us to 'imposing our own prejudices on it [the Old Testament]'.[10]

As already discussed, John Barton has written extensively on the ethics of the eighth-century prophets, and his works on Isaiah of Jerusalem and Amos's oracles against the nations are essentially descriptive rather than normative.[11] However, his more recent collection of these and other essays into one volume explores in more general terms the use of the Bible in ethics.[12] Of particular interest is

[6] Otto's focus on the legal traditions is in reaction to earlier German scholars such as Wellhausen who disparaged biblical law in favour of the ethical monotheism of the prophets, views that Otto regarded as anti-Semitic. By concentrating on parts of the Old Testament that offer *explicit* rules of conduct or norms, he hopes to avoid generalizing into the broader areas of history of Israelite religion or Old Testament theology (see Barton, *Understanding Ethics*, 163). The potential contribution of the narrative texts, in particular Genesis and Judges, to Old Testament ethics has been evaluated by Gordon Wenham (*Story as Torah*).

[7] Rodd, *Glimpses of a Strange Land*, 4.

[8] 'eine normative Applikation alttestamentlicher Handlungsanweisungen auf die heutigen' (Otto, *Theologische Ethik*, 11, 214).

[9] See esp. Otto, *Theologische Ethik*, 122–17, 266–7.

[10] Rodd, *Glimpses of a Strange Land*, 326–7.

[11] Barton, 'Ethics in Isaiah'; Barton, *Oracles against the Nations*.

[12] Barton, *Understanding Ethics*.

his discussion of virtue ethics and its suitability for articulating the Bible's moral perspective, which will be considered in more detail later in this chapter.

Bruce Birch, like Mein, situates ethics within Israel's community life, but unlike Mein sees relevance in a dialogue between 'the originating and the ongoing interpretive communities', from which Christian ethics can be derived.[13] Like others who consider the Old Testament to have currency in Christian ethical formation, Birch regards the inclusion in the canon of ethical material, whether or not it represents actual Israelite morality, as crucial, since this 'represents the judgement of the faith community that its witness is to be taken seriously by subsequent generations of the faithful in efforts towards the moral life'.[14] His approach is to use the Old Testament witness to the character and activity of God and the framework of the Israelites' story as the people of God as a moral resource.[15]

A few studies, such as that by Walter Kaiser, have sought to identify a central organizing feature or 'lodestone' through which to understand and apply Old Testament ethics. In Kaiser's case it is the principle of holiness as expressed in the biblical concept of holiness.[16] His study is based on a high view of biblical authority, and this theological perspective colours his selection and interpretation of texts.

Both Christopher Wright and Waldemar Janzen suggest that the biblical texts concerning Israelite morality provide concepts that are paradigmatic for the formation of ethics.[17] However, as Rodd notes, the manner in which they use the expression 'paradigm' differs. Janzen derives five paradigms or models of behaviour (familial, priestly, royal, wisdom and prophetic) from narrative texts as a means of presenting the ethics of the Old Testament. In contrast, Wright's paradigmatic approach is a selective, schematic account that

[13] B. Birch, *Let Justice Roll Down*, 31.

[14] Ibid. 37.

[15] Ibid.

[16] Based on the 'Law of Holiness' of Leviticus 18–20 and in particular the injunction 'You shall be holy, for I the Lord your God am holy' (Lev. 19:2) (Kaiser, *Old Testament Ethics*, 139; see also E. W. Davies, 'Walking in God's Ways').

[17] C. J. H. Wright, *Old Testament Ethics*; Janzen, *Old Testament Ethics*.

includes only such aspects of the Old Testament that fit his triangular model, YHWH—Israel—land.[18]

Focus on ecological ethics

The work of Rodd and Wright is particularly relevant for this study, since both focus specifically on ecological ethics as part of their task. In *Glimpses of a Strange Land* Rodd devotes an entire chapter to 'Nature', which takes as its starting point the current debate over the Old Testament and the environment. He also has a chapter dealing with the treatment of animals. While not disputing 'the wealth of imagery drawn from the natural world', Rodd takes issue with studies that approach the Bible with a view to finding an explicitly 'green' message.[19] In particular his concern is with anachronistic readings and proof-texting, and his conclusion concerning the Old Testament writers is unequivocal: 'It needs to be asserted as forcefully as possible that the question of safeguarding the environment did not enter into their thinking.'[20]

Rodd's critique of some of the authors he cites, in particular Lewis Regenstein, seems justified, but he fails to acknowledge the more nuanced perspective of others writing in this field.[21] In particular, his negative assessment of Sean McDonagh is in stark contrast to his positive endorsement of Robert Murray's *Cosmic Covenant*, even though both authors are advocating a similar sensitivity to the non-human world.[22] One wonders whether he objects more to the title and the overtly environmental agenda than to the content of McDonagh's book. Rodd is undoubtedly correct in his refusal to attribute specific modern environmental concerns to the Old Testament writers, but in his discussion appears to focus overmuch on the

[18] Rodd, *Glimpses of a Strange Land*, 319–20.

[19] Ibid. 319–20: 239. His particular focus is on the following works: Bradley, *God Is Green*; McDonagh, *Greening the Church*; Osborn, *Guardians*; and Regenstein, *Replenish the Earth*. Rodd accuses such authors of wishing 'to read the Old Testament as an environmentalist tract' (Rodd, *Glimpses of a Strange Land*, 239).

[20] Ibid. 249.

[21] Such as Bradley, *God Is Green*; McDonagh, *Greening the Church*; Osborn, *Guardians*.

[22] Murray, *Cosmic Covenant*.

use (or misuse) of certain biblical texts rather than the broader principles that might be present.

Wright's chapter on 'Ecology and the Earth' in *Old Testament Ethics for the People of God* draws on his earlier works on Old Testament society and ethics, to develop the notion of the 'triangle of creation' between God, humanity, and the earth.[23] The bulk of the chapter is an overview of a Christian understanding of creation within an ecological framework, rather than a detailed exegesis of individual texts. It is within this broad-brush approach that he finds the means of bridging the gap between the Old Testament world and ours:

> Ancient Israel may not have been anxious or fearful about the plight of the physical planet in the way we are, for the very good reason that we have made a far greater mess of it than the ancient world ever did. So to that extent many aspects of what we would regard as urgent ecological issues were not explicitly addressed within the Old Testament. Nevertheless, the theological principles and ethical implications that they *did* articulate regarding creation do have a far-reaching impact on how biblically sensitive Christians will want to frame their ecological ethics today. [Wright's italics][24]

Wright takes issue with Rodd on two counts: his confident and sweeping assertions (e.g. regarding the Israelite lack of concern for the environment), and his refusal to allow that Old Testament might have anything to say on matters of which the Israelites had no direct knowledge.[25]

In the end, as Wright himself points out, the difference between descriptive and normative approaches to Old Testament ethics is often a function of differing ideological perspectives.[26] This is clearly the case with the discussions of environmental ethics by Rodd and Wright that are outlined above. Rodd is sceptical of the role of the Bible as an external authority for moral decision-making, while Wright uses scripture to construct an environmental theology. Rodd focuses on specific individual biblical texts and rejects attempts

[23] C. J. H. Wright, *Old Testament Ethics*; see also C. J. H. Wright, *God's People* and C. J. H. Wright, *Ways of the Lord.* Wright's triangular paradigm is discussed in Chapter 2 of this volume.

[24] C. J. H. Wright, *Old Testament Ethics*, 144.

[25] Ibid. 104.

[26] Ibid. 446.

to find a Christian environmental ethic in them.[27] Although Wright uses a broader selection of texts, and a paradigmatic approach, it is his theology that clearly drives his biblical interpretation.[28] Yet since neither author engages in detailed exegesis of whole sections of the biblical material, the different conclusions that they each draw may represent an over-simplification of the complex and diverse biblical perspectives on the relationship between human beings and the earth.

In the light of the particular concerns of this volume, outlined in the Introduction, neither approach is sufficient in itself, although both offer welcome insights and each is indeed a counterbalance to the other's perspective. Rodd's rejection of the Old Testament as a source for environmental ethics places narrow constraints around the biblical text by focusing on just a few individual texts and by reading the texts in one direction only—from the ancient world to the contemporary—rather than engaging in a two-way conversation between text and reader. Wright's Christocentric theological interpretation offers a broader perspective and will be appealing to certain Christian constituencies, but does not leave the way open for those of different theological persuasions or those who would want to question the text itself.

A number of other assumptions have guided this volume. First, the recognition that, while the Bible is important as a sacred text within the Christian tradition, it is also the product of interpretive communities and has undergone a process of interpretation and reinterpretation across centuries of church history. This brings not only continuity of tradition, but also a healthy discontinuity as previous interpretations are challenged, and the text is not used to justify a status quo. Secondly, the need for a two-way dialogue between text

[27] Rodd, *Glimpses of a Strange Land*, 325.

[28] This tendency is exemplified in his treatment of texts such as Psalm 19 which seem to attribute personal capacities to nature (C. J. H. Wright, *Old Testament Ethics*, 111). For Wright, personalization of nature (as distinct from the literary device of personification of nature) is a form of idolatry, since personhood only rests in God, and, derivatively, in humans made in his image. That this is a theologically driven distinction is evident; close study of a text such as the book of Amos suggests both that there is more material attributing personal qualities to nature than has been hitherto realized, and that the issue is more complex than Wright suggests.

and reader that recognizes similarities and differences between the ancient and the contemporary and that enables each to 'speak' to the other. Walter Brueggemann calls for responsible Old Testament interpretation within the community of the church, which is 'interpretation done in an idiom that is congruent with the life setting of the community, but that is drawn from, informed by, and authorized by the idiom of the community of the text'.[29] Thirdly, ethical responsibility requires a willingness to challenge the anthropocentric, hierarchical perspective that has characterized much biblical interpretation and theological reflection across the centuries, and to engage in ethical reflection in the light of the relational perspective of the text. Finally, it recognizes that the Christian interpretive community, so often insular and isolationist, needs to undertake a 'double listening' whereby it hears the voices of its own cultural milieu as well as the voices of the text.

It is with the latter point in view that this discussion of environmental ethics and the biblical text will now be broadened into the realm of ethical theory in general and the ways in which this has been conceptualized within the environmental community. This will be the basis for exploring what common ground, if any, is to be found between contemporary environmental ethics and the biblical texts, and some of the issues that concern environmental philosophers will be examined in the light of the prophetic material that has been the focus of the exegesis. There are of course huge dangers in reading back into the text, as Rodd has so clearly articulated, but the aim of this process is to highlight potential starting points for a shared morality, intrinsic to human relationship with the rest of the created order.

ENVIRONMENTAL ETHICS

A brief background

The academic discipline of ecology as the science dealing with interrelationships in nature began to develop formally in the late

[29] Brueggemann, *Theology*, 746.

nineteenth century, and drew on a long tradition of natural history observation and writing.[30] Initially concerned exclusively with non-human life systems, it was in the period between the wars that interest in the social science field of human ecology developed in American institutions such as the University of Chicago.[31] It was only in the latter half of the twentieth century that 'the sense of ecology as a philosophy, a general worldview or a holistic vision' began to be articulated.[32] Among the most well-known of environmental philosophers is Aldo Leopold, described by Callicott as the 'father or founding genius of recent environmental ethics',[33] and as 'an environmental philosopher, before environmental philosophy came on the scene'.[34] Leopold stands in a long tradition of natural history writers on both sides of the Atlantic, naturalists whose work is both reflective and inspirational, and whose capacity to encapsulate in words the essence of human relationship with the natural world is remarkable.[35] In Leopold's seminal collection of essays, *A Sand County Almanac*, originally published in 1949, he argues that the basis of all ethics—'that the individual is a member of a community of interdependent parts'—should be extended to include the land.[36] The resulting 'land ethic' he maintains,

> changes the role of *homo sapiens* from conqueror of the land-community to plain member and citizen of it. It implies respect for his fellow-members and also respect for the community as such.[37]

Leopold sees that change in human ethics with regard to land will only take place if there is an internal change in human emphases and

[30] Cittadino, 'Ecology', 74–5.
[31] Ibid. 88–9.
[32] Ibid. 93.
[33] Callicott, 'Animal Liberation', 311.
[34] Callicott, *Beyond the Land Ethic*, 7.
[35] These include Henry David Thoreau (e.g. *Walden*, and *Essays and Poems*) and John Muir (e.g. *Mountains of California*) in the US, and Gilbert White in the UK (e.g. *Natural History of Selbourne*).
[36] Leopold, *Sand County Almanac*, 203.
[37] Ibid. 204.

convictions—and this will not happen until philosophy and religion enter the debate.[38]

In one respect at least, Leopold's desire has been fulfilled. The field of environmental ethics has spawned a vast and ever-increasing body of literature ranging from abstract philosophical treatises to applied works dealing with specific conservation issues. An impressive array of academic journals addressing theoretical and practical matters can be found on the shelves of university libraries.[39] A complex array of debates informs the working ethos of the various conservation organizations, and philosophical arguments are cited as the rationale behind some extreme forms of environmental activism.[40]

Broadly speaking, two fundamental and contentious issues can be identified, which form the basis of subsequent debate. The first is concerned with the rationale behind ethical judgements and the second with the object(s) of valuation. As Attfield puts it,

> Without some kind of ethic (a theory of right and responsibility) and some kind of axiology (or value-theory), we lack guidance and direction for tackling problems, whether global, environmental or otherwise.[41]

ETHICAL THEORIES

Discussions on the rationale for environmental decision-making draw on the three dominant conceptions of morality in western philosophical thought: consequentialism, deontology, and virtue ethics.[42] Each of these is briefly outlined below, together with an account of their relevance to environmental ethics. As with all attempts to systematize, there is overlap between these moral theories.[43] Some environmental ethicists adopt positions that seem to

[38] Ibid. 210.

[39] At least five journals in the field of environmental ethics are listed in the Cambridge University Newton Catalogue, *Environmental Ethics*; *Environmental Values*; *Ethics and the Environment*; *Ethics, Place and Environment*; and *Worldviews, Environment, Culture, Religion*.

[40] E.g. Animal Liberation Front, 'The Morality of Animal Rights'.

[41] Attfield, *Global Environment*, 27.

[42] Also called perfectionism (Ogletree, *Christian Ethics*, 19).

[43] Frasz, 'Environmental Virtue Ethics'.

straddle the conceptual boundaries, and at a pragmatic level policy-making and practical decisions may not be clearly related to any one concept.[44]

Consequentialism

Consequentialist ethical theories are predicated on the utilitarian principles of Jeremy Bentham and J. S. Mill who advocated the Greatest Happiness Principle 'that actions are right in proportion as they tend to promote happiness, wrong as they tend to produce the reverse of happiness'[45] and that 'the standard is not the agent's happiness, but the greatest amount of happiness altogether'.[46] A consequentialist approach therefore suggests that ethical behaviour is that which produces the best overall consequences. It calculates the likely results of actions and makes decisions based on their relative value for human well-being.[47] This approach has been critiqued for its 'narrowly anthropocentric and utilitarian worldview' which implies an instrumental view of non-human nature.[48] In response to such anthropocentrism, environmentalists have advocated extending the range of ethical awareness into the biological community of species and ecosystems.[49] Thus consequentialist environmental ethics is concerned with maximizing the benefits of action in terms of non-human as well as human interests, and in particular with the good of whole biota or ecosystems rather than an individual

[44] E.g. the 'humane holism' which Fern attributes to Rolston and Callicott (Fern, *Nature*, 66; see also Deane-Drummond, *Ethics of Nature*).

[45] J. S. Mill 'Utilitarianism' in Plamenatz, *English Utilitarians*, 169.

[46] Ibid. 173. See also discussion in Hare, 'Utilitarianism'. Interestingly, Mill extends this beyond human happiness, 'so far as the nature of things admits, to the whole sentient creation' (Plamenatz, *English Utilitarians*, 174), although he does not develop this idea.

[47] Ogletree, *Christian Ethics*, 20–1.

[48] Dryzek, 'Green Reason', 195.

[49] Palmer, *Environmental Ethics*, 125. The most militant anti-anthropocentrism is deep ecology (a phrase coined by Arne Naess, Naess, *Outline of Ecosophy*), which takes a radically ecocentric perspective, at times hostile to all human activity. See Devall, 'Deep Ecology'.

species.[50] However, there is great debate over the scope and nature of the 'good of the whole' in environmental terms, particularly when conflicting interests emerge.[51]

Deontology

Deontological ethics is concerned with rules of right and wrong as determinant of behaviour, independent of the consequences.[52] It draws on Kantian and neo-Kantian ideas concerning the principle of the rational being to suggest that '[f]undamental justice and fairness towards persons . . . takes priority over more encompassing visions of human well-being'.[53] Thus the moral considerability of others becomes paramount as a basis for ethical decision-making.[54] A number of environmental ethicists, seeking to counter the traditional anthropocentric tendencies in ethics, have expanded the parameters of moral considerability to include any living organism.[55] The attitude of reverence for life, first advocated by Albert Schweitzer, is the basis for moral obligations or 'rules of duty' towards the natural world.[56] Deontologists are divided between those who suggest equality of all living things and those who advocate a hierarchical system of moral considerability, with the criterion of sentience as a guiding principle.[57]

[50] E.g. Attfield, *Environmental Concern*. See also Attfield, *Value and Obligation*; Singer, *Animal Liberation*.

[51] Palmer, *Environmental Ethics*, 116.

[52] Ibid. 15.

[53] Ogletree, *Christian Ethics*, 23.

[54] Ibid.

[55] Palmer, *Environmental Ethics*, 58.

[56] Schweitzer adduces, 'It is *good* to maintain and cherish life; it is *evil* to destroy and check life' (*Philosophy of Civilisation*, 254; Schweitzer's italics), and '[The ethic of reverence for life] . . . inspires us to join in a search for opportunities to afford help of some kind or other to the animals, to make up for the great amount of misery which they endure at our hands' (*Philosophy of Civilisation*, 265). See also Taylor, *Respect for Nature*, 90–8.

[57] Taylor (*Respect for Nature*) is an example of the first position, and Regan (*All That Dwell*) of the second.

Virtue Ethics

Virtue ethics focuses on the character of moral actors rather than their actions. Its beginnings are found in the writings of Aristotle, who stated that 'moral or ethical virtue is the product of habit'.[58] The human self can be developed and trained to exhibit certain virtues—or their corresponding vices. In contemporary ethical thought, virtue ethics takes on various shades of meaning, but is concerned with the cultivation of character traits that enable human flourishing.[59] It is the regular exercise of such virtues—'the fixed and stable moral dispositions from which ethical decisions flow'—that result in the full realisation of human potentiality or flourishing.[60]

Environmental virtue ethics is a relative newcomer in the field of environmental ethics. Its focus is on 'building of human character structure to incorporate the virtues that will lead us to value and preserve the environment for its own sake and for the sake of becoming better and more joyful persons'.[61] Sandler puts it in starker terms. Since ecosystem sustainability is a pre-condition of the cultivation of flourishing, and genuine virtue includes the cultivation of flourishing as one of its goals, '*any genuinely virtuous agent* will exhibit environmental sensitivity and be disposed to promote ecosystem sustainability' [Sandler's italics].[62] His viewpoint is predicated upon the extension of the concept of flourishing to include non-human entities, which is a natural outcome of Leopold's land ethic. As Shaw points out, virtue ethics avoids some of the problems encountered by the land ethic in trying to ascribe values in the biotic community (as discussed below).[63]

Both Shaw and Sandler are among a number of environmental ethicists who suggest what could be termed 'land' or ecological

[58] Aristotle, *Eth. Nic. II*, 71.
[59] Barton, *Understanding Ethics*, 63–4.
[60] Ibid. 65.
[61] Holly, 'Virtue Ethics', 392–3.
[62] Sandler, 'External Goods', 284.
[63] Shaw, 'Land Ethic', 61.

virtues.[64] While there are obvious areas of overlap between these environmental virtues, the diversity among them highlights the subjective and potentially nebulous nature of virtue ethics. It is notable, however, that a number of them, including those suggested by secular environmentalists, have resonance with biblical themes and ideas, including those of the prophetic texts. Of them, three may be singled out as being of particular interest: the virtue of wisdom,[65] that of humility (or its opposite, pride)[66] and that of justice.[67] Just a few examples will demonstrate that ideas that resonate with each of these principles can be found in varying degrees in the prophetic books studied in this volume. The appeal to wisdom is evident in the parable of the farmer (Isa. 28:23–9), and in the comparison between Israel's foolishness and the natural wisdom of a ox or ass (Isa. 1:2). Pride (whether of Israel or the surrounding nations) is regularly condemned by the prophets (e.g. Isa. 2:12–17, 10:12–19; Hos. 5:5), while the call for justice in society is one of the prophetic themes of these books (e.g. Amos 5:24; Isa. 1:17).

ASCRIBING VALUE

The second contentious issue in environmental ethics concerns the concept of value and the origin of moral worth. A number of questions can be identified, which will be briefly detailed here, but not discussed in detail. First, does all non-human nature have intrinsic value or are some parts merely valuable in instrumental terms (e.g. as

[64] Ibid. 63–6. See also Bouma-Prediger, 'Constructive Proposal'; Deane-Drummond, *Ethics of Nature*; Sandler, 'Environmental Virtue'. Alongside this could be set the principles of the Earth Bible Project (see above, Chapter 3).

[65] Bouma-Prediger, 'Constructive Proposal'; Deane-Drummond, *Ethics of Nature*; Shaw, 'Land Ethic'.

[66] Bouma-Prediger, 'Constructive Proposal'; Nash, *Loving Nature*; Sandler, 'Environmental Virtue'.

[67] Bouma-Prediger, 'Constructive Proposal'; Deane-Drummond, *Ethics of Nature*; Sandler, 'Environmental Virtue'. Deane-Drummond notes that although justice is normally associated with a deontological position, the virtue of justice has been fruitfully combined with a neo-Kantian position by Onora O'Neill (Deane-Drummond, *Ethics of Nature*, 46).

a food source)?[68] This debate is often linked to that mentioned above on equality between sentient and non-sentient nature.[69] Secondly, how is value in nature ascribed? Is it a matter of degree, i.e. do some natural entities or communities merit more value than others, and if so on what grounds? Moreover is moral value in nature *subjective*, i.e. conferred by a (human) valuer on to that which is valued, or *objective*, i.e. intrinsic to or an emergent property of that which is valued?[70]

The debate is further polarized between *individualist* environmental ethics, concerned with actions involving individual organisms or entities, and *collectivist* (or ecocentric) ones, which deal with ecological groupings such as biota or ecosystems.[71] Advocates of an individualist approach strive to develop criteria for determining the moral value of individuals and are only secondarily concerned with species, which are regarded as collections of individuals.[72] In contrast, collectivists talk in terms of 'biotic communities' and land as 'organism', and seek to develop an ethic that 'preserves the integrity, stability and beauty of the land community'.[73] Collectivist approaches to environmental ethics tend also to be consequentialist, concerned with maximizing 'the good of the whole'. These two approaches surface in a number of practical contexts, for example whenever there is debate over whether an invasive non-native species

[68] Rolston, *Environmental Ethics*. See also Benzoni, 'Theological Ethic'; Dryzek, 'Green Reason'; LaBar, 'Nonhuman Organisms'. The charge made by Callicott ('Intrinsic Value') that this dichotomy represents a 'radical ontological dualism' has been refuted by Preston ('Epistemology').

[69] It particularly surfaces in the context of animal welfare issues (e.g. Attfield, *Environmental Concern*; Hill, 'Human Excellence').

[70] See Benzoni, 'Theological Ethic'; Dryzek, 'Green Reason'; LaBar, 'Nonhuman Organisms'.

[71] Palmer's use of the term 'collectivist' rather than the more usual 'systemic' is followed here for clarity (Palmer, *Environmental Ethics*, 116).

[72] E.g. Regan, *All That Dwell*; Taylor, *Respect for Nature*. See discussion in Palmer, *Environmental Ethics*, 59–82.

[73] Leopold, *Sand County Almanac*, 204. Leopold's work has been developed by Callicott in numerous publications (e.g. 'Animal Liberation'; *Defense of the Land Ethic*; *Beyond the Land Ethic*), including an attempt to construct a contemporary Judaeo-Christian environmental ethic based on applying nature writer John Muir's 'citizenship' ethic to a perceptive exegesis of the two Genesis creation accounts (Callicott, 'Genesis'). See also Dryzek, 'Green Reason'.

of plant or animal should be culled to reduce competition with native species.[74]

Questions surrounding the ascription of value to non-human entities not only occupy environmental philosophers; they also shape ecological policy.[75] In practical terms, organisations involved in environmental issues take a variety of positions across the anthropocentric–ecocentric spectrum.[76] The former can tend towards an instrumental view of non-human nature, in which its worth is construed in terms of benefits to human populations.[77] Current concerns over the effect of climate change on human poverty levels and the campaign for sustainable development are situated at this end of the spectrum.[78] An ecocentric outlook, whether individualist or collectivist, ascribes intrinsic value to non-human nature, and is exemplified by campaigns to 'save' endangered species.[79]

A number of scholars have explored such debates from a theological perspective, seeking to articulate an appropriate Christian response to environmental ethics.[80] In most cases, this is undertaken without reference to the Bible; where texts are mentioned, it is often as passing references.[81] The present task is to examine how these environmental questions might be more specifically addressed by the biblical texts. It should be stressed that the aim is not to look for some hidden environmental agenda in the message of the prophets, but rather for areas of convergence (or perhaps disparity). This is a reciprocal rather than one-way process, exploring how the texts

[74] E.g. the recent government decision to cull ruddy duck populations, see DEFRA, 'Ruddy Duck'; RSPCA, 'Ruddy Duck'.

[75] See discussion in Attfield and Dell, *Values*.

[76] See discussion in Brennan, *Nature*; Gruen, *Reflecting on Nature*.

[77] The 1987 Bruntland Report on sustainable development (WCED, 'Our Common Future') and, more recently, the Stern Review (HM Treasury, *Stern Review*) have both addressed environmental issues in terms of human need.

[78] It is notable that all the major aid charities in the UK now campaign for reduction in carbon emissions.

[79] E.g. the work done by campaigning organizations such as the World Wide Fund for Nature and the Royal Society for the Protection of Birds.

[80] A critique of various approaches can be found in Deane-Drummond, *Ethics of Nature*, 31–8; see also Hessel, *Christianity and Ecology*; Northcott, *Environment*; Palmer, *Environmental Ethics*.

[81] An exception is Bouma-Prediger, *Beauty of the Earth*, who, however, makes little reference to the biblical prophets.

might help human beings live more sustainably in the contemporary world as well as how the world might influence our reading of the texts.

ENVIRONMENTAL ETHICS AND THE BIBLICAL TEXTS

The preceding discussion on ethical theories has been couched in the language of contemporary ethics and philosophy, and as such contains both terminology and concepts that are, by their very nature, foreign to the biblical texts. The thought world of the Old Testament is concrete rather than abstract, rooted in the experiences of life in a particular context, rather than based on philosophical speculation. It is therefore not surprising that in the Old Testament questions about how to live, and how to do so well, are not expressed in an abstract philosophical manner. This does not mean, however, that the texts have nothing to contribute to an evaluation of ethical responses to our contemporary situation. Issues to do with morality and behaviour are very much the concern of the Israelite prophets. Moreover, the biblical account of their experiences of life lived in relationship with their God, as well as in close connection with the land that is his gift to them, offers important insights for twenty-first-century environmental ethics.

Continuity and discontinuity with the text

The starting point for the discussion is to establish the obvious points of continuity and discontinuity between the text and contemporary environmental issues. At its broadest level, continuity can be seen in the concept of interrelationship which governs both the prophetic depictions of the world and the understanding of it postulated by the science of ecology. Following on from this, however, is a major area of discontinuity, namely the religious dimension of the biblical texts: their perspective is wholeheartedly theocentric, while self-evidently that of ecology is not.

An interrelational perspective

Contemporary ecological science is based on 'the empirical and experimental study of the relations between living and nonliving organisms within their ecosystems'.[82] It is concerned with interrelationships within the natural world, both at the level of individual species and as part of larger biotic communities. Many ecologists are concerned purely with studying the natural habitats and relationships of species 'in the wild'. However, at the level of environmental policy the effect of human culture and technology is increasingly an important factor, as human impact on ecosytems and habitats continues to worsen.

In the biblical texts studied, as has been suggested in each of the exegetical chapters, the prophetic view of the world also presumes an inherent interrelationship in the world, whereby what happens in one sphere affects other areas too. Although not privy to such scientific and technological understanding as modern day ecologists, the ancient writers are also observers of the world they live in and aware of its natural rhythms and seasons, as well as its flora and fauna. Like most in a pre-industrial society, they rely on natural phenomena such as sun, moon, and stars for orientation and time-keeping, and on cloud formation and the behaviour of certain species to determine the weather. They are closely involved in the success or failure of crops and the welfare of livestock, since the community's livelihood and well-being depend upon them.

There is also a sense of the unknown, even danger about the world, which reflects the struggle to survive in what is often a hostile environment. Wild places are inhabited by wild animals (e.g. Isa. 30:6); extreme weather or natural disaster might cause sudden and devastating damage (e.g. Amos 8:8); always there is the threat that crops will be overgrown by 'thorns and briers' (e.g. Isa. 7:23–5). Underlying the prophets' experience of both wilderness and domestic life is an understanding of connectivity, of cause and effect, act and consequence, that encompasses the whole of the created order, not just its human population.

[82] M. Tucker and Grim, 'World Religions and Ecology', 15.

The picture presented by the prophetic texts of the interconnection between human beings and the non-human creation suggests that they are concerned with more than just survival. As has been demonstrated in the exegesis chapters the relationship between human and non-human is part of a fundamental order in the world.[83] When this works well, both human society and the rest of creation flourish (e.g. Isa. 32:16–20; Hos. 2:20 [18]); when the order breaks down, everything suffers (e.g. Isa. 24:3–6; Hos. 4:1–3). The knowledge that human behaviour impacts other parts of creation, and vice versa, and the presupposition that this is part of the moral order of the universe form a fundamental part of the prophetic message.

A theocentric foundation

In the prophetic texts, as indeed in the Old Testament in general, interconnection is a three-way relationship, one that incorporates YHWH as well as human and non-human creation. This clearly differs from an ecological understanding that is concerned solely with living organisms and their habitats. Furthermore, the biblical emphasis is on viewing life and the world from a *theocentric* perspective (as exemplified in the frequent designation of the prophetic word as 'the word of YHWH'). When crops fail, it is seen as the action of YHWH (e.g. Amos 4:6–10); the behaviour of both weather and the cosmos is understood in terms of theophany (e.g. Amos 1:2; Isa. 13:10, 13). This perspective 'co-orders both human and other creatures to their Creator'.[84] It contrasts with ecological debates couched in the language of ecocentric versus anthropocentric interests and reduces, and perhaps even eliminates, the need to prioritize one over the other.

[83] Von Rad suggests that 'the most characteristic feature of [Israel's] understanding of reality was the fact that she believed man to stand in a quite specific, highly dynamic, existential relationship with his environment' (*Wisdom in Israel*, 301).

[84] DeWitt, 'Behemoth and Batrachians', 297; see also Gustafson, *Theocentric Ethics*.

KEY ISSUES FOR THE TEXTS

In order to go beyond these basic broad areas of continuity and discontinuity, and to facilitate dialogue between the ancient and the contemporary, the core environmental ethics issues that were outlined above have been simplified to a number of seminal ideas or questions that can be posed to the biblical texts. These are:

1. The value ascribed to the non-human creation—whether it has intrinsic worth or merely instrumental value.
2. The ethics of human behaviour—whether morality is based on duty and legal observance, on consideration of best possible outcomes, or on the virtues that promote flourishing.
3. The relative importance of individual and community in ethical consideration.
4. Whether nature is a stable entity or a world in flux.
5. The tension between culture and nature.

Of these, the first three points clearly concern issues significantly addressed by the biblical texts. The latter two have less resonance with the texts but represent areas in which ambivalence or tension is present, both in the text and in the contemporary world.

The value of non-human creation

First impressions suggest that in the prophetic texts that we have examined the interaction between human and non-human creation portrays an instrumental view of the earth's resources, in which the non-human creation is valued primarily in terms of its ability to support human life or contribute to economic prosperity. The quantity of agricultural descriptions and motifs that feature extensively in First Isaiah, and significantly in Amos and Hosea, support this impression. The well-being or misery of the people (whether God's own people or other nations) is depicted in terms of the failure or success of their agriculture and husbandry (e.g. Isa. 5:8–10, 16:8–10, 30:23–4; Amos 4:7–8, 9:13–15; Hos. 2:11 [9], 14 [12], 23–5 [21–3]). Furthermore, wild animals are often regarded as a problem or threat and their encroachment on and destruction of the human urban environment as a result of God's judgement (e.g. Isa. 13:21–2, 34:13–15; Amos 5:19–20).

There are, however, a number of features that suggest that the non-human creation is regarded as possessing value in its own right. First, in all three books the language of the earth (or land) mourning creates an identity for the earth distinct from its human inhabitants (Amos 1:2; Hos. 4:3; Isa. 24:4).[85] Furthermore, on a number of occasions the cosmos functions as an independent referent. Heavens and earth are appealed to as witnesses (Isa. 1:2, 28:23, see also Mic. 6:2) or as partners in dialogue with YHWH (Hos. 2:23–4 [21–2]).

Secondly, the non-human creation provides a means of evaluating the challenges of human life (e.g. Amos 7:1–3, 8:1–2) and is even held up as a moral example for human conduct (Isa. 1:3; Amos 6:12). Thirdly, the association of non-human creation with descriptions of YHWH's might and activity suggests an understanding of the world that is not exclusively concerned with its social or economic value. This is exemplified by Hosea, in which figurative descriptions of YHWH almost always feature imagery of the natural world (e.g. 5: 12, 14, 11:10, 13:8), and by the hymnic fragments of Amos, where the non-human creation functions to demonstrate God's power to human beings (Amos 4:13, 5:8–9, 9:5–6).

In summary, the dominant role played by agriculture in ancient Israelite society might suggest that the earth's natural resources be regarded purely as a commodity.[86] This does not seem to be the perspective of the prophets, who not only recognize the material and economic value of the produce of the land, but also assign a place for the wider non-human creation in YHWH's story which far outstrips any utilitarian value.

The ethics of human behaviour

What governs human conduct according to Amos, Hosea, and First Isaiah? Is it adherence to a set of duties or laws that determine

[85] Hayes, *The Earth Mourns*.
[86] Borowski, *Agriculture*, 10.

priorities and assign moral value? Or does the prospect of certain consequences motivate behaviour—whether the desire to aim for the best possible outcomes or to avoid negative ones? Is there a virtue ethic operating, which advocates character qualities that enable the flourishing of all?

Old Testament morality has usually been described in terms of deontological and consequentialist ethical models, as noted by Barton, but there would seem to be hints in the prophetic texts of virtues that are implicitly valued for their own sakes rather than out of legal requirement or fear of consequences.[87] However, as is so often the case when applying external criteria to biblical material the whole picture cannot be defined in terms of one approach or another. Rather, as will be seen, the prophetic material exhibits features of all three philosophical positions—deontological, consequentialist, and virtue ethic.

Law and obligation to codes of behaviour play a significant part in the ethical mandate of these prophetic texts. In Hosea the peoples' sin is classed as lack of knowledge of God and failing to adhere to 'the teaching', which in turn is reflected in the well-being of the earth (Hosea 4). Yet this emphasis on the obligations of obedience is balanced by Hosea 2, in which the promise of restored relationship with YHWH and with the all creation is held up as an encouragement to Israel to respond to him (Hos. 2:16–21 [14–19]).

The prophets Amos, Isaiah and Micah all decry hollow cultic observance (Amos 5:21–3; Isa. 1:12–15; Mic. 6:6–7), in favour of obligations towards the poor (Amos 5:24; Isa. 1:16–17; Mic. 6:8). Both the religious and social practices outlined in these books might reasonably constitute an appeal to legalism or a sense of duty. Yet each prophetic book also contains a sense of the consequences of actions, whether positive or negative. In Isaiah, obedience to YHWH will result in eating 'the good of the land' (טוב הארץ) and failure to do so in violent death (Isa. 1:19–20). Amos advocates pursuit of goodness and justice as a means of securing divine presence and favour (Amos 5:14–15). Micah highlights the consequences of

[87] Barton, 'Virtue', 71. He suggests that narrative texts of the Old Testament might be fruitful for the identification of a virtue ethic at the implicit rather than explicit level.

dishonest and violent practices, as well as apostasy, in terms of material shortfall (Mic. 6:13–15). This might not exactly represent consequentialism in the utilitarian sense of contemporary ethics; however it does suggest that in these prophetic books the consequences of Israel's actions (whether good or ill) is regarded as of paramount importance.

In the light of the interest in virtue ethics that has developed among environmental ethicists in the past decade or so, slightly more attention will be given to exploring this with respect to the prophetic texts.[88] Aspects of a virtuous character are hinted at in each of the books. In Hosea it is by default—virtuous behaviour is notoriously absent and instead pride and faithlessness characterise Israel's behaviour (5:5, 7), as does the breakdown of society's moral values (4:2). Where positive virtues are advocated or looked for, it is couched in the language of both cause and effect (Hos. 10:12), and, in conjunction with the knowledge of God, of legal observance (4:1).

The humbling of the proud is a notable theme in Isaiah and to a lesser extent, Amos. Individuals who exhibit arrogance are brought down (Isa. 5:15, 13:11), and national pride is explicitly condemned—whether of Israel (Amos 6:6, see also 8:7) or of foreign nations (Assyria, Isa. 10:12–13; Babylon, 14:11; Moab, 16:16; Tyre 23:9). In restoration promises, those that are humble will receive favour (Isa. 11:4, 29:19). The antithesis between wisdom and foolishness also plays its part in Isaiah, both in proverbial material, which presents examples of right living (Isa. 1:2–3, 28:24–9) and in discourse (Isa. 32:4–8).

The word 'justice' (משׁפט) occurs frequently in the prophets, although not always in the sense of a character trait or virtue.[89] However, it seems to denote the active pursuit of virtue in Isa. 1:17

[88] Barton suggests that 'a deliberately imprecise set of ideas' should be adopted when exploring whether the concept of virtue ethics is anticipated in the Old Testament (ibid. 65). This perhaps reflects both the ambiguities inherent in understanding the concept of 'flourishing', as well as the difficulties in looking the Old Testament through the lens of Greek philosophy.

[89] In its pairing with 'righteousness' (צדקה) it more usually denotes a state of affairs or 'world order' (Schmid, *Gerechtigkeit*). Hosea's use of משׁפט is primarily to denote God's judgement (5:1, 11, 6:5).

where the injunction to 'seek justice' is paired with 'learn to do good'.[90] Likewise in Isa. 16:5, the ideal ruler is one 'seeking justice' and 'quick in righteousness' alongside the virtues of faithfulness and kindness. In Amos 5:15 the practice of justice is paired with love of good and hatred of evil, a theme that is also picked up in Mic. 6:8.[91]

None of these prophets is explicitly concerned about the effect of virtuous living on the non-human environment or indeed of duties to, or responsibilities for, its well-being. In this respect then their perspective is anthropocentric. Yet each portrays clearly human effect on the rest of the created order. In Hosea, when the virtues of truthfulness and kindness are abrogated, the whole environment suffers (Hos. 4:1–3); in Amos and Isaiah, when justice fails the earth is disrupted, the harvest fails, cosmic disturbance occurs, and urban infrastructure disintegrates (e.g. Isa. 24:1–13; Amos 8:4–10). The opposite is also true: the prospect of restoration—of the knowledge of God, and of human social structures—is accompanied by the promise of renewal of the whole creation. This finds its fullest and most detailed expression in Isaiah, which portrays the flourishing of sentient and non-sentient creation, wild and tame animals as justice, righteousness, and peace are restored (e.g. Isa. 11:1–10, 32:15–20, 35:1–10).[92]

In these biblical texts, ethical perspectives, whether virtues, duties, or consequences, come together in the theocentric perspective of their authors. Obedience to, and relationship with YHWH is held out as a means of ensuring well-being for all creation, human and non-human, sentient and non-sentient, agricultural and wild.[93]

[90] As already noted, there is overlap between deontological and virtue ethic concepts of justice. In these texts, the distinction between a just person and the practice of just acts is blurred.

[91] Cf. Mic. 3:1–2 which appears to be a reversal of Amos 5:14–15.

[92] Blenkinsopp notes that in First Isaiah, 'ecological transformation [is] always associated with the creation of a social order based on justice and righteousness' (Blenkinsopp, *Isaiah 1–39*, 434).

[93] See Fretheim's account of Israelite self-understanding which roots its law in creation theology (Fretheim, *God and World*, 133–56).

Individual and community approaches

The tensions in contemporary environmental ethics between collectivist and individualist perspectives do not find the same degree of parallel in the prophetic texts as the previous two points. This is because the contemporary debate on this issue is largely a factor of the negative effect of human impact on the natural world over the past century, and the need to monitor and regulate this.[94] Nevertheless, the texts hint at some principles that have application in today's context.

First, the message of the prophets is in most cases directed at communities (e.g. foreign nations, people of Israel, inhabitants of Jerusalem) or social groupings (e.g. priests, Hos. 4:4–10; landowners, Isa. 5:8–10) rather than individuals.[95] Secondly, for the prophets, the religious identity of Israel is based upon its status as the community of God's chosen people, exemplified by the great deliverance from slavery in Egypt (Hos. 2:25 [23] (cf 1:8), 11:1; Isa. 14:1; Amos 2:10). Thirdly, moral values and behaviour are worked out within the framework of this community, and it is on the community rather than on individuals that judgement is pronounced as well as, on occasions, promises of hope.[96] If, as Ogletree suggests, the moral soundness of a community is most clearly seen in the treatment of its most vulnerable members, then by Amos and Isaiah's accounts, both Israel and Judah are seriously flawed.[97]

The community focus that characterizes the message of the prophets does not denigrate the place of individual responsibility. Personal accountability and guilt are highlighted in the texts, both by messages addressing specific categories of people (e.g. Amos 4:1, 6:1) and by those listing specific wrongs (e.g. Hos. 4:2; Isa. 5:18–23). But 'moral responsibility is a corporate responsibility' and the interdependence

[94] Cittadino, 'Ecology'.

[95] Even in messages addressed to specific individual rulers (e.g. King Ahaz in Isa. 7–8) the individual's role as head of the society presupposes a community focus.

[96] G. Tucker, 'Role of Prophets', 165.

[97] Ogletree, *Christian Ethics*, 80.

of the community means that the failing of some part of it can bring consequences for the whole.[98] This highlights one of the serious ethical problems posed by the prophets' indictment against social injustice—that the punishments YHWH inflicts (e.g. with respect to Amos drought 4:7, flood 5:8, earthquake 8:8) are as devastating for poor as for rich.[99] This calls into question the very nature of the concept of justice, which seems to punish those least able to stand for themselves.[100]

The problem is explained in terms of theodicy by a number of scholars. Koch notes with regard to the act/consequence matrix in Hosea, 'Yahweh's action consists of the setting in motion of the consequences of a human action'.[101] As Barton suggests,

> The prophets' object is to demonstrate that not only is disaster coming, which many suspected, but that it is coming for a good reason ... and that it vindicates (rather than impugning) the justice of Yahweh.[102]

The interesting parallel in contemporary environmental ethics is with the inequity that ecological problems bring, since it is the world's poor who are the worst affected by anthropogenic environmental problems such as global warming.[103] Even the effects of so-called 'natural' disasters, which also have the most detrimental effects on those who are poor, weak, and vulnerable, are notably exacerbated by human actions.[104]

[98] B. Birch, *Let Justice Roll Down*, 258.

[99] Dempsey alludes to the problem of divine injustice towards the poor, but does not develop the issue (Dempsey, *Hope Amid the Ruins*, 61–3, 70). It is discussed more fully with respect to Ezekiel by Carley, 'Harsh Justice', 147–50.

[100] These issues are explored more fully in Marlow, 'Justice for Whom?'

[101] Koch, 'Doctrine of Retribution', 67.

[102] Barton, 'History and Rhetoric', 55; see also Koch, 'Doctrine of Retribution', 64–9; Crenshaw, 'Theodicy'.

[103] As a result of an increase in 'extreme' weather events (e.g. severe hurricanes, flooding), erratic rainfall leading to crop failure, desertification, etc.

[104] E.g. the destruction of mangrove swamps (nature's flood protection) in coastal regions to enable commercial development results in more devastating flooding than would otherwise occur, as demonstrated in the Indian Ocean tsunami of Dec. 2004, and Hurricane Katrina in 2005.

Ambiguity in the texts

These three issues—the value of non-human creation, the ethics of human behaviour and the importance of community in ethics—represent important categories in the discussion of the biblical texts in the light of such a pressing contemporary issue. Each category is predicated upon, and derives its weight from, the principle of interconnectivity—one of the basic tenets of the exegesis chapters. Before exploring the full implications of this, two further issues will be explored in brief. These represent two areas in which the prophetic texts exhibit a certain ambiguity: the ideal of the 'balance of nature' and the culture/nature dichotomy.

Balance of nature

Until relatively recently environmental science operated within the paradigm of stability and equilibrium in nature. This suggested that the natural world operated within self-regulating and stable closed systems, independently of human interference.[105] This model of the balance of nature has gradually given way to an understanding that ecosystems are in a state of continual flux and change, even apart from human interference, a paradigm known as *non-equilibrium.*[106] The implications of this gradual change in perspective are not inconsiderable for environmental ethics, at both a philosophical and a practical level.[107] However, the pressing question for this study is to what extent the prophets adopt a view of the world as a stable entity, or whether the new non-equilibrium model finds any currency.

The initial impression is that balance in the natural world is viewed as an ideal and as part of the outcome of restored relationship with YHWH (e.g. Hos. 2:20–4 [18–23]; Amos 9:13–15; Isa. 30:23–6). This balance is expressed from the human perspective in most instances, with freedom from weeds and wild animals as part of the ideal (e.g.

[105] Deane-Drummond, *Ethics of Nature*, 36–7.

[106] Lodge/Hamlin, *New Ecology*, 7.

[107] See the treatment of this by Deane-Drummond, *Ethics of Nature*, 37–8, and the more detailed analysis by Callicott, 'Balance of Nature'.

Isa. 35:9, 30:23–4). But on several occasions the anticipated restoration of cosmic harmony is described in terms well beyond human experience or understanding of the natural world. In particular this is true of Isaiah 11, which portrays a scene of paradisiacal peace in which the normal balance of predation and destruction is overturned and carnivorous eating habits transformed. Likewise, Isaiah 35 depicts the transformation of a whole ecosystem in the context of the miraculous reversal of human infirmities. These present a perspective in which the natural order of creation has been overthrown, and things happen contrary to the laws of nature. In these texts at least, the idea of a stable balanced world is no more a reality for the prophetic writers than it is for ecologists today.

A culture/nature divide

The polarization in environmental ethics between biocentric and anthropocentric positions is one that is read back into biblical texts by certain eco-hermeneutic interpretations.[108] However, as Brown observes, the category distinction is not one necessarily recognized by ancient authors, for whom the natural world and human civilization represent 'the inseparable products of divinely instituted creation'.[109]

Although the interconnection between the non-human creation and human society is clearly articulated in the prophetic texts, nevertheless there are clear boundaries between human experience in the settled, farmed land and the hostile territory of wild animals (e.g Hos. 2:14 [12]; Isa. 34:10–15 and Isaianic references to 'thorns and briars' in antithesis to vines). Wild animals and scrubland are portrayed as a threat to human civilization and survival, suggesting a thoroughly anthropocentric perspective to these texts, and a separation between human life (culture) and non-human (nature) that might conceivably have presaged current alienation from nature.

However, a number of factors suggest that this interpretation is too simplistic. First, it is evident from First Isaiah that familiarity

[108] Exemplified in the Earth Bible Project's category distinction between Earth and human beings (Habel, *Readings*).

[109] W. P. Brown, *Ethos of Cosmos*, 2.

with 'the wild' informed the prophetic vision. The sheer number of wild species named suggests that observation of the landscape outside the city formed part of daily life.[110] Secondly, the concept of wilderness is ambiguous in the prophetic texts. As discussed in the chapter on Hosea, it is both the place of barrenness and alienation, but also of divine encounter and renewal (Hos. 2:16 [14]; see also Hos. 13:5; Amos 2:10).[111] At a more mundane level, in each book human interface with the wilderness takes place in the context of the everyday reality of shepherding flocks, both in metaphor (e.g. Mic 7: 14) and in reality (Amos 1:2, 7:14–15). This is not to detract from its uncertain, even hostile characteristics. However, a part of Israelite community life is involved with, and dependent on the wild.

Thirdly, in Isaiah 34:14–17, although wild animals enter and settle in the urban domain, they do so in the context of divine initiation and order. Furthermore, the text indicates that this is a place of long-term rest and of fecundity for these wild species, suggesting that in this instance at least, human needs are not the main priority. These three examples of the blurring of parameters between nature and culture, non-human creation and community are evidence of what Brown calls 'the integral relationship between creation's ethos and human ethic'.[112]

ENVIRONMENTAL ETHICS AND THE OLD TESTAMENT

To sum up then, so far this chapter has sought to explore ways in which an environmental ethic for the contemporary world might engage with the textual material of the prophets, in particular Amos, Hosea, and First Isaiah. Most studies of the ethics of the Old Testament, while providing useful background and examples of a variety of approaches to the texts, are not addressed specifically to

[110] Approximately fourteen species of birds/mammals and seven of snakes (depending on identification of the correct species in translation). See Chapter 6.

[111] Discussed in Chapter 5.

[112] W. P. Brown, *Ethos of Cosmos*, 384.

environmental issues. The exceptions are studies by Rodd and by Wright, which both explore the possibility of using the Bible in ecological ethics, yet reach diametrically opposite conclusions. As already noted, this can be attributed to two distinct but connected factors. First, Rodd's treatment of individual texts which, in his opinion, fail to offer a satisfactory contemporary environmental ethic contrasts with Wright's broader thematic approach, which suggests the ancient Israelite world view as a paradigm for responsible living in today's world. Secondly, Rodd's starting point is the conviction that biblical ethics can only be descriptive, not normative, while Wright's is the theological endorsement of the Bible as a text for the contemporary church.

Diversity in environmental ethics

The burgeoning field of environmental philosophy covers a wide-ranging spectrum of concepts drawn from the field of ethical philosophy in general. Among environmental ethicists there is great variety in approach, based on the three broad theoretical areas of classical ethics—deontological, consequentialist, and virtue ethics. Each approach includes a range of opinions on questions of value and defining interest groups. Each leads to a plethora of applications in the highly contextual arena of environmental policy. None of these can be seamlessly or exclusively applied to the biblical texts, both on account of the conceptual differences between the ancient Hebrew and the modern worlds, and because the categories themselves are more fluid and overlapping than theorists maintain. Despite these difficulties, a number of points of connection between contemporary environmental ethics and the biblical prophetic books have been established.

A new model for reading the texts

Three main areas in which the worlds of the prophetic material and the twenty-first century intersect have been suggested: (*a*) the ascription of value; (*b*) reasons for human morality; and (*c*) the priority of

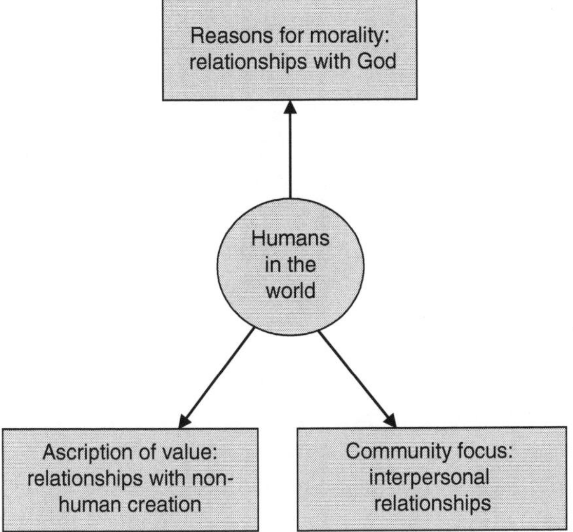

Figure 9. An interrelational Old Testament environmental ethic

community. These are not three arbitrary categories; rather they relate to and extend the triangular paradigm of ecological interrelationship that was discussed in Chapter 3, and which the exegetical chapters have explored, to suggest an interrelational model for deriving environmental ethics from the Old Testament. This model can be displayed diagrammatically as in Figure 9.

The model draws upon the principle of interconnectivity—which itself forms the basis both for the science of ecology and for the world view of the prophetic texts studied. It presumes the fundamental interrelationship between God, human beings and the natural world which the prophets so clearly articulate, but it develops and reconceptualizes this in a more specific way. As can be seen from the diagram, the central core of the model is human place in the world. This is not an attempt to undermine the theocentric concerns of the texts or to presume that an anthropocentric orientation is the primary consideration. It merely reflects the reality that ethics (insofar as human beings can conceive of it) is concerned with *human* morality and that human ethical reflection is by its very nature constructed from a human perspective. In this respect then the model is anthropocentric, but not in an exploitative or utilitarian sense.[113]

The central circle of the model is deliberately phrased in the plural: 'human*s* in the world' in order not to presuppose an exclusively individualistic understanding of human identity and behaviour—an unfortunate tendency that characterizes western society. How we understand our place in the world is at once both individual, dependent upon our own perceptions of reality, and communal, developed in the context of the social groups to which we belong (family, religious community, neighbourhood, etc.).

From this centre point of human 'being' in the world, human ethical reflection and decision-making must function in three directions—towards God, towards the non-human and towards other people (whether individuals or communities). As Figure 9 indicates, each of these directions concurs with one of the three areas of intersection between the prophetic texts and contemporary environmental ethics.

The *basis for morality* in a theocentric framework is predicated upon human understanding of, and relationship to, God. It is this characteristic above all that distinguishes between a Christian ethical framework and one couched in non-religious terms, just as it marks the discontinuity between the relational matrix of the prophets and that of ecological science. With regard to environmental concern, the Christian affirmation of obedience to God, combined with the belief in a creator God and a good creation which is shared by the other Abrahamic faiths, strengthens the case for responsible living in a world under stress.

The extent to which *value is ascribed* to the non-human world informs the way that human beings relate to the rest of the created order. The vision of the prophets is not of a utilitarian anthropocentricity, but one where human and non-human creation intersect, and are mutually dependent. In this 'landscape', to use Hailwood's term, the desolation and destruction that is the result of human hubris, greed or violence affects both human society and the natural world.[114] So too, the sense of hope that the prophets' messages of

[113] See the discussion on terminology in the Introduction to this volume.
[114] Hailwood, *Green Liberal.*

restoration convey concern all parts of the created order. The call for human ethical decision-making to move away from an exclusively utilitarian perspective on the non-human creation is one that finds resonance in the biblical texts.

The *role of communities* as the loci of ethical formation and action has already been discussed. The third direction of the model develops this beyond the local and cultural subgroups to which all human beings belong, to consider relationships within a broader framework. In the biblical prophets, the indictment against unethical living concerns attitudes both to those who are 'other', i.e. foreigners, and to those who are disadvantaged, i.e. widows and orphans. The global nature of the environmental issues faced today, coupled with the negative impacts on poor and marginalized populations worldwide, requires a fresh outworking of the prophetic call for justice and righteousness. This has enormous implications for the lifestyle choices of those living in the affluent west.

This ethical model, like most models, is partial and incomplete, and no doubt flawed in many respects. Nevertheless, it highlights the fact that the principles that govern ethical decision-making in the contemporary world are not foreign to the biblical text, and establishes important points of contact between the two. These points of contact invite a rereading of the biblical text in the light of current environmental concerns which is neither dependent on a few individual proof texts nor based on systematic theological interpretation. It opens the way for dialogue between ecology and religion, specifically the Judaeo-Christian tradition, by engaging in a real way with the ethical issues and principles as well as with the biblical texts. In the coming decades the impact of the projected dramatic increase in environmental refugees will have ethical implications for all nations and their citizens.[115] The challenge before religious communities such as the church is that of being prepared to exercise the moral leadership needed to prevent isolationist and reactionary attitudes to such changes, and to demonstrate an ethic which values all people and the whole of creation.

[115] Myers, 'Environmental Refugees'.

In 2007 an Environment Agency survey of leading environmentalists and scientists asked them to name fifty things that will save the planet. The role of faith communities and their leaders was listed second:

> It's time the world's faith groups reminded us we have a duty to restore and maintain the ecological balance of the planet. Christians, Muslims, Hindus and others already believe that it is morally wrong to damage the environment. The problem is that many people simply choose to ignore this.[116]

This survey highlights a remarkable shift among some sections of the conservation community. To respond to its challenge, it is vital that the church be better informed of the rich contribution of its own scriptures to a positive understanding of the creation as a basis for raising awareness of environmental issues and promoting good practice among its own members and the wider community. The texts of the biblical prophets are a rich source of reflection on ways in which human beings interact with the rest of creation as well as with God. Although the issues that their authors addressed are vastly different from those we face today, these texts invite us to rediscovery of our fundamental interconnection with the rest of creation and to discover ways to live more sustainably within it.

[116] Environment Agency, '50 Things That Will Save the Planet'.

Bibliography

Ackroyd, P. R. 'Isaiah I-XII: Presentation of a Prophet', in *Congress Volume, Göttingen 1977*, *VT* Supp. 29, ed. J. A. Emerton, 16–48. Leiden: Brill, 1978.

Aerts, Diederik et al. *Worldviews: From Fragmentation to Integration.* Brussels: VUB Press, 1994.

Aichele, G., ed. *The Postmodern Bible: the Bible and Culture Collective.* New Haven: Yale University Press, 1995.

Aitken, James, K. 'Jewish Tradition and Culture', in *The Early Christian World*, Vol. 1, ed. Philip Esler, 80–110. London and New York: Routledge, 2000.

Albrektson, Bertil. *History and the Gods: An Essay on the Idea of Historical Events as Divine Manifestations in the Ancient Near East and in Israel.* Lund: CWK Gleerup, 1967.

Albright, William Foxwell. *Yahweh and the Gods of Canaan.* London: Athlone Press, 1968.

Allen, Leslie. *The Books of Joel, Obadiah, Jonah and Micah*, NICOT. London: Hodder & Stoughton, 1976.

—— *Psalms 101–150*, WBC. Waco, Tex.: Word Books, 1983.

Alt, Albrecht. *Essays on Old Testament History and Religion*, trans. R. A. Wilson. Oxford: Blackwells, 1966 [Ger. 1953].

Alter, Robert. *The Art of Biblical Poetry.* New York: Basic Books, 1985.

—— and Frank Kermode, eds. *The Literary Guide to the Bible.* London: Collins, 1987.

Andersen, Francis, and David Noel Freedman. *Hosea: A New Translation with Introduction and Commentary*, AB. New York: Doubleday & Co, 1980.

—— *Amos: A New Translation with Introduction and Commentary*, AB. New York: Doubleday, 1989.

Anderson, G. W. 'Isaiah XXIV–XXVII Reconsidered', in *Congress Volume, Bonn 1962*, *VT* Supp. 9, ed. G. W. Anderson, 118–26. Leiden: Brill, 1963.

Anderson, Bernhard. *Creation versus Chaos.* Philadelphia: Fortress Press, 1987.

—— *From Creation to New Creation.* Minneapolis: Fortress Press, 1994.

—— ed. *Creation in the Old Testament.* London: SPCK, 1984.

Animal Liberation Front. 2007. 'The Morality of Animal Rights', http://www.animalliberationfront.com/Philosophy/Morality/Morality-index.htm.

Annas, Julia. 'Naturalism in Greek Ethics: Aristotle and After', in *Proceedings of the Boston Area Colloqium in Ancient Philosophy*, IV, ed. J. Cleary and D. C. Shartin, 149–71. Lanham, New York, and London: University Press of America, 1989.

Aquinas, Thomas. *Compendium of Saint Thomas's Theology in English*, ed. E. O'Donnell. Vol. 1. Dublin: James Duffy, 1859.

—— *Summa Theologica: Part I*, trans. Fathers of the English Dominican Province. London: Burns Oates & Washbourne, 1937.

—— *Summa Theologica: Part III (Supplement)*, trans. Fathers of the English Dominican Province. London: Burns Oates & Washbourne, 1942.

—— *Summa Theologicae: Cosmogony (1a. 65–74)*, ed. William Wallace. Vol. 10, *Summa Theologicae: Latin Text and English Translation*. London: Blackfriars, 1967.

Aristotle. *Nicomachean Ethics II*, trans. H. Rackam. 2nd edn. Vol. 19, LCL. Cambridge, Mass.: Harvard University Press, 1933.

—— *Politics*, trans. Peter L. Phillips Simpson. Chapel Hill: University of North Carolina Press, 1997.

Armstrong, Edward A. *Saint Francis, Nature Mystic: The Derivation and Significance of the Nature Stories in the Franciscan Legend*. Berkeley: University of California Press, 1973.

Armstrong, Regis J. *St Francis of Assisi: Writings for a Gospel Life*. Slough: St Paul's, 1994.

—— and Ignatius C Brady. *Francis and Clare: Complete Works*. London: SPCK, 1982.

Assman, Jan. *Ma'at: Gerechtigkeit und Unsterblichkeit im Alten Ägypten*. Munich: Verlag C. H. Beck, 1995.

Attenborough, Sir David. 'I'd show George Bush a few graphs', in *Natural World* (2005).

Attfield, Robin. *The Ethics of Environmental Concern*. Oxford: Blackwell, 1983.

—— *A Theory of Value and Obligation*. London: Croom Helm, 1987.

—— *The Ethics of the Global Environment*. Edinburgh: Edinburgh University Press, 1999.

Attfield, Robin, and Katharine J. Dell, eds. *Values, Conflict and the Environment*. 2nd edn. Aldershot: Avebury, 1996.

Augustine. *The City of God*, ed. Marcus Dods. Vol. 1, *The Works of Aurelius Augustine, Bishop of Hippo*. Edinburgh: T. & T. Clark, 1871.

—— *Confessions*, trans. Philip Schaff. Vol. 1, NPNF[1]. Peabody, Mass.: Hendrickson, 1886. Reprint, Peabody, Mass.: Hendrickson, 1994.

—— *The Literal Meaning of Genesis*, trans. John Hammond Taylor. 2 vols. New York: Newman Press, 1982.

—— 'Two Books on Genesis against the Manichees', in *Saint Augustine: Two Books on Genesis against the Manichees and On the Literal Interpretation of Genesis. An Unfinished Book*, ed. Roland J. Teske, 143–88. FC 84. Washington: Catholic University of America Press, 1991.

—— 'On the Literal Interpretation of Genesis: An Unfinished Book', in *Saint Augustine: Two Books on Genesis against the Manichees and On the Literal Interpretation of Genesis. An Unfinished Book*, ed. Roland J. Teske, 143–88. FC 84. Washington: Catholic University of America Press, 1991.

—— *On Genesis Against the Manicheans*, trans. Edmund Hill, *The Works of Saint Augustine: A Translation for the 21st Century*. New York: New City Press, 2002.

—— *On Genesis*, trans. Edmund Hill, *The Works of Saint Augustine: A Translation for the 21st Century*. New York: New City Press, 2002.

Bach, R. 'Bauen und Pflanzen', in *Studien zur Theologie der alttestamentlichen Überlieferungen*, ed. R. Rendtorff and K. Koch, 7–32. Neukirchen: Neukirchener Verlag, 1961.

Ball, Jim, and Steven Bouma-Prediger. 'An Urgent Call to Action: Scientists and Evangelicals Unite to Protect Creation.' Washington, D.C.: Centre for Health and the Global Environment/National Association of Evangelicals, 2007.

Ballard, Harold Wayne Jr. *The Divine Warrior Motif in the Psalms.* N. Ricjland Hills, Tex.: BIBAL Press, 1999.

Barker, William. 'Isaiah 24–27: Studies in a Cosmic Polemic.' Unpublished thesis, University of Cambridge, 2006.

Barr, James. *The Semantics of Biblical Language.* Oxford: Oxford University Press, 1961.

—— 'Revelation through History in the Old Testament and Modern Theology', *Int* 17 (1963): 193–205.

—— 'Man and Nature—the Ecological Controversy and the Old Testament.' *BJRL* 55 (1972): 9–32.

—— 'The Synchronic, the Diachronic and the Historical: A Triangular Relationship?' In *Synchronic or Diachronic? A Debate on Method in Old Testament Exegesis*, ed. Johannes C. de Moor, 1–14. London, New York, and Cologne: Brill, 1995.

Barstad, Hans. *The Religious Polemics of Amos*, VTSupp. 34. Leiden: Brill, 1984.

Barton, John. 'Natural Law and Poetic Justice in the Old Testament.' *JTS* 30 (1979): 1–14. Reprinted in: *Understanding Old Testament Ethics.* Louisville and London: Westminster John Knox Press, 2002.

Barton, John. '*Amos' Oracles Against the Nations: A Study of Amos 1.3–2.5.* Cambridge: Cambridge University Press, 1980. Reprinted in: *Understanding Old Testament Ethics.* Louisville and London: Westminster John Knox Press, 2002.

—— 'Ethics in Isaiah of Jerusalem,' *JTS* 32 (1981): 1–18. Reprinted in: *Understanding Old Testament Ethics.* Louisville and London: Westminster John Knox Press, 2002.

—— 'History and Rhetoric in the Prophets', in *The Bible as Rhetoric: Studies in Biblical Persuasion and Credibility*, ed. Martin Warner. London: Routledge, 1990.

—— *Reading the Old Testament.* 2nd rev. edn. London: Darton, Longman & Todd, 1996.

—— ed. *The Cambridge Companion to Biblical Interpretation.* Cambridge: Cambridge University Press, 1998.

—— 'Virtue in the Bible,' *Studies in Christian Ethics* 12 (1999): 12–22. Reprinted in *Understanding Old Testament Ethics.* Louisville and London: Westminster John Knox Press, 2002.

—— *The Nature of Biblical Criticism.* Louisville and London: Westminster John Knox Press, 2007.

Basil of Caesarea. *The Treatise De Spiritu Sancto: The Nine Homilies of the Hexaemeron and the Letters of Saint Basil the Great*, trans. Blomfield Jackson, NPNF^2. Oxford: James Parker, 1895.

Batto, Bernard. 'The Covenant of Peace: A Neglected Ancient Near Eastern Motif,' *CBQ* 49 (1987): 187–211.

Bauks, Michaela. '"Chaos" als Metapher für die Gefährdung der Weltordnung', in *Das biblische Weltbild und seine altorienalischen Kontexte*, ed. Bernd Janowski and Beate Ego, 431–64. Tübingen: Mohr Siebeck, 2001.

Baumgärtel, Friedrich. 'Zu den Gottesnamen in den Büchern Jeremia und Ezechiel', in *Verbannung und Heimkehr*, ed. Arnulf Kuschke, 1–29. Tübingen: JCB Mohr (Paul Siebeck), 1961.

Beed, Clive, and Cara Beed. 'Peter Singer's Interpretation of Christian Biblical Environmental Ethics,' *Worldviews, Environment, Culture, Religion* 2, no. 1 (1998): 53–68.

Begrich, Joachim. 'Die Priesterliche Tora', in *Werden und Wesen des Alten Testaments*, ed. P. Volz, F. Stummer, and J. Hempel, 63–88. Berlin: Alfred Töpelmann, 1935.

Benzoni, Francisco. 'Rolston's Theological Ethic,' *Environmental Ethics* 18, no. 4 (1996): 339–52.

Berchman, Robert M. *From Philo to Origen: Middle Platonism in Transition.* Vol. 69, Brown Judaic Studies. Chico, Calif.: Scholars Press, 1984.

Bergant, Dianne. *Israel's Wisdom Literature: A Liberation-Critical Reading.* Minneapolis: Fortress, 1997.

Bergey, Ronald. 'The Song of Moses (Deuteronomy 32:1–43) and Isaianic Prophecies: A Case of Early Intertextuality?' *JSOT* 28, no. 1 (2003): 33–54.

—— ed. *Environmental Stewardship.* London: T. & T. Clark, 2006.

Berry, Thomas. *The New Story.* Vol. 1, Teilhard Studies. Chambersburg, Pa.: ANIMA Books, 1978.

—— 'Economics: Its Effects on the Life Systems of the World', in *Thomas Berry and the New Cosmology*, ed. A. Lonergan and C. Richards, 5–26. Mystic, Conn.: Twenty-Third Publications, 1987.

—— *The Dream of the Earth.* San Francisco: Sierra Club Books, 1988.

Berry, Wendall. *The Gift of Good Land.* San Francisco: North Point Press, 1981.

Berry, R. J. *God's Book of Works: The Nature and Theology of Nature.* London: T. & T. Clark, 2003.

Beuken, William A. M. *Isaiah: Part II Chapters 28–39*, HCOT. Leuven: Peeters, 2000.

Birch, Bruce. *Let Justice Roll Down: The Old Testament, Ethics and Christian Life.* Louisville: Westminster John Knox Press, 1991.

—— 'Divine Character and the Formation of Moral Community in the Book of Exodus', in *The Bible in Ethics: The Second Sheffield Colloquium*, JSOT Supp. 207, ed. John W. Rogerson, Margaret Davies, M. Daniel, and R. Carroll, 119–35. Sheffield: Sheffield Academic Press, 1995.

Bjørndalen, Anders Jørgen. *Untersuchung zur allegorischen Rede der Propheten Amos und Jesaja.* Vol. 165, BZAW. Berlin: De Gruyter, 1986.

Black, Max. 'Metaphor,' *Proceedings of the Aristotelian Society* 55 (1954): 273–94. Reprinted in *Models and Metaphors: Studies in Language and Philosophy.* Ithaca, NY: Cornell University Press, 1962.

Blenkinsopp, Joseph. *Isaiah 1–39: A New Translation with Introduction and Commentary*, AB. New York: Doubleday, 2000.

Block, Daniel. *The Gods of the Nations: Studies in Ancient Near Eastern National Theology.* Grand Rapids and Leicester: Baker Academic/Apollos, 2000.

Boadt, Laurence. 'The Poetry of Prophetic Persuasion: Preserving the Prophet's Persona.' *CBQ* 59 (1997): 1–21.

Bonaventure. 'The Mirror of Perfection', in *The Little Flowers of St. Francis, The Mirror of Perfection, St. Bonaventure's Life of St. Francis*, 181–300, trans. Robert Steele. London: J. M. Dent & Sons, 1963.

—— *The Soul's Journey into God; the Tree of Life; the Life of St Francis*, trans. Ewert Cousins. London: SPCK, 1978.

Bornkamm, Heinrich. *Luther's World of Thought.* Saint Louis: Concordia, 1965.

Borowski, O. *Agriculture in Iron Age Israel.* Winona Lake, In.: Eisenbrauns, 1987.

—— 'The Sharon: Symbol of God's Abundance.' *BRev* IV, no. 2 (1988): 40–3.

—— *Every Living Thing: Daily Use of Animals in Ancient Israel.* Walnut Creek, Calif.: Altamira Press, 1998.

Boshoff, W. S. 'Yahweh as God of Nature: Elements of the Concept of God in the Book of Hosea,' *JNSL* 18 (1992): 13–24.

Bosman, Hendrik. 'Adultery, Prophetic Tradition and the Decalogue', in *Wünschet Jerusalem Frieden*, ed. Matthias Augustin and Klaus-Dietrich Schunck, 21–30. Frankfurt am Main: Verlag Peter Lang, 1986.

Boston, James R. 'Wisdom Influence upon the Song of Moses,' *JBL* 87, no. 2 (1968): 198–202.

Bouma-Prediger, Steven. 'Response to Louke van Weensveen: A Constructive Proposal', in *Christianity and Ecology: Seeking the Well-Being of Earth and Humans*, ed. Dieter Hessel and Rosemary Radford Ruether, 173–82. Cambridge, Mass.: Harvard University Press, 2000.

—— *For the Beauty of the Earth: A Christian Vision for Creation Care.* Grand Rapids: Baker Academic, 2001.

Bourke, Joseph. 'Le Jour de Yahvé dans Joël,' *RB* 66 (1959): 5–31.

Bourke, Vernon J. 'Natural Law', in *A Dictionary of Christian Ethics*, ed. John Macquarrie, 224–5. London: SCM, 1967.

Bovati, P. 'Le langage juridique du prophète Isaïe', in *The Book of Isaiah/Le livre d'Isaïe*, ed. J. Vermeylen, 177–96. Leuven: Leuven University Press, 1989.

Bovenkerk, Bernice et al. 'To Act or Not to Act? Sheltering Animals from the Wild: A Pluralistic Account of a Conflict between Animal and Environmental Ethics,' *Ethics, Place and Environment* 6, no. 1 (2003): 15–26.

Braaten, Laurie J. 'Earth Community in Hosea 2', in *The Earth Story in the Psalms and the Prophets*, ed. Norman Habel, 185–203. Sheffield: Sheffield Academic Press, 2001.

Bradley, Ian. *God is Green: Christianity and the Environment.* Darton, Longman & Todd, 1990.

Brennan, Andrew. *Thinking About Nature: An Investigation of Nature, Value and Ecology*. London: Routledge, 1988.

Brettler, Marc Zvi. *God is King: Understanding an Israelite Metaphor*. Sheffield: Sheffield Academic Press, 1989.

Brin, Gershon. *The Concept of Time in the Bible and the Dead Sea Scrolls*. Leiden, Boston, and Cologne: Leiden, 2001.

Brooke, George J. '4Q500 1 and the Use of Scripture in the Parable of the Vineyard,' *DSD* 2 (1995): 268–94.

Brooke, John H. *Science and Religion: Some Historical Perspectives*. Cambridge and New York: Cambridge University Press, 1991.

Brooks, Peter N. *Hymns as Homilies*. Leominster: Fowler Wright Books, 1997.

Broshi, Magen. 'Bread, Wine, Walls and Scrolls,' 145–55. Sheffield: Sheffield Academic Press, 2001.

Brown, William P. *The Ethos of the Cosmos: The Genesis of Moral Imagination in the Bible*. Grand Rapids: Eerdmans, 1999.

—— *Seeing the Psalms: A Theology of Metaphor*. Louisville: Westminster John Knox Press, 2002.

Brown, F., S. R. Driver, and C. A. Briggs. *A Hebrew and English Lexicon of the Old Testament*. Oxford: Clarendon, 1929.

Brownlee, William H. *The Meaning of the Qumrân Scrolls for the Bible with Special Attention to the Book of Isaiah*. New York: Oxford University Press, 1964.

Brueggemann, Walter. 'Amos IV 4–13 and Israel's Covenant Worship,' *VT* 15 (1965).

—— 'Unity and Dynamic in Isaiah,' *JSOT* 29 (1984): 89–107.

—— 'The Uninflected Therefore of Hos 4:1–3', in *Reading from this Place, Vol 1: Social Location and Biblical Interpretation in the United States*, ed. F. Segovia and M. A. Tolbert, 231–49. Minneapolis: Fortress, 1995.

—— 'The Loss and Rediscovery of Creation in Old Testament Theology,' *ThTo* 53, no. 2 (1996): 177–90.

—— *Theology of the Old Testament: Testimony, Dispute, Advocacy*. Minneapolis: Fortress Press, 1997.

—— *Isaiah 1–39*. Louisville: Westminster John Knox Press, 1998.

—— *The Land: Place as Gift, Promise, and Challenge in Biblical Faith*. Minneapolis: Fortress Press, 2002.

Budde, K. 'The Nomadic Ideal in the Old Testament.' *The New World* 4 (1895): 235–79.

Burtt, E. A. 'The Metaphysics of Newton', in *Science and Religious Belief: A Selection of Recent Historical Studies*, ed. C. A. Russell, 131–46. Sevenoaks: Hodder & Stoughton, 1973.

Buss, Martin J. *The Prophetic Word of Hosea: A Morphological Study*. Berlin: A Töpelmann, 1969.

Caird, G. B. *The Language and Imagery of the Bible*. London: Duckworth, 1980.

Callicott, J. Baird. 'Animal Liberation: A Triangular Affair,' *Environmental Ethics* 2 (1980): 311–38. Reprinted in: *In Defense of the Land Ethic*, New York: State University of New York Press, 1989.

—— *In Defense of the Land Ethic*. Albany: State University of New York Press, 1989.

Callicott, J. Baird. Genesis and John Muir', in *Covenant for a New Creation: Ethics, Religion and Public Policy*, ed. C. S. Robb and C. J. Casebolt, 107–40. Maryknoll, N.Y.: Orbis Books, 1991. Reprinted in: *Beyond the Land Ethic*, New York: State University of New York Press, 1999.

—— 'Rolston on Intrinsic Value: A Deconstruction,' *Environmental Ethics* 14, no. 1 (1992): 23–46.

—— *Beyond the Land Ethic: More Essays in Environmental Philosophy*. Albany: State University of New York Press, 1999.

—— 'From the Balance of Nature to the Flux of Nature: The Land Ethic in a Time of Change', in *Aldo Leopold and the Ecological Conscience*, ed. R. L. Knight and S. Reidel, 90–105. Oxford: Oxford University Press, 2002.

Calvin, John. *Institutes of the Christian Religion, Book I*, trans. F. L. Battles, ed. John McNeill. Vol. 20, LCC. London: SCM Press, 1960.

—— *Commentaries on the First Book of Moses called Genesis*, trans. John King. Vol. 1. Grand Rapids, Mich.: Baker Book House, 1993.

Cansdale, George. *Animals of Bible Lands*. Exeter: Paternoster Press, 1970.

Carleton Paget, J. N. B. 'The Christian Exegesis of the Old Testament in the Alexandrian Tradition', in *Hebrew Bible / Old Testament. The History of Its Interpretation*. Vol. 1: *From the Beginnings to the Middle Ages (Until 1300), Part 1*, ed. M Sæbø, 478–542. Göttingen: Vandenhoeck & Ruprecht, 1996.

Carley, Keith. 'Ezekiel's Formula of Desolation: Harsh Justice for the Land/ Earth', in *The Earth Story in the Psalms and the Prophets*, ed. Norman Habel, 143–57. Sheffield: Sheffield Academic Press, 2001.

Carone, Gabriela Roxana. 'Plato and the Environment,' *Environmental Ethics* 20, no. 2 (1998).

Carr, David M. 'Reading Isaiah from Beginning (Isaiah 1) to End (Isaiah 65–66): Multiple Modern Possibilities', in *New Visions of Isaiah*, ed. Marvin A. Sweeney and Roy F. Melugin. Sheffield: Sheffield Academic Press, 1996.

Carroll Robert P. Daniel. *Contexts for Amos: Prophetic Poetics in Latin American Perspective*. Sheffield: Sheffield Academic Press, 1992.

—— 'Night Without Vision: Micah and the Prophets', in *The Scriptures and the Scrolls: Studies in Honour of A. S. van der Woude on the Occasion of his 65th Birthday*, ed. F. Garcia Martinez, A. Hilhorst and C. J. Labuschagne, 74–84. London, New York, and Cologne: Brill, 1992.

—— 'City of Chaos, City of Stone, City of Flesh: Urbanscapes in Prophetic Discourses', in *'Every City shall be Forsaken': Urbanism and Prophecy in Ancient Israel and the Near East*, ed. L. L. Grabbe and R. D. Haak, 45–61. Sheffield: Sheffield Academic Press, 2001.

—— *Amos—The Prophet and His Oracles*. Louisville: Westminster John Knox, 2002.

Carson, Rachel. *Silent Spring*. Harmondsworth, Middlesex: Penguin Books, 1962.

Cassuto, U. 'The Second Chapter of the Book of Hosea (1927)', in *Biblical and Oriental Studies*. Vol. 1: *Bible*. Jerusalem: Magnes Press, 1973.

—— *Biblical and Oriental Studies*. Vol. 1: *Bible*, trans. Israel Abrahams. Jerusalem: Magnes Press, 1973.

Celano. *The Lives of S. Francis of Assisi*, trans. A. G. Ferrers Howell. London: Methuen, 1908.

Čern', Ladislav. *The Day of Yahweh and Some Relevant Problems*. Prague: Karlovy University Press, 1948.

Chadwick, Henry. *Early Christian Thought and the Classical Tradition: Studies in Justin, Clement and Origen*. Oxford: Clarendon Press, 1966.

Chaney, Marvin L. 'Whose Sour Grapes? The Addressees of Isaiah 5:1–7 in the Light of Political Economy', in *Semeia 85: The Social World of the Hebrew Bible*, ed. R. A. Simkins and S. L. Cook, 105–22. Atlanta: Society of Biblical Literature, 1999.

Charles, R. H., ed. *The Apocrypha and Pseudepigrapha of the Old Testament in English*. Vol. 1: *Apocrypha*. Oxford: Clarendon, 1913.

—— ed. *The Apocrypha and Pseudepigrapha of the Old Testament in English*. Vol. 2: *Pseudepigrapha*. Abridged edn. Berkeley: Apocryphile Press, 2004.

Childs, Brevard S. *Biblical Theology in Crisis*. Philadelphia: Westminster, 1970.

—— *Isaiah*. Louisville: Westminster John Knox, 2001.

Chilton, Bruce D. *The Isaiah Targum: Introduction, Translation, Apparatus and Notes*, ArBib. Edinburgh: T. & T. Clark, 1987.

Cittadino, Eugene. 'Ecology and American Social Thought', in *Religion and the New Ecology: Environmental Responsibility in a World in Flux*, ed. David Lodge and Christopher Hamlin, 73–115. Notre Dame, Ind.: University of Notre Dame Press, 2006.

Clark, Gordon R. *The Word Hesed in the Hebrew Bible*. Vol. 157, *JSOT* Supp. Sheffield: Sheffield Academic Press, 1993.

Clayton, Philip. *God and Contemporary Science.* Edinburgh: Edinburgh University Press, 1997.

Clement. *Exhortation to the Heathen.* Vol. 2, ANF. Peabody, Mass.: Hendrickson Publishers, 1994.

Clements, Ronald E. 'Understanding the Book of Hosea,' *RevExp* 72, no. 4 (1975): 405–23.

—— *Isaiah 1–39*, NCB. Grand Rapids: Eerdmans, 1980.

—— 'Beyond Tradition History: Deutero-Isaianic Development of First Isaiah's Themes,' *JSOT* 31 (1985): 95–113.

Clements, Ronald E. 'The Wolf Shall Live with the Lamb: Reading Isaiah 11:6–9 Today', in *New Heaven and New Earth: Prophecy and the Millennium*, ed. P. J. Harland and C. T. R. Hayward, 83–99. Leiden, Boston, and Cologne: Brill, 1999.

Clifford, Richard. 'The Unity of the Book of Isaiah and Its Cosmogonic Language,' *CBQ* 55 (1993): 1–17.

Clines, David. 'The Parallelism of Greater Precision: Notes from Isaiah 40 for a Theory of Hebrew Poetry', in *Directions in Biblical Hebrew Poetry*, ed. E. R. Follis, 77–100. Sheffield: JSOT Press, 1987.

—— 'Was There an *'bl* II 'Be Dry' in Classical Hebrew?' *VT* 42, no. 1 (1992): 1–10.

—— 'Beyond Synchronic/Diachronic', in *Synchronic or Diachronic? A Debate on Method in Old Testament Exegesis*, ed. Johannes de Moor, 52–71. London, New York, and Cologneöln: Brill, 1995.

—— and David Gunn. '"You tried to persuade me" and "Violence! Outrage!" in Jeremiah XX 7–8,' *VT* 28 (1978): 20–27.

Cohen, Jeremy. *'Be Fertile and Increase, Fill the Earth and Subdue It': the Ancient and Medieval Career of a Biblical Text.* Ithaca, NY: Cornell University Press, 1989.

Cohn, Robert L. *The Shape of Biblical Space: Four Biblical Studies.* Atlanta: Scholars Press, 1981.

Conrad, Edgar W. *Reading Isaiah.* Minneapolis: Fortress, 1991.

Conybeare, F. C., and St George Stock. *A Grammar of Septuagint Greek.* Grand Rapids: Zondervan, 1980.

Cornelius, Izak. 'The Visual Representation of the World in the Ancient Near East and the Hebrew Bible.' *JNSL* 20, no. 2 (1994): 193–218.

Cowdin, Daniel. 'The Moral Status of Otherkind in Christian Ethics', in *Christianity and Ecology: Seeking the Well-Being of Earth and Humans*, ed. Dieter Hessel and Rosemary Radford Ruether, 261–90. Cambridge, Mass.: Harvard University Press, 2000.

Cox, Harvey. *The Secular City.* New York: MacMillan, 1965.

Crenshaw, James. 'The Influence of the Wise upon Amos: The 'Doxologies of Amos' and Job 5:9–16, 9:5–10,' *ZAW* 79 (1967).

—— *Hymnic Affirmations of Divine Justice: The Doxologies of Amos and Related Texts in the Old Testament*, SBLDS 24. Missoula, Mt.: Scholars Press, 1975.

—— *Old Testament Wisdom*. Louisville: Westminster John Knox Press, 1998.

—— 'Theodicy and Prophetic Literature', in *Theodicy in the World of the Bible*, ed. Antti Laato and Johannes De Moor, 236–55. Leiden: Brill, 2003.

—— ed. *Studies in Ancient Israelite Wisdom*. New York: Ktav Publishing House, 1976.

Cripps, Richard. *A Critical & Exegetical Commentary on the Book of Amos*. London: SPCK, 1929.

Cross, Frank Moore. 'Yahweh and the God of the Patriarchs,' *HTR* 55 (1962): 225–59.

—— *Canaanite Myth and Hebrew Epic*. Cambridge, Mass.: Harvard University Press, 1973.

—— 'The Redemption of Nature,' *PSB* NS 10, no. 2, (1989): 94–104.

Crüsemann, Frank. *Studien zur Formgeschichte von Hymnus und Danklied in Israel*. Neukirchen: Neukirchener Verlag, 1969.

Cunningham, Lawrence. *Francis of Assisi: Performing the Gospel Life*. Grand Rapids and Cambridge: Eerdmans, 2004.

Daly, Herman E., and John B. Jr. Cobb. *For the Common Good: Redirecting the Economy towards Community, the Environment and a Sustainable Future*. London: Green Print, 1990.

Dampier-Whetham, W. C. D. *A History of Science and its Relations with Philosophy and Religion*. Cambridge: Cambridge University Press, 1930.

Daniels, Dwight R. *Hosea and Salvation History: The Early Traditions of Israel in the Prophecy of Hosea*. Berlin and New York: Walter de Gruyter, 1990.

Davies, Graham I. 'The Destiny of the Nations in the Book of Isaiah', in *The Book of Isaiah/Le livre d'Isaïe*, ed. J. Vermeylen, 93–120. Leuven: University Press, 1989.

—— *Hosea, NCB*. Grand Rapids: Eerdmans, 1992.

—— 'Introduction to the Pentateuch', in *The Oxford Bible Commentary*, ed. John Barton and John Muddiman, 12–38. Oxford: Oxford University Press, 2001.

Davies, Andrew. *Double Standards in Isaiah: Re-evaluating Prophetic Ethics and Divine Justice*. Leiden: Brill, 2000.

Davies, Eryl W. 'Walking in God's Ways: The Concept of *Imitatio Dei* in the Old Testament', in *In Search of True Wisdom: Essays in Old Testament*

Interpretation in Honour of Ronald E. Clements, ed. Edward Ball, 99–115. Sheffield: Sheffield Academic Press, 1999.

Davies, Philip R. 'The Wilderness Years: Utopia in the Book of Hosea', in *Utopia and Distopia in the Prophetic Literature*, ed. Ehud Ben Zvi, 160–74. Göttingen: Vanderhoeck and Ruprecht, 2006.

Davis, Ellen. *Scripture, Culture and Agriculture.* Cambridge: Cambridge University Press, 2009.

Day, John. 'A Case of Inner Scriptural Interpretation: The Dependence of Isaiah XXVI. 13–XXVII. 11 on Hosea XIII. 4–XIV.10 (Eng. 9) and its Relevance to Some Theories of the Redaction of the "Isaiah Apocalypse", *JTS* 31 (1980): 309–19.

—— *God's Conflict with the Dragon and the Sea.* Cambridge: Cambridge University Press, 1985.

—— 'Pre-Deuteronomic Allusions to the Covenant in Hosea and Psalm LXXVIII,' *VT* 36, no. 1 (1986): 1–12.

—— 'Baal', in *Anchor Bible Dictionary*, 1, ed. D. N. Freedman et al., 545–9. New York: Doubleday, 1992.

—— 'Ugarit and the Bible: Do They Presuppose the Same Canaanite Mythology and Religion?' In *Ugarit and the Bible: Proceedings of the International Symposium on Ugarit and the Bible, 1992*, ed. G. J. Brooke, A. H. W. Curtis, and J. Healey, 35–52. Münster: Ugarit-Verlag, 1994.

—— Robert Gordon, and H. G. M. Williamson. *Wisdom in Ancient Israel: Essays in Honour of J. A. Emerton.* Cambridge: Cambridge University Press, 1995.

De Moor, Johannes C., ed. *Synchronic or Diachronic? A Debate on Method in Old Testament Exegesis.* Vol. 34, *OtSt.* London, New York, and Cologne: Brill, 1995.

De-Shalit, A. *The Environment Between Theory and Practice.* Oxford: Oxford University Press, 2000.

De Vaux, Robert. *Ancient Israel: Its Life and Institutions*, trans. John McHugh. London: Darton, Longman, & Todd, 1965 [Fr. 1958].

De Waard, Jan. 'The Chiastic Structure of Amos V 1–17,' *VT* 27 (1977): 170–7.

Deane-Drummond, C. *The Ethics of Nature.* Oxford: Blackwell, 2004.

DEFRA 2002. U.K. Ruddy Duck Control Trial Final Report (2002). In DEFRA, http://www.defra.gov.uk/wildlife-countryside/scientific/ruddy/ruddy1/index.htm

DeGuglieilmo, Antonine. 'The Fertility of the Land in the Messianic Prophecies,' *CBQ* 19 (1957): 306–11.

Delitzsch, Franz. *The Prophecies of Isaiah*, trans. J. Martin. Vol. 1. Edinburgh: T. & T. Clark, 1881 [Ger. 1879].

Dell, Katharine J. *The Book of Job as Sceptical Literature.* Berlin and New York: De Gruyter, 1991.

—— 'Misuse of Forms in Amos,' *VT* 45, no. 1 (1995): 45–61.

—— 'The Use of Animal Imagery in the Psalms and Wisdom Literature of Ancient Israel,' *SJT* 53, no. 3 (2000): 275–91.

—— *'Get Wisdom, Get Insight': An Introduction to Israel's Wisdom Literature.* London: Darton, Longman & Todd, 2000.

—— 'Covenant and Creation in Relationship', in *Covenant as Context,* ed. A. D. H. Mayes and R. B. Salters, 111–33. Oxford: Oxford University Press, 2003.

—— The Book of Proverbs in Social and Theological Context. Cambridge: Cambridge University Press, 2006.

Dempsey, Carol. *Hope Amid the Ruins: the Ethics of Israel's Prophets.* St Louis, Miss.: Chalice Press, 2000.

Department of the Environment. *This Common Inheritance.* London: HMSO, 1990.

DeRoche, Michael. 'Zephaniah I 2–3: The 'Sweeping' of Creation,' *VT* 30, no. 3 (1980): 104–8.

—— 'The Reversal of Creation in Hosea,' *VT* 31 (1981): 401–9.

—— 'Structure, Rhetoric and Meaning in Hosea IV 4–10,' *VT* 33, no. 2 (1983): 185–98.

—— 'Yahweh's Rîb Against Israel: A Reassessment of the So-called "Prophetic Lawsuit" in the Preexilic Prophets,' *JBL* 102, no. 4 (1983): 563–74.

Devall, Bill. 'Deep Ecology and Radical Environmentalism,' *Society and Natural Resources* 4, no. 1 (1991): 247–57. Reprinted in: *Reflecting on Nature: Readings in Environmental Philosophy,* 115–22, ed. Lori Gruen and Dale Jamieson. Oxford and New York: Oxford University Press, 1994.

DeWitt, Calvin B. 'Behemoth and Batrachians in the Eye of God: Responsibility to Other Kinds in Biblical Perspective', in *Christianity and Ecology: Seeking the Well-Being of Earth and Humans,* ed. Dieter Hessel and Rosemary Radford Ruether, 290–316. Cambridge, Mass.: Harvard University Press, 2000.

Dines, Jennifer M. *The Septuagint.* London: T. & T. Clark Continuum, 2004.

Dorst, Jean. *Before Nature Dies,* trans. C. D. Sherman. London: Collins, 1970 [Fr. 1965].

Doyle, Brian. *The Apocalypse of Isaiah Metaphorically Speaking: A Study of the Use, Function and Significance of Metaphors in Isaiah 24–27.* Leuven: Leuven University Press, 2000.

Dozeman, Thomas B. 'Hosea and the Wilderness Wandering Tradition', in *Rethinking the Foundations: Historiography in the Ancient World and in the*

Bible, ed. S. L. McKenzie and T. Römer, 55–70. Berlin: Walter de Gruyter, 2000.

Driver, G. R. 'Two Astronomical Passages in the Old Testament,' *JTS* 4 (1953): 208–12.

—— 'Birds in the Old Testament I: Birds in Law,' *PEQ* (1955): 5–20.

—— 'Birds in the Old Testament II: Birds in Life,' *PEQ* (1955): 129–40.

Driver, S. R., and G. B. Gray. *A Critical and Exegetical Commentary on The Book of Job*, ICC. Edinburgh: T. & T. Clark, 1921.

Droge, Arthur J. *Homer or Moses? Early Christian Interpretations of the History of Culture*, HUT. Tübingen: Mohr Siebeck, 1989.

Dryzek, John. 'Green Reason: Communicative Ethics for the Biosphere,' *Environmental Ethics* 12 (1990): 195–210. Reprinted in: *Reflecting on Nature: Readings in Environmental Philosophy*, 159–174, ed. Lori Gruen and Dale Jamieson. Oxford and New York: Oxford University Press 1994.

Dyrness, William. 'Environmental Ethics and the Covenant of Hosea 2', in *Studies in Old Testament Theology*, ed. Robert L. Hubbard Jr., Robert K. Johnson and Robert P. Meye. Dallas: Word, 1992.

Eaton, Heather. 'Ecofeminist Contributions to an Ecojustice Hermeneutics', in *Readings from the Perspective of Earth*, ed. Norman Habel, 54–71. Sheffield: Sheffield Academic Press, 2000.

Eckersley, R. 'Beyond Human Racism,' *Environmental Values* 7 (1998): 165–82.

Ehrlich, Arnold B. *Randglossen zür Hebräischen Bibel: Textkritisches, sprachliches und sachliches*. Vol. 5. Hildesheim: Georg Olms, 1968.

Ehrlich, Paul. *The Population Explosion*. London: Arrow Books, 1991.

Eichrodt, Walter. *Theology of the Old Testament*, trans. J. A. Baker. 2 vols. Vol. 2. London: SCM Press, 1964 [Ger. 1933].

—— 'Prophet and Covenant: Observations on the Exegesis of Isaiah', in *Proclamation and Presence: Old Testament Essays in Honour of Gwynne Henton Davies*, ed. J. I. Durham and J. R. Porter, 167–88. London: SCM, 1970.

Eidevall, Gören. *Grapes in the Desert: Metaphors, Models and Themes in Hosea 4–14*. Stockholm: Almqvist & Wiksell International, 1996.

—— 'Images of God, Self and the Enemy in the Psalms: On the Role of Metaphor in Identity Construction', in *Metaphor in the Hebrew Bible*, ed. P. van Hecke, 55–66. Leuven: Leuven University Press, 2005.

Elert, Werner. *The Structure of Lutheranism*. Vol. 1: *The Theology and Philosophy of Life of Lutheranism especially in the Sixteenth and Seventeenth Centuries*, trans. Walter A. Hansen. Saint Louis: Concordia, 1962 [Ger. 1958].

Eliade, Mircea. *The Myth of the Eternal Return*, trans. Willard R. Trask. London: Routledge & Kegan Paul, 1955 [Fr. 1949].

Ellis, Peter F. *The Yahwist: The Bible's First Theologian.* London: Geoffrey Chapman, 1969.

Elvey, Anne. 'Earthing the Text? On the Status of the Biblical Text in Ecological Perspective,' *ABR* 52 (2004): 64–79.

Environment Agency. '50 Things That Will Save the Planet,' *Your Environment*, 17, Supp. (2007) (www.environment-agency.gov.uk/yourenv).

Environmental Audit Committee, House of Commons. 'Keeping the Lights On: Nuclear, Renewables and Climate Change.' London: House of Commons, 2006.

Eslinger, Lyle. 'Inner-Biblical Exegesis and Inner-Biblical Allusion: The Question of Category,' *VT* 42, no. 1 (1992): 47–58.

Evans, C. A. *Jesus and His Contemporaries: Comparative Studies.* London, New York, and Cologneöln: Brill, 1995.

Feliks, Jehuda. *The Animal World of the Bible.* Tel Aviv: Sinai, 1962.

—— *Nature and Man in the Bible.* London: Soncino Press, 1981.

Fern, R. *Nature, God and Humanity: Envisioning an Ethics of Nature.* Cambridge: Cambridge University Press, 2002.

Filoramo, Giovanni. *A History of Gnosticism*, trans. A. Alcock. Cambridge: Basil Blackwell, 1991.

Fiorenza, Schüssler Elizabeth. *Bread not Stone: The Challenge of Feminist Biblical Interpretation.* Edinburgh: T. & T. Clark, 1984.

Fischer, Georg. 'Die Redewendung דבר על-לבה im AT: Ein Beitrag zum Verständnis von Jes 40,2,' *Bib* 65 (1984): 244–50.

Flight, J. W. 'The Nomadic Idea and Ideal in the Old Testament,' *JBL* 42 (1923): 158–226.

Fohrer, G. 'Jesaja 1 als Zusammenfassung der Verkündigung Jesajas,' *ZAW* 74 (1962): 251–68.

Ford, David. 'God and Our Public Life: A Scriptural Wisdom.' Paper presented at the Ebor lecture series: 'Liberating Texts? Revelation, Identity and Public Life', York St John University, 8 November 2006.

Foster, M B. 'The Christian Doctrine of Creation and the Rise of Natural Science,' *Mind* xliii (1934): 446–68.

—— 'Christian Theology and Modern Science of Nature (I),' *Mind* 44 (1935): 439–66.

—— 'Christian Theology and Modern Science of Nature (II),' *Mind* 45 (1936): 1–27.

Francis, St. *Little Flowers of St Francis*, trans. R. Hudleston. London: Burns Oates, 1953.

Frankfort, H. & H. A., John A. Wilson, and Thorkild Jacobsen. *The Intellectual Adventure of Ancient Man.* Chicago: University of Chicago Press, 1946. Reprinted as *Before Philosophy.* London: Penguin Books, 1973.

Frasz, Geoffrey. 'Environmental Virtue Ethics: A New Direction for Environmental Ethics.' *Environmental Ethics* 15, no. 3 (1993): 259–74.

Freedman, David Noel. *The Nine Commandments: Uncovering a Hidden Pattern of Crime and Punishment in the Hebrew Bible.* New York, London, and Toronto: Doubleday, 2000.

Fretheim, Terence E. *The Suffering of God: An Old Testament Perspective,* OBT. Philadelphia: Fortress, 1984.

—— 'Nature's Praise of God in the Psalms,' *ExAud* 3 (1987): 16–30.

—— 'The Plagues as Ecological Signs of Historical Disaster,' *JBL* 110, no. 3 (1991): 385–96.

—— *God and World in the Old Testament: A Relational Theology of Creation.* Nashville: Abingdon, 2005.

Frick, Frank S. '"Oil From Flinty Rock" (Deuteronomy 32:13): Olive Cultivation and Olive Oil Processing in the Hebrew Bible—a Socio-Materialist Perspective,' *Semeia* 86 (1999): 3–17.

Frolov, Serge. *The Turn of the Cycle: 1 Samuel 1–8 in Synchronic and Diachronic Perspectives.* Berlin: De Gruyter, 2004.

Gadd, C. J. 'Epic of Gilgamesh, Tablet XII,' *RA* 30, no. 1 (1933): 127–43.

Gehman, H. S. 'Natural Law and the Old Testament', in *Biblical Studies in Memory of H. C. Alleman,* ed. J. M. Myers, O. Reimherr and H. N. Bream. New York: J. J. Augustin, 1960.

Gese, Hartmut. 'Der kosmische Frevel händlerischer Habgier', in *Prophet und Prophetenbuch: Festschrift für Otto Kaiser zum 65,* ed. Volkmar Fritz, Karl-Friedrich Pohlmann and Hans-Christoph Schmitt, 59–72. Berlin: De Gruyter, 1989.

Gesenius, W K. *Commentar über den Jesaia.* Leipzig: F.C.W. Vogel, 1821.

Geyer, John. 'Desolation and Cosmos,' *VT* 49 (1999): 49–64.

Gibson, J. C. L. *Canaanite Myths and Legends.* Edinburgh: T. & T. Clark, 1977.

Gilfillan Upton, Bridget. 'Feminist Theology as Biblical Hermeneutics', in *The Cambridge Companion to Feminist Theology,* ed. S. F. Parsons, 97–113. Cambridge: Cambridge University Press, 2002.

Gillingham, Susan. '"Who Makes the Morning Darkness": God and Creation in the Book of Amos,' *SJT* 45, no. 2 (1992): 165–84.

Gingerich, Owen. *The Book Nobody Read: Chasing the Revolutions of Nicolaus Copernicus.* London: William Heinemann, 2004.

Gitay, Yehoshua. *Isaiah and his Audience: The Structure and Meaning of Isaiah 1–12*, SSN. Assen and Maastricht: Van Gorcum, 1991.

Glacken, Clarence J. *Traces on the Rhodian Shore: Nature and Culture in Western Thought from Ancient Times to the End of the Eighteenth Century.* Berkeley: University of California Press, 1967.

Godfrey, Robert W. *God's Pattern for Creation: A Covenantal Reading of Genesis 1.* Phillipsburg, NJ: P. & R. Publishing, 2003.

Gordon, Edmund I. *Sumerian Proverbs: Glimpses of Everyday Life in Ancient Mesopotamia.* Philadelphia: University Museum, 1959.

Gordon, C. H. 'Poetic Legends and Myths from Ugarit,' *Ber* 25 (1977): 5–133.

Gossai, Hemchand. *Justice, Righteousness and the Social Critique of the Eighth Century Prophets.* New York: Peter D. Lang, 1993.

Gosse, Bernard. 'Isaïe 34–35: Le chatiment d'Edom et des nations, salut pour Sion,' *ZAW* 102 (1990): 396–404.

Gottwald, Norman K. *The Tribes of Yahweh: A Sociology of the Religion of Liberated Israel, 1250–1050 BCE.* New York: Maryknoll, 1979.

Grant, Robert M. *Irenaeus of Lyons.* London and New York: Routledge, 1997.

Gray, George Buchanan. *A Critical & Exegetical Commentary on the Book of Isaiah: I–XXVII*, ICC. Edinburgh: T. & T. Clark, 1912.

Gray, Mark. *Rhetoric and Social Justice in Isaiah.* New York and London: T. & T. Clark, 2006.

Green, Alberto W. *The Storm God in the Ancient Near East.* Winona Lake, Ind.: Eisenbrauns, 2003.

Greenfield, J. C. 'The Hebrew Bible and Canaanite Literature', in *The Literary Guide to the Bible*, ed. Robert Alter and Frank Kermode, 545–60. Cambridge, Mass.: Belknap, 1987.

Gregory of Nyssa. *Selected Writings and Letters of Gregory, Bishop of Nyssa*, trans. W. Moore and H. A. Wilson. Vol. 5, NPNF^2: Christian Literature Publishing Company, 1893. Reprint, Peabody, Mass.: Hendrickson, 1994.

Grigson, Caroline. 'Plough and Pasture in the Early Economy of the Southern Levant', in *The Archaeology of Society in the Holy Land*, ed. T. E. Levy, 245–68. London: Leicester University Press, 1995.

Gruen, Lori, and Dale Jamieson, eds. *Reflecting on Nature: Readings in Environmental Philosophy.* Oxford and New York: Oxford University Press, 1994.

Gunkel, Hermann. *Schöpfung und Chaos in Urzeit und Endzeit: Eine religionsgeschichtliche Untersuchung über Gen 1 und Ap Joh 12.* Göttingen: Vandenhoeck & Ruprecht, 1895.

—— 'The Prophets: Oral and Written', in *Water for a Thirsty Land: Israelite Literature and Religion*, ed. K C Hanson, 85–133. Minneapolis: Fortress Press, 2001. Reprint, of 'Die Propheten als Schriftsteller und Dichter', in *Die Propheten* 34–70, (Gottingen: Vandenhoeck & Ruprecht, 1923).

Gunkel, Hermann, and Joachim Begrich. *Introduction to Psalms: The Genres of the Religious Lyric of Israel*, trans. J. D. Nogalski. Macon, Ga.: Mercer University Press, 1998 [Ger. 1933].

Gunton, Colin. *Christ and Creation*. Carlisle and Grand Rapids: Paternoster/ Eerdmans, 1992.

—— *The One, The Three and the Many: God, Creation and the Culture of Modernity*. Cambridge: Cambridge University Press, 1993.

Gustafson, James M. *Ethics from a Theocentric Perspective*. Vol. 2, *Ethics and Theology*. Chicago and London: University of Chicago Press, 1984.

Habel, Norman. *The Land Is Mine: Six Biblical Land Ideologies*, OBT. Minneapolis: Fortress, 1995.

—— ed. *Readings from the Perspective of the Earth*. Vol. 1, *The Earth Bible*. Sheffield: Sheffield Academic Press, 2000.

—— ed. *The Earth Story in the Psalms and the Prophets*. Vol. 4, *The Earth Bible*. Sheffield: Sheffield Academic Press, 2001.

—— and Vicky Balabanski, eds. *The Earth Story in the New Testament*. Vol. 5, *The Earth Bible*. Sheffield: Sheffield Academic Press, 2002.

—— and Peter Trudinger, eds. *Exploring Ecological Hermeneutics*. Atlanta: Society of Biblical Literature, 2008.

—— and Shirley Wurst, eds. *The Earth Story in Genesis*. Vol. 2, *The Earth Bible*. Sheffield: Sheffield Academic Press, 2000.

—— —— eds. *The Earth Story in Wisdom Traditions*. Vol. 3, *The Earth Bible*. Sheffield: Sheffield Academic Press, 2001.

Hailwood, Simon. *How to be a Green Liberal: Nature, Value and Liberal Philosophy*. Chesham: Acumen, 2004.

Hammershaimb, Erling. 'On the Ethics of the Old Testament Prophets', in *Congress Volume Oxford 1959*, *VT* Supp. 7, ed. G.W Anderson, 75–101. Leiden: Brill, 1960.

—— *The Book of Amos: A Commentary*, trans. John Sturdy. Oxford: Basil Blackwell, 1970 [Dan. 1958].

Hampson, Daphne. *After Christianity*. London: SCM Press, 1996.

Hare, R. M. 'Utilitarianism', in *A New Dictionary of Christian Ethics*, ed. J. F. Childress and John Macquarrie, 640–3. London: SCM Press, 1986.

Harper, William Rainey. *A Critical and Exegetical Commentary on Amos and Hosea*, ICC. Edinburgh: T. & T. Clark, 1936.

Harrison, Peter. *The Bible, Protestantism and the Rise of Natural Science*. Cambridge: Cambridge University Press, 1998.

—— 'Subduing the Earth: Genesis 1, Early Modern Science, and the Exploitation of Nature,' *Journal of Religion* 79, no. 1 (1999): 86–109.

—— *The Fall of Man and the Foundations of Science.* Cambridge: Cambridge University Press, 2007.

Hayes, Katherine M. *'The Earth Mourns': Prophetic Metaphor and Oral Aesthetic.* Vol. 8, SBLABib. Atlanta: Society of Biblical Literature, 2002.

Hayward, T. *Political Theory and Ecological Values.* Cambridge: Polity Press, 1998.

Hecke, P. van. 'Living Alone in the Shrubs: Positive Pastoral Metaphors in Micah 7:14,' *ZAW* 115, no. 3 (2003): 362–375.

—— ed. *Metaphor in the Hebrew Bible.* Leuven: Leuven University Press, 2005.

Hegel, G. W. F. *The Philosophy of History*, trans. J. Sibree. New York: Dover Publications, 1956 [Ger. 1844].

—— *Lectures on the Philosophy of Religion*, trans. E. B. Speirs and J. B. Sanderson. 3 vols. Vol. 2. London: Routledge and Kegan Paul, 1962 [Ger. 1832].

Hempel, J. *Das Ethos des Alten Testaments.* 2nd 1964 ed. Vol. 67, BZAW. Berlin: Alfred Töpelmann, 1938.

Hendry, George S. *Theology of Nature.* Philadelphia: The Westminster Press, 1980.

Hessel, Dieter, and Rosemary Radford Ruether, eds. *Christianity and Ecology: Seeking the Well-Being of Earth and Humans.* Cambridge, Mass.: Harvard University Press, 2000.

Hiebert, Theodore. 'Theophany in the OT', in *Anchor Bible DIctionary*, VI, ed. D. N. Freedman et al., 505–11. New York: Doubleday, 1992.

—— *The Yahwist's Landscape: Nature and Religion in Early Israel.* New York: Oxford University Press, 1996.

Hill Jr, Thomas E. 'Ideals of Human Excellence and Preserving the Natural Environment', in *Reflecting on Nature: Readings in Environmental Philosophy*, ed. Lori Gruen and Dale Jamieson, 98–110. Oxford and New York: Oxford University Press, 1994.

Hillel, Daniel. *The Natural History of the Bible: An Environmental Exploration of the Hebrew Scriptures.* New York: Columbia University Press, 2006.

Hillers, Delbert R. 'The Roads to Zion Mourn,' *Per* 12, no. 1/2 (1971): 121–34.

HM Treasury. *Stern Review on the Economics of Climate Change.* Cambridge: Cambridge University Press, 2006.

Hoffmann, Yair. 'The Day of the Lord as a Concept and a Term in the Prophetic Literature,' *ZAW* 93 (1981): 37–50.

Hoffmeyer, Jeffrey. 'Covenant and Creation: Hosea 4:1–3,' *RevExp* 102, no. 1 (2005): 143–51.

Holly, Marilyn. 'Environmental Virtue Ethics: A Review of Some Current Work,' *Journal of Agricultural and Environmental Ethics* 19, no. 4 (2006): 391–424.

Holt, Else Kragelund. 'דעת אלהים und חסד im Buche Hosea,' *SJOT* 1 (1987): 87–102.

Holt, Else Kragelund. *Prophesying the Past: The Use of Israel's History in the Book of Hosea*. Sheffield: Sheffield Academic Press, 1995.

Hopkins, David. 'Bare Bones: Putting Flesh on the Economics of Ancient Israel', in *The Origins of the Ancient Israelite States*, ed. P. R. Davies and Volkmar Fritz. Sheffield: JSOT Press, 1996.

Horst, F. 'Die Doxologien im Amosbuch,' *ZAW* 47 (NF6) (1929): 45–55.

—— 'Naturrecht und Altes Testament', in *Gottes Recht: Gesammelte Studien zum Recht im Alten Testament*, ed. H. W. Wolff. Munich: Kaiser, 1961.

Houston, Walter. *Contending for Justice: Ideologies and Theologies of Social Justice in the Old Testament*. London and New York: T. & T. Clark, 2006.

Houtman, Cornelis. *Der Himmel im Alten Testament: Israels Weltbild und Weltanschauung*. Vol. 30, OtSt. London, New York, and Cologne: Brill, 1993.

Howell, Kenneth J. *God's Two Books: Copernican Cosmology and Biblical Interpretation in Early Modern Science*. Notre Dame, Ind.: University of Notre Dame Press, 2002.

Huffmon, Herbert. 'The Covenant Lawsuit in the Prophets,' *JBL* 78, no. 4 (1959): 285–95.

—— 'The Treaty Background of Hebrew YĀDA.' *BASOR* 181 (1966): 31–7.

Hugger, Pirmin. 'Das trauernde Land, der schreiende Stein', in *Künder des Wortes: Beiträge zur Theologie der Propheten*, ed. L. Ruppert, P. Weimar and E. Zenger, 301–13. Würzburg: Echter Verlag, 1982.

Hughes, J Donald. 'Frances of Assisi and the Diversity of Creation,' *Environmental Ethics* 18, no. 3 (1996): 311–20.

Humbert, Paul. 'Emploi et portée du verbe bârâ (créer) dans l'Ancien Testament,' *TZ* 6 (1947): 401–22.

Intergovernmental Panel on Climate Change. '4th Assessment Report' (2007).

Irenaeus. *Against Heresies*, ed. Alexander Roberts and James Donaldson. Vol. 1, *ANF: The Apostolic Fathers with Justin Martyr and Irenaeus*. Edinburgh: T. & T. Clark, 1994.

Irwin, W. H. *Isaiah 28–33: Translation with Philological Notes*. Rome: Pontifical Biblical Institute, 1973.

Jacob, Edmond. 'Du premier au deuxième chant de la vigne du prophète Esaïe, Refléxions sur Esaïe 27:2–5,' *ATANT* 59 (1970): 325–30.

—— Carl-A Keller, and Samuel Amsler. *Osée, Joël, Abdias, Jonas, Amos*, CAT. Neuchatel: Éditions Delachaux & Niestlé, 1965.

Janowski, Bernd, and Beate Ego, eds. *Das biblische Weltbild und seine altorientalischen Kontexte.* Tübingen: Mohr [Siebeck], 2001.

—— Ute Neumann-Gorsolke, and Uwe Glessmer. *Gefährten und Feinde des Menschen: Das Tier in der Lebenswelt des alten Israel.* Neukirchen: Neukirchener Verlag, 1993.

Janzen, Waldemar. *Old Testament Ethics: A Paradigmatic Approach.* Louisville: Westminster John Knox Press, 1994.

Jensen, Joseph. *The Use of tôrâ by Isaiah: His Debate with the Wisdom Tradition.* Washington, D.C.: Catholic Biblical Association of America, 1973.

Jeppesen, Knud. 'The Maśśā' Bābel in Isaiah 13–14,' *PIBA* 9 (1985): 63–80.

Jeremias, Jorg. *The Book of Amos: A Commentary*, trans. Douglas W. Stott, OTL. Louisville: Westminster John Knox, 1998 [Ger. 1995].

Jobling, David, and Nathan Loewen. 'Sketches for Earth Reading of the Book of Amos', in *Readings from the Perspective of Earth*, ed. Norman Habel, 72–85. Sheffield: Sheffield Academic Press, 2000.

Johnson, D. G. *From Chaos to Restoration.* Sheffield: Sheffield Academic Press, 1988.

Jones, Barry. *The Formation of the Book of the Twelve: A Study in Text and Canon.* Vol. 149, SBLDS. Atlanta: Society of Biblical Literature, 1995.

Jones, G. H. 'An Examination of Some Leading Motifs in the Prophetic Oracles against Foreign Nations.' Unpublished thesis, University of North Wales, 1970.

Kaiser, Otto. *Isaiah 13–39*, trans. R. A. Wilson, *OTL*. London: SCM, 1974 [Ger. 1973].

—— *Isaiah 1–12*, trans. John Bowden. 2nd edn., *OTL*. London: SCM, 1983 [Ger. 1981].

Kaiser, Walter C. *Towards an Old Testament Theology.* Grand Rapids: Zondervan, 1978.

—— *Toward Old Testament Ethics.* Grand Rapids: Zondervan, 1983.

Kang, Sa-Moon. *Divine War in the Old Testament and in the Ancient Near East.* Berlin: Walter de Gruyter, 1989.

Kapelrud, Arvid S. *Baal in the Ras Shamra Texts.* Copenhagen: G. E. C. Gad, 1952.

—— 'Central Ideas in Amos.' *Historisk-Filosofisk Klasse* 4 (1956): 1–86.

Karris, Robert J. *The Admonitions of St Francis: Sources and Meanings.* New York: The Franciscan Institute, 1999.

Kaufmann, Yehezkel. *The Religion of Israel: From its Beginnings to the Babylonian Exile*, trans. Moshe Greenberg. London: George Allen & Unwin, 1961 [Heb. 1937].

Kawall, Jason. 'Reverence for Life as a Viable Environmental Value,' *Environmental Ethics* 25, no. 4 (2003): 339–58.

Kelly, Joseph G. 'Interpretation of Amos 4:13 in the Early Christian Community', in *Essays in Honor of Joseph P. Brennan* by members of the faculty, Saint Bernard's Seminary Rochester, New York. Rochester, N.Y.: St Bernard's Seminary, 1976.

Kent, John. 'Eighteenth Century: An Overview', in *The Oxford Companion to Christian Thought*, ed. Adrian Hastings, Alistair Mason, and Hugh Pyper et al., 195–99. Oxford: Oxford University Press, 2000.

Kissane, Edward J. *The Book of Isaiah: Translated from a Critically Revised Hebrew Text with Commentary*, Vol. 1. Dublin: Brown and Nolan, 1960.

Knierim, Rolf. 'Cosmos and History in Israel's Theology,' *HBT* 3 (1981): 59–124. Reprinted in *The Task of Old Testament Theology: Method and Cases.* Grand Rapids: Eerdmans, 1995.

Knight, Douglas A. 'Cosmogony and Order in the Hebrew Tradition', in *Cosmogony and Ethical Order: New Studies in Comparative Ethics*, ed. R. Lovin and F. A. Reynolds, 133–57. Chicago and London: University of Chicago Press, 1985.

Koch, Klaus. 'Die Rolle der hymnischen Abschnitte in der Komposition des Amos-Buches,' *ZAW* 86 (1974): 504–37.

—— *The Prophets, Vol I: The Assyrian Period.* 2 vols, CCC. London: SCM Press, 1982.

—— 'Is There a Doctrine of Retribution in the Old Testament?' In *Theodicy in the Old Testament*, ed. J. Crenshaw, 57–87. Philadelphia/London: Fortress/SPCK, 1983.

—— 'Ba'al Sapon, Ba'al Šamem and the Critique of Israel's Prophets', in *Ugarit and the Bible: Proceedings of the International Symposium on Ugarit and the Bible, 1992*, ed. G. J. Brooke, A. H. W. Curtis and J. Healey, 159–74. Münster: Ugarit-Verlag, 1994.

Korpel, Marjo C. A. *A Rift in the Clouds.* Münster: Ugarit-Verlag, 1990.

Kraftson-Hogue, Michael. 'Toward a Christian Ecological Ethic: The Lesson of Old Testament Israel's Dialogic Relations with Land, History, and God,' *CSR* 28, no. 2 (1998): 270–82.

Krašovec, Jože. *La Justice (sdq) de Dieu dans la Bible Hébraïque et l'interprétation juive et chrétienne.* Frieburg/Göttingen: Vandenhoeck & Ruprecht, 1988.

Kratz, Reinhard G. 'Israel in the Book of Isaiah,' *JSOT* 31, no. 1 (2006): 103–28.

LaBar, Martin. 'A Biblical Perspective on Nonhuman Organisms', in *Religion and the Environmental Crisis*, ed. Eugene C. Hargrove, 76–93. Athens, Ga., and London: University of Georgia Press, 1986.

Lachenbacher, S. 'Note sur l'*ardat-lilî*,' *RA* 65, no. 1 (1971): 119–54.

Laetsch, Theodore. *Minor Prophets*. Saint Louis: Concordia, 1956.

Laks, André. 'Commentary on Annas', in *Proceedings of the Boston Area Colloqium in Ancient Philosophy*, IV, ed. J. Cleary and D. C. Shartin, 172–85. Lanham, New York, and London: University Press of America, 1989.

Lambert, W. G. 'The Cosmology of Sumer and Babylon', in *Ancient Cosmologies*, ed. C. Blacker and M. Loewe, 42–65. London: George Allen & Unwin, 1975.

Landy, Francis. *Hosea*, RNBC. Sheffield: Sheffield Academic Press, 1995.

—— 'Fantasy and the Displacement of Pleasure: Hosea 2:4–17', in *A Feminist Companion to the Latter Prophets*, ed. Athalya Brenner. Sheffield: Sheffield Academic Press, 1995.

Leal, Robert B. *Wilderness in the Bible: Towards a Theology of Wilderness*. New York: Peter Lang, 2004.

Leopold, Aldo. *A Sand County Almanac and Sketches Here and There*. Oxford and New York: Oxford University Press, 1987.

Leupold, H. C. *Exposition of Isaiah Volume 1*. Welwyn: Evangelical Press, 1968.

Levenson, Jon. *Creation and the Persistence of Evil*. Princeton, N.J.: Princeton University Press, 1988.

Lewis, C. S. *The Problem of Pain*. London: Centenary Press, 1943.

Lewis, Rhodri. 'The Enlightenment', in *The Oxford Handbook of English Literature and Theology*, ed. Andrew Hass, David Jasper and Elizabeth Jay, 97–114. Oxford: Oxford University Press, 2007.

Liebreich, L, J. 'The Compilation of the Book of Isaiah, Part 1', *JQR* 46 (1955): 276—77.

—— 'The Compilation of the Book of Isaiah, Part 2,' *JQR* 47 (1956): 126 –27.

Lieu, Judith M. *Neither Jew nor Greek? Constructing Early Christianity*. London and New York: T. & T. Clark, 2001.

Light, Gary W. 'The New Covenant in the Book of Hosea,' *RevExp* 90 (1993): 219–38.

Lindblom, Johannes. *Die Jesaja-Apokalypse: Jes. 24–27*. Lund: C.W.K Gleerup, 1938.

—— 'Wisdom in the Old Testament Prophets', in *Wisdom in Israel and the Ancient Near East*, ed. M. Noth and D. Winton Thomas, 192–204. Leiden: Brill, 1955.

Linzey, Andrew. *Animal Rights.* London: SCM Press, 1976.

—— *Animal Theology.* London: SCM, 1994.

Lodge, David, and Christopher Hamlin, eds. *Religion and the New Ecology: Environmental Responsibility in a World in Flux.* Notre Dame, Ind.: University of Notre Dame Press, 2006.

Long, A. A. *Hellenistic Philosophy: Stoics, Epicureans, Sceptics.* London: Duckworth, 1974.

Lovejoy, Arthur. *The Great Chain of Being: A Study of the History of an Idea* (William James Lectures, Harvard University 1933). Cambridge, Mass.: Harvard University Press, 1950.

Lovelock, James. *Gaia: A New Look at Life on Earth.* Oxford: Oxford University Press, 1979.

—— *The Ages of Gaia: A Biography of our Living Earth.* Oxford: Oxford University Press, 1988.

Lowth, R. *Isaiah: A New Translation.* Boston: Hillard, 1834.

Lust, J. 'Isaiah 34 and the *herem*', in *The Book of Isaiah/Le Livre d'Isaïe*, ed. Vermeylen J., 275–86. Leuven: Leuven University Press, 1989.

—— *Messianism and the Septuagint: Collected Essays*, ed. K. Hauspie. Leuven: Leuven University Press, 2004.

Lütgert, Wilhelm. *Schöpfung und Offenbarung: Eine Theologie des Erstes Artikels.* 2nd edn. Giessen: Brunnen Verlag, 1984.

Luther. *The Sermon on the Mount (Sermons) and the Magnificat*, ed. Jaroslav Pelikan. Vol. 21, Luther's Works. Saint Louis, Miss.: Concordia, 1956.

—— *Lectures on Genesis Chapters 1–5*, ed. Jaroslav Pelikan. Vol. 1, Luther's Works. Saint Louis, Miss.: Concordia, 1958.

—— *Table Talk*, ed. T. G. Tappert. Vol. 54, Luther's Works. Philadelphia: Fortress, 1967.

—— *First Lectures on the Psalms*, ed. Jaroslav Pelikan. Vol. 11, Luther's Works. Saint Louis, Miss.: Concordia, 1976.

Lyman, J. Rebecca. *Christology and Cosmology: Models of Divine Activity in Origen, Eusebius and Athanasius.* Oxford: Clarendon Press, 1993.

McCarthy, Dennis J. *Treaty and Covenant: A Study in Form in the Ancient Oriental Documents and in the Old Testament.* Rome: Biblical Institute Press, 1978.

McConville, J. G. *Deuteronomy.* Leicester: Apollos, 2002.

—— *God and Earthly Power: An Old testament Political Theology.* London and New York: T. & T. Clark, 2006.

McDonagh, Sean. *To Care for the Earth: A Call to a New Theology.* London: Geoffrey Chapman, 1986.

—— *The Greening of the Church.* London: Geoffrey Chapman, 1990.

McFague, Sallie. 'An Earthly Theological Agenda,' *The Christian Century* (1991): 2–15.

—— *A New Climate for Theology: God, the World, and Global Warming.* Minneapolis: Fortress Press, 2008.

McGrath, Alister. *Historical Theology: An Introduction to the History of Christian Thought.* Oxford: Blackwell Publishers, 1998.

—— *A Scientific Theology*, Vol. 1: *Nature.* Edinburgh: T. & T. Clark, 2001.

Macintosh, A. A. 'Hosea and the Wisdom Tradition', in *Wisdom in Ancient Israel: Essays in Honour of John Emerton*, ed. John Day, Robert Gordon, and H. G. M. Williamson, 124–32. Cambridge: Cambridge University Press, 1995.

—— *Hosea: A Critical and Exegetical Commentary*, ICC. Edinburgh: T. & T. Clark, 1997.

McKane, William. *Prophets and Wise Men.* London: SCM, 1965.

—— *Micah: Introduction and Commentary.* Edinburgh: T. & T. Clark, 1998.

McKenzie, John L. 'God and Nature in the Old Testament (Part 1),' *CBQ* 14, no. 1 (1952): 18–39.

—— 'God and Nature in the Old Testament (Part 2),' *CBQ* 14, no. 2 (1952): 124–45.

Maguire, Daniel. *The Moral Core of Judaism and Christianity.* Minneapolis: Fortress, 1993.

Marlow, Hilary. 'The Lament over the River Nile: Isaiah 19:5–10 in its Wider Context,' *VT* 57, no. 2 (2007): 229–42.

—— 'The Other Prophet! The Voice of Earth in the Book of Amos', in *Exploring Ecological Hermeneutics*, ed. Normal Hakel and Peter Trudinger. 75–84. Atlanta: Society of Biblical Literature, 2008.

—— 'Justice for Whom? Social and Environmental Ethics and the Hebrew Prophets', in *Ethical and Unethical Behaviour in the Old Testament: God and Humans in Dialogue*, ed. Katharine J. Dell. London: T. & T. Clark, 2009.

Martin, Luther H. 'Graeco-Roman Philosophy and Religion', in *The Early Christian World: Volume I*, ed. Philip Esler, 53–79. London and New York: Routledge, 2000.

Masenya, Madipoane. 'An Eco*Bosadi* Reading of Psalm 127.3–5', in *The Earth Story in the Psalms and Prophets*, ed. Norman Habel, 109–22. Sheffield: Sheffield Academic Press, 2001.

Masson, Scott. 'Romanticism', in *The Oxford Handbook of English Literature and Theology*, ed. Andrew Hass, David Jasper and Elizabeth Jay, 115–30. Oxford: Oxford University Press, 2007.

Mathews, Claire R. *Defending Zion: Edom's Desolation and Jacob's Restoration (Isaiah 34–35 in Context)*. Berlin and New York: Walter de Gruyter, 1995.

Matthews, Victor. 'Treading the Winepress: Actual and Metaphorical Viticulture in the Ancient Near East,' *Semeia* 86 (1999): 19–32.

Mathews, Victor. *The Social World of the Hebrew Prophets*. Peabody, Mass.: Hendrickson Publishers, 2001.

—— and Don. C. Benjamin. *The Social World of Ancient Israel, 1250–587 BCE*. Peabody, Mass.: Hendrickson Publishers, 1993.

Mauser, Ulrich. *Christ in the Wilderness*. London: SCM Press, 1963.

May, Gerhard. *Creatio Ex Nihilo: The Doctrine of 'Creation out of Nothing' in Early Christian Thought*, trans. A. S. Worrall. Edinburgh: T. & T. Clark, 1994.

Mays, James L. *Hosea: A Commentary*, OTL. London: SCM, 1969.

—— *Amos: A Commentary*, OTL. London: SCM, 1969.

Meadowcroft, Tim. 'Some Questions for the Earth Bible.' Paper presented at the ANZATS Conference, Christchurch, New Zealand 2000.

—— Review of *Readings from the Perspective of Earth*, in *Stimulus* (2001), 42–4.

Mein, Andrew. *Ezekiel and the Ethics of Exile*. Oxford: Oxford University Press, 2001.

Melugin, Roy F. 'Figurative Speech and the Reading of Isaiah 1', in *New Visions of Isaiah*, ed. Roy F. Melugin and Marvin A. Sweeney, 282–305. Sheffield: Sheffield Academic press, 1996.

—— and Marvin A. Sweeney, eds. *New Visions of Isaiah*. Sheffield: JSOT Press, 1996.

Miller, Patrick D. *The Divine Warrior in Early Israel*. Cambridge, Mass.: Harvard University Press, 1973.

—— 'Aspects of the Religion of Ugarit', in *Ancient Israelite Religion*, ed. Patrick D. Miller, Paul D. Hanson and S. Dean McBride Jr., 53–66. Philadelphia: Fortress, 1987.

—— 'Creation and Covenant', in *Biblical Theology: Problems and Perspectives*, ed. S. Kraftchick, C. D. Myers and B. C. Ollenburger, 155–68. Nashville: Abingdon, 1995.

Miranda, José Porfirio. *Marx and the Bible: A Critique of the Philosophy of Oppression*, trans. John Eagleson. London: SCM Press, 1977 [Sp. 1971].

Miscall, Peter D. *Isaiah 34–35: A Nightmare/A Dream*. Sheffield: Sheffield Academic Press, 1999.

Möller, Karl. *A Prophet in Debate: The Rhetoric of Persuasion in the Book of Amos*. Sheffield: Sheffield Academic Press, 2003.

Moltmann, Jürgen. *God in Creation: An Ecological Doctrine of Creation*, trans. Margaret Kohl, Gifford Lectures, 1984. London: SCM Press, 1985 [Ger. 1985].

Morenz, Siegfried. *Egyptian Religion*, trans. Ann E. Keep. London: Methuen & Co Ltd, 1973 [Ger. 1955].

Morgan, Donn F. 'Wisdom and the Prophets', in *Studia Biblica:1. Papers on Old Testament and Related Themes*, ed. E. A. Livingstone, 209–44. Sheffield: JSOT Press, 1978.

—— *Wisdom in the Old Testament Traditions*. Atlanta: John Knox Press, 1981.

Morgan, Robert, and John Barton. *Biblical Interpretation*. Oxford: Oxford University Press, 1988.

Morris, Gerald. *Prophecy, Poetry and Hosea*, *JSOT* Supp. Sheffield: Sheffield Academic Press, 1996.

Moughtin-Mumby, Sharon. *Sexual and Marital Metaphors in Hosea, Isaiah, Jeremiah and Ezekiel*. Oxford: Oxford University Press, 2008.

Mowinckel, Sigmund. *The Psalms in Israel's Worship*, trans. D. R. Ap-Thomas. Vol. 1. Oxford: Basil Blackwell, 1962 [Nor. 1951].

Muir, John. *The Mountains of California*. San Francisco: Sierra Club Books, 1988.

Mullen, E. Theodore Jr. 'Hosts of Heaven', in *Anchor Bible Dictionary*, III, ed. D. N. Freedman, 301–4. New York: Doubleday, 1992.

Munch, Peter. *The Expression Bajjôm Hāhū': Is It an Eschatological Terminus Technicus?* Oslo: Dybward, 1936.

Murphy, R. E. 'Wisdom and Yahwism', in *No Famine in the Land: Studies in Honor of John L. McKenzie*, 117–26. Missoula, Mt.: Scholars Press, 1975.

—— 'Wisdom Theses and Hypotheses', in *Israelite Wisdom: Theological and Literary Essays in Honour of Samuel Terrien*, ed. J. Gammie, 35–42. Missoula, Mt.: Scholars Press, 1978.

—— 'Religious Dimensions of Israelite Religion', in *Ancient Israelite Religion: Essays in Honor of Frank Moore Cross*, ed. Patrick D. Miller, Paul D. Hanson and S. Dean McBride Jr., 449–58. Philadelphia: Fortress, 1987.

—— 'Wisdom in the O.T.', in *Anchor Bible Dictionary*, VI, ed. D. N. Freedman et al., 920–31. New York: Doubleday, 1992.

Murray, Robert. 'Prophecy and the Cult', in *Israel's Prophetic Tradition: Essays in Honour of Peter R. Ackroyd*, ed. R. Coggins, A. Phillips, and M. Knibb, 200–16. Cambridge: Cambridge University Press, 1982.

—— *The Cosmic Covenant: Biblical Themes of Justice, Peace and the Integrity of Creation*, HeyM 7. London: Sheed & Ward, 1992.

Myers, Norman. 'Environmental Refugees: A Growing Phenomenon of the 21st Century,' *Philosophical Transactions B* 357, no. 1420 (2002): 609–13.

Naess, Arne. *Ecology, Community and Lifestyle: Outline of an Ecosophy*, trans. David Rothernberg. Cambridge: Cambridge University Press, 1989 [Nor. 1976].

Nash, James, A. *Loving Nature: Ecological Integrity and Christian Responsibility*. Nashville: Abingdon, 1991.

—— 'Seeking Moral Norms in Nature: Natural Law and Ecological Responsibility', in *Christianity and Ecology: Seeking the Well-Being of Earth and Humans*, ed. Dieter Hessel and Rosemary Radford Ruether, 227–50. Cambridge, Mass.: Harvard University Press, 2000.

Nash, Roderick F. *The Rights of Nature: A History of Environmental Ethics*. Madison: University of Wisconsin Press, 1989.

Neusner, Jacob. *Judaism's Story of Creation: Scripture, Halakkah, Aggadah*. Vol. 3, Brill Reference Library of Ancient Judaism. Leiden: Brill, 2000.

Newman, Barbara. *Sister of Wisdom: St Hildegard's Theology of the Feminine*. Aldershot: Scolar Press, 1987.

Nichols, Aidan. *Discovering Aquinas: An Introduction to his Life, Work and Influence*. London: Darton, Longman & Todd, 2002.

Nicholson, Ernest. *God and His People: Covenant and Theology in the Old Testament*. Oxford: Clarendon, 1986.

—— 'Israelite Religion in the Pre-Exilic Period: A Debate Reviewed', in *A Word in Season*, ed. James D. Martin and Philip R. Davies, 3–34. Sheffield: JSOT Press, 1986.

Niehr, H. 'God of Heaven', in *Dictionary of Deities and Demons in the Bible*, ed. K. van der Toorn, Bob Becking, and P. W. van der Horst, 370–72. Leiden: Brill, 1999.

Nielsen, Kirsten. *Yahweh as Prosecutor and Judge: An Investigation of the Prophetic Lawsuit (Rîb-Pattern)*. Sheffield: JSOT Press, 1978.

—— *There is Hope for a Tree: The Tree as Metaphor in Isaiah*. Sheffield: Sheffield Academic Press, 1989.

Norris, Richard A. *God and World in Early Christian Theology*. London: Adam & Charles Black, 1966.

Northcott, Michael S. *The Environment and Christian Ethics*. Cambridge: Cambridge University Press, 1996.

—— *A Moral Climate: The Ethics of Global Warming*. Maryknoll, N.Y.: Orbis Books, 2007.

Nötscher, Friedrich. *Die Gerechtigkeit Gottes bei den vorexilischen Propheten*. Münster: Aschendorffsche Verlagsbuchhandlung, 1915.

Nwaoru, Emmanuel. 'Building a New World Order: A Perspective from Isaiah 11:6–9,' *BN* 119/120 (2003): 132–46.

O'Meara, John J. *Understanding Augustine.* Dublin: Four Courts Press, 1997.

Oden Jr., Robert A. *The Bible Without Theology: The Theological Tradition and Alternatives to It.* San Francisco: Harper & Row, 1987.

Oestreich, Bernhard. *Metaphors and Similes for Yahweh in Hosea 14:2–9 (1–8).* Frankfurt: Peter D Lang, 1998.

Ogletree, Thomas. *The Use of the Bible In Christian Ethics.* Philadelphia: Fortress, 1983.

Olley, John W. '"The Wolf, the Lamb and a Little Child": Transforming the Diverse Earth Community in Isaiah', in *The Earth Story in the Psalms and the Prophets,* 4, ed. Norman Habel, 219–29. Sheffield: Sheffield Academic Press, 2001.

Olmo Lete, Gregorio del. *Canaanite Religion: According to the Liturgical Texts of Ugarit.* Winona Lake, Ind.: Eisenbrauns, 1999.

Olson, Roger E. *The Story of Christian Theology.* Leicester: Apollos, 1999.

Olyan, Saul M. *Biblical Mourning.* Oxford: Oxford University Press, 2004.

Origen. *Origen on First Principles: Being Koetschau's Text of the De Principiis,* trans. G. W. Butterworth. London: SPCK, 1936.

—— *Contra Celsum,* trans. and ed. Henry Chadwick. Cambridge: Cambridge University Press, 1953.

Orr, David. 'Armageddon Versus Extinction.' *Conservation Biology* 19, no. 2 (2005): 290–2.

Osborn, Lawrence. *Guardians of Creation: Nature in Theology and the Christian Life.* Leicester: Apollos, 1993.

Osborn, E. F. *Irenaeus of Lyons.* Cambridge: Cambridge University Press, 2001.

Oswalt, John N. *The Book Of Isaiah: Chapters 1–39,* NICOT. Grand Rapids: Eerdmans, 1986.

Otto, Eckart. *Theologische Ethik des Alten Testaments.* Stuttgart: Kohlhammer, 1994.

Paas, Stefan. *Creation and Judgement: Creation Texts in Some Eighth Century Prophets.* Leiden: Brill, 2003.

Paley, William. *Natural Theology: Selections.* New York: Library of Liberal Arts, 1963.

Palmer, Clare. *Environmental Ethics and Process Thinking,* Oxford Theological Monographs. Oxford: Clarendon Press, 1998.

Pangritz, Walter. *Das Tier in der Bibel.* Munich and Basel: Ernst Reinhardt Verlag, 1963.

Park, Aaron W. *The Book of Amos as Composed and Read in Antiquity.* New York: Peter D. Lang, 2001.

Parmalee, Alice. *All the Birds of the Bible.* London: Lutterworth Press, 1959.

Passmore, J. *Man's Responsibility for Nature: Ecological Problems and Western Traditions.* 2nd edn. London: Duckworth, 1980.

Paul, Shalom M. *Amos: A Commentary on the Book of Amos.* Minneapolis: Fortress Press, 1991.

Peels, H. G. L. *The Vengeance of God: The Meaning of the Root NQM and the Function of the NQM-Texts in the Context of Divine Revelation in the Old Testament.* Vol. 31, OtSt. London, New York, and Cologne: Brill, 1995.

Peet, Garnet. 'The Protestant Churches in Nazi Germany' (1987), http://spindleworks.com/library/peet/german.htm

Pelikan, Jaroslav. *Luther the Expositor: Introduction to the Reformer's Exegetical Writings*, Luther's Works. Saint Louis, Miss.: Concordia, 1959.

—— *The Christian Tradition: A History of the Development of Doctrine.* Vol. 1, *The Emergence of the Catholic Tradition (100–600).* Chicago: University of Chicago Press, 1971.

—— *The Christian Tradition: A History of the Development of Doctrine.* Vol. 3, *The Growth of Medieval Theology (600–1300).* Chicago: University of Chicago Press, 1978.

—— *Christianity and Classical Culture: The Metamorphosis of Natural Theology in the Christian Encounter with Hellenism.* New Haven: Yale University Press, 1993.

Pennington, Jonathan. 'Dualism in Old Testament Cosmology: *Weltbild* and *Weltanschauung*,' *SJOT* 18, no. 2 (2004): 260–77.

Perdue, Leo G. *The Collapse of History: Reconstructing Old Testament Theology.* Minneapolis: Fortress, 1994.

—— *Wisdom and Creation: the Theology of Wisdom Literature.* Nashville: Abingdon, 1994.

—— *Reconstructing Old Testament Theology: After the Collapse of History.* Minneapolis: Fortress Press, 2005.

Perlitt, Lothar. *Vatke und Wellhausen.* Berlin: Alfred Töpelmann, 1965.

—— *Bundestheologie im Alten Testament*, WMANT. Neukirchen-Vluyn: Neukirchener Verlag, 1969.

Petersen, Allen Rosengren. *The Royal God: Enthronement Festivals in Ancient Israel and Ugarit?* Sheffield: Sheffield Academic Press, 1998.

Pettinato, Giovanni. 'Pre-Ugaritic Documentation of Ba'al', in *The Bible World: Essays in Honor of Cyrus H. Gordon*, ed. G. Rendsburg et al., 203–09. New York: Ktav Publishing House, 1980.

Pfeifer, Gerhard. 'Jahwe als Schöpfer der Welt und Herr ihrer Machte in der Verkündigung des Propheten Amos,' *VT* 41, no. 4 (1991): 475–81.

Philo. *On the Account of the World's Creation given by Moses.* Vol. 1, LCL. Cambridge, Mass.: Harvard University Press, 1981.

—— *On the Creation of the Cosmos according to Moses: Introduction, Translation and Commentary by David T. Runia.* Vol. 1, Philo of Alexandria Commentary Series. Leiden and Boston: Brill, 2001.

Plamenatz, John, ed. *The English Utilitarians.* Oxford: Basil Blackwell, 1949.

Plato. *The Phaedo of Plato*, trans. Patrick Duncan. London: Oxford University Press, 1928.

—— *Timaeus*, trans. R. G. Bury. Vol. 9, LCL. Cambridge, Mass.: Harvard University Press, 1929.

Pois, Robert A. *National Socialism and the Religion of Nature.* London and Sydney: Croom Helm, 1986.

Porteous, Norman W. 'Jerusalem-Zion: The Growth of a Symbol', in *Verbannung und Heimkehr*, ed. Arnulf Kuschke, 235–52. Tübingen: J. C. B. Mohr (Paul Siebeck), 1961.

Preston, Christopher J. 'Epistemology and Intrinsic Value: Norton and Callicott's Critique of Rolston,' *Environmental Ethics* 20, no. 4 (1998): 409–28.

Preuss, H. D. 'Das Gottesbild der älteren Weisheits Israels', in *Studies in the Religion of Ancient Israel*, *VT* Supp. 23, ed. G. W. Anderson, 117–45. Leiden: Brill, 1972.

Preuss, H. D. 'Erwägungen zum theologischen Ort alttestamentlicher Weisheitsliteratur,' *EvT* 30 (1970): 393–417.

Primavesi, Anna. *Sacred Gaia: Holistic Theology and Earth System Science.* London and New York: Routledge, 2000.

Pseudo-Dionysius. *The Complete Works*, trans. Colm Luibheid, ed. Paul Rorem. New York: Paulist Press, 1987.

Quasten, J. *Patrology*, vols. 2–4. Allen, Tex.: Christian Classics, 1983–6.

Quistorp, Heinrich. *Calvin's Doctrine of the Last Things*, trans. Harold Knight. London: Lutterworth Press, 1955. Translation of *Die Letzten Dinge im Zeugnis Calvins.*

Rasmussen, Larry L. 'Ecology and Morality: The Challenges to and from Christian Ethics', in *Religion and the New Ecology: Environmental Responsibility in a World in Flux*, ed. David Lodge and Christopher Hamlin, 246–78. Notre Dame, Ind.: University of Notre Dame Press, 2006.

—— 'Symbols to Live By', in *Environmental Stewardship*, ed. R. J. Berry, 174–84. London: T. & T. Clark, 2006.

Raven, Charles E. *Natural Religion and Christian Theology: Science and Religion*, Gifford Lectures 1951, Series 1. Cambridge: Cambridge University Press, 1953.

Ray, John. *The Wisdom of God Manifested in the Works of the Creation.* London: Ray Society, 2005. Reprint of 1826 edn.

Redditt, Paul L. *Haggai, Zechariah, Malachi*, NCB. Grand Rapids: Eerdmans, 1995.

Regan, Tom. *All That Dwell Therein: Animal Rights and Environmental Ethics*. Berkeley, Los Angeles, and London: University of California Press, 1982.

Regenstein, Lewis G. *Replenish the Earth: A History of Organized Religion's Treatment of Animals and Nature—Including the Bible's Message of Conservation and Kindness to Animals*. London: SCM, 1991.

Rendtorff, Rolf. *The Old Testament: An Introduction*, trans. John Bowden. London: SCM Press, 1985.

—— *The Covenant Formula*. Edinburgh: T. & T. Clark, 1988.

—— *Canon and Theology*, trans. Margaret Kohl. Edinburgh: T. & T. Clark, 1994 [Ger. 1991].

Reventlow, H. G. *Problems of Old Testament Theology in the Twentieth Century*, trans. John Bowden. London: SCM, 1985 [Ger. 1982].

—— 'Righteousness as Order of the World', in *Justice and Righteousness*, ed. H. G. Reventlow and Y. Hoffman, 163–72. Sheffield: JSOT Press, 1992.

Richards, Ivor A. *The Philosophy of Rhetoric*. London: Oxford University Press, 1936.

Ricoeur, Paul. *Freud and Philosophy: An Essay on Interpretation*, trans. Denis Savage. New Haven and London: Yale University Press, 1970 [Fr. 1965].

—— *The Rule of Metaphor: Multi-disciplinary Studies of the Creation of Meaning in Language*, trans. Robert Czerny, with Kathleen McLaughlin and John Costello. Toronto: University of Toronto Press, 1977 [Fr. 1975].

Riede. *Im Spiegel der Tiere: Studien zum Verhältnis von Mensch und Tier im alten Israel*. Göttingen: Vandenhoeck & Ruprecht, 2002.

Rignell, L. G. 'Isaiah Chapter 1: Some Exegetical Remarks with Special Reference to the Relationship Between the Text and the Book of Deuteronomy,' *ST* 11 (1957): 140–58.

Robbins, Frank Engleton. *The Hexaemeral Literature*. Chicago: University of Chicago Press, 1912.

Robinson, G. D. 'Paul Ricoeur and the Hermeneutic of Suspicion,' *Premise* II, no. 8 (1995).

Robson, Michael. *St Francis of Assisi: The Legend and the Life*. London: Geoffrey Chapman, 1997.

Rodd, Cyril S. *Glimpses of a Strange Land: Studies in Old Testament Ethics*. Edinburgh: T. & T. Clark, 2001.

Rogerson, John W. 'The Old Testament View of Nature: Some Preliminary Questions', in *Instruction and Interpretation: Studies in Hebrew Language, Palestinian Archaeology and Biblical Exegesis*, OtSt 20, ed. H. A. Brongers et al. Leiden: Brill, 1977.

—— *Theory and Practice in Old Testament Ethics*, *JSOT* Supp. London: T. & T. Clark, 2004.

—— and Judith M. Lieu. *The Oxford Handbook of Biblical Studies.* Oxford: Oxford University Press, 2006.

Rolston III, Holmes. *Environmental Ethics: Duties to and Values in the Natural World.* Philadelphia: Temple University Press, 1988.

—— 'Does Aesthetic Appreciation of Landscapes Need to be Science-Based?' *British Journal of Aesthetics* 35, no. 4 (1995): 374–86.

—— 'Caring for Nature: What Science and Economics Can't Teach Us but Religion Can,' *Environmental Values* 15 (2006): 307–13.

Ross, J. P. 'Jahweh Seba'ot in Samuel and Psalms,' *VT* 17 (1967): 76–92.

RSPCA Science Group. 'Ruddy Duck Cull' (2007), http://www.rspca.org.uk/servlet/Satellite?pagename=RSPCA/RSPCARedirect&pg=sciencegroup&marker=1&articleId=1086681282101.

Rudolph, Wilhelm. *Hosea.* Gütersloher: Verlagshaus Gerd Mohn, 1966.

Ruether, Rosemary Radford. *Liberation Theology: Human Hope Confronts Christian History and American Power.* New York: Paulist Press, 1972.

—— *Gaia & God: An Ecofeminist Theology of Earth Healing.* London: SCM, 1992.

—— ed. *Women Healing Earth: Third World Women on Ecology, Feminism, and Religion.* London: SCM, 1996.

—— 'Conclusion: Eco-Justice at the Center of the Church's Mission', in *Christianity and Ecology: Seeking the Well-Being of Earth and Humans*, ed. Dieter Hessel and Rosemary Radford Ruether, 603–13. Cambridge, Mass.: Harvard University Press, 2000.

Runia, David T. *Philo of Alexandria and the Timaeus of Plato.* Leiden: Brill, 1986.

Sakenfeld, Katharine Doob. *The Meaning of Hesed in the Hebrew Bible: A New Enquiry.* Missoula, Mont.: Scholars Press, 1978.

Sandler, Ronald. 'The External Goods Approach to Environmental Virtue Ethics,' *Environmental Ethics* 25, no. 3 (2003): 279–93.

—— 'A Theory of Environmental Virtue,' *Environmental Ethics* 28, no. 3 (2006): 247–64.

Santmire, H. Paul. *The Travail of Nature: The Ambiguous Ecological Promise of Christian Theology.* Minneapolis: Fortress Press, 1985.

Sawyer, John F. A. *Isaiah Volume 1.* Louisville: Westminster John Knox Press, 1984.

Scheffczyk. *Creation and Providence*, trans. R Strachan. London: Burnes & Oates, 1970.

Schmid, Hans Heinrich. *Wesen und Geschichte der Weisheit: eine Untersuchung zur altorientalischen und israelitischen Weisheitsliteratur.* Berlin: Alfred Töpelmann, 1966.

—— *Gerechtigkeit als Weltordnung: Hintergrund und Geschichte des alttestamentlichen Gerichtigkeitsbegriffes*, BHT 40. Tübingen: Mohr [Siebeck], 1968.

Schmid, Hans Heinrich. Creation, Righteousness, Salvation: 'Creation Theology' and the Broad Horizon of Biblical Theology', in *Creation in the Old Testament*, ed. Bernard W. Anderson, 102–17. London: SPCK, 1980 [Ger. 1973].

Schneemelcher, ed. *New Testament Apocrypha: Gospels and Related Writings.* Vol. 1. Cambridge and Louisville: James Clarke & Co./Westminster John Knox Press, 1991.

Schneidewind, William M. 'The Evolution of Name Theology', in *The Chronicler as Theologian*, ed. M. P. Graham, S. L. McKenzie and G. N. Knoppers, 228–39. Edinburgh: T. & T. Clark, 2003.

Schwartz, Joshua. 'Treading the Grapes of Wrath: The Wine Press in Ancient Jewish and Christian Tradition,' *TZ* 49 (1993): 215–28.

Schweitzer, Albert. *Civilization and Ethics: The Philosophy of Civilisation, Part II*, trans. John Naish. London: A. & C. Black, 1923 [Ger. 1922].

Seeligmann, Isac Leo. *The Septuagint Version of Isaiah and Cognate Studies*, ed. R. Hanhart and H. Spieckermann, FAT. Tübingen: Mohr [Siebeck], 2004.

Sheehan, Jonathan. *The Enlightenment Bible: Translation, Scholarship, Culture.* Princeton, N.J., and Oxford: Princeton University Press, 2005.

Segundo, Juan Luis. *Liberation of Theology.* Maryknoll, N.Y.: Orbis Books, 1976.

Seifrid, M. 'Righteousness Language in the Hebrew Scriptures and Early Judaism', in *Justification and Variegated Nomism: The Complexities of Second Temple Judaism*, 1, ed. D. A. Carson, P. T. O'Brien and M. A. Seifrid. Grand Rapids: Baker Academic, 2001.

Seow, C. L. 'Lord of Hosts', in *Anchor Bible Dictionary*, III, ed. D. N. Freedman, et al., 304–07. New York: Doubleday, 1992.

—— 'Lilith', in *Dictionary of Deities and Demons in the Bible*, ed. K. van der Toorn, Bob Becking and P. W. van der Horst, 973–6. London, New York, and Cologne: Brill, 1995.

Shaw, Bill. 'A Virtue Ethics Approach to Aldo Leopold's Land Ethic,' *Environmental Ethics* 19, no. 1 (1997): 53–67.

Sheppard, Gerald T. 'The Anti-Assyrian Redaction and the Canonical Context of Isaiah 1–39,' *JBL* 104, no. 2 (1985): 193–216.

Sherwood, Yvonne. *The Prostitute and the Prophet: Hosea's Marriage in Literary-Theoretical Perspective.* Sheffield: Sheffield Academic Press, 1996.

Shields, Mary E. *Circumscribing the Prostitute: The Rhetorics of Intertextuality, Metaphor and Gender in Jeremiah 3:1–4:4*, *JSOT* Supp. London and New York: T. & T. Clark, 2004.

Siegert, Folker. 'Early Jewish Interpretation in a Hellenistic Style', in *Hebrew Bible / Old Testament. The History of Its Interpretation.* Vol. 1: *From the Beginnings to the Middle Ages (Until 1300), Part 1*, ed. M Sæbø, 130–98. Göttingen: Vandenhoeck & Ruprecht, 1996.

Simkins, Ronald. *Yahweh's Activity in History and Nature in the Book of Joel.* Lewiston: E. Mellen Press, 1991.

—— *Creator and Creation; Nature in the World View of Ancient Israel.* Peabody, Mass.: Hendrickson, 1994.

Singer, Peter. *Animal Liberation: Towards an End to Man's Inhumanity to Animals.* Wellingborough: Thorsons, 1983.

Sire, James. *The Universe Next Door.* Leicester: InterVarsity Press, 1976.

Smelik, K. A. D. 'Ma'at', in *Dictionary of Deities and Demons in the Bible*, ed. K. van der Toorn, Bob Becking and P. W. van der Horst, 534–5. Leiden: Brill, 1999.

Smith, Duane Andre. 'Kinship and Covenant in Hosea 11:1–4,' *HBT* 16, no. 1 (1994): 41–53.

Smith, Ralph L. *Micah-Malachi*, WBC. Waco, Tex.: Word, 1984.

Snow, D. W., and C. M. Perrins. *The Birds of the Western Palearctic.* Concise edn. Oxford: Oxford University Press, 1998.

Soggin, J. Alberto. *The Prophet Amos: A Translation and Commentary*, trans. John Bowden. London: SCM, 1987 [It. 1982].

Soskice, Janet M. *Metaphor and Religious Language.* Oxford: Clarendon, 1985.

Southgate, Christopher. 'Stewardship and its Competitors: A Spectrum of Relationships between Humans and the Non-Human Creation', in *Environmental Stewardship*, ed. R. J. Berry, 185–95. London: T. & T. Clark, 2006.

Stadelmann, Luis J. *The Hebrew Conception of the World.* Rome: Biblical Institute Press, 1970.

Stamm, Johann J., and Maurice E. Andrew. *The Ten Commandments in Recent Research.* London: SCM, 1967.

Steck, O. H. *Bereitete Heimkehr: Jesaja 35 als Redaktionelle Brücke zwischen dem Ersten und dem Zweiten Jesaja.* Stuttgart: Verlag Katholisches Bibelwerk, 1985.

Stevenson, Kalinda Rose. 'If Earth could Speak: The Case of the Mountains against YHWH in Ezekiel 6:35–36', in *The Earth Story in the Psalms and the Prophets*, 4, ed. Norman Habel, 158–71. Sheffield: Sheffield Academic Press, 2001.

Stock, Konrad. 'Welt/Weltanschauung/Weltbild,' *TRE* 35 (2003): 536–8.

Strawn, Brent A. *What is Stronger than a Lion?* Göttingen: Vandenhoeck & Ruprecht, 2005.

Strong, Maurice. 'Beyond Rio: New World Order, or Lost Opportunity?' *The Fourth Kew Environmental Lecture* (1993).

Stuart, Douglas. *Hosea-Jonah*, WBC. Waco, Tex.: Word Books, 1971.

—— 'The Sovereign's Day of Conquest,' *BASOR* 221, no. February (1976): 159–64.

Stuart, Simon et al. 'Conservation Theology for Conservation Biologists: A Reply to David Orr,' *Conservation Biology* 19, no. 6 (2005).

Stuhlmueller, Carroll. *Creative Redemption in Deutero-Isaiah.* Rome: Biblical Institute Press, 1970.

Sweeney, Marvin A. *Isaiah 1–39 with an Introduction to Prophetic Literature.* Grand Rapids: Eerdmans, 1996.

—— *The Twelve Prophets: Volume One, Berit Olam: Studies in Hebrew Narrative and Poetry.* Collegeville, Minn.: Liturgical Press, 2000.

—— 'Micah's Debate with Isaiah,' *JSOT* 93 (2001): 111–24.

Talmon, Shemaryahu. 'The "Desert Motif" in the Bible and in Qumran Literature', in *Biblical Motifs: Origins and Transformations*, ed. A. Altmann. Cambridge, Mass.: Harvard University Press, 1966.

Taylor, Paul W. *Respect for Nature: A Theory of Environmental Ethics.* Princeton, N.J.: Princeton University Press, 1986.

Teilhard de Chardin, Pierre. *The Phenomenon of Man*, trans. Bernard Wall. London: Collins, 1959 [Fr. 1955].

Terrien, Samuel. 'Amos and Wisdom', in *Israel's Prophetic Heritage: Essays in Honour of James Muilenberg*, ed. B. W. Anderson. London: SCM, 1976.

Thiessen, Matthew. 'The Form and Function of the Song of Moses (Deuteronomy 32:1–43),' *JBL* 123, no. 3 (2004): 401–24.

Thomas, Keith. *Man and the Natural World: Changing Attitudes in England 1500–1800.* London: Penguin Books, 1986.

Thoreau, Henry David. *Collected Essays and Poems.* New York: Library of America, 2001.

—— *Walden.* New Haven: Yale University Press, 2004.

Toorn, K. van der. 'Yahweh', in *Dictionary of Deities and Demons in the Bible*, ed. K. van der Toorn, Bob Becking and P. W. van der Horst, 910–19. Leiden: Brill, 1999.

Toulmin, Stephen. *Cosmopolis: The Hidden Agenda of Modernity.* New York: Free Press, 1990.

Trapè, Agostino. 'Saint Augustine', in *Patrology*, IV, ed. Johannes Quasten, 342–462. Allen, Tex.: Christian Classics, 1986.

Trigg, Joseph W. *Origen: The Bible and Philosophy in the Third-century Church.* London: SCM Press, 1983.

Tristram, H. B. *The Natural History of the Bible.* London: SPCK, 1889.

Tsumura, David. *Creation and Destruction: A Reappraisal of the Chaoskampf Theory in the Old Testament.* Winona Lake, In.: Eisenbrauns, 2005.

Tucker, Gene M. 'The Role of the Prophets and the Role of the Church', in *Prophecy in Israel*, ed. David L. Petersen, 159–74. London: SPCK, 1987.

—— 'Creation and the Limits of the World: Nature and History in the Old Testament,' *Horizons in Biblical Theology* 15, no. 2 (1993): 105–18.

—— 'Rain on a Land Where No One Lives: The Hebrew Bible on the Environment,' *JBL* 116 (1997): 3–17.

—— 'The Peaceable Kingdom and a Covenant with the Wild Animals', in *God Who Creates: Essays in Honor of W. Sibley Towner*, ed. William P. Brown and S. Dean McBride Jr., 215–25. Grand Rapids: Eerdmans, 2000.

Tucker, Mary Evelyn, and John Grim. 'The Emerging Alliance of World Religions and Ecology,' *Daedalus* 130, no. 4 (2001): 1–25.

Urbrock, William J. 'Angels, Bird-droppings and Fish Liver: The Earth Story in Tobit', in *Readings from the Perspective of Earth*, ed. Norman Habel, 125–37. Sheffield: Sheffield Academic press, 2000.

Vallance, J. T. 'Animals', in *The Oxford Classical Dictionary*, ed. S. Hornblower and A. Spawforth, 90–3. Oxford: Oxford University Press, 1996.

van Dyke, Fred, et al. *Redeeming Creation: The Biblical Basis for Environmental Stewardship.* Downers Grove, Ill.: InterVarsity Press, 1996.

Van Ruiten, J. T. A. G. M. 'The Intertextual Relationship between Isaiah 65:25 and Isaiah 11:6–9', in *The Scriptures and the Scrolls: Studies in Honour of A.S. van der Woude on the Occasion of his 65th Birthday*, ed. F. Garcia Martinez, A. Hilhorst, and C. J. Labuschagne, 31–42. London, New York, and Cologne: Brill, 1992.

van Wensveen, Louke. 'Christian Ecological Virtue Ethics: Transforming a Tradition', in *Christianity and Ecology*, ed. Dieter Hessel and Rosemary Radford Ruether, 155–71. Cambridge, Mass.: Harvard University Press, 2000.

van Wieringen, Archibald L. 'Jesaja 6–12: Die Vegetationsbildsprache und die prophetische Struktur', in *The Book of Isaiah/Le Livre d'Isaïe*, ed. J. Vermeylen, 203–7. Leuven: Leuven University Press, 1989.

van Zijl, Peter J. *Baal: A Study of Texts in Connection with Baal in the Ugaritic Epics.* Neukirchen-Vluyn: Neukirchener Verlag, 1972.

Vannier, M. A. 'Origène et Augustin, interprètes de la création', in *Origienta Sexta: Origène et la Bible/Origen and the Bible*, ed. Gilles Dorival and Alain Le Boulluec, 723–36. Leuven: Leuven University Press, 1995.

Vermeylen, J. *Du Prophète Isaïe à l'Apocalyptique: Isaïe I—XXXV, Miroir d'un demi-millénaire d'expérience religieuse en Israël, Vol 1.* Paris: Librairie Lecoffre, 1977.

Vermeylen, Jacques, ed. *The Book of Isaiah / Le livre d'Isaïe.* Leuven: University Press, 1989.

von Rad, Gerhard. 'The Origin of the Concept of the Day of Yahweh,' *JSS* 4, no. 2 (1959): 97–108.

—— *Old Testament Theology, Vol 1,* trans. D. M. G. Stalker. Edinburgh: Oliver and Boyd, 1965 [Ger. 1957].

von Rad, Gerhard. *Genesis: A Commentary,* trans. J. H. Marks. 3rd edn. London: SCM Press, 1972 [Ger 1971].

—— *Wisdom in Israel,* trans. J. Martin. London: SCM Press, 1972 [Ger. 1970].

—— 'Some Aspects of the Old Testament World View', in *The Problem of the Hexateuch and Other Essays,* 144–65, trans. E. W. Trueman Dicken. London: SCM Press, 1984 [Ger. 1964].

—— 'The Theological Problem of the Old Testament Doctrine of Creation', in *The Problem of the Hexateuch and Other Essays,* 131–43, trans. E. W. Trueman Dicken. London: SCM, 1984 [Ger. 1936].

von Waldow, Hans Eberhard. 'Israel and Her Land: Some Theological Considerations', in *A Light Unto My Path: Old Testament Studies in Honor of Jacob M. Myers,* ed. H. N. Bream, R. D. Heim, and C. Moore, 493–508. Philadelphia: Temple University Press, 1974.

Vriezen, T. C. *An Outline of Old Testament Theology.* Oxford: Basil Blackwell, 1970.

Walsh, Carey Ellen. *The Fruit of the Vine: Viticulture in Ancient Israel.* Winona Lake, Ind.: Eisenbrauns, 2000.

Wambacq, B. N. *L'épithète divine Jahvé Seba'ôt.* Paris: Desclée de Brouwer, 1947.

Watson, Rebecca S. *Chaos Uncreated: A Reassessment of the Theme of 'Chaos' in the Hebrew Bible.* Berlin and New York: De Gruyter, 2005.

Watts, John D. W. 'An Old Hymn Preserved in the Book of Amos,' *JNES* 15 (1956): 33–39.

—— *Vision and Prophecy in Amos.* Leiden: Brill, 1958.

—— *Isaiah 1–33,* WBC. Waco, Tex.: Word Books, 1985.

—— *Isaiah 34–66,* WBC. Waco, Tex.: Word Books, 1987.

Weber, Max. *Ancient Judaism,* trans. H. H. Gerth and D. Martindale. Glencoe, Ill.: Free Press, 1952 [Ger. 1921].

Weeks, Andrew. *German Mysticism from Hildegard of Bingen to Ludwig Wittgenstein: A Literary and Intellectual History.* Albany: State University of New York Press, 1993.

Weeks, Noel. *Admonition and Curse: The Ancient Near Eastern Treaty / Covenant Form as a Problem in Inter-Cultural Relationships.* London: T. & T. Clark, 2004.

Weinfeld, M. '"Justice and Righteousness"—משפט וצדקה—The Expression and its Meaning', in *Justice and Righteousness: Biblical Themes and their Influence*, ed. H. G. Reventlow and Y. Hoffman, 228–46. Sheffield: JSOT Press, 1992.

—— *Social Justice in Ancient Israel and in the Ancient Near East.* Jerusalem, Minn.: Magnes Press/Fortress Press, 1995.

Weiss, Meir. 'The Origin of the "Day of the Lord"—Reconsidered,' *HUCA* 37 (1966): 29–60.

—— 'Methodologisches über die Behandlung der Metapher dargelegt an Am. 1:2,' *TZ* 23 (1967): 1–25.

—— 'The Decalogue in Prophetic Literature', in *The Ten Commandments in History and Tradition*, ed. Ben-Zion Segal, 45–81. Jerusalem: Magnes Press, 1985.

Wellhausen, Julius. *Prolegomena to the History of Israel*, trans. J. S. Black and A. Menzies. Edinburgh: Adam & Charles Black, 1885 [Ger. 1883].

—— *Die Kleinen Propheten übersetzt und erklärt.* 4th edn. Berlin: Walter de Gruyter, 1963.

Wendel, François. *Calvin: The Origins and Development of his Religious Thought*, trans. Philip Mairet. London: Collins, 1963 [Fr. 1950].

Wendland, Ernst R. 'The "Word of the Lord" and the Organisation of Amos: A Dramatic Message of Conflict and Crisis in the Confrontation between the Prophet and People of Yahweh,' *JOTT* 2, no. 4 (1988): 1–51.

Wenham, Gordon. *Story as Torah: Reading the Old Testament Ethically.* Edinburgh: T. & T. Clark.

Weren, W. J. C. 'The Use of Isaiah 5:1–7 in the Parable of the Tenants (Mark 12:1–12; Matthew 21:33–46),' *Bib* 79 (1998): 1–26.

Westermann, Claus. 'Das Reden von Schöpfer und Schöpfung in Alten Testament', in *Das Ferne und Nahe Wort: Festschrift L. Rost*, ed. Fritz Maass, 238–44. BZAW 105. Berlin: A Töpelmann, 1967.

—— *Creation*, trans. J. Scullion. London: SPCK, 1974 [Ger. 1971].

—— *Blessing in the Bible and the Life of the Church*, trans. Keith Crim. Philadelphia: Fortress Press, 1978 [Ger 1968].

—— *Elements of Old Testament Theology*, trans. Douglas W. Stott. Atlanta: John Knox Press, 1982 [Ger. 1978].

—— *Genesis 1–11: A Commentary*, trans. J. Scullion. London: SPCK, 1984 [Ger. 1974].

—— *Roots of Wisdom: The Oldest Proverbs of Israel and Other Peoples*, trans. J. Daryl Charles. Edinburgh: T. & T. Clark, 1995 [Ger. 1990].

Wharton, James A. 'Hosea 4:1–3', *Int* 32, no. 1 (1978): 78–83.

Whedbee, J. William. *Isaiah and Wisdom.* Nashville and New York: Abingdon, 1971.

White, Gilbert. *The Natural History and Antiquities of Selbourne.* London: Routledge, 1890.

White Jr., Lynn. 'Natural Science and Naturalistic Art in the Middle Ages,' *AHR* 52, no. 3 (1947): 421–35.

—— 'The Historical Roots of Our Ecologic Crisis,' *Science* 155, no. 3767 (1967): 1203–7.

White, Peter S. 'Disturbance, the Flux of Nature, and Environmental Ethics at the Multipatch Scale', in *Religion and the New Ecology: Environmental Responsibility in a World in Flux,* ed. David Lodge and Christopher Hamlin, 176–98. Notre Dame, Ind.: University of Notre Dame Press, 2006.

Whitten, Tony, and Bryony Morgan, eds. *Faiths and the Environment: World Bank Support 2000–05.* Washington: The World Bank, 2006.

Whybray, R. N. 'The Sage in the Israelite Royal Court', in *The Sage in Israel and the Ancient Near East,* ed. J. Gammie and Leo G. Perdue. Winona Lake, Ind.: Eisenbrauns, 1990.

Wilch, John. *Time and Event: An Exegetical Study of the Uses of 'ēth in the Old Testament in Comparison to Other Temporal Expressions in Clarification of the Concept of Time.* Leiden: Brill, 1969.

Wildberger, Hans. *Isaiah 1–12,* trans. T. H. Trapp. Minneapolis: Fortress, 1991 [Ger. 1972].

—— *Isaiah 13–27,* trans. T. H. Trapp. Minneapolis: Fortress, 1997 [Ger 1978].

—— *Isaiah 28–39,* trans. T. H. Trapp. Minneapolis: Fortress, 2002 [Ger. 1982].

Williams, Arnold. *The Common Expositor: An Account of the Commentaries on Genesis 1527–1633.* Chapel Hill: University of North Carolina Press, 1948.

Williams, Gary Roye. 'Frustrated Expectations in Isaiah V 1–7: A Literary Interpretation,' *VT* 35, no. 4 (1985): 459–65.

Williams, Rowan. *Arius: Heresy and Tradition.* London: SCM Press, 2001.

Williamson, H. G. M. *The Book Called Isaiah: Deutero-Isaiah's Role in Composition and Redaction.* Oxford: Clarendon, 1994.

—— 'Relocating Isaiah 1:2–9', in *Writing and Reading the Scroll of Isaiah: Studies of an Interpretive Tradition,* ed. C. C. Broyles and C. A. Evans, 263–77. London, New York, and Cologneöln: Brill, 1997.

—— 'Isaiah 1 and the Covenant Lawsuit', in *Covenant as Context: Essays in Honour of E. W. Nicholson*, ed. A. D. H. Mayes and R. B. Salters, 393–406. Oxford: Oxford University Press, 2003.

—— *Isaiah 1–5*, ICC. London and New York: T. & T. Clark, 2006.

Willis, John T. 'The Genre of Isaiah 5:1–7,' *JBL* 96, no. 3 (1977): 337–62.

Wilson, Robert. 'Ethics in Conflict: Sociological Aspects of Ancient Israelite Ethics', in *Text and Tradition*, ed. S. Niditch, 193–205. Atlanta: Scholars Press, 1990.

Witmer, Stephen E. 'Taught by God: Divine Instruction in Early Christianity.' Unpublished thesis, University of Cambridge, 2006.

Wolff, Hans Walter. '"Wissen um Gott" bei Hosea als Urform von Theologie,' *EvT* 15 (1952–3): 533–54. Reprinted in *Gesammelte Studien zum Alten Testament*, 182–205. München: Chr Kaiser Verlag, 1964.

—— *Amos the Prophet: The Man and his Background*, trans. John Reumann. Philadelphia: Fortress Press, 1973 [Ger. 1964].

—— *Hosea*, trans. Gary Stansell. Philadelphia: Fortress Press, 1974 [Ger. 1965].

—— *Anthropology of the Old Testament*, trans. Margaret Kohl. London: SCM, 1974 [Ger. 1973].

—— *Joel and Amos: A Commentary on the Books of the Prophets Joel and Amos*. Philadelphia: Fortress Press, 1977 [Ger. 1975].

Wood, Joyce Rilett. *Amos in Song and Book Culture*. Sheffield: Sheffield Academic Press, 2002.

World Commission on Environment and Development (WCED). 'Our Common Future,' ed. Gro Harlem Brundtland. Oxford: Oxford University Press, 1987.

Wright, G. E. *God Who Acts: Biblical Theology as Recital*. London: SCM, 1952.

—— 'The Lawsuit of God: a Form-Critical Study of Deuteronomy 32', in *Israel's Prophetic Heritage*, ed. Bernhard Anderson and Walter Harrelson, 26–67. London: SCM, 1962.

—— *The Old Testament and Theology*. New York: Harper and Row, 1969.

Wright, Christopher J. H. *Living as the People of God: The Relevance of Old Testament Ethics*. Leicester and Downers Grove, Ill.: InterVarsity Press, 1983. (US title: *An Eye for an Eye: The Place of Old Testament Ethics Today*.)

—— *God's People in God's Land*. Grand Rapids: Eerdmans, 1990.

—— *Walking in the Ways of the Lord*. Leicester: Apollos, 1995.

—— *Old Testament Ethics for the People of God*. Leicester: InterVarsity Press, 2004.

Wright, David F. 'Augustine: His Exegesis and Hermeneutics', in *Hebrew Bible / Old Testament. The History of Its Interpretation* Vol. 1: *From the*

Beginnings to the Middle Ages (Until 1300), Part 1, ed. M Sæbø, 701–30. Göttingen: Vandenhoeck & Ruprecht, 1996.

Wright, J. Edward. 'Biblical Versus Israelite Images of the Heavenly Realm,' *JSOT*, no. 93 (2001): 59–75.

Yee, Gail A. 'A Form-Critical Study of Isaiah 5:1–7 as a Song and a Juridical Parable,' *CBQ* 43 (1981): 30–40.

Young, Edward J. *The Book of Isaiah: The English Text, with Introduction, Exposition, and Notes, Vol II chapters 19–39*. Grand Rapids: Eerdmans, 1969.

Zimmerli, Walther. 'The Place and Limit of the Wisdom in the Framework of the Old Testament Theology,' *SJT* 17 (1964): 146–58.

—— *Old Testament Theology in Outline*, trans. D. E. Green. Edinburgh: T. & T. Clark, 1978 [Ger. 1972].

——'Mensch in Rahmen der Natur nach den Aussagen des erten biblischen Schöpfungsberichtes,' *ZTK* 76 (1979): 139–58.

—— 'Das Gottesrecht bei den Propheten Amos, Hosea und Jesaja', in *Werden und Wirken des Alten Testaments: FS Claus Westermann*, ed. Rainer Albertz, 216–35. Neukirchen-Vluyn: Neukirchener Verlag, 1980.

—— 'The 'Land' in the Pre-Exilic and Early Post-Exilic Prophets', in *Understanding the Word*, eds. James Butler et al., 253–54. Sheffield: JSOT Press, 1985.

Index

Scripture Index

Printed and bound by CPI Group (UK) Ltd, Croydon, CR0 4YY